ENDGAME

INSIDE THE *IMPEACHMENTS* OF DONALD J. TRUMP

REP. ERIC SWALWELL

ABRAMS PRESS, NEW YORK

Paperback ISBN: 978-1-4197-4549-2
eISBN: 978-1-68335-932-6

Printed and bound in the United States
10 9 8 7 6 5 4 3 2 1

Abrams books are available at special discounts when purchased in quantity for pre-
miums and promotions as well as fundraising or educational use. Special editions can
also be created to specification. For details, contact specialsales@abramsbooks.com
or the address below.

ABRAMS The Art of Books
195 Broadway, New York, NY 10007
abramsbooks.com

For my dad, who boldly risked everything to do what was right; my mom, who raised four boys to always do good; my wife, Brittany, who inspires me to fight harder not just for our children, Nelson and Cricket, but everybody's children; and for the public servants, who proved courage beats corruption.

CONTENTS

PART 3: ALL ROADS LEAD TO PUTIN

PART 4: UKRAINE

PART 5: IMPEACHING THE PRESIDENT

PART 6: A SECOND IMPEACHMENT

On January 15, 2020, Adam Schiff came looking for me on the House Floor. He wanted to talk to me one-on-one. Earlier that day, Speaker of the House Nancy Pelosi had announced the seven impeachment managers she had selected to argue the case before the U.S. Senate in the impeachment trial of President Donald Trump—and I was not among them. As one of only two members on both the Intelligence and Judiciary Committees, I had spent many hours working to keep a corrupt president in check, and I was crushed not to have been chosen—even if I was proud of the elite team the Speaker had put together under the leadership of Schiff, Chairman of the Intelligence Committee.

"You'd have been a terrific manager," Chairman Schiff told me.

I thanked him, not only for his words but also for making a point of searching me out to help cushion the blow. We talked a little about the historic proceeding about to take place, but I didn't want to keep him. He had a lot of work to do, preparing for the trial.

"And you know what, who knows? It's Donald Trump," Adam said as he turned to leave. "Maybe he'll be impeached again."

We both laughed. It was kind of Adam to say, his way to try to make me feel better.

Adam would go on to make a blistering case against Trump, impassioned and cogent and eloquent, and his prescient warnings about Trump in the Senate trial would be validated by history—including his well-meaning quip to me. Almost one year to the day after that conversation, Speaker Pelosi asked me to serve as a manager in Donald Trump's second impeachment trial, this time for inciting an insurrection at the U.S. Capitol. I would be part of the team, under the leadership of my colleague Jamie Raskin of Maryland, that would detail the astonishingly lurid and undeniable case against Trump in directly working to undermine our democracy. I'm proud of the case we presented, and proud that when my son, Nelson, and daughter, Cricket, look back on these years, they will see that we held Donald Trump accountable.

As I write, it's spring, a time of healing and of new life. We've made progress as a country in immunizing our people and fighting against a global pandemic challenging every nation on the planet. After years of Trump using the Oval Office to spread lies, incite fear, and stoke hatred, President Joe Biden has restored faith in government and in basic human decency and kindness. He has enjoyed far broader support than his predecessor ever once claimed in his four years in office. Already, despite the nakedly cynical obstructionism of panicked House Republicans, we have passed landmark legislation to help get people back on their feet and remain in their homes, to help tackle child poverty and inequality, and to reopen schools. President Biden has reminded people all across this great land that empathy is a sign of strength, not weakness, and that we are all in this together.

That's not to say we can now take a long victory lap. We have a lot more to do to heal the wounds of the past four years. No matter how tempting, we can't just turn the page and move on. We can't forget. Sometimes it's hard to believe it all happened. It's as if we're waking from a nightmare. But it was entirely foreseeable. I kept telling myself throughout the Trump years, *This isn't happening.* I just didn't want to see it.

On November 8, 2016, I was huddled in a small kitchen behind a banquet room. I was with my wife, Brittany, and my longtime political advisor, Alex Evans. I tried to assure Brittany that everything was going to be okay. But I didn't really know that it was. We had a television on in the background, and it was clear that Donald Trump was about to become president.

This isn't happening.

I had panned Trump's 2015 announcement, delivered after he descended that Trump Tower escalator, as a stunt to raise his profile. Sure, he "won" each debate, but that was because he was the most entertaining candidate in a field of stiff, uninspiring politicians. Once he started winning primaries, it was as if every Democrat's wish had been granted. We would be able to face the worst GOP candidate in the general election. A cakewalk! The Billy Bush tape? Game over!

But Trump never lost momentum. A snowball turned into an avalanche. And there I stood with Brittany and Alex, forced to accept the impossible. Our great country, my fellow citizens, had elected Donald Trump as president.

This isn't happening.

Just a little over four years later, I was overtaken by the same feeling. I was on the Floor of the House of Representatives, about to certify the Electoral College votes for the 2020 election. We were finally done with Donald Trump, but my phone was blowing up with alerts about threats to the Capitol. Pipe bombs had been found outside my office building, Cannon. Thousands of rioters had moved from Trump's White House rally to the Capitol. Next thing I knew, Speaker Pelosi was being ushered out of the Chamber by her security detail. A security officer was now telling me and my colleagues to get our gas masks out and be prepared to duck in case of gunfire. Trump's mob was hell-bent on taking over the Capitol and stopping our count. The House Chaplain started praying—last rites of sorts. The seat of government for the greatest country in the world was about to be overrun by terrorists inspired and sent by the loser of a free and fair election. My colleagues and I were soon running to a secure location, running for our lives. For hours we would wait for an all-clear signal declaring that the Capitol had been secured.

This isn't happening.

Just like four years before, I didn't want to accept that, as a country, we had again found ourselves in such an awful, impossible position. Our Capitol had been breached. For the first time in our country's history, we would not see a peaceful transition of power.

This isn't happening.

I had naïvely believed that a country as great as ours was immune from such ruin. But I would realize weeks after I fled the Floor, as I prepared to try the second impeachment trial against Trump, that everything about January 6 was foreseeable. We had become blinded by the inertia of democracy. We had assumed that it was as reliable as a western sunset. We had let our guard down. And evil had tried to take over.

I'm a sports fan, a former Division I soccer goalkeeper, and I can remember how sometimes, doing my job in goal meant a tie in regulation and a game going to overtime (or extra time, as you'd say in soccer). That's where we are now as a country, I think. Biden's victory did not win the game. It was more like it knocked in a header as the time expired, sending the game into overtime We fought back Trumpism and the cult of disinformation that fueled it and took the House back in the 2018 elections. Then we fought it back again and brought the nefarious activities of Trump and so many of his enablers to light, impeaching him for abuse of power and obstruction of justice. The American people saw Trump for who he was, saw the crooked playbook he hoped to use to sway the 2020 election—and resoundingly voted him out of office. And when he made his pathetic, desperate attempt to thwart the will of the people by inciting an insurrection at the Capitol, we stood up to him again.

It's tempting to say, *Time to move on. Let the past be the past.* But the danger, to our present and to our immediate future, is too real for us to forget. Biden won the 2020 election by more than 7 million votes and received 306 Electoral College votes (to Trump's 232), but the Senate is split 50–50, and we have a 4-vote edge in the House. November 3, 2020, was anything but the end. We are squarely in overtime.

In this book, originally published in June 2020, I set out to capture the historic events of the first impeachment from my vantage point in the House. I wanted to write a detailed account of those days because, even as they were happening, it was clear that the tornado of scandal and lies whipped up by Trump and his cronies was overwhelming for many people. It was hard to keep up with all of it. I wanted to give the reader a better understanding of impeachment itself, thankfully uncommon enough to require some explanation. And I hoped this book would give some insight into what I believe in and into the courage of those, like Fiona Hill and Lt. Col. Alexander Vindman, who stood up to a bully in the most powerful office in the world.

Little did I know when the book was first published that that bully would incite his supporters to storm the Capitol, or that Adam Schiff's quip about a second impeachment would come true. So, for this edition, I've added my account of those tumultuous days.

I had a front-row seat. I'll never forget, and I don't want you to forget, either.

—Eric Swalwell
Dublin, California
April 2021

PART 1: MUELLER DAY

CHAPTER 1

JULY 24, 2019

Mueller Day started for me when my two-year-old son, Nelson, woke me up before dawn. I had a big day ahead, but the most important thing that morning was his sore pointer finger. He'd been sent home from preschool the day before with the injury. He seemed fine when we put him to bed, but Brittany and I feared he'd wake up in pain and we'd have to take him in for X-rays. What did we know? As young parents, everything feels like a crisis. But I could see from the way he was throwing his trucks around that his finger was just fine. Relief! Instead of worrying about a trip to urgent care, I'd be able to focus on questioning Special Counsel Robert Mueller later in the day in two separate Congressional hearings watched live by millions of people.

Nelson wanted to watch *Cars*. (He'd only seen it 1,800 times at that point.) He also wanted a cookie. "No chance," I said. Next, he wanted pancakes. I wanted time for a little more Mueller prep work, but he was insistent. I made a counteroffer. Maybe Cheerios and milk could work today? As a former prosecutor in Alameda County in Northern California, I felt like I had some experience in being persuasive when I really needed to be. Not that morning, though. Nelson held firm. (Stubbornness is an inherited trait.) So, I whipped up a batch of pancakes, and he seemed appeased.

He didn't eat a single one. What parent doesn't know how that goes? But he was satisfied enough for me to leave and make my way over to Capitol Hill not too far behind schedule.

The whole month of July 2019 was like that for me, feeling caught between two places, or several, always playing catch-up. Two and a half weeks earlier, I'd still been out on the stump campaigning for the Democratic nomination for President of the United States. I was bummed to be off the trail, but I had zero regrets about having gone for it. I ran inspired by the power of young people to rise up and demand change in politics and government. I first ran for my House seat against an older incumbent from my party who had been in Congress too long and had fallen out of touch with his constituents. My surprise win in that race was all about the value of new energy and new perspectives. I believe in being bold and insisting on real change, even if that means taking some heat or falling short. After all, I'd grown up in the San Francisco Bay Area, surrounded by a culture of try, fail, try again, fail again, try another time . . . and you're Google.

I'd had my say in a televised Democratic presidential debate and taken my shot. I had good reason to believe the country wanted generational change. In 2018, I led an effort that helped elect twenty-nine new members of Congress in their forties and younger, who delivered us a crucial majority in the House. I made ending gun violence my top issue and had the National Rifle Association on the run when I pushed for an assault weapons ban. I became a favorite target of theirs on social media, which I saw as a badge of honor. My dad even called me in December 2018 to tell me the NRA had put me on the cover of their magazine. He knew because he is a member.

As much as I hoped it would take off, my presidential campaign wasn't breaking through. Besides, it was hard to be away from Washington with so much coming to a boiling point there, when I was one of only three members of Congress to serve on both the Intelligence and Judiciary Committees. I asked myself a lot of tough questions about whether I still had a shot to win the Democratic nomination for President. By early July 2019, I realized it was time to get back to Washington full time.

"Today ends our presidential campaign," I announced in my hometown of Dublin, California, on Monday, July 8, "but it is the beginning of an opportunity in Congress."

Weeks later, as I was making Nelson pancakes that morning of the Mueller hearing, it struck me that for the first time, I felt relieved not to be running for President anymore. I was going to be part of an effort to find out if Congress could do its constitutional duty of checking a corrupt President. We were up against the incalculable power of systematic disinformation and blatant lies in the social media age. We had to prevail.

We didn't know how much of a difference Mueller's live testimony to the nation would make, but we knew this was our best shot to take all the work that had gone into his investigation and showcase it for the American people. We were well aware of the challenge we faced, breaking through layers of complacency to drive home the truth of Donald Trump's guilt. We were very organized in our preparations for questioning Mueller. I hadn't seen a prep effort like that since former FBI director James Comey testified before the House Intelligence Committee in March 2017 on Russia's interference in the 2016 elections.

Trump fired Comey suddenly and impulsively on May 9, 2017. A week later, it was revealed that Trump had pressured Comey in a White House meeting to hold back an investigation of former White House National Security Advisor Michael Flynn, telling the FBI director, "I hope you can let this go."

A day after those revelations were made public, Mueller, a lifelong Republican and former FBI director, was appointed by Acting Attorney General Rod Rosenstein to oversee an investigation into any ties between the Trump campaign and Russia's intervention into our 2016 elections. Mueller had a reputation for being honest, tough, and thorough. As Republican Senator Ben Sasse told the *New York Times* when Mueller was appointed, his "record, character, and trustworthiness have been lauded for decades by Republicans and Democrats alike."

By the following year, as Mueller's all-star lineup of investigators moved toward a conclusion, indications emerged that for all the wrongdoing Mueller was uncovering, leading to a dizzying total of thirty-four different indictments, Trump himself might not be held accountable. A May 2018 *New York Times* article quoted former New York City Mayor Rudy Giuliani, by then working as Trump's personal lawyer—important to note: *personal*, not official—bragging that he'd heard from Mueller's team that "they can't indict" Trump because of Justice Department guidelines against indicting a sitting President. The headline on the article: CONGRESSIONAL CANDIDATES, NOT MUELLER, COULD DECIDE TRUMP'S FUTURE.

Most astonishing about the Mueller Report was that not a single piece of it leaked. Sure, reporters tried to glean what Mueller was up to, staking out the special counsel's office to see who was going in for interviews. But we truly had no idea on the House Intelligence Committee. As Mueller conducted his investigation, we hoped he would aggressively use the subpoena power that we in Congress were not ourselves using under a Republican majority. We also falsely assumed Mueller was following the most important evidence in a white-collar crime: the money. Money is all Donald Trump cares about. If you want to know what Trump has done, look at where his money comes from and where it goes.

I'll never forget the day Mueller finally delivered his report to Attorney General William Barr. It was on March 22, 2019, and I was in Los Angeles. I knew I'd have to get to a television studio to let the public know that we were going to fight like hell to let them see the report as soon as possible.

The scene was just so perfect. As I was walking up the stairs to the CNN studio, I saw someone walking down the stairs: It was none other than John Dean, Nixon's former White House counsel and the witness who testified before Congress and broke open the Watergate investigation. We stopped and talked. Dean told me he thought the Mueller Report was a ticking time bomb. He encouraged me to keep holding this President accountable.

"We want the full report, we want it now, we want it before the President is going to get it or able to make any edits," I told Wolf Blitzer and the CNN audience a few minutes later.

I was wary of Trump trying to pull a fast one. Wolf asked if I had confidence in Barr to give Congress as much information from the report as he possibly could, and in a timely way.

"With Mr. Barr, look, I'll trust, but we have to verify," I said. "So, we will ultimately see the full report because the President is outnumbered. We have now the subpoena power and a judiciary that will uphold the precedents from the Nixon era."

In retrospect it should have been more obvious that Barr would spin the Mueller Report as falsely as he did. Two days later, he released a letter saying the report cleared Trump on collusion with Russia. His letter also seemed to suggest it cleared him on obstruction, though it did include a snippet from Mueller specifying that "while this report does not conclude that the President committed a crime, it also does not exonerate him."

Barr went to great lengths to assert that there had been no obstruction offense for which Trump could be charged, taking it upon himself to make that claim despite a clear conflict of interest.

Mueller, not one to speak out if he could avoid it, felt compelled to release a four-page memo complaining about Barr's characterization of his report, saying it "did not fully capture the context, nature, and substance" of the report and lamenting, "There is now public confusion about critical aspects of the results of our investigation."

I'd been suspicious of Barr since Day One. I was assured by every Washington establishment Republican I knew that he was a "Republican's Republican." Barr was respected for his prior service under President George H. W. Bush. One lawyer friend of mine said, "He's not a Trump guy. He's his own man." If that was the case, then why did Trump want him, I wondered?

I was most concerned that Barr had sent, in the middle of the Mueller investigation, an unsolicited letter to Acting Attorney General Rod Rosenstein, claiming that the Mueller probe was illegitimate. Barr subscribed to the unitary theory of the executive, which called for sweeping powers for the President, and that worried me. Trump is a child. He's corrupt. But he's not stupid. If he can get guys on his team who believe he is supreme and untouchable, he's going to hire them. That's what he saw in Barr.

My first reaction as I read the Mueller Report inside the Judiciary Committee conference room was "That's it?" This was an investigation that had lasted nearly two years and included five hundred interviews and more than thirty-five hundred subpoenas. Yet, the report boiled down to 448 pages, many of which had thick black lines through them, blocking me and my colleagues from seeing the text. As we understood it, Mueller wrote the report, sent it unredacted to Barr, and Barr chose the redactions and determined whether to level charges for any of the conduct. Barr did a hit job on the report—just as he had been appointed to do. He blocked out 20 percent of the text and determined that despite Mueller's laying out ten instances of obstruction of justice, Trump would not be charged with any of them.

I had a lot of questions. So did my colleagues. We knew we couldn't change Barr's judgment that Trump couldn't be charged with a crime. That was a given. But there was a sense among Speaker of the House Nancy Pelosi, Chairman Adam Schiff of the Intelligence Committee, and Chairman Jerry Nadler of the Judiciary Committee that we should fight like hell to get as much of the information about the investigation into the public realm as possible.

I was in a unique position. I served on Speaker Pelosi's leadership team and was a member of both the Intelligence and Judiciary Committees.

We agreed early on that Intel would take on the counterintelligence aspect of the report, seeking to answer the question "Is Donald Trump a counterintelligence risk?" Is he jeopardizing our national security via his Russia connections? The Judiciary Committee, in considering whether we should proceed with an impeachment inquiry, would seek to get the underlying evidence of the Mueller Report that Barr hid from the public. The evidence of most interest was the FBI's 302s, which are the agents' interview notes, and the grand jury material. Typically, grand jury material is sealed from the public. However, the Nixon impeachment inquiry established the precedent that Congress could see it.

As both committees pressed, Barr's DOJ started to drip out information. But Judiciary Committee members had to go to the Department of Justice and sit in a secure room to read the materials provided. It was a frustrating process. I would set an appointment to go to "Main Justice," the Robert F. Kennedy Department of Justice Building on Pennsylvania Avenue, enter through a nonpublic, police-guarded door and walk down a long corridor to a small office room where they were stored. I sat at a long wooden table on a wobbly wooden chair and reviewed FBI agent interview notes for a handful of witnesses. I was not even allowed to take my own notes on what I saw or have my cell phone, which I left outside. There was absolutely no purpose or order to why those were the notes the DOJ was allowing us to see. Even more frustrating, the notes were heavily redacted. This whole experience was supposed to give a peek behind the curtain of the Mueller Report that was out of public view. But we pulled back the curtain to find only more curtains. Redactions within redactions.

"There's more materials for you upstairs, sir," a DOJ aide said to me on one of my trips there.

"I'm sorry?" I said, confused.

"You're on Intel, too," the aide continued. "You're allowed to see the materials upstairs. But your Judiciary staffer has to stay here."

What the hell was upstairs? I wondered. I went up to the sixth-floor SCIF, or Sensitive Compartmented Information Facility. The aide handed me a folder marked top secret. The document consisted of just a few pages underneath the cover sheet. *Again, why this document?* I wondered. *Where did this fit into the whole report?* That's how our Congressional review of the redacted Mueller Report mostly went: Disorientation. Difficulty making any sense of why the DOJ provided what it provided. Doubt about what we were missing. We went to court, determined to get as much as we could. Intentionally, or unintentionally, the DOJ would be more cooperative with some of the Freedom of Information Act requests from the free press. The Trump administration hated the press, yet the press had been prioritized above Congress's lawful subpoenas? *They must really hate Congress,* we thought.

We ultimately voted to hold Attorney General Barr in contempt for his refusal to work with us. As to our counterintelligence concerns, the Intel Committee was provided a single briefing regarding counterintelligence. We walked away with more questions than answers, and concerned that no counterintelligence investigation of Donald Trump was ever conducted.

That was why Mueller's testimony to us on July 24 was so important, and why we were going to be absolutely as prepared as we could be, even understanding as we did that preparations carried you only so far. What was that quote from Mike Tyson? "Everybody has a plan until they get punched in the mouth." We were sure the Republicans were going to try to punch us in the mouth with their antics, and it would be up to us to respond—or not.

The lighter moments are the ones you remember. The day before we questioned Mueller, we had a two-hour mock hearing in Judiciary. One of our staffers played Republican Jim Jordan, which meant the staffer was not wearing a suit jacket, obviously, and was jumping up and down and screaming, objecting to everything. Norm Eisen, the Judiciary Committee's oversight consultant, who was playing Mueller, at one point interrupted "Jim Jordan."

"Mr. Chairman, I don't know the rules of the committee, but shouldn't the gentleman from Ohio have to wear a coat?" he asked, and we cracked up.

I stopped a couple times to take pictures of us rehearsing, reminding myself, *This is a moment in history.* You've got the majority on the Democratic side preparing for Mueller, and the other side, where Republicans would be, was empty. I asked my questions on Judiciary and then ran over to Intel for its prep session. That meant going three floors below the Capitol, into another SCIF.

For Intel's mock hearing, the part of Robert Mueller was played by former Southern District of New York prosecutor Dan Goldman, who was on our staff. Dan was very committed to the part. Over the previous two weeks, he had engrossed himself in learning the style of Bob Mueller. There were times in between questions when we would ask him something completely unrelated to Mueller, and needed Goldman to be Goldman. He couldn't help himself. He'd still answer like Mueller.

"Dan!" we'd call out. "Break out of Mueller!"

That had to have been about the best Method acting anyone had seen from a Congressional staffer, and it fit with the intensity in the room. Every member was scrutinizing the questions of the other members, not in a malicious way, but constructively. There was so much pressure to get it right. We were all giving each other notes on our questions, like in a writing seminar: "I like it when you did that" or "You need to pare down that section."

Adam Schiff, our Chairman, reminded us to take a step back and think about how viewers at home would process the hearing. Yes, we had a role to play as Intelligence Committee members, but he was also very aware of the need to reach more people.

"These are all fact-based questions," he said. "We'll be getting mostly yes, no, yes, no, yes, no, out of Mueller, so make sure you really listen to the answers. Don't feel like you're so confined to the script we've all worked on. If you see an opportunity to ask him something outside of the script, don't miss that."

He was right. If Mueller ended up just repeating "I refer you to the report" one hundred times the next day, that would be a loss for us. We could all have spared ourselves the trouble of questioning him.

I had one idea I'd been working on. Barry Berke from Judiciary staff had told me about a letter signed by a thousand former federal prosecutors, some Republican, some Democrat, some neither, attesting that, in their professional view, the information contained in the Mueller Report had more than enough evidence to indict President Trump on multiple charges of obstruction of justice. The list included former senior officials at the Justice Department, special prosecutors, and U.S. attorneys.

"Let me see the letter," I said.

It was a good letter. "As former federal prosecutors," they wrote, "we recognize that prosecuting obstruction of justice cases is critical because unchecked obstruction—which allows intentional interference with criminal investigations to go unpunished—puts our whole system of justice at risk."

The prosecutors who signed the letter were experienced, top-level people. I noticed that the letter included each prosecutor's years of service: thirty, thirty-five, forty. I kept thinking: *What would have an impact?* I asked my staff to add up the numbers. We practiced how the questioning could go.

"Are you familiar with this letter?" I asked in the mock session. "You know some of the people who signed this letter. You respect people in this letter who say it's a crime."

I liked how it was going. I was into it. So, almost without thinking, I added one more question for our Mueller stand-in.

"Sir, do you want to sign this letter?"

Everyone loved that, and I wondered if I could pull off asking that of the real Mueller.

The night before Mueller testified, I remember thinking that success the next day would be based on people wanting to know more. Mueller was act 1. He was setting the table. Our job? The next act would be to fill the chairs with all of the people in the report. That's how it was supposed to go.

CHAPTER 2

GRADUALLY, THEN SUDDENLY

No matter how the press might play it, no matter what cable TV chose to emphasize, the day Robert Mueller testified before Congress was the beginning of the end for Donald Trump. As I saw it, there was always a real chance he would be impeached by the House. It wasn't a shock that a corrupt businessman who had moved on to be a corrupt President was going to wind up in serious trouble. The only questions were when he would get caught and how much damage he would do first. To tweak that old Hemingway quote from *The Sun Also Rises,* how did he get impeached? Two ways. Gradually, then suddenly.

Until then, Trump had kept everyone's head spinning. Whether it was by design or a combination of weakness and dumb luck, the Trumpist outrage-a-day strategy—sometimes it felt like one an hour—was oddly effective. No one could keep up. Trump, a guy who obviously never believed he would actually win the presidency, bought himself time to scam money for himself and his family and turn the office of President of the United States into a reality TV prop he would use to his personal advantage at every turn. The longer he held the reins of power, it was clear, the more damage he would do and the worse it would be for my children and their generation when their time came to pick up the pieces.

Trump was elected three weeks after Brittany and I got married at the René C. Davidson Courthouse on Lake Merritt in Oakland. Nancy O'Malley, my former boss at the Alameda County District Attorney's Office, officiated before family and a few colleagues and close friends. I was happy that colleagues from Congress—Nancy Pelosi, Anna Eshoo, Ruben Gallego, and Seth Moulton—and my former boss Ellen Tauscher could be there. It was great to see Pelosi and O'Malley together, both strong women and important mentors who had taught me so much. Later, at the reception held at Wente

Vineyards, in my Congressional district, I toasted them: "To the two Nancys who have always kept me straight."

Brittany and I never had a honeymoon. We figured we'd put everything into the 2016 campaign and then, after Hillary was elected, we'd find time to go away together. Well, I went away, but not with my wife, and certainly not to any beach. With Donald Trump as President, almost every question I fielded from constituents was some form of "How do we stop him?" There was a lot we could do to minimize his damage, pressure we could apply to slow him down, but only one way to really stop him: we had to beat him, first by winning the House. Brittany and I agreed the best thing I could do was spend as much time as I could on the road helping candidates running for Congress to flip the House. As I went across the country talking with voters, I would tell them, "Give Democrats the majority, and we can cut our time in hell in half."

I'd had a whirlwind return to the halls of Congress that summer. The Capitol you see on TV is beautiful, historic, and majestic. It's all that, for sure, but it's also a series of catacomb-like tunnels and hallways where you spend a lot of time as a Congressman walking from one meeting to another. So much of being in Congress has to do with trust and relationships, and those relationships are built during those little unplanned conversations you have with one another when you meet in a Capitol hallway. As soon as I left the presidential campaign trail, those relationships, which had been put briefly on hold, were back in full swing. They had to be, as we all geared up for the chance to pose questions to Robert Mueller, the man at the center of a swirling Category 5 political storm.

At stake was nothing less than the nature of truth. Washington, DC, has long been a place where in the war between perception and reality, perception often came first. Ronald Reagan kept saying, "It's morning in America," delivering the line like the former actor and pitchman he was. And with time, more and more people said, "Well, I guess it *must* be morning in America." After John F. Kennedy was brutally murdered in 1963, his wife, Jacqueline, set about framing her husband's time in office as a modern-day Camelot. It was a time, Jackie urged reporters to write, of mythic figures come to life, locked in heroic struggle through events like the Cuban Missile Crisis of 1962.

Looking back now, we see that period a little through Jackie's eyes. Time and again in Washington, through periods like the civil rights struggle, a battle raged over who could convince the public that their version of reality was the more resonant and the more authentic.

What had changed in the Trump years, right before our eyes, was the extent to which out-and-out lies—just making shit up left and right—became not just accepted, but widespread. Lies had long been a Washington art form, honed to polished perfection in the salons of Georgetown, but they were generally employed with a certain amount of style and finesse. As the former Washington correspondent Allen Drury summed it up in his doorstop 1959 novel *Advise and Consent*, "Son, this is a Washington, DC, kind of lie. It's when the other person knows you're lying, and also knows you know he knows."

What was truly new to the U.S. political stage was the idea, up until then associated only with totalitarian regimes, that truth was irrelevant, that all that mattered was the word of the leader, and that it was essential to show your loyalty by believing the lie of the day. If that lie was contradicted by the one from a day earlier, then it was your duty to get with the program and vouch for the new lie. It got hard to keep track of so many lies. In fact, it was exhausting. The lies were just too numerous to process.

That was why, in my time questioning Mueller that day at the Capitol, I focused on the sheer, blinding scale of Trump's lies.

I had submitted Exhibit 8 to be flashed up on the screen: photos of numerous Trump associates. I felt like I was back in court. Mueller probably did, too. "Director Mueller, I'm showing you campaign Chairman Paul Manafort, political advisor Roger Stone, deputy campaign manager Rick Gates, National Security Advisor Michael Flynn, Donald Trump's personal attorney Michael Cohen, and foreign policy advisor George Papadopoulos," I said.

"These six individuals have each been charged, convicted, or lied to your office or other investigators," I said. "Is that right?"

Mueller tried to slow down my line of questioning.

"That's all—I look askance at Mr. Stone because he is . . . a different case here in DC."

I moved right on, speaking slowly but firmly.

"So, National Security Advisor Flynn lied about discussio sian Ambassador related to sanctions," I continued. "Is that ri

"That's correct," Mueller said.

"Michael Cohen lied to this committee about Trump Tower Moscow," I asked. "Is that correct?"

"Yes," Mueller said.

"George Papadopoulos, the President's senior foreign policy advisor, lied to the FBI about his communications about Russia's possession of dirt on Hillary Clinton," I asked. "Is that right?"

"Correct," Mueller said. "Yes."

"The President's Campaign Chairman Paul Manafort lied about meetings that he had with someone with ties to Russian intelligence," I pressed on. "Is that correct?"

"That's true," Mueller said.

The exchange was somewhat dry, devoid of the drama that makes a sure-fire, top-of-the-cable-news-hour highlight, but it was also utterly damning, especially to anyone who had spent much time around a courtroom. Lies are to lawyers what smoke is to firefighters. Systematic, coordinated lying in the upper reaches of government is a five-alarm fire. This kind of conflagration should trigger a national emergency, but only if the alarm is connected and loud enough that the country can be awakened.

I knew the print and TV reporters covering Mueller Day had a tough job. Since Trump's inauguration, they, too, had struggled to keep up with the deluge of dishonesty coming from his administration and his allies in Congress. But as the day went on, I worried that the media was focusing on all the wrong things.

One cable news anchor called me during a break in the Mueller testimony.

"He doesn't look well," she said.

"But are you listening to what he's saying?" I replied. "He's not trying to win a Tony Award."

The narrative shaping up among the press on the day of Mueller's testimony was summed up by these *New York Times* headlines: THE BLOCKBUSTER THAT WASN'T: MUELLER DISAPPOINTS THE DEMOCRATS, over a news analysis by Peter Baker; and LACK OF ELECTRICITY IN MUELLER HEARING SHORT-CIRCUITS IMPEACHMENT, over a Carl Hulse piece.

We'd known going in that Mueller's testimony would not be riveting political theater in the manner of, say, Supreme Court nominee Brett Kavanaugh going from meek and polite to yelling about beer and fuming with rage in nothing flat. That wasn't the point. This was an investigation of an attack on our 2016 presidential election by Russia, a blow to what we as a people have always held most sacred, our unmatched tradition of democratic succession every four years. This wasn't a trip to the movies. A blockbuster? No Democrat had built it up as that. What we did say was that if you tuned in and paid attention, you would be left with a stunning, unmistakable picture of a President with nothing but contempt for accountability who insisted on breaking laws at almost every turn. Mueller also established that Trump had asked for and benefited from Russia's help.

From where I sat on the House Judiciary and Intelligence Committees, which by then had both been investigating the epic wrongdoing of the Trump administration for months, I had a palpable sense that the country was moving closer to impeachment. Yet many reporters weren't seeing what I was seeing, focused as they were on Mueller's "performance."

"President Trump was probably never going to be impeached by the House of Representatives before the 2020 elections," Carl Hulse wrote in the *Times*. "The testimony by Robert S. Mueller III, the former special counsel, makes that a near certainty."

In another exchange with a news anchor that day, I made clear I thought coverage of Mueller's testimony was missing the point. "So here's the deal," I texted. "If you were to read a transcript of Mueller today, you would conclude the President should be removed from office. If you watched it on TV, you would offer a style critique. I think you guys are missing what he said and focusing on how he said it."

"I hear you," the anchor wrote back, "but wasn't the whole point having him say out loud what was in the report? He didn't do a good job of it."

By the next day, the Washington buzz was all about style, with close to nothing being said about substance. There had to be room for the truth to land somewhere in the middle. Yes, as we all expected going in, Mueller's testimony was an acquired taste, too important to ignore, but for some viewers, not as compelling or memorable as it could have been. At the same time, we knew conclusively that we had a rogue President, one incapable of following the law or putting the needs of the country before his own. We knew that he was highly vulnerable to further scrutiny. And those of us in Congress knew that, despite the media spin, more scrutiny was coming.

To me, Trump's impeachment was inevitable. Congress would hold him accountable for his crimes, his misdeeds, and his betrayal of the public trust and the Constitution one way or another—and not because we're Democrats and he's a Republican, but because our Constitution demands it. As Speaker Pelosi would say the day she endorsed impeachment, citing Thomas Paine, "The times have found us."

Pelosi gave a press conference a few hours after Mueller's testimony that was widely misunderstood. While some portrayed the day as a vindication of her reluctant stance on impeachment, the Speaker was looking to next steps. Support among House Democrats for an impeachment inquiry was growing by the day. In the week after Mueller appeared before our committees, two dozen more House members would come out in public in support of an impeachment inquiry, "a notable spike," as the Associated Press would dub it. This was a clear sign that my colleagues weren't basing their views on public polls. The media kept saying that as a political issue, impeachment was a dud, but this wasn't about politics. If my colleagues had been finger-in-the-wind types, they'd have avoided impeachment. But we didn't retreat; we moved forward. Ideally, history will judge Mueller's "performance" not by TV ratings, but by how he moved Congress to act.

Pelosi knew not to come out strongly for impeachment unless she had a convincing, easy-to-communicate story to tell about Trump's misconduct. She also knew that Trump, a man who had abused his office every single day, was out of his depth. Damning revelations were a daily fixture of life in Trump's Washington.

Yet, what jumps out at me, looking back on Mueller Day, is the way the media spin set Donald Trump up. The coverage pushed the line that impeachment seemed less likely, rather than more, after Mueller's testimony. I thought that spin was dead wrong, and I said so at the time—but Trump fell for it.

"The Democrats had nothing and now they have less than nothing," he said at the White House the day Mueller testified, before heading to West Virginia for a fund-raising event.

The following day, July 25, Trump was clearly flush with a feeling of "victory." He was up early at the White House that Thursday, watching *Fox & Friends*, and he started his daily stream of tweets at 7:06 a.m. with one quoting host Ainsley Earhardt saying of the Mueller hearing, "Yesterday changed everything, it really did clear the President. He wins."

Later that morning, Trump tweeted, "TRUTH IS A FORCE OF NATURE!" For a change, he actually had a good point, better than he knew.

Trump would also tweet about a Fox News poll citing positive numbers for the President on his handling of the economy, with 52 percent approving, making that his best issue with voters. That same poll also showed former Vice President Joe Biden as the front-runner at that point in the Democratic presidential race, with more support for him than for his next two competitors combined. And perhaps most important of all the numbers, the poll gave Biden a 10 percentage point edge over Trump if they were to face off against each other in the 2020 presidential election.

In Trump's mind, based on Mueller's performance, impeachment was behind him. He was doubly emboldened. Not only wasn't he worried about impeachment, but despite the ten possible criminal acts of obstruction of justice identified in the Mueller Report, the special counsel had testified before Congress that Trump could not be charged, as his Department of Justice was acting on its own policy that no President could be indicted. Trump now believed he could commit crimes with impunity.

CHAPTER 3

"I WOULD LIKE YOU TO DO US A FAVOR THOUGH"

The morning after Robert Mueller appeared before our committees on Capitol Hill, President Trump had a call scheduled with the President of Ukraine. Volodymyr Zelensky was newly elected and desperate for U.S. public backing as his country tried to fend off military incursions from its much larger neighbor, Russia. The call began at 9:03 a.m. and was monitored by an assortment of individuals, including multiple White House officials. (I'll assume Vladimir Putin himself was not actually listening in real time, smirking to a roomful of acolytes at the Kremlin.)

"We are trying to work hard because we wanted to drain the swamp here in our country," said Zelensky, clearly doing his best to butter up the easily flattered Trump, according to the "rough transcript" of the call later released by the White House.

Trump vented about Angela Merkel and the Germans not doing enough to help, and Zelensky said he agreed.

"I would also like to thank you for your great support in the area of defense," Zelensky told Trump. "We are ready to continue to cooperate for the next steps, specifically we are almost ready to buy more Javelins from the United States for defense purposes."

Trump's immediate reply to the request for Javelin anti-tank missiles, as we would all later discover, was a stone-cold shakedown.

"I would like you to do us a favor though because our country has been through a lot and Ukraine knows a lot about it," Trump said, alluding to nonsensical conspiracy theories about the 2016 presidential election (which we know to have been hatched as Russian intelligence service disinformation). "I would like you to find out what happened with this whole situation with Ukraine.... The server, they say Ukraine has it.... As you saw yesterday, that whole nonsense ended with a very poor performance by a man named Robert Mueller, an incompetent performance, but they say a lot of it started with Ukraine. Whatever you can do, it's very important that you do it if that's possible."

We'll never know how much Trump's tongue was loosened on that call by his giddy mood following Mueller coverage that made him feel everything was at last breaking his way. Maybe he would have been just as blunt and brazen about using an official government call to strong-arm an ally into digging up political dirt on his likely 2020 opponent no matter how the press had spun Mueller's testimony.

After saying he would like his personal lawyer, Rudy Giuliani, and Attorney General Barr to call Zelensky, here's what Trump said, according to the call summary the White House released: "[T]here's a lot of talk about Biden's son, that Biden stopped the prosecution and a lot of people want to find out about that so whatever you can do with the Attorney General would be great. Biden went around bragging that he stopped the prosecution so if you can look into it . . . It sounds horrible to me."

One hour later, Biden was in Indianapolis for a National Urban League forum of candidates for the Democratic presidential nomination. Biden predicted that Russia would "pay a price" for its blatant attack on the 2016 U.S. elections, and he sharply criticized Trump for saying he would gladly accept dirt on political opponents from other countries.

"It is outrageous, it is un-American, and it's close to treasonous," the former Vice President said.

Two hours after Trump's conversation with Zelensky, the White House officially called on the Defense Department, through its Budget Office, to "hold off" on sending nearly $400 million in badly needed security assistance to Ukraine, so Trump could maximize leverage in pushing Zelensky for his "favor."

One day later, in Kyiv, Zelensky met with two Trump representatives, Gordon Sondland, U.S. Ambassador to the European Union, and Kurt Volker, U.S. special envoy for Ukraine. The two men, as we would later find out, gave the new Ukrainian President advice on how to stay on Trump's good side. By all accounts, the meeting went well, and afterward, Sondland went to lunch with a group that included David Holmes, the embassy's counselor for political affairs.

At one point, Sondland called Donald Trump himself.

Zelensky, Sondland told Trump, "loves your ass!"

"So, he's gonna do the investigation?" Trump asked—so loudly that Holmes heard every word.

"He's gonna do it," Sondland told him, adding his belief that Zelensky, needing America's help so badly, would do "anything you ask him to."

We didn't know the Ukraine shakedown had already been set in motion the day after Mueller testified, but we did know that the more you connected the dots, the more unmistakable proof you gathered of Trump's criminal conduct as President. If you use force to hide the truth, time is your enemy. In Washington, where conventional wisdom can flip like a leaf in the wind, the thinking up to then had been that impeachment had to happen fast or it wouldn't happen at all. I disagreed with the idea that "the clock was running out," and with the notion that Democrats had to spend 2020 focused only on elections and not on holding Donald Trump accountable.

"If the truth comes out, I just don't see how an impeachment proceeding helps Donald Trump during the election," I told my former Chief of Staff, Alex Evans, the night after Mueller testified. "If Trump wants to fight everything in the courts, and we don't get rulings until 2020, how does he look better when a cascade of court decisions comes down against him just before the election?"

I thought Trump had more of an incentive to get ahead of the story, before the election, than we did. Mueller had made clear to me that the more we continued to dig, the more we would find. I asked him if it was true that he and his investigators "cannot rule out the possibility that the unavailable information would shed additional light. Is that correct?"

Many of Mueller's answers had been halting, as if to avoid a good sound bite, but this time he was crisp.

"That is correct," he said. "We don't know what we don't know."

It was clear from Mueller's testimony that there was a trove of "what we don't know." Mueller's team had conducted 500 interviews, issued more than

3,500 subpoenas, and produced thousands of pages of interview notes, but they didn't look at Trump's finances. It was a gap as big as the Grand Canyon.

"Why is it so important that witnesses cooperate and tell the truth in an investigation like this?" I asked Mueller next, my last question.

"Because the testimony of the witness goes to the heart of just about any criminal case you have."

Too few took the time to listen closely to Mueller that day. Reporters and political operatives who should have known better thought they could get on just fine not knowing what they didn't know. They were wrong. They miscalculated. Politics is not just about politics, it's also about the truth, and it's about principle, and it's about courage. The American people would ultimately demand that the crimes of Donald Trump be pursued.

This is the story of how the forty-fifth President of the United States was finally held accountable, how courageous public servants stood up and spoke truth to power, and what it means for our future that they did. I will share insights from my work with the House Intelligence and Judiciary Committees and our investigations of the Trump presidency, but I will not pass on any confidential or classified information and I will not pass on compromising items from behind closed committee doors merely for entertainment value. I pledge upfront to do my best to get the facts down as well as I know them, to steer clear of spin or gratuitous Republican bashing, and to stay open, always, to interpretations of events I might at first have missed and that might challenge me to reassess my views. I wrote this book to help sort out a vast and varied narrative that unfolded at lightning speed, with as many vertiginous twists and turns as a roller coaster ride, and I hope that by following my own path through these events, readers can put those twists and turns in a context that can lead to thoughtful reflection. I spent this period of time looking for signs of courage, real courage, and found it repeatedly, and some of what I saw behind the scenes may help put that courage into focus.

I believe we as a country will find a way to come together again. I believe in the power of the young to pull us into the future and move us past the mistakes of previous generations. I believe in remembering, and learning from where we've been, and not letting the power mongers of any era claim a monopoly on truth. They never have, and they never will. The truth belongs to all of us.

I've spent much of my life surrounded by Republicans—from my parents and two of my brothers to my lifelong best friend who went on to be the top White House speechwriter for President George W. Bush. Most important, I married a Hoosier from Southern Indiana who grew up with the Pence family. I would like to see a Republican Party that purges itself of the taint of Trumpism and asks the American people for its trust again.

I would like to see our elected officials talking about basic values and looking to our better natures, even when that feels like an impossible challenge. Courage matters. Courage is our only hope.

Think of the courage it took for Lt. Col. Alexander Vindman to testify before the nation knowing what that might cost him. Think of Dr. Fiona Hill and all that she risked. Think of the courage Senator Mitt Romney showed when he shocked Trump and his party by voting for impeachment and delivering a speech so powerful and unforgettable it left one of his fellow Senators in tears. Courage is not dead. Honor is not dead, not yet.

This is not a story of cynicism. It is a story of how much of a difference courageous individuals can make.

As I said in my Floor speech before I voted to impeach, "Standing up works! Now is the time to summon the courage those patriots showed against Donald Trump's corruption. If they can risk their careers, even their lives, to do the right thing, why can't my Republican colleagues? After all, more is on the line than just military aid to an ally. To protect our national security, stand up. To secure our elections, stand up. To honor our oath to the Constitution, stand up."

PART 2: NO ONE IS ABOVE THE LAW

CHAPTER 4

WHAT MY DAD TAUGHT ME

Going into the first night of televised debate on the first articles of impeachment, I kept thinking about the best way to put into context why it was so important that we fight for the principle that we all must follow the rules. Then it hit me: I'd been raised to think that way. One of my first memories is of being a kid in Algona, Iowa, where my dad was chief of police starting in 1982. My father was a stickler for the rules. He believed that no one was above the law—not the mayor, not the mayor's good old boys, not anyone. That conviction ended up costing him his job.

I was born, the first of four boys, when my parents were living in Sac City, Iowa, where my dad spent a year as a police officer before taking a job with the Iowa Department of Corrections. Then he heard of an opening in Algona, a northern Iowa town of a little more than six thousand people, and he went there for an interview with the mayor and city council. He was only thirty-five, but this young guy from California with a strong law-and-order reputation was just what the council wanted. They thought he could bring technology and innovation to Algona, which didn't even have 911 service back then.

My father got off to a good start as chief of police in Algona. As expected, he was able to implement a 911 system. "Because of its being so new," my mother remembers, "all the teachers in the schools were teaching the kids about how to use 911."

One morning, my father was in his office at the Police Department when his secretary told him he had a call. "Your son is on the 911 line," she told him. I was four years old at the time.

"You'd been naughty," my mother remembers.

My dad says, "You were upset that I didn't kiss you good-bye and tell you that I loved you that morning on my way to work." So, I had called 911 and got my dad on the phone. Not bad for a four-year-old. I now joke with my dad that I was really just auditing his fancy new 911 system.

There had been a rash of petty crimes in Algona dating back to before my father was hired. People reported the theft of tape decks (this *was* the '80s), mopeds, bicycles, and, most dramatically, a snowmobile, which was recovered from the Des Moines River. Enough complaints came in that my father started an investigation soon after he took over as police chief, one that he says "just kept mushrooming." More than two hundred charges were filed against a dozen local youths. "But it was not crimes committed that stirred emotions here as much as the persons accused of perpetrating the unlawful acts—local lads of fine standing, all age fifteen," the *Des Moines Register* reported. "Reason given: boredom."

My dad used the situation to rally people to make some positive changes. Growing up in California with a single mother, he had learned the hard way about the positive difference a group like the Boys & Girls Clubs of America could make. A juvenile officer had taken him to one. That changed his life. He developed a lifelong admiration for law-enforcement officers and the good they and the organization can do. So, in Algona, when all these fifteen-year-olds from good families were getting into trouble, my father decided to organize a local chapter of the Boys & Girls Clubs.

The year before my dad arrived in Algona there had been only a handful of drunk-driving arrests, and over his first year there, there were more than fifty. The surge in arrests was because my father made sure that if he or one of his officers pulled someone over for driving while intoxicated, that person would be held accountable. Most people saw that as a good thing, but not the local firemen, who didn't like the way their new police chief reacted when a fireman driving home from a Fire Board meeting was arrested for drunk driving.

Art Cullen, a reporter for the *Algona Upper Des Moines* who went on to win a Pulitzer Prize for editorial writing, took to my father right away when he arrived in town, and the two worked as partners trying to bring about change. "He told the firemen they couldn't drink at the Fire Department anymore, that's what ultimately did him in," Art says.

My father also ran afoul of the mayor, who liked to drive around town with a gun on his dashboard. "Swalwell said, 'You can't do that anymore,'" Art remembers. "Well, that was his boss. Even though you should let it slide, he wouldn't let it slide. He really believed no one was above the law."

My father came to realize that the good old boy network didn't want a chief who was actually going to enforce the law. It wanted someone it could bend to its will, someone who would look the other way.

Everything came to a head in a very Iowa way, with the Kossuth County Fair in August 1985. People drive in from all over the county, and there were cars parked everywhere, many of them illegally. A sergeant came to the house and knocked.

"Chief," he told my dad, "we're getting a lot of complaints. People are parking in the fire lane. What do you want me to do?"

The worry was that fire trucks wouldn't be able to drive down the street. If a fire broke out, it could put people's lives at risk.

"Give them a few minutes, and then ticket and tow them," my dad said.

Local officers wrote twenty-one tickets that day. On Monday morning, the mayor came into my father's office to raise hell.

"I've been getting a lot of calls about people complaining about these tickets," he told my dad.

"Oh, really?" my father answered.

"I expect those tickets to be taken care of," the mayor said.

My father didn't say anything. He had no intention of doing anyone any favors and canceling the tickets. He called over to the county clerk's office and found out that people had already started paying off the tickets. So, what was the problem?

When the mayor found out my father had refused to cancel the tickets, he blew his top. He told my dad that unless he reversed the tickets, he would be fired. My dad stood firm. Some of the city council members stuck up for my father, dragging the whole thing out.

Iowa newspapers picked up the story as an example of obvious corruption. In early September, the *Algona Upper Des Moines* newspaper ran an editorial backing my father and calling on the mayor to resign. The *Des*

Moines Register reported on the standoff, noting that my father had recently received a $400 merit raise on his salary of $23,800 a year.

"The community has been very supportive," my father told the *Register*.

Twice my father went to court and received injunctions to keep the mayor from firing him, but by January 1986, he'd given in to the inevitable and reached a settlement to leave his job. "I told your mom we need to just get out of here," my dad remembers. "It was a great city, I loved the people there, but it was just too much of a good old boy network."

My dad wasn't very political. He didn't go to college, and he didn't go to law school. But in his way, I think he passed the test. He stood up for what was right and lost his job for it. He believed no one was above the law, and he insisted on sticking to that principle. My father never talked much about what happened in Algona—I think he was a little embarrassed—but even after we moved back to California and started a new life, I always remembered what he taught me about holding firm and sticking up for what's right. No one is above the law—not the mayor of a small town in Iowa and not, as I would grapple with three decades later, the President of the United States.

I remember one other thing my dad taught me when I was a boy: You have to stand up to bullies. Back in elementary school, there were a couple times where I was picked on and pushed around by older kids. I remember once when I was ten and playing basketball, someone taller and bigger than me was pushing me around. My brother Josh, nine at the time, saw what was happening, came out of nowhere, and decked the kid pushing me around. It's kind of embarrassing when your younger brother stands up to the bully for you, but I saw that my dad was right: The bully backed down.

A few years later, I was in middle school and told my dad that an older student was getting in my face every day and shoving me around. "Well that's because you haven't stood up to him," my dad said. So, the next time the bully got in my face, I pushed him back. Other students started to gather around. The bully was shocked. I got in trouble at school for that, but I remember my dad's reaction. Which was basically: *I'm supposed to be upset with you, but I'm glad you did that.* And you know what? That was it. That kid never bothered me again.

CHAPTER 5

MY BEST FRIEND THE REPUBLICAN

My involvement in the impeachments of Donald Trump has nothing to do with party politics, nothing to do with Democrats versus Republicans. That's because I've been raised by Republicans and close to Republicans my whole life. I've been *debating* with Republicans my whole life. My friendship with Chris Michel, going back to when we were both young boys growing up in Northern California, started with an argument. He was pitching in a Dublin Little League game. I was the home plate umpire, and he didn't like my ball and strike calls—and he let me hear about it. I was twelve years old, Chris was eleven, and both of us were in the same grade. Chris and I had never hung out. I knew him from class as a smart, studious kid who was maybe a little bit shy. He sure wasn't shy complaining about my umpiring, though.

My family had settled down in Dublin, a small bedroom community about thirty-five miles east of San Francisco, in the summer of 1992. After going to nearly a dozen schools in Iowa, Oregon, and up and down California, and living in nearly a dozen houses, I had finally found a lasting home. It was kind of cool seeing different parts of the country, at least in retrospect, but as a kid the nomadic life sucked. Just when you started to make new friends and settle in, you were moving again. For me, that made the few close friendships I developed feel even more precious.

When we came to town, Dublin was best known for having the most fast-food restaurants per capita in the United States. We had no Main Street, but we did have a street with a McDonalds, a Jack in the Box, a KFC, a Taco Bell, a Wendy's, and a Carl's Jr. The burgeoning economic engine of Silicon Valley was not far away, but by and large, I went to school with students from working-class families, mostly white, but also Hispanic, Filipino, and African American. There were a lot of churches in town. We went to Resurrection

Lutheran, which was across the street from the Chuck E. Cheese, always a powerful motivator to get us up and to church on a lazy Sunday morning.

By middle school I tended to hang out with the troublemakers, figuring they had to be cool and maybe I could pick up some of that by association. Hanging out with someone as smart as Chris Michel scared me. Sheesh, the guy could probably run circles around me academically.

Dublin didn't have a competitive traveling soccer team, so I had to try out in neighboring San Ramon. My new teammates called me "Scrublin," since I came from Dublin, a place of fast-food burger joints and blighted schools. I resented the nickname, but my teammates were friendly enough to invite me over to their houses, which felt palatial compared to where I lived. I took "Scrublin" on the chin, brushed it off, and rolled with it.

After leaving Iowa, my family had rented, never owned. Finally, when I was in high school, we moved into our first house—on the same street as Chris's. That's when he became a big influence on me. We were in freshman English together and both swooned for our teacher, Ms. Gray. She was young, wickedly smart, and a great teacher. Chris and I were competing to be her favorite student. We knew that she taught older grades a class we would love to get accepted into, Speech and Debate. Freshman English was almost an audition to get into that class.

Jean-Pierre Lacrampe, Chris, our other great high school friend Jeff Crawford, and I all did well in speech. By our senior year in mock trial, we had made it to the attorneys' tables, but my first opening statement as a mock trial attorney was a disaster. I started choking on water as I was speaking to the jurors, local attorneys who'd volunteered to come in and score us. Chris stared at me for a minute and then whacked me hard on the back to try to stop my coughing fit. I've never again choked on water in front of a jury.

Both my parents were registered Republicans, and if I thought about it at all growing up, I probably expected I'd be a Republican as well. Chris was politically conservative, but it wasn't something that we ever really thought or talked about much. He was never rigid in his ideas. We were constantly turning things around in our minds, looking for different insights, different ways to frame important questions. Having a great English teacher like Ms.

Gray helped open up a world of ideas to us. She made it all feel very real and urgent.

Through our economics teacher, Tim Sbranti, an important mentor who later became the Mayor of Dublin, we started getting involved in local political races. Tim was helping run the campaign of a candidate for Dublin City Council, Claudia McCormick. It was a nonpartisan race, not about Democrat or Republican, and Tim asked some of the students to get involved—and we did.

As we looked beyond high school graduation in 1999, Chris and I both wanted to go straight to a four-year college, something no one in either of our families had done. For me, my hands were my ticket. I earned a soccer and academic scholarship to Campbell University, a small Division I school in North Carolina, where I'd play goalkeeper. Campbell was a Southern Baptist university divided into men's and women's campuses. Women were not allowed to enter the men's dorms, and men were certainly not allowed into women's dorms. All I really had time to focus on was playing soccer and doing all I could to keep that scholarship and fulfill my parents' dream for me to go to college.

Prior to college, neither Chris nor I had ever visited Washington, DC. Now that we were both on the East Coast, Chris at Yale, me at Campbell, we decided to meet in the middle and explore DC together. We talked about what it would be like, walking by the White House, the Capitol Rotunda, the Washington Monument, the Lincoln Memorial, and so much else. For all the different waves of history, the different administrations that had come and gone, Washington was still the city of its namesake, the city of the Founders. It was the city of believers in a Constitution crafted with an eye to human nature and human foibles. Our Founders laid the groundwork for a democratic system built on a separation of powers doctrine, the three branches of government balancing each other out, to guard against abuse. They had gone to great trouble to rid themselves of one king and did not want to see their fine new experiment in democracy taken over by another one.

Our chance to visit came in early 2001. President George W. Bush, the son of a President, had been named the winner of the contested November 2000 presidential election. The inauguration was scheduled for Saturday, January 20, 2001, and every political figure in America had descended on the capital city. I was twenty then, and Chris was nineteen. We found the only hotel we could, a Days Inn deep in Virginia, and couldn't wait to take it all in, the pageantry and speeches, the spectators, the unfolding of history.

Chris was a Republican, but I didn't know what I was. A Republican like my parents? A Democrat like my mentor Tim Sbranti? I'd have to work that one out. In the meantime, I was going to stand in the cold with Chris and three hundred thousand others for Bush's inaugural address.

I liked what I heard that day. "We have a place, all of us, in a long story—a story we continue, but whose end we will not see," Bush said, expanding on the "American story" as one of a "flawed and fallible people, united across the generations by grand and enduring ideals."

It was a cold day, with some fog and a little rain, and we were way back on the Mall. I mostly remember loving being close to the action, feeling something stir inside me, a need to be involved, to play some part in the story of our country. "We were about ten thousand rows back, but you could see what was happening on the big screens, if you really squinted enough," Chris says.

Chris loved Bush's closing, which was both idealistic and powerful. "Americans are generous and strong and decent, not because we believe in ourselves, but because we hold beliefs beyond ourselves," he said, his voice echoing around us on the Mall.

"It was a typical Bush-at-his-best sort of speech," Chris says now, looking back. "It had a religious tone to it, a religious touch to it that reflected him, but it wasn't in your face. It wasn't over the top. It was in keeping with the tradition of the best American presidential rhetoric."

We squinted to see Bill Clinton step forward to shake the new President's hand and congratulate him on the speech, with Hillary, then a newly elected Senator, nearby. New First Lady Laura Bush stood and applauded.

Chris had also lined up tickets for us that night for something called the Fiesta Americana Inaugural Ball, hosted by the Organization of American States. I was really excited looking at the long list of special guests on the invitation, from President Bush to Colin Powell—until I noticed the asterisks after all the big names: for "invited" guests. Yeah, they weren't coming.

Invited, but not coming: a Washington trick. We were rookies and should have known better. But one thing the ball did have was margaritas, a lot of margaritas. We ate and drank our share.

In 2001, Chris and I both landed the Washington summer jobs we wanted. I interned in the office of Ellen Tauscher of California, a House Democrat, and Chris worked at an intelligence agency. That summer, we would take the Metro back to College Park, Maryland, where we were staying in a fraternity house, and talk about what we'd seen and done that day. We'd cook some chicken or fish on our George Foreman Grill and argue about what government was about and how it could best serve the people.

To help feed myself that summer, I took an early morning job handing out towels at the Washington Sports Club, a gym around the corner from the Capitol. I met a lot of members of Congress and a lot of Congressional aides in my work-issued gym shorts and gym shirt. I tried to learn as many of their faces and names as possible. I remember the intensely competitive Levin brothers—Carl and Sandy, a Senator and a Congressman—coming in often to play squash. They were loud. They shouted at each other. Then they'd finish up, come out smiling, and soon enough walk out of the locker room in suits and head up to the Capitol.

I also worked evenings that summer at Tortilla Coast, a Tex-Mex restaurant around the corner from the Capitol, where I was constantly taking taco orders from members of Congress. I would study the Congressional "facebook," a directory of every member, Republican and Democrat, with his or her photo and biographical information. I figured if I memorized their names and faces, I could call them by name—and get better tips. Shocking! Members of Congress were so easily flattered. What hit me reading their biographies was how many of them had gone to Ivy League schools or came from wealth, and how many had a parent or other family member who had served in Congress before.

I often saw Republicans and Democrats eating dinner together at Tortilla Coast. That made a big impression on me. Before that, I tended to think they were always enemies. But when I saw them talking and laughing together, often with their spouses, it opened my eyes to how important it was to build relationships, make friends, learn about others, talk a lot and listen more.

I had a good model in my boss, Representative Ellen Tauscher. I think I saw her hanging out with more Republicans that summer than Democrats. She was the living embodiment of bipartisanship. That was the Washington I came to know.

Fresh out of Yale in the summer of 2003, Chris was accepted for an internship at the White House working in the speechwriting department. He made the most of the chance and parlayed it into a full-time job. That winter, Chris was amazed to be handed an invitation, with a plus one, to a White House Christmas party. His then girlfriend, Emily Kropp, whom he'd met working at the White House, was already invited, so I got to be his date for the night.

Driving over to the White House wearing my rented tux, I'd heard on the radio that the deposed Iraqi dictator Saddam Hussein had been captured near his hometown of Tikrit. Everyone was talking about Hussein at the White House that night. I was nervous waiting in line to meet the President and First Lady and pose for a picture. Finally, a Marine guard read aloud from a card.

"Mr. President," he said. "Chris Michel and his guest, Eric Swalwell."

George Bush gave Chris a funny look—like "Who the hell is this guy you've brought to the White House?" To me, the President looked ten feet tall. I'd never met a President before. I must have found something to say to him, a joke about baseball maybe, but I was so nervous I forgot to say hello to the First Lady. Laura Bush held her hand out, patiently waiting for me to shake it.

"Hiiiiiii, Eric, I'm over here," she said finally, in that friendly Southern accent, flashing a warm smile. She was kind and gracious. I wasn't the first White House visitor to go blank in the big moment.

I knew by this time that I was a Democrat. I disagreed with a good number of the policies my friend and his boss advocated, but I had deep respect for what Chris was doing. Everything he did was rooted in his faith; then as now, it guided him, and that made Chris a perfect match for a President who was comfortable talking about his faith to the American people.

Chris and I argued the most over the Bush administration's approach to Iraq. Aside from my objections to how we went into Iraq—under the false pretense that Hussein had weapons of mass destruction—I believed we had no plan to rebuild the country and that our presence there was only help-ing terrorists recruit more followers. Today, we're still paying the price for invading Iraq in such a muddle. The Middle East is no more stable, ISIS was created, and we damaged our moral standing in the world. (In January 2020, when Trump gave the order to kill Iranian general Qasem Soleimani at Baghdad Airport, the argument between Chris and me continued—again, over the longer-term consequences, which I argued could be devastating.)

I was honored when Chris asked me to be co–best man at his July 2008 wedding to Emily, attended by some of the White House senior staff. The wedding was at the Cathedral of St. Matthew the Apostle in Washington, and the reception afterward was at the Mayflower Hotel, a Washington landmark. Unfortunately, the hotel had been in the news recently, with disclosures about New York Governor Eliot Spitzer meeting sex workers there.

"I must admit, I'm very impressed with the Mayflower's hospitality," I said at the start of my toast, pausing a beat. "They asked me if I wanted an escort up to my room."

The line drew an odd mixture of nervous laughs and mortified looks. Chris had a big smile on his face, but his eyes looked a little uncertain.

"The only person that's been more nervous about this speech than me is Chris," I continued, earning some laughs. "He even offered to write it. In my line of work, we call that consciousness of guilt." I paused. "Maybe he's concerned that my speech did not go through some of the same rigorous fact-checking methods used at the White House. Or maybe he's concerned that it did."

Chris stayed with the President all the way until the end of his admin-istration, finishing up as Bush's top speechwriter. The two were so close, in fact, that Bush asked Chris to help him write his memoir, *Decision Points*. Chris and Emily, newly married, moved to Dallas so Chris could work with the President every day. Emily would help the First Lady with her book, *Spoken from the Heart*.

The times have brought challenges to our friendship, but Chris remains my best friend, someone I've consulted on almost every important decision I've ever made.

CHAPTER 6

"WE DO JUSTICE"

I learned as a politically active student at the University of Maryland that you can't change people's minds unless you can first get them to pay attention. In May 2003, I dressed up in swim trunks, a Hawaiian shirt, and a black wig and showed up with a bullhorn outside the governor's office in Maryland to mock Bob Ehrlich, Republican Governor of Maryland, as "Bahama Bob." Ehrlich had just announced new plans to slash higher education spending, which we knew would mean higher tuition, and then had immediately gone on vacation in the Bahamas. We had a field day skewering him for that, making the local TV news and newspapers.

I'd gotten involved in politics soon after I arrived at Maryland (I transferred after an injury cost me my soccer scholarship), working with a young city councilman named Eric Olson and helping him to win reelection. Together we launched the idea of a nonvoting student representative on the city council. It took months, but eventually the legislation passed, and I was approved as the first city council liaison. I continued to work at Congresswoman Tauscher's office, going into DC three days a week, usually after an early morning class, and then sticking around for a shift at Tortilla Coast. I owned all of two suits, though I learned that if you invest in belts and shoes and a variety of ties, no one will notice you have only two suits.

One Tuesday in September 2001, I woke up early and was in my room at my fraternity house, Alpha Sigma Phi, ironing my suit pants before class and watching the *Today* show on my little thirteen-inch TV. A plane had just hit the North Tower of the World Trade Center. *Who could be so stupid?* I thought. Then another plane hit the South Tower. It was pretty clear this was an attack, but I was confused and didn't know what to think.

I had a government class that morning and didn't think of skipping it. It's hard to believe now that we went to class at all, and even harder to believe that in that class, the attacks were barely mentioned. But that was how far terrorism was from our minds. We just didn't grasp what had happened.

After class, I took the Metro over to the Hill in my pinstriped suit to work in Tauscher's office. I had no idea that at 9:43 a.m., an order had gone out to evacuate the White House and Capitol Building. When I arrived at the Capitol South Metro station, I got word that Tauscher's office was closed, and I caught another train home, where I learned that the Pentagon had also been hit.

Many of my fraternity brothers were from New York and New Jersey. We all sat in the living room of the house and watched the unbelievable images: a crumbled World Trade Center, a flaming Pentagon, and scattered fragments of a 757 in a field in Shanksville, Pennsylvania. Later that day, we found out that the father of one of our housemates, Ben, had been at the Pentagon that day and was missing. Seeing Ben lose his father shook me. Soon, I set to work establishing a scholarship fund, publicly and privately funded, for the families of 9/11 victims.

One memory of 9/11 stands out for me. After the Capitol was evacuated, sending me and so many others home, some 150 members of Congress assembled on the East Front steps of the Capitol, held a moment of silence for the fallen, and then spontaneously broke into "God Bless America." This was Republicans and Democrats together, holding hands and singing to honor the dead and show our enemies the force of unity. I couldn't believe it. The same members who had so often been at one another's throats were now banding together.

The following week, when I returned to Capitol Hill, I was struck by how dramatically things had changed. Washington had become a much darker place. Anxiety had taken over. There were temporary barriers everywhere, and people were jumpy about everything: a slammed door, a dropped book, a plane flying low. We were jolted so easily. The nation was traumatized, and we all feared the next attack was imminent.

Then news started breaking of anthrax being sent to people on Capitol Hill, including to Senators Tom Daschle and Pat Leahy, and to various news organizations. The white powder containing spores of anthrax, a highly lethal strain of weaponized bacteria, killed five people and infected many others.

ANTHRAX IS FOUND IN HOUSE BUILDING was the pulse-quickening *Washington Post* headline on Sunday, October 21, 2001.

One of my duties as a Congressional intern, besides answering phones and giving tours, was opening the mail. It was nerve-wracking, to say the least. Every time I opened a letter, I expected a powdery substance to spill out. If I started sniffling a little with a slight cold, I was paralyzed with anxiety. Had I been poisoned? Did I need to go stand in the long lines at the health clinic where nurses and doctors were evaluating staffers for signs of anthrax exposure?

It was a scary time that made me, like so many others, take stock of what was really important. I'd enjoyed my free-spirited summer of exploring Washington, from its corridors of power to its intern-filled bars, but now I was forced to grow up and see the world as it was, not as I wanted it to be. The aftermath of September 11 was a turning point in my life. We were at war with terrorists and the countries that supported them. I wanted to better understand this new threat to America. I got more serious about my studies, and settled on a vision for my future that would, somehow, involve running for office and making sure that the energy and fresh perspective of young people were represented.

I'd be lying if I said that as an intern in Washington it had never been a dream of mine to one day be in Congress myself, but I also dreamed of playing for the San Francisco Giants and hanging out with Will "the Thrill" Clark. I knew Congress was mostly closed to people like me who weren't rich or well connected. I certainly hadn't grown up knowing anyone who could get me into Congress. But the dream still grabbed me. Back home for Christmas 2001, I was high on my internship experience and told my dad and his conservative friends that when I was old enough, I would run for Congress. They all had a good laugh.

"I could see why you became a Democrat," my dad says now. "Ellen Tauscher was a great woman, and I think that played a big part in your decision. She was somewhat of a mentor to you. That's probably where the 'Democrat' came in."

I'd developed a passion for national security issues from being in Washington on 9/11, and that continued during my first term at law school. I hoped one day to work for the U.S. Attorney's Office. I wanted to be a part of the prosecution team that put America's enemies away. I signed up for a Homeland Security course, taught by national security expert Michael Greenberger, that focused almost exclusively on September 11.

We delved into a detailed study of the work of the 9/11 Commission—its inception, its challenges, and its report. What struck me most about the commission was the unity its members showed in working together to protect our country. That kind of unity took time and effort to pull together.

When it came time to focus on where I wanted to spend a summer as a law clerk, I zeroed in on home. The Alameda County District Attorney's Office had a reputation for being ethical and training and developing trial lawyers. It was the place for me, I knew, if only I could persuade them of that. I'd made it to the final interview, with Nancy O'Malley, the number two in the office, and felt it was going well. I was sure I had the job . . . until Nancy threw me a curve ball. She had a hypothetical question for me, and it was a tough one.

"What would you do," she asked, "if you were given a case where a police officer made a stop on a known drug dealer and found a lot of cocaine in the car, only to be told by the cop before he testified that he really didn't have a reason to stop the car, just that he knew the suspect was dirty. Would you proceed or drop the case?"

I had never met Nancy, and she was a tough read. I knew the Alameda County DA's Office had a reputation for integrity, but I also feared I would come across as weak, not enough of a go-getter, if I told her what I believed, which was that I should drop the case. I took a half second to think about it, gulped hard, and gave an answer I really thought might doom my chances.

"No case is more important than doing the right thing," I told her. "I'd dismiss it. We'll get that guy the next time."

Nancy gave me her best poker face—*Oh shit,* I was thinking—and thanked me for interviewing.

Nancy laughs thinking about that moment now. She knew I thought I had screwed myself with the wrong answer, thinking I'd lost the job.

I had no idea, for months, whether my answer had helped or hurt my application. Only once I was hired and spoke to Nancy at a summer law clerk happy hour did I bring up how nervous I'd been answering that question.

"You'd be surprised how many people say to proceed with the case," she told me that evening. "Some even say, 'You have to break a few eggs to make an omelet.'" She paused for impact, taking a sip of her drink. "You'll never meet those people," she continued. "I didn't hire them."

The office was highly regarded for the on-the-job training it offered its lawyers. Every summer law clerk was essentially guaranteed a shot at trying a jury trial. A supervisor would sit with the public, but the jury would never know the prosecutor was still in law school. You didn't get to pick your case, though. You had to make the best of whatever you were given.

My case involved a defendant accused of evading the police. "The police tried to pull this guy over, he didn't stop, and they chased him," I was told when I was given the case. "Pretty cut and dried."

Actually, the case was anything but cut and dried. Yes, the defendant was told to pull over. The officer turned on his lights. The defendant didn't pull over. The officer chased. The chase went so long it was finally called off. The defendant was later arrested on a warrant. Slam dunk, right? Not by a long shot.

I learned during the trial that the officer, who was white, had encountered the defendant, who was black, earlier in the evening. The defendant was pulling into a bar parking lot and had words with the officer over the speed he was driving into the lot. The officer felt disrespected. Some time passed, and as the defendant was leaving the bar, the officer was back in the area—throughout the trial, it looked more and more like the officer may have waited for the defendant to leave. The officer said the defendant committed a traffic violation as he was pulling out. The officer tried to pull him over. The defendant testified that he felt as if the officer had been waiting for him and that he feared for his life, which was why he hadn't pulled over. Instead, he said, he drove to a nearby police station.

I was skeptical, but when I checked, I found that the defendant had indeed gone to a police station. At trial, he was acquitted in about an hour. I was crushed because I "lost" the case, and I feared I wouldn't be hired.

I had it all wrong. The only person who should have been upset was the defendant, who had to go through that ordeal. Looking back on that case, I realize now that I wasn't mature enough to understand all that was going on.

I can't imagine what the black defendant felt as he pulled out of the parking lot and saw the same officer he'd had words with earlier now driving behind him. That's something most white men don't experience.

Nancy told me not to worry about losing the case, or my decision to find exonerating evidence to help the defendant. "In this office it's not about 'winning' and 'losing,'" she told me. "We do justice."

One of my first cases as a lawyer involved a public employee's abuse of power. It was the retrial of a firefighter arrested for driving under the influence. The jury in the first trial, handled by another prosecutor, had been hung 11 to 1 for guilt. Typically, for a misdemeanor case, if there is a hung jury, you would dismiss the case. But I wasn't dismissing this one. As soon as it came across my desk, what jumped off the page for me was the fact that when the firefighter, a battalion chief, was pulled over, instead of showing his driver's license to the police officer, he flashed his badge.

He thought his position entitled him to do whatever he wanted and not be held to account. Thankfully, the police officer wasn't corrupt. He was having none of it. The battalion chief's blood alcohol level was well over the legal limit and he had been pulled over because as he was driving on the freeway, he swerved out of his lane and almost swiped and killed two California Highway Patrol officers who were on the side of the road.

The battalion chief went to great lengths to try and beat the case, bringing in a Yale-trained gastroenterologist to claim that he'd had only one drink, but that because he had gastroesophageal reflux disease, also known as acid reflux, the blood alcohol test results had been exaggerated. The jury didn't buy this and convicted the battalion chief in about a half hour.

CHAPTER 7

"CONGRESS DOESN'T TAKE RESERVATIONS"

I wanted to run for Congress because I believed that young people with new energy and new ideas could shake things up and demand better of their elected leaders. You had to keep people in Congress on their toes. You had to remind them of the people back home counting on them to do their job. The more that elected representatives lost that connection to their constituents and became creatures of Washington, the more likely they were to put their own power and position first. It was especially important to keep young voters active and engaged and feeling that their core concerns were being represented. Young voters were the future, the ones least likely to give into cynicism and most likely to protest and oppose a lawless, rogue President like Donald Trump, as they did in large numbers from early in his presidency.

Pete Stark, my first opponent in a Congressional race, was the dean of the California delegation, first elected in 1972. By 2011, when I was starting to kick around the idea of running for Congress myself, Stark was eighty years old and had served in Congress for forty years. I thought that was too long. How could someone still be effective after serving that long? What about making way for the next generation, who may be more in touch with current issues?

In June 2010, California voters passed Proposition 14, which called for open primaries. Starting in 2011, all voters in the California primary would receive the same ballot, regardless of party affiliation. And instead of the top candidate from each party going through to the general election, the two candidates with the most votes, regardless of party, would run in the general. The Top Two Candidates Open Primary Act allowed a candidate to get out there and talk to voters from all parties; they could all vote for you.

Redistricting had so dramatically reshaped Stark's district going into the November 2012 elections that nearly half of it would consist of voters he hadn't represented for the past ten years. More than half these new voters were from the Tri-Valley area where I grew up, played soccer, and worked in the local courthouse as a prosecutor. Because I'd also served as planning commissioner and arts commissioner and, in 2010, was elected to the Dublin City Council, I knew the area and its needs.

In July 2011, I flew to Washington, DC, to represent the Dublin City Council in our pursuit of an economic development grant and meet with every member of Congress from the Tri-Valley area. The last meeting on my schedule was with Pete Stark. I didn't have high expectations, but I was curious to meet the man who would be representing me after redistricting. I sat in the waiting room of his Capitol Hill office for close to half an hour. Finally, a staff member came out to tell me that the Congressman would not be coming into the office that morning. I was told, though, that he wanted to speak to me on the phone.

I was invited into Stark's office, which was as grand and lavishly decorated as you'd expect from one of the wealthiest members of Congress. What an unusual scene it was. We were all there, Stark's staff and me and the city of Dublin's Washington lobbyist, but no Congressman Stark. I sank into a leather couch that probably cost as much as most people's cars and tried to figure out what was going on.

"I'm at home," Stark told me when he called in.

"California?" I asked.

"No, Maryland."

My head hurt, I was so confused. It was a busy day at the Capitol. People were moving around at a dizzying pace. The clock in the office was constantly buzzing all morning, indicating there were votes on the Floor. What the hell was Stark doing at home, missing votes? I would find out later that over the course of his career, Stark had missed more than *four thousand* votes, one of the worst records in Congress.

How did it happen? Back in 1972, Fortney Hillman Stark Jr. was the brash upstart. He grew up in Milwaukee, studied engineering at MIT, and then, after a stint in the air force in the late 1960s, moved to California to earn his MBA at UC Berkeley. He wasn't easy to figure out. On the one hand, he was a banker who had founded the Security National Bank in

Walnut Creek in 1963. On the other, he was a strong opponent of the U.S. war in Vietnam. In fact, he erected a huge peace sign on top of his bank, and he switched from Republican to Democrat in the 1960s. In 1970, the *San Francisco Examiner* dubbed Stark "an anti-establishment bank president," and the *Los Angeles Times* gently mocked his split personality: "Fortney H. (Pete) Stark can't seem to decide whether to make a lot of money or save the world." In 1972, at age forty, Stark defeated fourteen-term Congressman George Miller of Alameda after claiming in campaign flyers that the eighty-one-year-old Miller often "dozes through Congressional debates." (At least Miller showed up!)

Since redistricting, I'd been seriously mulling a run against Stark, and the visit to DC convinced me that at the very least, we should not have him representing us. I spoke to my high school friends Chris and Jeff about running, and they were skeptical that I had any kind of shot. They said the party would castigate me for running against a fellow Democrat. How would I raise the money? What about my $100,000 in student debt? What about my job at the District Attorney's Office? Surely, my higher-ups there wouldn't let me stay if I ran for Congress. The questions went on and on. But we talked each one through. Both friends offered me their full support. I made a big ask of each of them. I'd need a contribution from Jeff. He said, "No problem." And I'd need Chris to help me draft my announcement speech. He agreed—and promised not to add any Bush-isms. The next two people I needed to talk to were my two key mentors up until then, my former high school teacher Tim Sbranti and my boss, Alameda County district attorney Nancy O'Malley. When I had them both on board, I knew this was really happening.

I'll never forget the day I called Pete Stark as a courtesy to give him a heads up.

"Sir . . . I am going to make a public announcement today that I'm running for Congress," I told him. "I just want you to hear it first and from me."

"You don't stand a chance," he said. "I've locked up all the endorsements."

He had a point there. No question—statewide California Democratic leaders and members of Congress were behind Stark against a young unknown challenging him in a primary, but my feeling on that was: So what? I wasn't banking on having any of them. To me, those endorsements just branded Stark as an establishment candidate. I was going for local endorsements: mayors, city council members, school board members. Hell, I might even sweep the Mosquito Abatement Board.

One big problem I had was money. Stark had a war chest of more than half a million dollars and I'd need to raise at least a hundred thousand to have any shot at holding my own. I did what you do, which is pursue every possible lead of financial support, including flying back to Washington to line up support from college and law school friends.

I was out in the district campaigning for long hours, and Stark was paying close attention. He'd call my boss and complain. "Your boy is violating the rules, he's campaigning while on county time," Nancy remembers him saying. "And I said, 'No, no, Pete, he's not. I know exactly what he's doing.'"

I met with the *San Francisco Chronicle* Editorial Board during the campaign, led by longtime Editorial Page Editor John Diaz, who I'd been reading for years.

"Other Democrats are saying you should wait your turn, considering the long line of more senior Democrats waiting in line for Stark to retire," John said. "How do you respond to that criticism?"

"Congress doesn't take reservations," I said. "It's walk-ins only."

To put together a campaign team, I was lucky to convince Lisa Tucker, a political advisor to Ellen Tauscher, to come work for me, even though I was only a city council member at the time. Lisa would pay a heavy price for that, losing clients in her consulting business after being blacklisted for taking on a Democrat who was challenging another Democrat. She and a pollster she asked me to hire, Alex Evans, were about the only two experienced people who would agree to help. I was also lucky to have TJ Daly, husband to fellow Tauscher intern alum Melinda Mills, serve as my campaign manager.

Lisa told me we needed to do a poll. What she and Alex found out was that nobody knew who I was; my name identification stood at about 4 percent. I said that meant it was time to pack things up. Alex stared at me with a quizzical expression.

"You're looking at the poll the wrong way," he told me. "Stark's reelect number is about 41 percent. That's the number who say they're inclined to vote to reelect him. That's not catastrophic for him, but it's pretty bad."

I needed to build on my strengths, which were my work as a prosecutor and city council member and my community involvement as a local soccer coach. I also needed to point out Stark's two major weaknesses: that he didn't vote in Washington and that he had stopped coming home to work in the district.

"I understand what I'm supposed to tell the voters about Congressman Stark's work," I said to Alex, "but if they ask me something about myself, what should I say?"

Alex stared at me a minute. "You should remind them that Pete Stark doesn't vote in Washington and doesn't come to the district."

His point was that this was a referendum on the incumbent. Of course, I had to be credible and qualified, but this was really about whether Stark was serving his constituents.

When Stark and I met for what turned out to be our only debate, he was as nasty as Nancy O'Malley had warned me he might be, calling me a "pipsqueak" and a "Junior-Leaguer" all in the early going, earning a reprimand from the moderator for his personal attacks. He even, at one point, accused me, without evidence, of taking "hundreds of thousands of dollars" in bribes. It was a foolish blunder on his part. I knew I had a strong legal case to sue him for defamation, but I started by demanding a retraction—and so did the *Oakland Tribune*. Five days later, Stark had to retract his accusation. Pundits were speculating that he might be on the ropes.

I knew, given the new primary rules, that all I had to do was make a strong enough showing in the June primary to position myself as a viable alternative to Stark. Sure enough, Stark finished first that June, with 41.8 percent. I was at 36 percent, and knew I was within striking distance. Third-place finisher Chris Pareja would not be on the November ballot, and I was sure I could pick up many of his voters, people who had already cast a ballot against the forty-year incumbent Stark. Before Election Day in November, I kept knocking on doors and I picked up key endorsements from the *San*

Francisco Chronicle and the San Jose *Mercury News* editorial boards. I was elected with 52.1 percent of the vote.

I'll never forget, after being sworn in, Alex pulled me aside. "Don't take away the wrong lesson about what happened in your election," he told me, deadpan. "This election was not about you; it was about him," Alex said, and I knew he was right. "What happens next, the next two years, that will be entirely about you."

CHAPTER 8

I.T. HELP DESK, CAN I HELP YOU?

My class of Congress, elected in November 2012, had in common a searing experience. Just five weeks after the election that month, a national tragedy occurred in Newtown, Connecticut. On December 14, a twenty-year-old went on a shooting spree at Sandy Hook Elementary School, leaving twenty-six people dead, six adults and twenty children. Even now it's painful to think of Sandy Hook. At the time, I was devastated. I wanted to channel that grief into action in Congress.

Naïvely, I thought that I'd be able to get all my freshman colleagues on board with an assault weapons ban. I didn't know much about "whipping" (the art of asking colleagues to support a particular piece of legislation, tracking the count, and bringing it over the finish line for passage), but I did feel comfortable talking about guns from my work as a prosecutor. During a post–Sandy Hook early meeting with members interested in ending gun violence, Minority Leader Pelosi invited freshman members to her office. I remember Pelosi looking to a senior, more conservative Democratic member to understand, genuinely, why people needed assault weapons.

"Tell me," she said, "what is the purpose of these assault weapons? Do you use them to hunt? What's the purpose?"

The Blue Dog member looked at Leader Pelosi, then around the table, then back at the Leader. "Well, Madam Leader, they're just cool to shoot."

"So, it's a machismo thing?" Leader Pelosi asked without missing a beat.

The Blue Dog member nodded. "Exactly."

Leader Pelosi, mindful that banning assault weapons was not popular everywhere, encouraged us to keep our focus on background checks and said that individual members could focus on the assault weapons legislation. I continued to work my friends—but to little avail. I was shocked at how few of my freshman colleagues felt comfortable signing onto an assault weapons ban. It was seen as a political liability.

Toward the end of my first term, a young Pelosi Floor aide approached me. "The Minority Leader would like to see you," I was told.

Was I in trouble? Was the Leader upset with a vote I'd made or something I'd said? What other possible reason could she have to want to meet with me? I was still getting to know her, but I understood that she was a quick and methodical worker. I'd have to pay attention to exactly what she said, because she would make her point, no words wasted, then move on. She had dozens of other meetings with other members awaiting her.

"You wanted to speak with me, Leader?" I said, taking a seat.

"Oh, hi dear," she said, looking up and smiling. "Seeing that there are a lot more younger members now with this recent 2014 election, why don't you take the young members, start a group, and lead them in listening to young people across the country?"

I was still digesting what she said.

"I think that would be good for you," she added. "Thank you, dear." And with that, she was done, and soon speaking to another member.

Leader Pelosi was asking me to organize our youngest members to go out and listen to and speak for young people across the country. It was up to me to figure out the rest. Her suggestion could not have come at a better time. In the House Democratic Caucus, a debate was raging about our seniority system. Many younger members were frustrated that they were having to wait years, possibly decades, before they could join the leadership ranks or, if we took over the majority, chair a committee.

Frankly, my early days in Congress felt more like working at an I.T. Help Desk. As one of the younger members, I was often asked by more senior members to set up Facebook accounts, sign them up for "Snapshot"—"Er, that's Snapchat, sir"—and even help adjust their phones to silent mode so they wouldn't ring in the middle of committee hearings. I was eager to take on a bigger leadership role.

I saw this as an opportunity to get something done, and recruiting other younger members was easy. We were all eager to do *something*. The hardest part in launching it was naming the group.

One of my early mentors in Congress was Anna Eshoo, from the Bay Area, whose district included Silicon Valley cities like Mountain View, site of Google's headquarters. On one long flight back home from Washington, Anna brought me a *New York Times Magazine* article about Anthony Shore, a brilliant Madison Avenue type with a genius for branding and naming.

Handing the article back after I was done, I said absently, "Boy, wouldn't it be great if we could get a guy like him to help us name our group?"

She stared at me as if I had three heads. "Eric, that's why I gave you the article!" she said. "Call him and have him work on it."

I really thought she had to be kidding. "Anna, this guy is not going to take my call. He names Fortune 100 companies," I said.

"Eric, you're a member of Congress," Anna said firmly, a little edge to her voice. "You may not know who he is, but he will respect who you are."

So, I found Anthony Shore on Twitter, and within about twenty-four hours we connected. Anthony was thrilled to help me name the group. We talked through the group's goals and priorities, and a few weeks later he sent me a long list of possible names. One jumped out at me: Future Forum. The word *future* had to be in the name, and *forum* conveyed a conversation. We weren't going to classrooms, brew pubs, and workplaces to tell young people what they needed to know; we were going to listen and have a conversation.

The Millennial generation is the largest, best educated, and most diverse generation ever in American history. We put together a group that was going to reach out to them, listen to them, learn from them, and speak for them as their representatives in Washington. Over the next two years, we went to more than fifty cities across the country, with a particular focus on the Midwest, the Southwest, and places where young people felt especially left out of the conversation about America's economic future.

"What should I do about this Antarctica trip request?" my scheduler asked.

I was wrapping up my first term in Congress, had survived a primary challenge from the Majority Leader of the California State Senate (backed by Pete Stark, out for revenge), and was finally beginning to get my sea legs.

"Antarctica? What in the world are you talking about?" I asked.

"The Science Committee is going to Antarctica. You're too junior to be invited, but there's a waitlist, and I need to know if I should put you on it."

I didn't track what any of that meant, but the more I asked, the more I learned: The United States has a serious climate mission in Antarctica that Congress has jurisdiction over.

"Sure, put me on the list," I said, having no expectation of making the cut.

A few months later, in November 2014, my scheduler came back and told me, "A bunch of members dropped out. You're in."

Why not, I thought. It was an interesting mission of Congress. I was not married, had no kids, and was eager to get out of Washington. Next thing I knew, I was dressed in polar gear and boarding an LC-130, a large military transport plane on skis, for the flight to McMurdo Station, Antarctica, via Christchurch, New Zealand.

It was only a nine-hour flight from Christchurch to McMurdo, a few hours more than my weekly flights back and forth between San Francisco and Washington. But it turns out, it wasn't as easy to fly to Antarctica from New Zealand as I had thought. The Congressional delegation was made up almost entirely of Science Committee members, led by Chairman Lamar Smith of Texas. Joining us was the National Science Foundation (NSF) President Dr. France Córdova and a NASA astronaut. Turns out, Antarctica is the place on earth NASA considers most like Mars.

We had to wait a few days in New Zealand for the Antarctica weather to clear, so the control officer representing our embassy suggested one day that we go out and see New Zealand. I was interested. So was Southern California Republican Darrell Issa. We were the only takers. Next thing I knew, Darrell and I were changing into wetsuits and diving into a New Zealand sea. Our guide told us to make sounds, to sing, to flail around—basically to do any embarrassing thing we could to attract dolphins. We finally found them.

Darrell dubbed me "the Dolphin Whisperer," and it was the beginning of the oddest of friendships. After the dolphin swim, we grabbed a beer near the pier and chatted about our upbringings and what had brought us to Congress. We'd later go on to work on a number of tech-related bills together.

Our group finally made it to McMurdo Station, our plane landing on the Ice Princess runway on skis. We were then taken to our dorms. I was fascinated to learn that the mission in Antarctica works only because of the Antarctic Treaty System. Countries we rarely see eye to eye with otherwise work with us to carry out our joint missions. So far south, in such harsh conditions, we all need one another.

After a few days on the continent, I started to notice that there was very little we were seeing related to climate change. Some of the Democrats on the trip started to talk. One of the principal rebels among us was former Maryland Congresswoman Donna Edwards. She asked, "Doesn't it seem odd we aren't seeing or hearing anything about climate change?" *Yes*, I thought. But who would I register that complaint with? Finally, Edwards confronted the NSF director. "We've been here for days," Edwards said. "When do we hear about climate change?" Dr. Córdova didn't know how to answer that. Although she had served in the Obama administration, her funding was at the whim of a Republican-controlled Congress. She told Donna that she was under orders from the Science Committee Chairman to keep the itinerary climate change free.

What the hell? I wondered. *We've come all the way to Antarctica, and we aren't going to learn about climate change? What kind of fucked-up trip is this?* We had helicopter tours, saw penguins, visited Ernest Shackleton's cabin, and even flew to the South Pole. But no climate change. I also started noticing something that seemed out of place. Dr. Córdova, during all our travels, was always reading some trashy entertainment magazine—*People, US Weekly*, those types.

"Keeping up with the Kardashians there, Doc?" I asked her.

She turned red, opened her magazine, and revealed that it was hiding a copy of *Scientific American*.

"Don't tell the Chairman," she joked, referring to Lamar Smith.

I couldn't believe it. The ice caps were melting, seawater was rising, fires were burning across America, and our own science director couldn't even be seen reading a magazine on science?

As we shuttled across the continent on helicopters, you couldn't miss the massive ice sheets at risk of melting and dramatically increasing sea level rise because of the warming ocean. But my Republican colleagues weren't interested in facts. It was a theme I'd see in years to come.

CHAPTER 9

NATIONAL SECURITY DEMOCRAT

As my first term was coming to a close, former Alabama Congressman Bud Cramer, a friend and mentor and a true Blue Dog Democrat, asked me to lunch. He knew that in my second term, I might have access to better committee assignments, and he wanted me to consider Intel, the House Permanent Select Committee on Intelligence. Like me, Bud was a former prosecutor. He'd served on Intel and told me about the good, bipartisan work it did. He told me that my staff would probably object to my wanting to join; every staff does, he said. Intel is a committee unlike any other in the House. For one, it locks out your own office staff from what you're doing, because committee members and committee staff have access to classified information. Congressional staff doesn't. Bud told me that my office staff would not be allowed to accompany me to hearings, could not be told what I had learned, and would not be able to know where I'd be traveling.

The committee meets in a SCIF, where you are sealed off from the world without any electronic devices. You can't multitask. Bud also told me that if I joined, I'd have to do my homework. The materials associated with the briefings we'd be participating in were dense reading on the most sensitive national security programs the United States conducts. The public, Bud told me, counts on Congress to have oversight of these programs. No one else gets to see them. If Congress doesn't check them, no one will.

I also sought out Anna Eshoo's advice. She had served on Intel and answered question after question on the long flights we took together to California and back. The more we talked, the more I was convinced that Intel was the right fit for me. I was reminded of how 9/11 had been a wake-up call for me and how afterward I'd vowed to try to make a difference with my career. I approached Leader Pelosi, who had previously served on Intel and risen to be Ranking Member, and let her know of my interest. Unlike any other committee in Congress, Intel members are selected by direct appointment by the Speaker and Minority Leader. Months later, I was stunned to discover that I'd been given the honor of serving on the committee.

It was a brave new world for me. To give one example I can share, in early April 2015, I flew from Washington, DC, to Vienna, Austria, to Erbil, Iraq, on my first Intelligence Committee trip. One other committee member, Congressman Mike Pompeo, joined me in Erbil, and we flew to Baghdad together on a small military plane. I asked the pilot to let me join him up front, and from the copilot seat, I watched dusk descend over the desert landscape. As I was staring out, I was jolted by the sight of flashes of light down below us.

"Gunfire?" I asked the pilot.

"Just fireworks," he said.

I wondered if he was just trying to make me feel better. I tried to take in every detail I could on the drive through Baghdad to the U.S. embassy, which loomed ahead like a giant fortress as we approached it. I had mixed feelings. Though I was just a college student at the time, I had been against the Iraq War from the beginning, an invasion justified on false pretenses. Twelve years after we invaded, here I was in Baghdad, a member of Congress staying in a multibillion-dollar embassy that housed thousands of U.S. personnel and soldiers behind high walls, with security sentries everywhere.

I'd finally fallen asleep that first night when, not two hours later, a security alarm woke me up.

"Stay away from windows," a voice said over the loudspeaker in my room.

There was gunfire in the area. I got up, bleary eyed, and tried to figure out if I should be worried. After a few minutes, we were given the all-clear. The next morning, I learned that the sounds I heard had been "celebratory gunfire." A local team had won a soccer game, so afterward, someone had to fire a few rounds into the air. They just happened to be a little too close to the embassy.

I wanted to get outside beyond the walls and see Baghdad. U.S. Ambassador to Iraq Stu Jones, a former Ambassador to Jordan, offered to have Iraqi

Vice President Ayad Allawi join us for dinner at the embassy. I wanted to get out of the complex. We agreed on dinner at Allawi's house.

Knowing I was from California wine country, Allawi offered me a California red. I knew Muslim countries had strict rules about alcohol consumption, but I didn't want to offend my host. "I'll have whatever you're having," I told the Vice President. He chose some California wine. He didn't drink it, but I'll credit him with being a good host.

As we were leaving, I watched with fascination as Ambassador Jones pulled the Vice President aside and had sharp words for him. Jones was professional and composed, but he raised his voice, telling Allawi in no uncertain terms that the Iraqis needed to start delivering on what they'd promised. I was taken aback, but I could see that the Vice President respected this direct approach.

We were in Baghdad for Easter, and were able to attend an outdoor sunrise service at the embassy. The Iraq visit gave me a chance to get to know Pompeo. I found him to be a laid-back, easygoing guy who was obviously very close to his family. I didn't agree with him on much of anything policy-wise. Trips like that one are important for building up relationships across the aisle. Little did I know, though, that Pompeo and I would be on a collision course before long.

I'd gotten into politics to focus on national security issues, and the longer I served in Congress, the more I came to understand how broad a challenge it was. On that Iraq trip, we'd been alerted to a potential humanitarian disaster on a mind-numbing scale: Mosul Dam was cracking, and if it gave out, a million people could die. Our billion-dollar embassy would be flooded. I worked with Republican colleagues on the issue, looking for solutions, and had a newspaper op-ed ready to go when I asked a GOP Congressman on Intel who'd expressed interest in the issue to sign it with me. He balked, saying his constituents might complain about spending money in Iraq rather than at home. Politics trumped the urgency of the issue. It was frustrating. I'd run for Congress to break through that bullshit.

On a trip to Beirut, Lebanon, a few months after the Iraq trip, I was able to visit the memorial to the 241 Marines, sailors, and soldiers killed in

1983 when a truck bomb was detonated at the Marine barracks, the largest single-day death toll for the U.S. Marines since the Battle of Iwo Jima. I was a toddler at the time, and of course don't have any recollection of the reaction to that unprecedented act of terrorism, but then, neither does anyone else, it seems. Why is that? The Reagan administration, desperate to avoid answering questions about how it let such a terrible thing happen, staged an epic distraction the day after news of the bombing broke by invading the tiny Caribbean island nation of Grenada. The fate of the Marines who died in Beirut was mostly forgotten.

Taking a proactive approach to national security meant trying to figure out what issues would become important before they reached the critical stage. I spent a lot of time thinking about the issue of scarcity of resources. It wasn't enough to think about petro-states and war; we had to see national security in a broader, international context.

From 2013 to 2014, the *San Francisco Chronicle* did a multipart series on rare earth elements, seventeen elements on the periodic table that most of us never paid attention to in chemistry class—at least I didn't. The *Chronicle* series offered a fascinating rundown of how important these elements are to manufacturers of laptops, jet engines, and antimissile systems. The problem: China controlled about 97 percent of the exports, and was reducing them to increase the cost to U.S. manufacturers. We had other options. According to the *Chronicle* piece, there were mines that weren't being harvested for these elements because China had so cornered the market. I certainly didn't know much about rare earth elements, but I knew a few things about China. It cheats the markets and has a lot of government money to do so.

I wrote legislation that would have the Department of Energy create a Rare Earth Elements program to spur private development. It also provided for loan guarantees for the earliest investors. To my surprise, Science Committee Chairman Smith took me up on the idea. He said that if I took the loan guarantees part out of the bill, he would recommend it for a vote on the House Floor. No problem! Democrats were in the minority. We had to compromise and collaborate. I just wanted to see progress on the issue.

I was excited when it was finally time for the bill to be heard on the Floor. It was scheduled for the first day of voting in that week's session, so I took the red-eye back from California to be on the Floor to manage debate. The bill had gotten the approval of new Majority Leader Kevin McCarthy to be "voiced," basically passed unanimously "without objection." That was a win, but I was disappointed. Selfishly, I wanted to have a recorded vote, just to be able to vote on my own bill.

I landed at 6 a.m., slept for a few hours, and showed up at the Capitol around 11 a.m. I checked my phone and saw that my staff had sent me about a dozen emails while I was resting from the red-eye. Uh-oh. My bill was being "scored," they informed me. That was not good.

Andrew Ginsburg, my legislative director, explained that two outside, "dark money" groups, Club for Growth and Heritage Action, a sister organization of the Heritage Foundation, had sent alerts to their hundreds of thousands of members telling them to contact their members of Congress and urge them to vote against my bill, which was no longer going to be voice-voted and was probably in trouble.

I was sure I could convince some Republican friends to stick with me. I read the emails sent out against my bill. They were just lies. They said the legislation had loan guarantees, which was false. Those had been negotiated out. Chairman Smith told me my bill's chances of passing were fading fast. To his credit, he stuck with me and said he would still press to have a voice vote.

When I saw Representative Mick Mulvaney walk onto the Floor, I should have known the jig was up. Mulvaney was a perennial shit stirrer for the right-wing Freedom Caucus, the kind of guy who would throw lit firecrackers into a dinner party and then walk away smirking. He loved the attention, the action, and seemed devoid of any interest in ever solving a problem or getting anything done.

"You're not here to blow up our bipartisan agreement, are you, Mick?" I asked him.

He wasn't coy. "Hey Eric, Club for Growth asked me to just come down and call for a recorded vote," he said. "I'm not going to speak against it or anything. Just calling for a vote."

"What do you have against the bill?" I asked.

"I don't really know much about it. Again, they just asked me to call for a recorded vote. Don't take it personally."

"This is real personal," I told him. "If you call for this vote, you're going to blow up a good deal both sides worked on to address a real problem. Tell me your problem with the bill, and maybe we can address it."

He had no idea. I could have had the cure to cancer in the bill, for all he knew. As far as he was concerned, if Club for Growth was telling him to ask for a vote, those were his marching orders. He was one of their faithful soldiers.

He called for the vote. I had about an hour to approach my GOP friends. Many stuck with me. Too many looked me in the eye and said some variation of "Eric, I like your bill, I hate losing to China, but I'm worried about my score with these guys."

Chairman Smith advised me to pull the bill, because it was going to lose. I told him no way, the issue was too important, and I wanted to see who had courage and who didn't. The rare earth elements bill lost by nine votes. A week later, the World Trade Organization ruled against China for its rare earth elements export practices. We'd had an opportunity to give America an edge, but the outside groups had won.

I shouldn't have been surprised, I guess. Mulvaney was remarkably open about being corrupt. In April 2018, when he was interim director of the Consumer Financial Protection Bureau, a body whose mission he actively sought to undermine, he came clean in a talk to the American Bankers Association conference in DC.

"We had a hierarchy in my office in Congress," Mulvaney told the bankers, as reported in the *New York Times*. "If you're a lobbyist who never gave us money, I didn't talk to you. If you're a lobbyist who gave us money, I might talk to you."

The Mulvaneys of the world think they have the game fixed, but they have no clue. They feast at the trough for as long as they can, and then move on. I could work for real change in Washington, but I could never forget Mulvaney and people like him and all the damage they could do.

CHAPTER 10

LAND GRAB

Like most people born in the 1980s, I never imagined I would have to think much about Russia and Russian influence. Russia didn't seem scary at all anymore. More of a punchline. A sad Borat joke. I didn't grow up hiding under my desk at school during air-raid drills. When President Reagan stood near the Berlin Wall and said, "Mr. Gorbachev, tear down this wall!" I was six years old. I knew the Cold War was a big deal for my parents. They were lifelong Republicans who loved Reagan for his talk about the Soviet Union being an "Evil Empire." They knew all about the time of Stalin and millions dying in the gulags.

I was eight when the Eastern Bloc fell apart. Democracy and freedom arrived first in Poland, and then country after country rose up. This wasn't like Prague Spring in 1968, when Russian tanks rolled in to crush a flowering of democratic freedom. Events in 1989 were beyond the Kremlin's control. My parents were thrilled by the November 1989 fall of the Berlin Wall. As for me, I was a lot more interested in Joe Montana throwing to Jerry Rice in those years. The bad guys were the Los Angeles Dodgers, not Communist dictators like Nicolae Ceaușescu of Romania. I harbored no antagonism toward Russia growing up. I saw it as a failed, irrelevant state, a relic of a tragic, misguided past.

Vladimir Putin changed my thinking. He was calculating and dangerous. President George W. Bush met Putin for the first time at a summit and announced he was trustworthy. That was a mistake. Putin was a ruthless former KGB agent who understood the U.S. far better than we understood him. Even Reagan had said of Russia, "Trust, but verify."

Conservative *New York Times* columnist William Safire, a former Nixon speechwriter, put the spin from Bush in devastating context. "'I like Old Joe,' said F.D.R. about Joseph Stalin," Safire wrote that month in the *Times*.

"Carrying on that self-deluding tradition of snap judgments, George W. Bush looked into the eyes of Vladimir Putin and announced, 'I was able to get a sense of his soul.' . . . The American gave the Russian what he most needs: public deference that salves Russia's wounded pride, and respect to its leader abroad as Putin methodically chokes off opposition at home."

Sound familiar? The shock of recognition in reading those words now, nearly twenty years after Safire wrote them, reinforces the need for us to be wary of a particularly American virtue that can make us vulnerable in foreign affairs: our frequent inability to see darkness for what it is.

We are such an optimistic people, we Americans. Believing in the best in humanity, we are often blind to the worst. It is so deeply engrained in our national psyche to give people the benefit of the doubt, to assume they are acting in good faith, that we can be completely outmaneuvered by sociopaths, cynics, and others for whom bad faith comes easily. It's a lesson we have to relearn constantly as a people, the need to see not only the Stalins and Hitlers and Mussolinis, but also the Kim Jong-uns and the Vladimir Putins as a different breed, unbound by sentimental notions of right and wrong, morality, or even decency.

Communism crashed and burned, but from its ashes, republics and satellite states such as Ukraine and Poland were becoming democracies. Sure, there were growing pains. In Ukraine, a country of forty-two million that is the largest geographically in Europe, a pro-Russian President, Viktor Yanukovych, had been elected in February 2010, and set about pushing the country away from democracy. Finally, after he strong-armed a set of laws through Parliament to cut back on basic democratic rights like freedom of speech and freedom of assembly, he was forced from office in February 2014. Since the previous November, the people of Ukraine had been gathering in Kyiv's Independence Square by the thousands, despite the obvious risk they ran by protesting. Day after day, protesters showed up in the bitter cold. After he was impeached, Yanukovych fled Kyiv in a three-car convoy, sought for "mass murder" following the deaths of more than one hundred Ukrainians.

The *New York Times* headline that February 24 was bizarre: UKRAINIAN EX-LEADER VANISHES INTO THIN AIR. But Yanukovych washed up a few days later in the Russian city of Rostov-on-Don, appearing on Russian television.

Times reporter Alison Smale summed up the challenges facing the new government: "how to guarantee law and order in a country where discredited police and politicians of all stripes command no loyalty; a crumbling economy veering on bankruptcy; a yawning cultural gap between east and west."

Then, in March 2014, Putin announced that Russia was annexing part of Ukraine, the Crimea. It was a stunning, historic land grab, the most blatant such land grab in Europe since World War II, and violated multiple agreements and treaties. First, Putin sent in special forces to secure strategic territory and staged an obviously bogus referendum in which 97 percent of Crimea residents were alleged to have voted in favor of leaving Ukraine and joining Russia. Then Putin made it official with an announcement that was heavy on self-pitying remarks about Russian humiliation, commenting, "Crimea has always been an integral part of Russia in the hearts and minds of people."

That April, U.S. Vice President Joe Biden flew to Ukraine, directed by President Obama, to show the United States' commitment to democracy in Ukraine and to resisting Russian aggression and meddling. "It's still too early to tell if this is going to succeed," U.S. Ambassador to Ukraine Geoffrey Pyatt told the Associated Press. "The ball is really in Moscow's court in terms of whether they're going to take this diplomatic off-ramp."

Up until I took an Intel Committee trip to Poland and Ukraine in late summer 2015 with a small group led by Republican Congressman Lynn Westmoreland of Georgia, I did not fully appreciate how dangerous Putin's Russia had become. Our first stop on our trip that August was in Poland, where our Polish hosts and the State Department gave us a sobering walk through the history of Russian aggression. Poland joined the European Union in 2004 and has been a key member of NATO, whose creation in the aftermath of World War II was one of the finest moments in the history of U.S. diplomacy and statecraft. Poland has a thousand-year history and centuries of experience in dealing with Russian attempts to undermine or subvert it.

I was eager to go to Ukraine and learn more about recent Russian aggression in Crimea. It should have been clear to me and others that this recent land grab was a sign of further Russian aggression to come. In Kyiv, we met with Ukrainian military leaders who were rightfully frustrated that the United States had not done more to counter Russia. It was brutal hearing how much we had let them down and how far Russian aggression had set back their country. The Kremlin under Putin, we were told repeatedly on that trip, responds only to direct confrontation. You can't pussyfoot with them. They will bully their way to advance their agenda. They are a destructive force that thrives on chaos and division. They only respond to pushback.

Incidentally, while I was in Ukraine, I got word from Intel Committee staff that President Obama was trying to reach me. At dusk, on our final day in Kyiv, I was able to connect with the President from my hotel room. I'd been told in blunt terms that the line was not secure, so I should make sure not to touch on any sensitive topics. I assumed the Ukrainians (and Russians) were probably listening. Obama said he had called to thank me for my support of the Iran nuclear deal reached in Vienna in 2015 and urged me to stand strong as efforts in Congress progressed to undermine it. I assured him that I would. But I didn't miss the chance to tell him I was in Kyiv, had met with the Ukrainians, and that they needed our help to hold out against mounting Russian aggression. He said he understood, but I sensed he also was mindful that we couldn't discuss too much on an open line. I never did get a chance to talk to President Obama about it further. Neither of us knew that it was almost too late.

CHAPTER 11

RED SQUARE

Vladimir Putin has been in charge of Russia almost my entire adult life, but from 2008 to 2012, he stepped down from the presidency and handed it over to his handpicked successor, Dmitry Medvedev, who served as President. Though he was largely a puppet, Medvedev did have some influence, and Russia in those years was relatively quiet. Ever since Putin took the presidency back in 2013, though, he has been on a mission to subvert democracy and the rule of law, consolidate his power ever more brazenly, and, we now know, project Russian power and stir up trouble abroad in previously unimaginable ways.

Early on in the transition from the Soviet state to what followed, Putin gained from the rise of a group of oligarchs who "privatized" Russian industry, from gas companies to mining to television networks, and became the richest men in the country, its key power brokers. Putin mostly left them alone as he consolidated power. Then he turned on them, sending some into exile and throwing some into jail. When Putin found himself embarrassed by Russian TV coverage of a nuclear-powered Russian submarine's sinking, he moved in to assert state control of all media. As a former KGB officer, Putin sees everything through the eyes of information warfare.

In addition to my duties on the House Intelligence Committee in 2015, I was chosen to serve as Ranking Member, or top Democrat, on the sub-committee charged with overseeing the Central Intelligence Agency. As Russia moved into Syria later that year, asked by the Assad regime to offer air support, it became clear to me that the Russians under Putin were escalating their aggression across the globe. They had moved into Ukraine and shot down a Malaysian airliner over eastern Ukraine, killing 298 innocent people. Now they were joining a crowded battlefield in Syria.

Around then, I was encouraged by committee staff to read *Red Sparrow,* an award-winning spy novel by former CIA agent Jason Matthews, who had worked in Russia House, the Agency's Russian mission center. Soon, most Democratic members and staffers on the Intelligence Committee were reading the book, and asking our professional staffers, many of whom had worked at various U.S. intelligence agencies, which parts of it were true and which parts fiction.

Reading the book felt like taking a journey into the past and seeing the world of the Cold War years through the perspective of the Soviet Union. But if I was really going to gain perspective I could use on Russia, I felt I had to go there. I submitted a formal request for a meeting with senior leaders at Russia's Ministry of Foreign Affairs, sure my offer would be summarily rejected. Russian authorities surprised me by saying yes, and in October 2015 I was off to Moscow, joined by Democratic Representative Dutch Ruppersberger of Maryland, former Ranking Member on Intel. He and I connected at Frankfurt Airport and flew Aeroflot together to Moscow's Sheremetyevo Airport.

We were probably already under surveillance on the flight from Germany, but once we landed it was obvious. For that entire visit, we were under 24/7 surveillance, and there was nothing subtle about it. I counted as many as ten different Russians, agents of some sort, following us or waiting for us at every stop along the way. They wanted to make sure we knew they were there. It was a little unnerving at first, but you got used to it.

We arrived at our hotel, across Red Square from the Kremlin, early in the evening. We were beat and had a full day of meetings the next day, but I was too excited to sleep. The energy of Red Square was like caffeine. We decided to drop off our bags in our rooms up on the ninth floor, freshen up, and then go explore.

"What room are you in, Dutch?" I asked.

He pulled out his room key envelope. "Nine-eleven," he read.

"Oh, they're definitely messing with you, Dutch," I said.

Once outside, we strolled across Red Square and viewed the Kremlin up close. We went inside Saint Basil's Cathedral and did some shopping at the ornate GUM, formerly the "State Department Store," which in Soviet days had a special section only for high-ranking Communist Party members.

I was determined to eat anywhere but at the hotel; I wanted an authentic Russian dining experience. So Dutch and I walked about a mile up Tverskaya

Street in search of the Russian restaurant recommended by hotel staff. It was almost comical. We'd go into a restaurant thinking we were in the right spot, only to discover we weren't. Our surveillance detail was always about twenty feet behind and twenty feet ahead. Finally, we found a place that fit the description we'd been given. We entered at street level and took a flight of stairs down to a basement dining room.

"This is it, Dutch," I said.

But again: wrong place. Out we went, back to the street—only, this time, our detail had assumed we were staying and had posted up right outside the front door. We surprised the hell out of them when we suddenly reappeared. It was hilarious watching them scramble to look as if they were doing anything but surveilling us. Four guys in black leather coats suddenly all had phones to their ears.

"Can we just ask them to take us to this place?" Dutch suggested. "They probably know where we're supposed to be going."

The next day, we went to the U.S. embassy, where our State Department team briefed me on Russia's involvement in Syria. I met with Ambassador John Tefft at his residence, and we talked at length about how Russia viewed its role in the world and what its objectives were in Syria. I told the Ambassador that I was concerned that even a mishap over Syrian airspace could lead to conflict. He agreed. I did not think to ask him about the Russians being bold enough to intervene in a U.S. election.

The day ended with a meeting in the Russian Ministry of Foreign Affairs, one of the tallest buildings in Moscow, just off the Moskva River. It was a massive building from an era long past, one of Stalin's "Seven Sisters" skyscrapers. I felt like I was walking into 1953, the year the building opened. Not much had changed inside, it appeared. I met with Georgy Borisenko, director of the Department of North America, and Alexey Isakov, deputy director. In our conversation, I expressed concern about Russia's role in Syria and Ukraine.

"My constituents are losing patience with Russia, but we want to avoid conflict," I told them.

They insisted Russia was interested only in fighting ISIS. I played my part and stressed that the evidence proved the contrary. This led to a lecture on U.S. involvement in the Middle East from Iraq to Afghanistan. I left unconvinced I had connected at all, but I had wanted them to hear from an American lawmaker—one with the power to vote to authorize military force—to understand that there were a lot of opportunities for us to work together if they genuinely wanted to defeat ISIS. They didn't seem interested. The whole meeting felt like a sham. Little did I know, as I sat there, that less than five hundred miles northwest of us, in Saint Petersburg, hundreds of Russians operating on orders of the Kremlin were hard at work hacking a candidate for President of the United States. They were infiltrating computer systems and stealing documents that would be used in just a few months to disrupt our election and create havoc.

Dutch Ruppersberger and I closed out the day with a visit to our hotel's rooftop bar to take in the sweeping view of Red Square. Back in my room, I watched one of the Democratic primary debates. No one on that stage, and not even a Congressman near the scene of the crime, had the slightest inkling that the democracy we'd always taken for granted was about to be upended.

CHAPTER 12

DIVIDE AND DEMEAN

The days after Donald Trump was elected President of the United States were a blur. Millions of stunned voters were in a fog, and so were many in Congress. How had this happened? What did it mean? How much had Russia helped Trump? How could we work with somebody as impulsive and self-centered as Trump, a figure who'd embarked on a strategy of divide and demean?

During the transition, days before inauguration, our Democratic leader, Nancy Pelosi, had a vision. We would look for ways to deal with Trump, but above all we'd fight for the priorities of the people who elected us. In the days leading up to Trump's inauguration in January 2017, Pelosi urged our caucus to focus on health care. She had buttons made that read PROTECT OUR CARE, making them available to every Democratic member to wear for the inauguration. It was a cold day, and many members wore overcoats, which happened to cover up the buttons they'd put on their suit coats. That morning, proudly wearing her button, Pelosi greeted members of our caucus and, with an inspecting eye, looked to see if each was wearing the button. "Where's your button, dear?" she would ask any member without one visibly displayed.

It was Day One of the Trump presidency, and she wanted us totally focused on the challenge at hand. Pelosi believed Trump would try to repeal the Affordable Care Act and that our first major fight would be protecting it. She was right. It was barely repealed in the House, and by the grace of God, Senator John McCain was healthy enough to live to vote against the repeal in the Senate.

I didn't want to be anywhere near Donald Trump taking the oath of office. I was sickened by the very idea of it. As a twenty-year-old, I had stood with Chris and watched George W. Bush take the oath. Weeks after I was sworn in to Congress, I had watched Barack Obama take his second oath as President. I went to those ceremonies full of pride in the power of

high ideals. This felt more like witnessing a hostile takeover by an unscru-
pulous corporate raider intent on gutting everything most Americans
held dear.

Understandably, many of my colleagues boycotted the swearing-in. In
the end, more than sixty-five announced they were not attending, including
civil rights icon John Lewis, who had denounced Trump as an "illegitimate"
President because of Russia's interference in the election. Hell, a good number
of my constituents urged me not to attend. They tweeted at me, posted on
my Facebook wall, called the office, asked me personally at my town halls.
One group was even sending around a petition.

I understood why my colleagues and constituents felt that way, but I saw
things differently. Donald Trump was not being sworn in as king, whatever he
himself might have thought. He was being sworn in to lead the second branch
of government for a four-year term. We, in Congress, are the preeminent, first
branch of government, as established by Article I of the Constitution. Our
Founders designed a system in which Congress made the laws and served
as a check on executive power. So I was going to show up and check Donald
Trump on Day One. He needed to see me. He needed to see the check.

Being on the House leadership team, I was given an assigned seat eight
rows behind the presidential podium. It was the oddest of scenes: former
Presidents, Supreme Court justices, and, most awkwardly, Hillary Clinton,
all standing stiffly in the bitter cold. Obviously, she was there in her capacity
as former First Lady, Senator, and Secretary of State. *If Hillary can be here,*
I thought, *I can be here.*

Donald Trump's inaugural address was as bad as I imagined it would
be. It felt like a dream that had gone off the rails. If you tried not to listen
closely to what he was saying, or trying to say, it was almost tolerable for a
few seconds at a time, but then you'd tune back in to discover that it was so
much worse.

Trump's brief address, a mash-up of phony bromides and strange insults,
with talk of "American carnage" and "America First," squandered any chance
he might have had of bringing the country together. There was none of the
eloquence or feeling of the first George W. Bush inaugural address, or of
Barack Obama's masterful laying out his vision of the life of the nation as a

"never-ending journey." Trump demeaned and coarsened his own presidency from the get-go, then proceeded to lie about the size of his crowd.

The last thing I wanted to do after that speech was remain anywhere near Donald Trump, now President Trump. But in for a penny, in for a pound(ing), I suppose. After a President is sworn in, it's custom for the leadership teams from both parties in both chambers to host the President and his family for lunch. This nightmare had a sequel, and it felt like a bad sign of things to come.

After the ceremony, I walked from the West End of the Capitol to Statuary Hall, which had served as the House Chamber from 1807 to 1857. The open hall, with statues of dignitaries that each state's legislature had sent to the Capitol, had been converted for the day into a dining room, with round tables seating eight set up throughout the room. At the head table sat the President and Vice President and their families. As I entered, I checked in and was given a card directing me to table number 8.

Who could I possibly be seated with? I wondered. After scanning the room, I located my table 8 and made my way toward it. I was the last to arrive, and looked at the seven guests sitting around the table with one empty chair.

You have got to be kidding me. This cannot be happening.

Former Speaker John Boehner was the first person I saw. He was with his wife.

Fine, I thought. *At least he'll make sure we're drinking good wine.*

Then I spotted octogenarian billionaire Sheldon Adelson, seated with his wife on one side and an empty chair on the other. Adelson had contributed at least $25 million to help elect Trump. He'd then set a record with a $5 million donation to the Trump Inaugural Fund, and for that, what did he get? He'd be sitting next to me, a Democratic Congressman from California. My stomach sank. Two hours with Sheldon Adelson? *How will I do this?* I thought. Then I remembered that the Oakland Raiders were considering a move to Las Vegas, and that Adelson, Chairman and CEO of the Las Vegas Sands Corporation, was in talks to finance their stadium. *At least we can talk sports,* I thought.

Then I looked to the left of my chair. There, without her spouse, sat Kellyanne Conway, the former pollster who took over as Trump's campaign manager when Paul Manafort quit in August 2016. Was Nancy Pelosi responsible for this? Who was my torturer? Was I being punished for something? *I even wore my button*, I thought.

I sheepishly took my seat, trying to be invisible.

I turned toward Kellyanne: "Hi, I'm—"

She smiled. "I know who you are."

I tried to lighten the mood.

"You know, Kellyanne," I said, "I'm sorry that you worked so hard, saw your candidate elected for President, and your first reward is lunch with me."

She did not laugh. She did not smile. She just looked away.

Oh boy, I thought. *This is going to be a long lunch.* (It could have been worse, as I found out later. That night at the Inaugural Ball, Conway ended up making headlines after stepping between two scuffling men. As the New York *Daily News* reported, "Conway apparently punched one of them in the face with closed fists at least three times, according to the stunned onlooker.")

As for the guest on my right, Sheldon had no idea who I was. That was probably a good thing. Who would want to be on that political predator's radar? He asked who I was, and I used the opportunity to try to learn about his intentions for the Raiders. I learned he really didn't like football at all and his stadium financing was motivated mostly by his son's interest. He was skeptical the deal would ever go through.

Before I could learn more, Kellyanne leaned across my plate, telling Adelson, "You know, Sheldon, you can call anytime if you need anything."

Sheldon complained about how hard it was to get ahold of anyone senior on the Trump team. He recommended that Kellyanne give everyone sequential phone numbers, so they'd be easy to remember.

"You know, like 555-1000, and 555-1001," he said. "That way I can just call down the order of seniority until you get who you need. That's how I do it with my team."

"That's a *great* idea, Sheldon," said Kellyanne. "I'll tell *him* you suggested that," she said.

This was ten minutes in. I was looking at roughly seventeen billion more years of this agony. I prayed someone would pull the fire alarm and clear the room.

Please, get me out of here, I thought. I sat for about an hour and then decided I had done my duty. I walked out—but not without running into a couple I knew, Greg and Denise Pence. Greg had just been elected to Congress in my wife's hometown of Columbus, Indiana. He'd won his younger brother's old seat.

My wife, Brittany, and Greg and Denise's daughter, Nicole, had grown up together and were still close friends, but I had never met Nicole's parents before this, which now seemed more important, as her dad was going to be a colleague. I congratulated Greg, who regaled me with stories of my father-in-law. Now I was interested in staying a little longer just to get some good dirt.

I was booked on the last flight out of Dulles to SFO that day. I wasn't going to stick around in Washington to toast the new President at any inaugural balls. I would much rather sit at the Dulles Airport bar and people-watch. Just looking around, my spirits were lifted. A bunch of flights must have landed at the same time, setting a flood of passengers in motion.

Suddenly, I saw hundreds of women walking through the terminal, moving at a steady clip, many of them wearing pink caps. The Women's March! In the tumult, I had forgotten that it was the next day. A million women were to converge on Washington the day after Trump's inauguration to show America who was going to save us. (Hundreds of marches would occur all over the country, including one in Northern California's East Bay that I joined, glad to be part of the largest single-day political protest in U.S. history with 3 to 5 million participants.) For about twenty minutes, I sat on that barstool as the cold beer warmed in my hand, and watched women march through the terminal with determination and purpose. To fight back against Trumpism, it was going to take a lot of work and a lot of organizing. This was a start, but the question was: Could this energy be sustained?

CHAPTER 13

PRESIDENT DONALD J. TRUMP? REALLY?

My hometown NBA team, the Golden State Warriors, did not come to Washington, DC, often, but as it happened, they were in town on February 28, 2017, to take on the Wizards. President Trump was also set to address Congress for the first time that night. I was hell-bent on catching at least the first part of the Warriors game. I needed my spirits lifted. Washington was a dark place in the first month of the Trump regime, and the Warriors were the perfect mood enhancer. I wasn't going to miss out on a chance to watch Splash Brothers Stephen Curry and Klay Thompson swish three-pointers from all over the court.

I managed to pull myself out of the game as planned—the Wizards beat the Warriors by four, a loss somehow not attributed by any sportswriters to the disappearance of the Warriors' biggest fan one quarter in—and hailed a cab to head back to the Capitol. The taxi made it only a few blocks away from the arena and then stopped. The traffic lights kept switching—red, green, red, green—but cars weren't moving. I rolled down my window and stuck my head out to see what the hell was the problem. No one was budging. I glanced at the time, and then jumped out and made a run for it, even though it was raining hard. As I was sprinting up the hill toward the Capitol, I heard a scolding voice in my head: *You'd better not miss this, Eric.*

I was running seriously late for, as weird as it seemed to me, an appointment to meet the President of the United States. I darted between idling cars, all of them stopped in their tracks as the presidential motorcade made its way to the Capitol Building. A phalanx of red brake lights lit up the street. My Nordstrom Rack suit was soaked in no time. My favorite brown leather shoes, which I'd already had resoled twice, were taking on water. I should have been better prepared. I cursed myself for, once again, trying to do too much with too little time. In minutes, President Trump would deliver his first address to Congress, about a month after being inaugurated, and I was doing the hundred-yard dash in the rain up Capitol Hill in dress shoes.

Tradition dictated that the House and Senate leaders greet the President before he was to speak, and then escort him to the House Chamber before the address. Trump was entitled to respect as President, but already in the first weeks of his administration, he'd gone out of his way to make it impossible to afford him that courtesy. Within days of being sworn in, Trump announced a Muslim ban, prohibiting travel to the United States by citizens from seven countries.

Deputy Attorney General Sally Yates, showing tremendous courage, refused to carry out the order. She was fired. America, a country defined by adding freedoms and multiplying opportunity, was entering an era of subtraction and division. I went to San Francisco International Airport to join thousands of protesters. Brittany insisted on coming, too, despite being six months pregnant. I also brought Mallory De Lauro, my district director and a lawyer in our office who handles immigration cases. I had to fly back to Washington soon after, but I told Mallory to set up a pop-up office at the airport, urging her, "Stay as long as you can and offer services to any person or family who needs them." Fortunately, we in San Francisco weren't alone. Across America, people had converged on airports to support Muslims who were being denied entry.

Trump stood for hate, and we had to show that we stood against him, even as we showed respect for the office of President. Many of my House colleagues had announced that they would boycott the Trump address to Congress, and we respected that choice, but the leadership needed to come up with an approach. Pelosi, then the House Minority Leader, proposed that we greet the President before the speech in a holding room just off the House Floor, but not walk in with him. Rather, we would hold back and let the Republicans escort him.

"Wait, we will be meeting him and talking to him?" I'd asked on a conference call of the leadership. I had never met Trump.

"Yes, of course. He's coming to our chamber," Pelosi said.

When the call wrapped, I called Pelosi directly.

"I want to give him a letter," I told her.

"What do you mean?" she asked me. "What kind of letter?"

I told her that a Muslim constituent had written a very personal letter to me, and I wanted to get it into Trump's hands.

"Secret Service will never let you do it," Pelosi warned. She would know. She'd been a House Leader for three Presidents. She knew protocol and security.

"I want to try," I said. "He needs to read this."

Days after Trump was elected, my office had received a letter from a man named Hazem Shaban, who lived in San Ramon, a growing Muslim community in my Northern California district. Mr. Shaban wrote to me that in 1990, he fled Kuwait during Iraq's invasion and was received as a refugee in the United States. "With the sense of honor and pride to my new adopting country I felt I had to service my new country so I joined the U.S. Navy in 1992," Mr. Shaban went on. He later married and raised three children in the Bay Area. Mr. Shaban's letter explained that he had become concerned about his family's safety.

"Donald Trump has been spreading fear and bigotry regarding immigrants and deportation of Mexicans and Muslims from the U.S. I had no answers to my fearful kids and wife[,] especially being Muslims[,] when they hear that Muslims may have to register and may have to leave the country when the only place they have ever lived is in the USA. And they always knew they were Americans."

My hand was shaking as I read the letter. I was so angry that it had come to this. But Mr. Shaban hadn't absolved me of responsibility. He'd sent his letter because he expected me to do something.

"I would like you to tell me where you stand on the subject and what should I tell my kids and family?" he implored me.

When I received the letter, I called Mr. Shaban immediately and told him that I would fight like hell every day to make sure that he and his family were still welcome in America.

"You fled to our open arms, you started a family here, and you signed up to defend our country in the armed services," I told him. "This is your country, Hazem."

I had Mr. Shaban's letter in my pocket as I raced in the rain toward the Capitol that night after leaving the Warriors game. I entered the Capitol on the empty Senate side and started looking for a bathroom, so I could pull myself together. I was by no means looking forward to meeting President Trump, but I also didn't want to do so looking like a wet dog.

Before I could find a men's room, I ran into Virginia Senator Tim Kaine, Vice-Presidential candidate on the 2016 Democratic ticket.

"Hello, Senator," I said.

"Eric, you're soaked!" he said.

I would have loved to have had time to talk with him, to get his perspective on where we were as a country, but I looked ridiculous, so I excused myself to head off in search of paper towels to swab away some of the water.

Speaker of the House Paul Ryan took to the back podium at the rostrum in the well of the House of Representatives.

"Will the following members please make their way to escort the President?" Ryan intoned, reading the names of the Senate and House Leaders on the escort committee.

". . . and Eric Swalwell of California."

The escort committee made its way through the Speaker's Lobby, just off the House Floor and behind the podium where Ryan now stood. The Democrats on both sides, House and Senate, held back. We were in no hurry, torn between our constitutional duty and our absolute disgust for the man who now presided over the executive branch of our government.

I had complained to Brittany for weeks about having to meet Trump. "He's a pig. He bragged about grabbing women by the pussy. He's awful," I told her.

"You just have to do it," she said. "For your constituents." She was right. And I had to do it for Mr. Shaban.

Right before I was to meet Trump, Pelosi walked over to me. "Do you have your letter, dear?"

"Yes, Leader." I smiled. She'd remembered. Of course, she had.

I almost hadn't brought the letter, worried that her warnings were right and that Trump would never take it. And then I almost hadn't made it to the Capitol because of the traffic and the rain. But I had kept the letter inside my coat pocket, and somehow it had stayed dry. Now I was stepping forward to meet the President.

"I know who you are," he said. "I know who you are."

I had my hand out, waiting for Donald Trump to shake it.

"I know who you are," he said again. "Eric Swalwell, California. I've seen you on TV!"

I half-laughed at the way he said it, like a boast. Of course he'd seen me on TV. I had been on Fox News with Tucker Carlson just the night before, talking about Trump's first proposed budget and worrying about the increase in military spending.

I reached into my jacket and pulled out the letter. "Mr. President, this is a letter from a Muslim refugee who served in our Navy," I said respectfully. "He's from San Ramon, California. I want you to read this letter, and I hope you'll speak to his concerns."

I handed it to Trump. It felt like it was just the two of us in the room. An aide stood in the distance. A cameraman was positioned behind a video camera. I looked around, expecting a nearby aide or Secret Service agent to dive in front of me and take the letter.

Nothing. Awkward silence.

Trump finally reached for the letter and held it up with both hands, kind of like he was trying to see what was inside.

"I will read this letter," he said as he waved it. "I will read this letter."

I had the feeling he thought it might be a check—or possibly a subpoena.

I walked away and Pelosi came over to me.

"Did he take it?"

I nodded yes. She lit up and gave me a big smile, grabbing my arm. She was excited for me. I was excited for Mr. Shaban. I called him immediately after the address. He told his kids. They were deeply grateful. Mr. Shaban told me he still believed in America.

PART 3: ALL ROADS LEAD TO PUTIN

CHAPTER 14

INVESTIGATING RUSSIA'S INTERFERENCE

So many people around the country, including members of Congress, had trouble believing that Donald Trump had been elected in a fair and clean way. His win defied reason. They kept asking: How did this happen? As a member of the House Intelligence Committee, I soon started getting some answers.

In late 2016 and early 2017, the committee was given numerous classified briefings rich in detail that made clear, beyond even the slightest shadow of a doubt, that Russia had pulled off a large-scale interference campaign, ordered by Vladimir Putin, seeking to help Donald Trump and hurt Hillary Clinton. How far had that interference campaign reached into the United States? That was not yet clear. Had any U.S. citizens worked with the Russians? Did anyone within the Trump campaign do so? Were voter systems penetrated? Was it possible that vote tallying was in any way affected? Remember, Trump lost the popular vote by more than 2.8 million votes—and still won the presidency, thanks to fewer than 80,000 votes in just three swing states. Even a small amount of direct intervention could swing an election that close.

I don't think I'd have believed it was possible if I hadn't lived through the Intel Committee briefings on Russia's interference myself. It was almost as if the Republicans on the committee knew what was coming and had spent time developing a cover story for the President, to block any scrutiny of the dirty truths behind his victory. Again and again, as Democrats on the committee attempted to pose necessary and important questions early in 2017, Republicans would interrupt, resorting to a sneering, nasty tone. If you've only seen politicians on TV, that might not sound surprising. But in a government proceeding, such as a closed-door, secure briefing with intelligence professionals, it's rare to see so stark a break with collegiality.

"Get over it!" we kept hearing. "Trump won. You're just being a poor sport."

All my instincts as a former prosecutor kicked in and told me that something wasn't right. Why was I smelling fear in the room? What had impelled the Republicans to move so quickly to adopt such a wild and desperate position? I didn't know, but I knew there was more to what was going on than met the eye—and that I would not rest until I did my part to help us find some answers.

A whiff of totalitarianism was in the air. Democracy thrives on the truth, on asking and answering legitimate questions. A profoundly antidemocratic spirit was driving Republicans in an odd and ugly direction. The more I thought about it, the more it dawned on me that the only reason Republicans would be so desperate to avoid any questions on the legitimacy of Donald Trump's election was that they themselves knew it was of questionable legitimacy. That realization shook me to the core.

I immediately thought of the 9/11 Commission, which had been widely hailed for its thorough, valuable, bipartisan work. If we needed a commission then, we needed one now. We had been attacked by terrorists on September 11, 2001, and we had been attacked in the run-up to the 2016 presidential election. As different as the two attacks were, they were similar in, apparently, catching us off guard. As defensive as some of my Republican colleagues on the Intelligence Committee were being, I believed that we could find common ground to come together against a hostile foreign power. I truly believed that they would care about protecting the integrity of our elections, preserving the absolute core of our democracy. Boy, was I naïve.

"Russia, if you're listening, I hope you're able to find the thirty thousand emails that are missing," Trump had said at a Florida press conference in July 2016. Yes, Russia had been listening, and wasted no time getting to work to electronically attack Hillary Clinton's candidacy. (As the Mueller Report would explain, "Within approximately five hours of Trump's statement, GRU officers targeted for the first time Clinton's personal office.")

The 2016 election campaign season had been mostly dominated by coverage of Trump's circus-like showmanship. He had been able to smear his opponent as "Crooked Hillary," helped along by a mass media that amplified his taunts because they made good copy or good TV. As then CEO of CBS Les Moonves said in February 2016, two years before he resigned in disgrace following multiple sexual misconduct allegations, Trump's run "may not be good for America, but it's damn good for CBS."

Sure, emails had been hacked, social media had been weaponized, and Russia was suspect number one, but little attention had been given in the media to Russia's role or intent. Much more coverage had been devoted to Hillary's email server and the contents of the emails Russia's hackers stole from the DNC and disseminated via WikiLeaks. A media analysis by the *Columbia Journalism Review* found that "in just six days, the *New York Times* ran as many cover stories about Hillary Clinton's emails as they did about all policy issues combined in the sixty-nine days leading up to the election."

Candidate Trump had said throughout the campaign that the election was going to be rigged. Clearly, he knew something the rest of us didn't. We would later learn that although our intelligence community knew the Kremlin was responsible, there was a debate inside the community about whether to publicly attribute the attack to Russia. Intelligence officials feared that doing so could play into Mr. Trump's hands. They were paralyzed by indecision. While they waited, Russia turned up its hacking and release efforts.

Candidate Trump was all too happy about that. "I love WikiLeaks!" he actually yelled on a public stage. Just imagine how cheered on all the hackers in Russia must have felt by clips of that moment.

In the months after the election, the Republicans knew that if they made a lot of noise and made a great show of their outrage and exasperation, "Russia" would become a very charged word. If you even mentioned Russia—the country that we *knew* had attacked our country's free and fair election—Republicans would act it as if we were trying to undermine the legitimacy of Trump's election. Their first reaction was to be hyperpartisan, and they didn't seem to want to take a step back and look at the bigger picture.

I wanted to create a bipartisan, professional inquiry so that we could learn exactly what had happened and take the necessary steps to mitigate our vulnerability to further attacks. I knew it was going to take work to get an independent investigation launched, but I would never have been able to live with myself if I had backed off from a challenge so critical to the country. I decided I'd go see Lee Hamilton, who had been vice chair of the 9/11 Commission, to pick his brain about what had made the Commission he'd helped lead so successful. I thought it could serve as a model for the commission I wanted to set up.

When my wife and I were in Indiana for the holidays that year, I took the opportunity to go to Bloomington to meet with Lee. He couldn't have been more helpful. He gave me background on how the 9/11 Commission was established, how it functioned, and what he learned from the investigation that should inform my thinking as I worked on legislation to create a new commission. He encouraged me to give any commission I created wide latitude for its inquiry. He impressed upon me the need to make sure it had the freedom "to follow the evidence," even if that led in unpredictable directions, and he warned me not to draw any conclusions or hint at any in the legislation establishing the commission.

Pelosi liked my idea, but she was also skeptical that it would actually happen any time soon. "The September Eleven Commission wasn't formed on September twelfth," she told me, and I got the point.

She went on to explain how hard and long she fought Republicans and the Bush administration to get an independent commission after 9/11. One was finally created in late November 2002, thanks to her persistent advocacy.

Pelosi didn't believe the Republicans would ever go for a commission now. They were going to protect Trump, she warned. But she said it was still worth trying.

"Go to one of your senior colleagues as a partner on this," she said. "You know, Elijah would be great. This is what he does on Oversight."

I knew Elijah Cummings, the senior Democrat on the Oversight and Government Reform Committee, from my days as a law student in Baltimore. He was an impassioned fighter and a gifted lawyer, and his speeches were thunderous, often bringing crowds to their feet. I needed a more senior partner if I wanted the bill to be taken seriously, and Elijah eagerly joined.

We had one final challenge in drafting the bill: Did we call the commission, factually, an "Independent Commission on Russian Interference," or the more diplomatic "Independent Commission on Foreign Interference"? We went back and forth. I decided to ask Lee Hamilton for his advice.

"Who the hell cares what it's called?" he said. "Do all you can to get Republicans on board."

He was right. We introduced our "foreign interference" bill in December 2016 before the 114th Congress concluded, knowing it would have little chance of passing in a lame-duck Congress. However, we felt it important to show the world an immediate response to the attack on our democracy so we could take steps to guard against similar attacks in the future. To do that we needed a spirit of unity. I went to work to find Republican co-sponsors, starting with my friends on the Intelligence Committee. There was widespread acknowledgment that Russia had attacked us, but also reluctance on their part to do anything publicly about it. One GOP member of the committee told me that she had already gone against Trump during the campaign, speaking out against some of his offensive comments, and she was afraid.

"I can't afford to have my head lopped off again," she told me.

Twitter as guillotine?

Another Republican member was close to signing on as a co-sponsor, but texted me in December: "I may need more time, but I can also co-sponsor later on." He added: "Want to make sure that what you're proposing is the best solution. Obviously I agree with the goal. . . . Clearly there are Members of Congress who are willing to be objective and apolitical on this issue—on both sides."

Another member, who had worked for the Intelligence Community prior to coming to Congress, told me that he, too, was bothered by what Russia had done, but that he would first have to talk to the Speaker of the House, Paul Ryan, to get his okay on moving forward. I waited a few days. He told me that Speaker Ryan thought Congress was up to the job. I went to Speaker Ryan on the Floor, told him about my bill, explained my hope that it could be bipartisan, and referenced the 9/11 Commission.

"Speaker, I want this to work," I told him. "I'll work with you to make any productive changes you'd like to see."

Speaker Ryan promised he would consider it and follow up with me. I knew he would be under pressure to quash any such investigation, but I also knew it was the right thing for the country—and knew Paul Ryan understood that.

I waited, and waited, and waited. The Speaker never followed up. He would eventually take the public stance that he didn't see the need for either an independent commission or a joint House-Senate investigation. I hope that, like me, Ryan will one day put down on paper his memories of that period and give us a deeper look into his thinking.

I moved on, and was startled to see so much fear from my Republican colleagues. No one wanted to cross Donald Trump and provoke a tweet. One member told me he would give consideration to co-sponsoring our legislation, but he wanted to wait for more evidence to come out.

Yet, there was no shortage of evidence, as I kept reminding him. As each outrageous news story broke—ranging from General Flynn's calls to Russian Ambassador Sergey Kislyak to the firing of James Comey—I'd go to this member and ask, "Are you ready now?"

"Almost," he kept saying. "Almost."

He never did join. He kept telling me he was close. (Ultimately, he was voted out of office, defeated by a Democratic challenger.) It might have helped bring him and others along if members of Congress had felt more pressure from the press to pursue an investigation. Oddly, the media seemed intent on giving credence to the self-serving Trump line about Democrats as sore losers.

In December 2016, four U.S. Senators came out with a remarkable joint statement that took a strong stand and showed real courage. All four signing the statement were senior, respected figures: Arizona Senator John McCain, the Republican Party's nominee for President eight years earlier; Democrats Chuck Schumer of New York and Jack Reed of Rhode Island; and GOP Senator Lindsey Graham of South Carolina. (Yes, *that* Lindsey Graham.) "Recent reports of Russian interference in our election should alarm every American," the statement read. "Democrats and Republicans must work together, and across the jurisdictional lines of the Congress, to examine these incidents thoroughly."

I recognize the problem the papers had in keeping up. There was a lot going on. It had just been revealed that Trump often skipped his daily intelligence briefing. His explanation—and this is not from the *Onion*—ran, "I'm, like, a smart person. I don't have to be told the same thing in the same words every single day for the next eight years." Also, that weekend, the *Washington Post* had reported that a CIA analysis had determined the Russian influence campaign was specifically targeted at boosting Trump's chances of winning.

This was obvious, and on the Intel Committee we'd already been briefed, but for the public at large, it was a dramatic revelation.

John McCain, appearing on *Face the Nation*, called Putin a "thug" and a "murderer," and said he could not fathom why Trump would pretend not to accept the analysis of intelligence professionals.

"I don't know what to make of it, because it is clear the Russians interfered," McCain said. "The facts are there."

An *LA Times* article reported that McCain called for a select committee to investigate, and added that "Several House members, including Rep. Eric Swalwell, D-Calif., have called for an independent commission to investigate."

Oddly, other than that, my push for a commission mostly earned mentions in opinion articles. A December 8, 2016, piece by Right Turn columnist Jennifer Rubin in the *Washington Post* ran under the headline EVEN IF TRUMP WOULD RATHER NOT, CONGRESS MUST INVESTIGATE RUSSIAN HACKING, with a photograph of street art, from Lithuania, of Putin and Trump locked in a deep kiss. Rubin also mentioned our call for an independent commission. John Podesta, whose emails had been hacked by the Russians, wrote a mid-December *Washington Post* op-ed calling for several steps, including endorsing the legislation Elijah Cummings and I had introduced.

When the new, 115th Congress convened in early 2017, Elijah and I reintroduced our bill. That February, I got a call out of the blue from Republican Representative Walter Jones of North Carolina. He wanted to sign on to my bill. I remembered Jones from my days as an intern. He served on the Armed Services Committee with my boss, Representative Tauscher, and I admired his independence of mind and willingness to cross the aisle. Back then, as an intern on a budget, I often ate dinner at the various evening receptions on the Hill, and I remembered running into Jones from time to time. He would even say hello and engage me in conversation. Not many members did that.

I also remembered him as one of the first Republicans to speak out against the Iraq War. I was honored to have him as the first Republican co-sponsor of our bill. He would pay a price at home for it, attracting a primary opponent, who would claim that Jones didn't support President Trump enough. Fortunately, Jones fended off the challenge. The voters respected his independence. I told him I'd go down and campaign for him, if he liked.

Or I'd campaign for the other guy, if that would help him more. Jones was reelected, but sadly died in February 2019 from ALS. Congress needs more members with his political courage.

It would be a few more months before we landed our second Republican co-sponsor. Then Justin Amash of Michigan quietly signed on to the bill. There is probably very little Justin and I agree on. But he is a principled legislator and one of the House's loudest champions of civil liberties. For him, our bill was about making sure that the executive branch had an independent check on it.

Throughout the 115th Congress, Pelosi continued to support my legislation. She urged every Democratic member to co-sponsor it. They did. She routinely tried to force votes for it on the Floor through procedural motions. And anytime she was asked publicly about the Russia investigation, especially in the early days, she would mention the independent commission proposal. I'm still convinced, to this day, that we would be in a different place as a country had the proposal been adopted. We could have taken the Russia investigation outside Congress and put it in the hands of experts, scholars, and statespersons. That would have meant no Devin Nunes nonsense, no blind Republican loyalty to the President at all costs, no spewing Russian propaganda.

I'd joined the Intelligence Committee to work on counterterrorism, but my work on that committee has been largely defined by an attack that neither I nor most Americans ever saw coming. Our democracy has been in turmoil ever since. As we learned what Russia had done, I believed that unity among Republicans and Democrats in Congress would be the best protection against future attacks—attacks that are certain to come. I thought back to watching Republicans and Democrats sing "God Bless America" together on the Capitol steps after the September 11 attacks. Sure, this attack did not take a single life, but it was a blow to our democracy. Firm in my belief that we would unite again, I worked hard for more than a year to move forward my legislation to create an independent commission. Eventually, I gave up and changed tack. If I couldn't change minds, my best bet was to try to change seats instead, and elect a new Congress that would protect us and protect the Constitution.

CHAPTER 15

COMEY'S BOMBSHELL

Despite all the stunts the Republicans were pulling, both parties on the Intel Committee had agreed to explore what Russia had done, the adequacy of the government's response to the Russia interference campaign, potential collusion between Trump team members and the Russians, and leaks to the media regarding the investigation. From November 8, 2016, until mid-March 2017, nearly all our work on that investigation would be conducted in secret. Some of what we learned early on came from explosive media reports. The most alarming was on January 12, 2017, when David Ignatius of the *Washington Post* reported that incoming National Security Advisor Michael Flynn had been in contact with Russia's Ambassador to the United States Sergey Kislyak during the transition period. The initial report did not indicate what Flynn and Kislyak discussed, but an update the following day included denials from the administration that they had discussed sanctions. Two days later, Vice President Mike Pence said that Flynn had told him that he had not discussed sanctions with Kislyak. But on February 9, the *Post* broke the story that Flynn had indeed urged the Russian Ambassador not to retaliate against the United States for sanctions related to election meddling. Some officials alleged that Flynn had in fact urged Russia not to overreact to sanctions because they would be revisited in the Trump administration. And within weeks, Flynn had resigned, provoking more questions, from Congress and the media, as to the depth of cooperation between the Trump team and the Russians.

James Comey's testimony before our committee on Monday, March 20, would be the public's first opportunity to hear what, if anything, the FBI had. In the week leading up to the hearing, anticipation ran high as to what Director Comey would say. Many of us speculated on what he wouldn't be willing to say. Many of my Democratic colleagues and I figured that if there was an investigation, he wasn't going to be able to tell us. After all, that was protocol. The FBI doesn't talk about investigations. Period. I was only in my third year on the committee, but I knew that. The Bureau didn't leak. It didn't tell.

Even before the hearing, Ranking Member Schiff began to say publicly that he had seen "circumstantial evidence of collusion" between the Trump campaign and the Russians. He had seen the evidence, he said, in a classified setting. I had seen much of the same evidence, though as a Ranking Member and a part of the Gang of Eight, the eight members of the U.S. Congress who are briefed on intelligence matters by the executive branch, Schiff had the deepest access of anyone in Congress.

I was the first Dem to publicly back up Schiff with the "circumstantial evidence" assertion. He and I were the only two prosecutors on the Democratic side of the Intelligence Committee, and I felt confident that we had seen, at the very least, circumstantial evidence of collusion. I was also careful to explain that evidence is not a conclusion. Evidence has to be tested. But from what I was briefed on and what I viewed in a windowless CIA reading room, I believed we were completely justified in probing for collusion. On the Sunday before Comey testified, Chairman Devin Nunes went on *Fox News Sunday* with Chris Wallace and said the exact opposite, claiming that Schiff, and anyone backing him up, was dead wrong. Nunes told the nation with a straight face that there was no evidence of collusion. The media was now thoroughly confused. How could we all look at the same evidence but reach such different conclusions?

Because the Intelligence Committee works in secret, we don't have our own public hearing room. Comey testified before us in the Ways and Means Committee room, a scene we would revisit over two years later.

"I have been authorized by the Department of Justice to confirm that the FBI, as part of our counterintelligence mission, is investigating the Russian government's efforts to interfere in the 2016 presidential election," Comey said in his testimony to us that Monday.

I wasn't surprised to hear that. We had already seen strong evidence in our earlier closed-door briefings that the Bureau was dutifully looking at what Russia had done.

Comey went on: "And that includes investigating the nature of any links between individuals associated with the Trump campaign and the Russian government and whether there was any coordination between the campaign and Russia's efforts."

The room fell silent. I can still hear his words ringing in my ear: *links between individuals associated with the Trump campaign and the Russian government.*

Director Comey changed the direction of our investigation and the course of history when he uttered those words. I looked over at my Republican colleagues, and they were stunned. After all, Chairman Nunes had just insisted to America, a day before on Fox, that there had been no evidence of collusion. None. Nada. They didn't seem prepared to hear that an investigation was ongoing. And they certainly had no idea where to go next. Comey was about to toss back to the committee members, and it was going to be up to us to decide in what direction the hearing next would go. Fortunately, while we had not prepared for him to confirm an investigation, we had prepared as if he would.

Television broadcasts of Congressional hearings are rarely about the witnesses. They're usually dominated by showboating members of Congress whose questions are longer than the answers the witnesses provide. It's common for the same question to be asked over and over and over. It's pretty well known that if you ask your version of the same question the most articulate way, it's yours that will make the nightly news. Of course, *I've* never done this.

Schiff wanted our hearing with Comey to be nothing like a typical Congressional hearing. We held a number of prehearing meetings to develop a game plan and assign roles. We agreed that our objective was to lay out, based on what we could say publicly, the case of Russia's interference and Trump coordination. We wanted the public to hear the strong evidence that existed that Russia did indeed attack us. We were mindful that most Americans aren't briefed every day on Russia's intelligence capabilities and objectives. To most, Russia was a distant adversary. Sure, it had recently invaded Ukraine and was wreaking havoc in Syria, but that was far removed from most Americans' lives.

We viewed it as our job to tell the American people how Russia's intelligence officers operated: why it's in Russia's interest to develop American assets (government, political, and business) and tactics employed to lure an asset, such as investing in the financially distressed as a recruiting tool. Then we'd lay out the case of the personal, political, and financial ties between Donald Trump (and his family, businesses, and campaign) with the Russians. We would tell this story by eliciting the information from Comey and the other witness, National Security Agency director Mike Rogers. We'd ask them open-ended questions about the Russian strategy and tactics, and the Trump team, and let their answers inform the American people.

Schiff and our staff suggested that rather than having each member jump around complicated subject areas, with limited time, we should assign each member a different section. If we stuck to our assigned sections, Schiff urged, and resisted the temptation to ask red-meat questions, we could paint an effective narrative. We all agreed. Too much was on the line to freelance. And while we didn't know it at the time, our open, public hearing would be one of the few opportunities we would get to tell the American people what had happened.

At one point in the hearing, I stepped out for a bathroom break and had to make my way through a scrum in the anteroom of the committee hearing room. I didn't pay too much attention to the gang of men who had gathered around the television, silent and picking their jaws off the floor as Comey testified live to Congress. I could see the chyron at the bottom of the screen: BREAKING—FBI DIRECTOR TO CONGRESS: TRUMP CAMPAIGN UNDER FBI INVESTIGATION. As I passed, I noticed that the men watching the television were Republican members of our committee. Why weren't they inside? The unwillingness of so many of the Intelligence Committee Republicans to be in the hearing as the FBI director historically told Congress that a sitting President's campaign was under investigation was a harbinger of how they'd conduct themselves over the next four years.

President Trump, true to form, added his own plot line to the hearing. Just days before, he had absurdly tweeted that President Obama had had his "wires tapped" at Trump Tower. What the hell was Trump talking about? Hard to say. But as the country would come to learn, painfully, it doesn't pay to waste your time trying to decipher the latest weird Trump riff. His outrageous statements are most often intended to distract.

I think of Trump as having an endless supply of smoke bombs, and every time he sees a shadow or hears a voice getting closer, he drops one of them and runs away. And for days, the whole country, including Congressional and federal investigators, is confused, trying to see through the smoke to understand what just happened.

We cleared up with Comey that the FBI had indeed not "wiretapped" Trump Tower. Just to make sure the public understood the intent behind Trump's claim and what it should mean for his credibility on the Russia investigation, I fell back on my prosecutorial training, thinking back to an instruction that every juror in America is given during a trial: If a witness deliberately lies about a material fact in a case, you, the juror, can consider not believing the witness about anything. I asked Comey if he remembered that instruction. He revealed a slight smile. I could see the boyish former prosecutor coming out.

"Yes, that's familiar to me," he said.

I didn't have to say anything more. It was clear to all who were listening that the President had lied, and the way we treat liars is to not listen to them. Inside courtrooms and in the court of public opinion.

After I put to bed the outrageous claim that Trump Tower had been wiretapped, I quickly moved to the area I had asked to be assigned: financial distress as a recruiting tool. "To land on Russia's radar as somebody that they may want to recruit, would you agree that being a businessperson, a prominent businessperson is something that would be attractive to them?" I asked Comey. From everything I knew about the Russians, their intelligence services were masterful at using financial need as a foot in the door to land a potential asset. The approach was common: Reach out to that person, invest, overpay, and draw them in. It wasn't as sexy as *kompromat*, the art of using blackmail to line up an asset. But most intelligence experts believe kompromat is the least effective way to get someone to work for you. After all, the premise of the relationship is that you "caught" the asset doing something embarrassing. They may *have* to work with you, but they certainly won't *want* to work for you.

Financial targeting is different. It allows the recruiter to develop a bond with the asset. Through investment and overpaying, a bond cements, trust grows, and a friendship forms. Then, whether the asset is witting or not, he becomes loyal to his Russian handler. The handler can ask the asset for information on anything of importance to which he or she has access. Or, financial targeting can be a long bet on someone who may be in a position of power or knowledge at a later date.

With Trump, it was clear to me from our investigation that he had long-standing ties to Russia. For years, he had tried to invest in Russia and had allowed Russians to invest in him. Indeed, Russians had invested in Trump Tower and occupied many of its condos. Russians had financed Trump SoHo, another Trump property. Most curious was the Palm Beach property on North County Road. In 2004, Donald Trump purchased a 62,000-square-foot home for $41.35 million. In 2008, at the peak of the financial collapse, during a year of severe financial distress for the real estate market, he sold the home for nearly $100 million to a Russian oligarch. He credits this sale to his being a "great negotiator," but it sure smelled bad. The more we learned about his efforts to invest in Russia or to let Russians invest in him, the more the whole thing looked like a Russian intelligence operation.

Everything in the Russia hacking investigation changed with Comey's testimony. Any chance of having a bipartisan investigation, where both parties would unite to tell America what had happened, was out the window. The Republicans were caught completely flat-footed. They had blindly followed their Chairman, who had confidently asserted "no collusion," and were ambushed by the FBI Director's confirmation of an investigation into collusion and his dismissal of the bogus Trump claims about Obama administration wiretapping. From that day forward, the Republicans would do all they could to hinder any progress that Democrats, and the public, tried to make to understand the depth of Trump's ties to Russia.

The day after the Comey hearing, Devin Nunes, bizarrely, made a secret midnight trip to the White House. He then claimed, without any evidence, that the Obama administration had essentially spied on and "unmasked" the names of U.S. persons in intelligence reports. He raced to the White House the next day and held a press conference on the White House grounds to announce an investigation into what he had learned.

"What the hell is he doing?" was a common question among Democratic members on the committee. We had access to the same information as Nunes. There was no evidence of what he was claiming. Was he mimicking Trump's same smoke bomb approach? Nunes had embarrassed himself at the March 20 hearing, and his members looked foolish, wholly unprepared for the FBI Director's testimony. Was this his rip cord? It only got more bizarre. Our investigation rolled on, but every time we made progress or the press pulled a new thread, Nunes found a new, inventive way to obstruct.

I'll never understand why my Republican colleagues on the Intel Committee went along with Nunes's obstruction. They were each deathly afraid to stand up for what was right. What I saw, as I briefly stepped out of the Comey hearing for that bathroom break—Republicans too ashamed to appear publicly at their committee hearing, but too curious not to watch it footsteps away on TV—was cowardice.

They were all deathly afraid of Trump attacking them on social media. "If he tweets at you, he wins," one Republican committee member told me. I didn't understand the reasoning. Was keeping the job more important than doing the right thing? These were members of the United States Congress! I would hope this wasn't the only job they could land. And if they did do the right thing, I would hope they'd be rewarded for it.

I love my job. But the day I have to abdicate my responsibilities and look the other way out of fear—forget it. I'll walk away. And maybe that's the best lesson I've taken away from this. Don't be the guys watching the show from outside the room. Either get your ass in the arena, or leave it.

CHAPTER 16

THE JOKER

"Okay, okay, enough, you can answer the question," Steve Bannon's lawyer, Bill Burck, told his client, as if Bill were a homeroom teacher trying to get the class clown to focus. Bannon didn't heed his advice. He leaned over, covered his mouth with his hand, and whispered into Bill's ear. Bannon started laughing, but Bill was white as a ghost. It was sick. We were interviewing the Joker, I thought. "Okay, Steve, okay," Bill said. "I think you should answer the question."

We were in hour six of a ten-hour interview. Bannon was refusing to answer many of our questions, and at this point, had resorted to just trying to irritate the committee with long pauses and horsing around between questions. This was one of our first interviews of 2018 (January 16 to be exact), as our investigation of Russia's interference moved into its second year, and Bannon had done something no other witness in the investigation had been able to achieve: He united Republicans and Democrats. Both sides were equally frustrated with his stunts and refusal to answer questions. But if his goal was for us to give up and stop asking questions, he had bet wrong.

Our goals for Bannon were simple: To understand his role in Trump World (campaign, transition, White House), learn how close he was with Trump and what discussions they had about Russia during the campaign and presidency, and find out what Bannon knew about other Trump principals who had shady dealings with Russia, like Flynn and Kushner, and the truth behind the Comey firing.

I sat about ten feet across the table from Bannon, toward the front of our side of the conference table. I had a copy of *Fire and Fury* sitting in front of me. Our committee wanted to know just how much of the book's explosive revelations relating to Russia's interference—and the attributions to Bannon—were accurate. Bannon saw my copy of the book and shot me a smirk. In the end, he didn't dispute much of anything that was in it when confronted by me and my Democratic colleagues. It was clear he was a likely source for Michael Wolff's bestseller. But for most of our questions related to Russia, Bannon was going to hide behind bogus legal privileges. He was "under orders from the White House," his lawyer would tell us.

Donald Trump was impeached in the second Article for his categorical refusal to cooperate with Congress. He had done this throughout his presidency, but with Bannon he claimed new ground as to where he would assert executive privilege. During our interview, Bannon asserted executive privilege not only for the period covering his time working at the White House, but also for the time he worked on the transition team before the inauguration, and most astoundingly, for the time after he left the White House. Under Bannon's orders from the White House, Bannon could not share anything he said to anyone in the world even after he was fired. That doesn't sound so stunning now, seeing how powerful Trump thinks he is and how little he believes he has to be held accountable for. But at the time, it sounded crazy, not only to Democrats but to some Republicans as well. Like, "They don't really think that, do they?" And that was where maybe the oddest chapter of the whole Russia investigation occurred.

Mike Conaway of Texas, the Republican sitting in as chair for the recused Devin Nunes, was so frustrated by Bannon's refusal to answer questions, he called for a recess. He needed the break to figure out what to do. The nine Democrats on the committee and our staff were puzzled. Bannon wasn't the first one to refuse to answer questions.

The previous summer, Jared Kushner had smugly walked into the House Intelligence conference room for hours of "I don't recall." As Ranking Member Schiff pressed Kushner on the campaign's connections to Russia, Trey Gowdy helped Trump's son-in-law to take the stonewalling to a new low. "Mr. Kushner," he said, "you're kind to sit here and answer these questions, but let me just break this to you. You're going to be here all night. They're not going to stop. This is a voluntary interview."

I couldn't believe it. We were trying to find out what Russia did and who, if anyone, they worked with. And as soon as Schiff started to zero in, Gowdy told Kushner to pull the rip cord. Schiff asked a few more questions. Gowdy interrupted and made the point again. Kushner finally said something to the effect of, "I think I'm going to take Mr. Gowdy's advice." And that was it. He abruptly ended the interview. We'd never see him again.

Just a few weeks before we interviewed Bannon, Don Jr. had claimed he didn't have to answer questions about conversations he had with his dad about the Trump Tower meeting with the Russians. He cited no legal privilege. He didn't think he had to bother; he just wasn't answering it. I called it the "Privileged's Privilege" because only the Trump family would think up such above-the-law nonsense.

So why did the Republicans care so much about Bannon? Confused as we were, we welcomed their cooperation to try and force him to answer questions. Conaway seemed uncertain how to proceed. Again and again throughout the investigation, we found that Conaway had no power. He was ceremonially chairing the committee, but any request we made of him would be tabled for later. Which was odd if Nunes was truly recused. Recusal doesn't mean you don't show up, but still pull the strings above the stage. It means you have no involvement in making decisions. The tenth time Conaway told us, "That's above my pay grade," we realized who was running the show.

During the recess, Democrats huddled in Schiff's Ranking Member office, which is just outside the committee conference room. Bannon was with Burck in a conference room next door. As we walked back to the conference room to see what was going on, Schiff saw Conaway talking to his staff in the hallway between Schiff's office and the conference room.

"Mike, we have to subpoena him," Schiff said. "You guys can't let someone make such a sweeping claim of executive privilege."

"How do we do this?" Mike asked. That was concerning. *How do we do this?* He didn't know how you actually went about issuing a subpoena? Two years into our investigation, Intel Committee Republicans had not used the subpoena power. They were rusty.

It was as if Schiff were the Chairman. He walked Mike through how he would do it: Draw up a subpoena, sign it, and serve it right there on Bannon. Mike agreed and his staff scrambled to make it happen. I'm convinced if you looked at the GOP Intel staff Google search history that day you would find, "how to subpoena a witness" on ten of their computers.

We weren't completely naïve as to what the Republicans were up to, but if it could aid the investigation and answer some of our questions, we were willing to go along. After all, the Republicans in Congress had their own motives for wanting to stick it to Bannon. He had shredded many of them for years, and now they couldn't resist confronting Bannon with questions about his prior attacks on Republicans. Don't get me wrong, it was entertaining to see Republicans go after someone as evil as Bannon. But two things about their Bannon bashing bothered me. First, they weren't going after him about inconsistencies or gaps in his testimony relating to Russia. That would have been helpful. Instead, they were only interested in defending themselves against the attacks he had made against them over the years. It was purely to land punches while they had him stuck in their witness chair. Second, they didn't go after Bannon because they believed he was a bad person enabling a corrupt President. No, it was only because he had attacked them and they wanted payback.

After about an hour, we returned to the Committee room. A young aide who worked as a nonpartisan staffer for the committee was tasked with serving the subpoena. Members from both sides all felt bad for him. He was nervous and unsure how Bannon would receive it. I'd served hundreds of witnesses before as a prosecutor. Some friendly, most not. But I knew it was not as dramatic as it was depicted on television. "You're going to be fine," I said. "It's not a big deal and happens every day." He didn't seem convinced.

The aide slowly walked over to Bannon and stood behind him. Like a restaurant waiter setting down an entree, he set the paper in front of Bannon and his lawyers. Conaway told Bannon he was being subpoenaed. Bannon was unmoved. He would have to return a few weeks later to testify. He would still refuse to answer our questions, and the Republicans would never move to hold him in contempt, the only remedy to force him. As I said, we weren't naïve as to why the Republicans wanted to push with the subpoena. I had hoped we had reached a milestone of bipartisanship we could build on for other witnesses, but I should have known better. They had no intention of making Bannon tell the committee what he knew. In fact, they were well aware he would refuse. His attorney had told them as much before he testified. The Republicans just wanted to get their licks in on Bannon, and then get back to licking Trump's boots.

CHAPTER 17

TAKING ON TUCKER

"I'll make a deal with you, Congressman," the familiar, grating voice declared, "if you show me any evidence of collusion . . . any evidence at all, I'll give you a half hour of my show."

I'd found myself, once again, in a verbal jiujitsu match with Tucker Carlson of Fox News. Since the March 20 Comey hearing, I had become a frequent guest on Tucker's show. And my appearances usually went like this: "So X (Trump official) talked to Y (Russian) during the campaign," Tucker would whine. "So what? Where's the collusion?"

I would lay out for him why it was a problem. Tucker would interrupt, laugh, scowl, roll his eyes. And we'd go back and forth, the question-and-answer exchanges getting shorter and shorter the longer we went.

It always felt like my best shot with Tucker was to get as much information out as early as possible. This offer—show proof and get a half hour—I wasn't going to miss.

"You've got a deal, Tucker," I told him. And like a prosecutor who had just been challenged by a judge to have a motion filed by the end of the day, I went to work.

If I'm going on Tucker's show, my staff prepares as if a hurricane is about to hit our office. When you're the opposition guest on Fox News, the phones will light up. Twitter will explode. And, sadly, death threats come in. We could probably justify hiring a full-time staffer just to deal with the post–Fox News appearance storm. But millions of honest, hardworking Americans watch Fox. Why miss a chance to speak to them directly? It's also the only way my conservative parents will see me on TV. Plus, I get to speak directly to the President.

I don't mind defending myself against what I believe to be the harshest, most contrarian of critics. In fact, I welcome it. It makes me a better legislator. Tucker Carlson is obnoxious, but he's not dumb. He recognizes logical fallacies. Sometimes he exploits them, just for the prurient pleasure of seeing his guest defend the absurd. But sometimes, sometimes, he helps me sharpen my point.

Republican colleagues would often come up to me after a Tucker appearance. "Man, I don't agree with you, but you're brave to go on that show," they'd say.

"I do Fox more than you guys do," I'd kid them. "And he's on *your* team!"

It didn't take much work to put together evidence of collusion to send him. I had already been compiling it, and updating it regularly, on my Congressional website. I wanted my constituents to understand why I was spending so much time on the Russia investigation. What it meant to them and why it mattered for our democracy. So, I did what I knew best: I laid out the case as if my constituents were a jury.

For our office's website, I put together an interactive Trump-Russia guide. I didn't expect it would take so much work to keep up to date though. Every single day, there was something, either new press reporting, new Trump team disclosures, or new indictments. I called it "Connecting the Trump-Russia Dots"; I laid it out in a few sections, starting with "Russia: Not Our Friend." I felt it was important for people, especially Millennials (people like me who did not necessarily grow up believing Russia was an adversary), to understand why Russia was dangerous.

I even asked Comey about the danger of Russia during our hearing. Did he view contacts a prominent American had with Russians differently from contacts that American had with a Brit, a Mexican, or an Aussie? He said yes, and explained that because Russia was an adversary, and because of its aggressive efforts to recruit American intelligence assets, it must be viewed skeptically. I also wanted people to know that the Russians have been a disruptive force in Syria, supporting the Assad regime; invaded a sovereign ally in Ukraine; and were supporting the Taliban in Afghanistan.

I next laid out Trump's ties to Russia, but not just his ties—his family's, his businesses', and his campaign's. It seemed that in the Trump forest, if you shook a tree, a Russian would fall out. Sure, I'd been in Washington for only a few terms in Congress, but I knew you never saw the Russians come out to play. They were PNG in Washington: persona non grata. They knew that, and government officials knew that.

"You know, Eric, I've been on the Hill for decades, and I've asked around," now Intel Staff Director Tim Bergreen told me. "I asked my peers: how many Russians have you interacted with or worked with in your career? And you know what they told me? Exactly what I expected. 'Zero. We don't deal with the Russians.'" He was right. So, for Donald Trump and his team to draw themselves so damn close to so many Russians was deeply suspicious.

Although it was obvious, my website next explained what exactly Russia had done in our last election: the combination of stealing documents and disseminating them to undermine Hillary Clinton; Russia's weaponization of social media to boost Trump and hurt Hillary; and its efforts to poison the public square with vile rhetoric on social media, in order to turn Americans against one another. Finally, I connected the long-standing Trump-Russia ties to what Russia had done during the election: the June 9 Trump Tower meeting; candidate Trump inviting the Russians, on a public stage, to hack more; the repeated offers from the Russians to connect Donald Trump and Vladimir Putin. And then the payback for Russia: Flynn waving off the Ambassador, Trump spilling secrets in the Oval Office.

And that's not even the obstruction evidence, the evidence juries may consider to weigh consciousness of guilt. They're told that if a witness lies or obstructs, that may be used as evidence of his or her guilt. Boy, did we have evidence of that. And it was updated every single day.

By the morning after offering his deal, Tucker had the case for collusion in his inbox. I reminded him that evidence is not a conclusion, but that it sure as hell warranted probing deeper. And for our deal, the evidence I presented meant he clearly owed me thirty minutes on television.

Then . . . crickets. Nothing.

I tweeted at him, along with a link to a slide deck of the evidence, taunting him not to make a promise he didn't intend to keep. I heard nothing back.

A week later, a producer emailed and asked me to come on the show to discuss some other issue. I firmly said no—not until Tucker lived up to his promise.

My communications team, Josh Richman and Cait McNamee, assured me that Tucker had never intended to honor the deal. He was just being theatrical on television. I should drop it, they said. No way. I told them I wasn't doing the show until I got to present the case I'd made. If I were to appear on Tucker's show again for a second less than the promised thirty minutes, it would be a concession from me that I hadn't had sufficient evidence. But I did have the evidence. So why cave?

There were always other opportunities to go on TV. Up until 2017, I was like most members of Congress, doing only the occasional national TV interview. The Russia investigation changed everything. As my Intel colleagues and I witnessed Republicans doing all they could to bury the evidence in the case, we were compelled to make sure the American people knew what was going on.

The Republicans effectively kept our investigation underground. After March 20 with Comey, there were few public hearings. Meanwhile, they were toiling away to protect the President. So we were faced with a choice. Say nothing, honoring the long-standing tradition of not speaking publicly, especially to the press, about the workings of the Intel Committee. Or speak up. We all agreed we had to speak now, and speak loudly. So we took to the airwaves to make the case to the American people.

Ranking Member Adam Schiff, up to his eyeballs in media requests, gave the eight other Democratic members on the committee a green light to give him air support, and off we went. I took on as many requests as I could to help sound the alarm:

Russia attacked us.

Trump wanted to work with the Russians.

Act now, or lose our democracy.

Predictably, a line of attack against Democrats on the committee was that we were camera hungry. I never understood that attack. Because the Republicans were unable to knock down the substance of what we were telling the American people, they attacked the fact that we were speaking up at all? What does that say to the millions of people who watch the news? Especially considering that the GOP were unwilling to honor their oaths of office and use subpoena power to truly understand what happened in the 2016 election.

I approached my new mission as if I had to deliver a closing argument every night. Just as I used to try to persuade a jury, I now sought to persuade the American people. After all, they didn't follow this stuff every day. They weren't in the briefings. They were too busy working hard at their jobs and taking care of their loved ones. And to tune in or zone out, they'd watch the nightly news and cable programming. So they counted on those of us in the arena to explain what was happening and what it meant to them.

In May 2018, Tucker's executive producer reached out directly to me. He told me he loved having me on the show, but didn't understand why I hadn't been back on for a few months. He even suggested that my staff may not have been telling me about the requests in order to protect me. I told him I'd taken Tucker's on-air promise seriously and had provided him with a slide deck containing the promised evidence. I had lived up to my end of the deal. I now proposed a compromise: We do thirty minutes, some of that time devoted to the evidence I'd sent, and then we could move on to any news of the day. The producer promptly wrote back, accepting my offer.

I stuck to my guns and got my thirty minutes. I even brought Brittany to the studio. She watched from behind the camera, five months pregnant and white as a ghost. Tucker tried to make small talk with her beforehand. She nervously responded with short, one-word answers. I think she was afraid for me, but I was ready to go. Thirty minutes, one-on-one, with the largest prime-time audience. I welcomed the opportunity to make my case. And I felt strongly that the evidence was on my side. I wouldn't have agreed to do it unless I felt that way.

I'm 99 percent sure I didn't change Tucker's mind. He huffed. He interrupted. He rolled his eyes. He raised his voice. But that didn't stop me. When my time was up, it felt as if I'd just been on a roller coaster ride: It was thrilling, but I wished it had been longer. *Next time,* I thought, *I'll insist on the whole hour.*

CHAPTER 18

LIMITS TO THE LYING: HOPE HICKS

Hope Hicks was not like the other witnesses who came to our committee to lie for Donald Trump. For one, she was the youngest and the greenest. In February 2018, when she appeared before the House Intelligence Committee for eight hours of interrogations in our ongoing investigation of Russian interference in the 2016 election, Hicks was twenty-nine years old. She was not a creature of politics, but had worked with Ivanka Trump on her clothing line and come over to work on the Trump campaign because the family trusted her—and they valued trust over expertise or prior experience. It fell to Hicks to make assurances like her statement in November 2016 that "there was no communication between the campaign and any foreign entity during the campaign," a clear falsehood, something she may or may not have known at the time.

Others who had come before us—Donald Trump Jr., Jared Kushner, Steve Bannon—were, by comparison, grizzled old pros. Lying did not seem to faze them. They'd been in depositions before, and they knew the lengths to which Republicans would go to protect them. As long as Republicans held both houses of Congress, they would never be subpoenaed. They knew what that meant. Even if they did testify, and they didn't want to answer a question, they could just say, as Corey Lewandowski told us, "I'm not answering your fucking question." They just had to show up in front of us, sit down for an interview to be able to say they did, and then report back to the Trump team what we had. Then they'd do media interviews, hitting the same old talking points about how the Russia investigation was a big waste of time.

Hope Hicks was different. I saw a young, smart woman who was in way over her head and running with the wrong crowd—you know, like Karen in *Goodfellas*. She starts out as a nice girl from Long Island, gets taken in by the glitz and glamour of Henry Hill's mob life, and the next thing you know, she's hiding Henry's gun and flushing cocaine down the toilet. As communications director, Hope's job was to hide the gun. When she came into our interview room, our job was to see if she'd tell us where she put it.

"Would you consider yourself close to Donald Trump?" I asked.

Here we go, I thought. *Let's see where this takes us.*

I had the benefit, when I asked that question, of already watching Hope be questioned for the first two hours by Jim Himes. Jim represented the district where Hope grew up, in tony Greenwich, Connecticut. He was followed by Ranking Member Adam Schiff. A few hours in, and we had so much more to learn from Hope to understand the campaign's contacts with the Russians and the work the administration had done to cover those up.

How had she come to know the Trump family? Why had she stayed on? Why had the President said, "Russia, if you're listening . . ." and did you write that for him?

I observed Hope to have the best memory of any witness we had interviewed. Where other witnesses were well trained in the "I don't recall" shield, Hope rarely raised that to protect herself from perjury. She knew the answers, the cities, the exact dates and times for some questions. She was Donald Trump's brain, his institutional well of knowledge, a memory bank. She also was putting on a charm offensive, smiling and looking at everyone at the table. It was the best-attended interview we had. Republicans who never had an interest in the Russia investigation and who had shown up to almost none of our interviews showed up for this one.

"Would you describe your relationship with Donald Trump as a typical employer-employee relationship?" I asked her.

"I would say our relationship is anything but a typical employer-employee relationship," she said, going on to explain how much time they had spent together during long days on the campaign trail and at the White House.

"Are you loyal to Donald Trump?" I pressed further.

"What do you mean by loyal?" she asked.

I'd seen this tactic before. After all, as candid as I believed she had been up to that point, she was still the communications director of the Trump White House. I turned her question back on her.

"Well, what does loyalty mean to you?" I asked.

She paused and thought about it. "Loyalty is being committed to someone," she declared.

"Are you committed to Donald Trump?" I asked.

"Yes," she said firmly.

"Is he committed to you?" I pressed.

"Yes," she said again.

"Has Donald Trump ever asked you to lie for him?"

That broke up the cadence. Hope sat up straight. For the first time during the interview, she looked over at her lawyer. She leaned toward him, and they whispered back and forth. After more whispering, she asked to take a break and stepped out with her lawyers. I looked at the clock. Minutes ticked by. When she came back in, I noted the amount of time that had passed—to make sure that anyone reading the transcript would be aware of the passage of time. We had no cameras in the witness room. No audio recording. Just the stenographer's notes. And I wanted it to be clear for posterity that when she was asked whether Donald Trump had ever asked her to lie for him, Hope Hicks had needed a nearly ten-minute break.

"Has Donald Trump ever asked you to lie for him?" I asked again when she came back in.

She whispered again to her lawyers, then refused to answer the question. Her lawyer, for the first time, said it was too broad a question.

"Has Donald Trump ever asked you to lie about the Russia investigation?" I asked.

I figured I'd narrow it to just that. More whispering. She asked for another break and stepped out. I noted the time again. After another five minutes passed, she would again refuse to answer the question.

I tried again. "Have *you* ever lied for Donald Trump?" I asked her.

More stammering. More whispering. She became visibly stirred and started stuttering that she was a good person and had told "white lies" for the President. I sought to drill down and learn what exactly that meant. Most important, what did it mean for the Russia investigation and the many false statements she had given around it?

"Has Jared Kushner ever asked you to lie?" I asked.

"I refuse to answer that question," she said.

"Steve Bannon?" I asked

She refused to answer.

"Paul Manafort?"

Again, she refused.

"Michael Cohen?"

One by one, I went through the names of the Trump family members and the senior campaign and business officials she had worked with. Again and again, she repeated, "I refuse to answer." Each time she said it, she got more upset, raising her voice each time and sending me a very angry stare.

I was sitting about fifteen feet away from her, but I could see that she was upset. She had become unnerved. I could imagine it wasn't comfortable to sit in front of Congress and have to defend your boss and what you had done for him. But this was a serious investigation, and few were closer to Donald Trump than Hope Hicks.

Each time she refused to answer, I looked to the Acting Chairman overseeing the hearing, Mike Conaway, and said, "Mr. Chairman, can you instruct the witness to answer the question?"

But Hope had learned what Don Jr., Jared, and Bannon had learned. The Republicans would protect her. She could just refuse to answer.

That refusal seemed to cost her. The next day, after brutal headlines about her "white lies" testimony, Hope Hicks resigned—shocking news and a blow to Trump, who considered her invaluable, one of the very few aides he truly liked and trusted.

Early on, as a prosecutor working in Oakland, I'd often taken the "How close are you?" approach. It was a common line of questioning, good for testing how close an alibi witness, best friend, or spouse was to a defendant.

First, you established closeness, but you didn't do it in a stiff, lawyerly way. You put that persona aside and did your best to be human: "So, you guys seem like you were pretty close, right?" I might ask. "Were you always together? And you trusted each other? He trusted you? You trusted him? Like loyal to each other, right? Were you so close you'd lie for him?"

This classic test also helps you understand what the witness would be willing to do for the other person. I'd done it dozens of times in court. It was usually pretty effective at helping the jury understand the relationship between the two people in question and the actions the witness was willing or not willing to take.

Hope Hicks was in a dynamic like many I'd seen before between two people who were very close—except she happened to be very close to the President of the United States.

Later, in June 2019, we brought Hicks (now in a new job) back to Washington to testify before the House Judiciary Committee on issues including whether Trump's campaign worked with the Russians and if he sought to cover that up. She sat for seven hours of questioning, led by Sarah Istel and Norm Eisen of the Judiciary Committee staff, but did her best not to say anything. Hicks said she would follow Trump's orders to her, although she no longer worked for the White House, and refused to answer even basic questions, such as the location of her office in the West Wing.

Repeatedly, Hicks cited a magical concept the White House team had come up with, the notion of "absolute" immunity—which of course has no basis in the Constitution and, in fact, goes against everything the Framers had in mind. No one is above the law. No one in our system is "absolutely immune" from accountability.

On February 13, 2020, the *New York Times* reported Hicks would return to the White House as Counselor to the President. I don't know who Hope Hicks was before she worked for Donald Trump. But like so many exposed to him, she would evolve in the wrong direction. The sense of wrong and right we saw when she came before our committee, and the emotional toll of lying for someone else, must no longer be a concern to her, based on her decision. I'd thought she was different, but in the end she's just another victim of the Trump corrupting virus.

CHAPTER 19

THE MAN WITH THE NIXON TATTOO

The January 2019 indictment of onetime Nixon henchman Roger Stone surprised no one. Stone had a long track record of sleazy tricks and dirty deeds, going all the way back to Richard Nixon. By the time of his September 26, 2017, interview before the House Intelligence Committee, Stone had become a caricature of himself, a cartoon villain who dressed like the Penguin from the old *Batman* TV show. I led that interview, and in my preparations, I fully expected Stone to come swaggering in the way he usually did. It didn't go that way.

Stone was nervous the whole time, a completely different person than I expected. I guess if you were facing Congress under oath and telling lie after lie you might be nervous, too. Before we got started, Stone read an opening statement that was all over the place. One minute, he was demanding an apology from Hillary Clinton—I didn't see her anywhere on the dais—and the next, he was singling me out for attack.

"And then there is Congressmen Eric Swalwell," he droned, quoting me as having said, "From Roger Stone, we hope to learn the same things we learned from Paul Manafort, Carter Page, Don Jr., and others who were particularly active in their dealings with Russians during the summer of 2016." The quote was accurate, as the world knows now.

"Has Mr. Swalwell read my exchange with the Twitter persona which he alleges constitutes collusion?" Stone actually said that with a straight face before the Intel Committee. "The exchange is innocuous at best. Since I had no other contact with Russians, what could he be referring to?" He then went on an unpersuasive riff, ostensibly trying to convince us that he always saw the notorious hacker Guccifer 2.0 not as "a Russian asset," but as "benign." Yeah, right.

I heard him out, keeping my best prosecutor's poker face, letting him assume what he wanted to assume about what was coming next. Stone, like many of the witnesses, expected that I would come out hard-charging, but I had a surprise or two for him.

My overriding goal in leading the Roger Stone interview was to get as much information from him as possible. Considering how much he'd gone after me on Twitter and fringe news programs, I figured he would come into the interview room swinging. If I swung back, it would just be a mess. Sure, that might be fun fireworks, and would play well on TV and online, but what would it achieve for our investigation? Absolutely nothing. So, when Stone began his testimony swiping at me, I did what I always did when attacked in the courtroom, I bit my lip and told myself to stay focused.

Don't get me wrong. I wanted to rake Stone over the coals and expose him for the disgusting fraud he is. But that wasn't my job. My job was to learn what he knew. And if he didn't want to tell us, if he preferred to tell us lies, then the goal was to create a clean record to make sure he'd be held accountable.

"Congratulations" was my first word to Stone.

He looked at me quizzically.

"You're friends with Donald Trump, right?" I asked.

Stone nodded.

"Known him for years?"

Stone glanced around, as if looking for help, unclear where I was going. He had not prepped for this moment, nor anticipated for a second the proceedings veering in this direction.

"Yes," he answered, confused.

"And you helped elect your friend, of a long time, President of the United States," I said. "That's a big deal. Congratulations."

He nervously said thank you—this from a man who'd just gone on a Buffalo radio show to call me a "lightweight, mannequin, pretty boy from California . . . a yellow-bellied coward."

I'd disarmed Roger Stone with the approach he least expected: smiles and encouragement. For the next several hours, my Democratic colleagues and I questioned Stone about his long-standing ties to Trump, Paul

Manafort, and others on the campaign; to Russians who'd interfered; and to Julian Assange."

TV Stone didn't show up that day. The overdressed, overconfident, bombastic, bullying operative used to swaggering through quick media hits was nowhere to be seen. Sure, once we were done with him, he walked out of the interview room and tried to make a show of declaring victory to the television cameras. Then, over the next few months, drip by drip, he sent multiple letters to the committee to adjust his bullshit story. Lying can be a lot of work.

One interesting footnote to Roger Stone's performance that day: For all his denials, he was proving with his words just how in sync with the Russians he was. Back in 2017, he was parroting a Russian propaganda line later adopted by Donald Trump himself: "Based on what we know now, it is clear that there was a foreign nation which was colluding with a presidential campaign in an attempt to influence the outcome of the 2016 presidential election," he said late in his opening statement. "Therefore, I strongly urge this committee to investigate the numerous, publicly documented contacts between Ukraine and the Clinton campaign, particularly in light of recent public reports that Ukraine is now providing sophisticated missile technology to North Korea."

Lie upon lie upon lie—it was clear he had gone to great lengths to bury the evidence of the work he had done to obtain Russian-hacked emails to help Donald Trump. Why would someone lie, obstruct, and tamper if he was innocent? Was that easier than telling the truth?

The historical verdict on Roger Stone was devastating, as the wily old operator had surely known it would be. ROGER STONE JOINS THE REMARK-ABLE UNIVERSE OF CRIMINALITY SURROUNDING PRESIDENT TRUMP was the *Washington Post* headline on November 15, 2019, after Stone was found guilty of lying in his testimony to us.

Stone had now joined a gallery of convicted former Trump campaign associates: Paul Manafort, who had served as Trump's presidential campaign chairman and was by then behind bars; Manafort's deputy, Rick Gates, who pleaded guilty to a conspiracy charge and would finally, in December 2019, be sentenced to forty-five days in jail; Michael Flynn, Trump's National Security

Advisor during the transition, pled guilty to lying to federal investigators; George Papadopoulos, a campaign aide, who served twelve days in prison for lying to FBI investigators about his contacts; and finally, Michael Cohen, Trump's longtime lawyer and fixer, whom I'll get to soon.

Roger Stone stood out from the crowd not least for what his sleazy presence told us about Trump. Generally, if you're clean, you don't boast in public, "I am not a crook," the way President Richard Nixon famously did in November 1973, less than a year before he resigned in disgrace. And if you're clean, you don't boast about your ties to Richard Nixon, the way Stone repeatedly did. He was proud of having learned the art of political sleaze as a young operative cooking up dirty tricks for Nixon's 1972 campaign.

"By night, I'm trafficking in the black arts," Stone would later gush about those years. "Nixon's people were obsessed with intelligence." After Nixon resigned, Stone found work with Bob Dole, doing who knows what, until he was fired after investigative columnist Jack Anderson outed him as a Nixon "dirty trickster."

Stone egged Trump on to run for President, flattering him and revving him up with advice like "Attack, attack, attack—never defend" and "Admit nothing, deny everything, launch counterattack." He provided a bridge between Trump's reality TV persona and the blunter, less airbrushed menace of Nixonian skullduggery. There was about Stone, as there always had been about Nixon, a naked, desperate yearning to have a seat at the table.

Even for those of my generation—for whom the whole Nixon era, Watergate and all that, feels like ancient history, Boomer lore—it was still weird to see the way Roger Stone clung to the memory of his Nixon glory days. He had even had Nixon's face tattooed on his back.

Roger Stone clearly believed that, at some point, as President Gerald Ford had pardoned Stone's disgraced former idol Nixon, Donald Trump would pardon him.

"Have there been any discussions at the [Justice] Department about pardons for Paul Manafort, Roger Stone, Michael Flynn or Michael Cohen?" I asked Acting Attorney General Matthew Whitaker during his February 2019 testimony to the Judiciary Committee.

"Congressman, we have a very well-worn system for—" he began, lamely.

I cut him off. "That the President doesn't follow. But have there been discussions about pardons for those individuals that you're aware of? Yes or no?"

"Congressman, as I've been Acting Attorney General, I have not been involved in any discussions of any pardon even—including the ones you're discussing."

We all took that as a yes. Whitaker, roundly mocked for his sweaty, blustering, middle-linebacker-on-Super-Bowl-Sunday demeanor that day, did not lie very well.

If you asked me a decade ago if I thought a president would ever pardon one of his associates, indicted on federal charges for actions taken to help that president's campaign, I would have told you that you were crazy. But by the time I interviewed Whitaker, it was no longer so shocking to imagine Trump abusing the great powers of his office to help cover up his crimes.

What happened next, though, was actually worse than that. And I should have seen it coming. Because, as has become his custom, instead of doing his own dirty work, Trump used his lackies to do his bidding for him.

On February 10, 2020, four federal career U.S. Attorneys filed a sentencing recommendation for Stone in court, recommending seven to nine years in prison for Stone's crimes, consistent with established sentencing guidelines. They did their jobs.

The next day, just hours after Trump tweeted criticizing that sentencing recommendation on Twitter as "horrible and very unfair," Attorney General Barr intervened, overruling the career prosecutors. Suddenly, instead of seven to nine years, the Department recommended a more lenient, unspecified term of incarceration for Stone. And this wasn't the first time. The previous month, the Justice Department intervened in the sentencing recommendation for Michael Flynn after he pled guilty to federal charges, including lying to the FBI. The original recommendation was six months in jail; the Department's latest filing now says probation will do just fine.

Since the Attorney General's intervention, all four career prosecutors have withdrawn with public filings from Stone's case. One of those prosecutors resigned from the Department, too. Because this isn't okay. The Attorney General is not the *President's* attorney. He is the Attorney for the American people. And if we lose the Justice Department's ability to enforce the law, free of political interference, we lose our rule of law.

Trump wants us to stay quiet. He tries to ensure loyalty by threatening and attacking those against him, including career officials from both sides of the aisle, and the Purple Heart veteran Lt. Col. Alexander Vindman, who told the truth in our impeachment investigation about Trump's crimes.

Despite Trump's vicious attacks, we will stand against him. The same day the Attorney General intervened, Senator Kamala Harris—who worked in the same California District Attorney's office that I did—continued to do her job. She bravely spoke out, demanding that Attorney General Barr testify about his Department's handling of the Stone case.

Our committee *will* hear from the Attorney General. As this book goes to bed, he is scheduled to testify before the Judiciary Committee in March 2020. As I said via Twitter when I heard the news, "Can't wait." My father taught me to speak truth to power regardless of the cost. As Senator Harris stated, it is our duty to ensure that the integrity of the Department and our system of justice is upheld. And that includes making sure Trump doesn't use our nation's Department of Justice as his own personal henchmen. Because neither Trump, nor the DOJ, is above the law. And when someone like Stone, or Manafort, or even the President commit crimes, they must be held accountable.

Despite Barr's machinations, on February 20, District Judge Amy Jackson sentenced Stone to forty months in prison. Blasting his lies and his witness tampering, Judge Jackson emphasized that justice demanded Stone's punishment be decided by a neutral party, and not be swayed by the tweets of someone with a "long-standing" relationship to him. "The court cannot be influenced by those comments. They were entirely inappropriate." If Stone's actions went unpunished, she noted, "it will not be a victory for one party over another. Everyone loses . . . For that reason, the dismay and disgust at the defendant's belligerence should transcend party."

The punishment of Stone carried an important message. So did Judge Jackson's words. "The truth still exists," she said during the sentencing hearing. "The truth still matters."

CHAPTER 20

THE YEAR OF THE WOMAN

The Founders had seen the potential for a dangerous con man like Donald Trump, a lifelong grifter ready to run a confidence game on the American people. What they had not envisioned were the extremes of power-mad partisanship one political party would pursue to back up a man who most privately held in contempt. They had not anticipated so many key figures disavowing their most deeply held views to treat the U.S. Constitution with all the reverence of paper used to wrap an In-N-Out burger.

The only fixed point in the madness of our time, the only thing we could count on, was the upcoming November 2018 midterm elections and the chance they gave the voters to offer their verdict on the Trump presidency and its priorities. "Hold on tight," I'd tell activists across America, evoking the Rev. Martin Luther King Jr. "Let's keep moving our feet to the ballot boxes. That's where change will come."

If we could make our case to voters and pick up enough Democratic seats to win control of the House of Representatives, there would be hope. If we won the House, we would have subpoena power. We would have control of the committees, which meant we could investigate the giant network of corruption and criminal behavior presided over by Donald Trump from the first day he entered the White House. But first we had to win. If we picked up seats—that much seemed certain—but fell narrowly short of a majority, Trump would be a runaway train, freed from any accountability or constitutional checks and balances.

House Democrats had gone through a soul-searching leadership showdown just after Trump was elected in 2016. The halls were filled with whispers of who might be challenging Nancy Pelosi for Minority Leader. I was never worried. I knew that at such a difficult and pivotal point in our national history, Congressional Democrats needed a leader of Pelosi's skill and experience to counter not only Speaker Ryan but also President Trump. Pelosi understood people, inside and outside Congress, and had the best political antennae around.

I was on Pelosi's whip team working to count her votes and convince others that they should be with us. Theoretically, every conversation I had with her at that time should have been about her race, but that was just not Nancy. She was always more interested in talking about other House business. In her mind, yes, she wanted to win reelection as Minority Leader, but she had many more important duties to carry out. By the end of November 2016, she'd carried the vote, beating back a challenge from Tim Ryan of Ohio, and the leadership team could get down to plotting a course for the next two years.

The more we toiled away in the House Intelligence Committee on the Russia investigation, the more questions we had about the President's relationship with Russia and its President, Vladimir Putin. Yet with very few rights and powers as the minority party in Congress, we were nearly helpless, watching every day as the Republicans took out the shovels to bury any evidence of Trump's guilt. Fortunately, as we fought on the inside, with the few resources afforded the minority, candidates across America were stepping up on the outside. These patriots, many of whom had served in the military or the intelligence community, answered the call to service when our country needed it most.

In a clear act of desperation, the House Republican campaign arm decided to shift all its resources to making the midterm a referendum on Pelosi as Speaker and Trump's being impeached. Negative ads around the country sought to paint a vote for the Democratic candidate as a vote for Speaker Pelosi. A *USA Today* analysis in April 2018 found that to that point, Pelosi had been featured in fully 34 percent of all broadcast ads for House races, compared to 9 percent in 2016. Trump was desperate, and doing his part to convince Americans that if Pelosi won, Democrats were sure to impeach him.

I was surprised, as I campaigned across all corners of America for Future Forum candidates, at how much anxiety I heard expressed about Pelosi. Though we would see later that the GOP attacks obviously didn't work on everyday voters, I saw firsthand how they were affecting traditional

Democratic supporters and donors in the run-up to the midterms. Long-time supporters of Pelosi's would pull me aside after an event to tell me they were concerned about the impact Trump's attacks were having in battleground states.

"We've known her forever," I kept hearing. "We love her. But if she were to announce she wasn't running for Speaker, we would win the House."

The first few times I heard that—mostly from older, white men—I held my tongue. I didn't want to push back and alienate a good Democrat whose support we needed. The more I heard it, though, the more frustrated it made me. I have to credit a very bright young woman on our finance team, Yardena Wolf, for giving me the courage to speak up. She spent most of 2018 traveling the country with me to support Democratic candidates and sat through all the same sharp critiques of Pelosi that I had to endure. After weeks of this, she asked if she could tell me what she really thought.

"Of course," I told her.

"I think it's bullshit that all these men just trash Pelosi," she said. "They'd never say this about a man."

She was right. I felt cowardly for having kept quiet. Not anymore. That summer and all the way through the midterms, I didn't miss a chance to vigorously defend Pelosi.

"Do you really think that if she steps aside," I asked one donor, "Trump and the GOP will say, 'Thank you. We will stop attacking Democrats now'? They're attacking her because she's effective."

By the summer of 2018, it was looking like we had at least a 50 percent shot of winning back the House. That August, Nate Silver's FiveThirtyEight was forecasting that we'd pick up eight seats in the West and nine each in the Northeast, Midwest, and South, for a net gain of thirty-five, which would comfortably put us back in control. But given the predictions ahead of 2016, we couldn't rest easy.

By any measure, Pelosi's leadership of the Democrats that election cycle was brilliant. She urged message discipline on everyone running for office, putting out the word for candidates to focus on health care, health care, health care and to talk about Republican efforts to repeal and replace the

Affordable Care Act, emphasizing, especially, the justifiable fears of people with preexisting conditions that they could lose their coverage. Her message was "Don't take the bait"—don't let it be the Donald Trump reality TV show, keep talking to voters about what matters most to them.

The last weeks before the 2018 midterm elections were a blur for me. No one wanted me out fighting for our candidates more than Brittany, but she was due with our second child, expected close to Election Day. Anytime I was out on the campaign trail, we both worried she'd go into labor early and I'd miss the birth. That had almost been the case with our first child.

In 2016, nothing ended up as planned. Instead of a honeymoon and a Hillary Clinton presidency, Brittany and I had spent the first year of our marriage mostly apart from each other as I helped Democrats win the House. On top of that, we were expecting. Being on the road or in Washington, I missed most of Brittany's doctor's appointments. That was hard, getting updates on the road, FaceTiming during appointments, opening texts to see pics of a sonogram. The last week before the delivery, I decided to stay home. I was going to miss votes so I wouldn't miss my son's birth. At Brittany's fortieth week appointment, she excitedly shared with her OB-GYN that I'd be around all week and home for the birth.

"You're going to miss the health care vote?" her doctor, Sara Skolnick, asked.

Uh-oh. She was referring to a potential vote that week to repeal the Affordable Care Act.

"Yes. I'm not missing the birth of my son."

The doctor was not moved. "How about we make a deal?" she countered.

"Wait," Brittany cut in, "there might be a health care vote this week?"

I hadn't wanted to say anything. But yes, the GOP repeal vote was imminent.

"How about this?" Dr. Skolnick said. "You do your job. And I'll do mine."

I was puzzled.

She continued: "You go back to Washington and make sure they don't take away my patients' health care," she said, "and I'll see your wife every single day, and I promise you won't miss the birth."

"Babe, you have to go," Brittany told me.

I had no choice. Doctor's orders. I went back to Washington, and Dr. Skolnick kept her word. I woke up early on the morning of May 18 to a spate of texts from Brittany: "Call me." She was going into labor. I didn't even shower. I called an Uber and went directly to Dulles. I somehow made it across the country and to the hospital with three hours to spare. I was there for Brittany, witnessed the birth of my son, and saw how much saving health care meant to a doctor. Most important, I learned that my wife was willing to sacrifice my missing one of the most important moments in our lives if it meant I would help others.

I didn't have to go through anything so dramatic to be there with Brittany for the birth of our second child. Nelson had a little baby sister, and we were overjoyed. On October 24, 2018, I posted a baby picture on Facebook: "Meet Kathryn Watts Swalwell—we'll call her 'Cricket.' Mama and baby are doing great. And I'm thrilled that for the first time in as long as anyone can remember in my family, a male had a girl. #YearOfTheWoman"

No Swalwell male had ever had a daughter. I went as far back as I could on Ancestry.com and found nothing, nada, no girls. I never expected it would be any different for me. We were stunned to learn at ten weeks that we were having a girl, and overjoyed.

I knew what gift I wanted for Cricket, and it came on November 6, 2018: a resounding setback for Trumpism in the midterm elections and a Year of the Woman in politics. I watched the results come in from a Dublin union hall, where I had rented a couple of thousand square feet of office space for a "Red to Blue Headquarters." Hundreds of volunteers had descended that year to make phone calls, send text messages, and write postcards to help win the House. It was such a thrill to watch with those volunteers as the results rolled in and the races were called across the country.

"Colin Allred has won in Dallas," Brian Williams announced on MSNBC, referring to the former NFL linebacker and Democrat who'd won a seat in the House.

We cheered. We had put a lot of work into helping Colin in Texas's 32nd Congressional District. His win was America's win. And it was one seat closer to the twenty-four we needed to win the House. Hour by hour, new results came in as polling places closed. We watched with growing excitement as all the major news outlets declared that the Democrats had won the House and the screen cut to Nancy Pelosi taking the stage at a victory party in Washington.

"Today is about more than Democrats and Republicans, it's about restoring the Constitution's checks and balances to the Trump administration," she said.

The biggest winner was democracy itself: There had been a huge turnout, with 49 percent of eligible voters casting a ballot, the most in a midterm election since 1914. Polls showed that fully two thirds of voters saw this as the most important midterm election of their lives. They were taking a stand against Trump's disastrous and destructive politics, but more than that, against the bigotry, the hate, and the unending corruption.

I'd spent a lot of time on the road, meeting with and supporting candidates running in the most flippable seats in the country. Most of them never imagined themselves as candidates for Congress. Most of them stepped up when they saw their democracy on the ropes and wanted to defend it. And they were young. I launched an initiative called Future40 to focus on the forty youngest candidates, in their forties or younger. They brought bursts of new energy, new ideas, and a much-needed new confidence. Diverse in ethnicity, religion, geography, sexual orientation, and professional background, they represented the best of their generation. And America needed them.

Democrats picked up forty-one seats in the House, more than enough to take control, and also gained seven governorships, which would protect against partisan gerrymandering in the next decade. A record thirty-six women were elected to the House for the first time, meaning we would have at least one hundred and two women in the House over the next two years, also a record. No Muslim woman had ever been elected to the U.S. Congress. Now we had two. Same for Native American women, and now we had two.

The GOP strategy, running on Nancy Pelosi and against impeachment, had been a flop. People wanted a check on Trump. They wanted accountability. They wanted investigations that could give them some answers, wherever that led us as a nation.

CHAPTER 21

THE TRUMP SHUTDOWN

One thing Democrats knew we needed was a leader strong enough to face off with Donald Trump and not blink. We needed a leader who had the experience to take Trump on, but to do it in a smart and purposeful way. We needed Nancy Pelosi as Speaker of the House to fight for constitutionally mandated oversight of an executive branch making a naked power grab. Pelosi saw right through Trump, and he knew it, and it unnerved him. With Republicans all-in on power for power's sake, it was going to take a scrappy and crafty leader who could make Trump feel political pain. That was what happened with the Trump Shutdown, a crucial step in holding the President accountable.

But before Pelosi could become the first Speaker to win two separate terms in that office since Sam Rayburn in 1955, she would have to line up some votes. Two weeks after the 2018 election, sixteen House Democrats released a letter thanking Pelosi for her service, but saying they wanted new leadership and would not support her for Speaker. I didn't like how this was shaping up. I'd traveled the country pushing for new leadership and new faces in Congress, but Nancy Pelosi was the leader we needed to go toe-to-toe with Trump. And Pelosi had just led us in taking back the House. To me, sacking her would have been the equivalent of firing a football coach the day after he'd won the Super Bowl.

The argument against Pelosi was that we needed generational change. As the leader of Future Forum, I talked every day about that topic—with the caveat that change simply for the sake of change is worthless. When I ran for Congress against an eighty-year-old incumbent, it wasn't about his age. It was about his mind-set. It was the fact that he'd lost touch with his district. I saw the opposite in Pelosi. Not only was she sharp and energetic, not only did she work hard to empower younger members like me, but she cared about the issues of my generation: climate action, money in politics, and ending gun violence and student debt. She was the opposite of out of touch.

Once again, I signed up to be part of the team working to elect Nancy as Speaker, and found that her attitude about the challenge was just as it had been two years earlier. She was not overly concerned. She took seriously the need to win each member's vote, but she wasn't tabling her other responsibilities to focus solely on running. To her, that would have been a dereliction of duty—and a sign of weakness. She was the leader of the Democratic Party. She'd led the effort to win back the House. Donald Trump and the Republicans told every American that if the Democrats won the House, Nancy Pelosi would be Speaker. The Democrats won the House, and as far as she saw it, and as far as I saw it, that meant the American people wanted a "Speaker Pelosi."

No one I've observed in politics understands the art of leverage and finding an opponent's weaknesses better than Nancy Pelosi. That was on display December 11, 2018, nearly five weeks after we won the midterms, when she was invited to the White House along with Senate Minority Leader Chuck Schumer to negotiate a way out of a pending government shutdown, brought about because Trump was holding out for funding for his proposed wall along the border with Mexico. Trump wanted cameras in the room. Pelosi was all too ready. She knew who was holding the cards and who was weak, and she went right at one of the President's weaknesses, his vanity. Put his name on it, and he'd proudly own it. Just like Trump Vodka, or Trump Steak, or Trump Ties, it didn't matter how bad the product. If there was going to be a shutdown, he'd have to own it.

"I think the American people recognize that we must keep government open, that a shutdown is not worth anything, and that you should not have a Trump shutdown," Pelosi said. "You have the White House."

Trump took the bait immediately. The video of the exchange was an instant classic: You had Pelosi on the left, composed and in control; Vice President Pence sitting between Pelosi and Trump, a prop more than a participant; and then Trump on the right. His reaction was delayed, weirdly. Pelosi was speaking clearly and loudly, but Trump didn't seem to hear at first.

The President leaned forward and demanded "A what?" Then he seemed to mumble, "Did you say 'a Trump shutdown'?"

Pelosi finished her point, reminding the President that with Republicans in control of the White House, the Senate, and the House (until the newly elected Congress convened in January 2019), he had no room for excuses. Trump, fixated on his campaign pledge to build a wall along our border with Mexico, bounced around from defiant to sarcastic, unable to hide his clear sexism in finding it difficult to have a woman standing up to him in a firm and always dignified way. He especially didn't like it when Pelosi called his obvious bluff in claiming he could get Republicans to vote immediately on a spending bill.

"Okay, then do it, then do it," she said.

Riled, Trump thought he could score points by assuming he knew things he didn't about Pelosi's standing in the Democratic caucus.

"I also know that, you know, Nancy's in a situation where it's not easy for her to talk right now, and I understand, and I fully understand that," Trump said sarcastically.

"Mr. President, please don't characterize the strength that I bring to this meeting as the leader of the House Democrats, who just won a big victory."

Pelosi had tried to save him, warning him that they shouldn't have a conversation like this in front of the press. But there was no saving him. Pelosi and Schumer did not even have to work all that hard to put Trump on record saying that he was proud to shut down the government to chase after his wall.

"Yes, I'll take it!" Trump declared at one point. "If we don't get what we want one way or the other . . . I will shut down the government, absolutely. . . . I am proud to shut down the government!"

In just a few unforgettable minutes, Pelosi had not only asserted her power as Speaker-elect, but she'd gotten President Trump to own the approaching shutdown. Most who were on the fence about her as Speaker moved toward supporting her.

As I told the *New York Times* that day, "I think she sealed the deal."

Republican Senator Lindsey Graham, who had gone from declaring Trump unfit for office before he won to sucking up to him at every turn, even admitted to the press that Pelosi had schooled the reality TV star. "I think she gave as good as she got," he told the *Times*.

And *Times* reporters Sheryl Gay Stolberg and Annie Karni even acknowledged that the exchange would "send a message to Democrats and Republicans alike that Ms. Pelosi is fully capable of taking on Mr. Trump and brushing off his lecturing, or in this gender-charged case, mansplaining."

I brought my baby girl, Cricket, to Nancy Pelosi's historic swearing-in as Speaker of the House for a second term on January 3, 2019. The roll call vote took hours, but I held Cricket in my arms the whole time. She was two and a half months old, looking sharp in a white wool onesie and wearing a pink bow. I knew she would have no recollection of the event, but I wanted to be able to tell her when she was older that she was on the House Floor when Nancy Pelosi was sworn in as Speaker.

If you had asked me that day if Speaker Pelosi would lead the impeachment of Donald Trump, I would have told you, "That will depend on Donald Trump." She hadn't led us into the majority to impeach Donald Trump. In fact, throughout the summer of 2018, in our private meetings, as she was attacked by some Democrats for not supporting impeachment, Pelosi would always refocus the conversation.

"Health care, jobs, corruption," she would remind us. "That's what people care about. Protecting health care. Creating jobs. Fighting corruption."

Pelosi was absolutely right to remind people at every turn that this fight was about the voters, not us. It wasn't about our personal differences with a contemptible President. Impeachment wasn't Pelosi's thing. Back in 2007 to 2009, before I was elected to Congress, she had been under immense pressure to impeach George W. Bush for lying about the Iraq War. She deftly resisted. She trusted the voters.

As soon as we gained the majority in January 2019, the press, many Americans, and members of Congress would call for Trump's impeachment. At her Election Night party, Michigan Representative Rashida Tlaib told her supporters she was ready to "impeach the motherfucker." Within hours of being in power, House Democrats were being asked, "Are you going to impeach the President?"

Pelosi told us to keep our eyes on the ball. We had been elected, under her "For the People" agenda, to lower the cost of prescription drugs, clean up government, expand voting rights, pass background checks on the sales of firearms, allow DREAMers to stay in America, and finally, to ensure that women received equal pay for equal work. We would get to work in the months ahead to pass legislation to do all that, much of it with bipartisan support. If we ever brought up impeachment in our leadership meetings, or even seemed to be broaching the subject, Pelosi didn't miss a chance to remind us: "Make sure you're talking about our 'For the People' agenda." She was adamant that we show our constituents and the public that while we would hold the President accountable, we were doing much more.

Pelosi's leadership was decisive in ending the Trump Shutdown, which had gone into effect on December 22, 2018, when Trump, for a change, held to his word on something and showed that he was indeed happy to own a government shutdown. He didn't get the funding for his symbolic, obviously ineffective border wall, so he took his toys and went home. As Chuck Schumer had put it earlier that month, "President Trump is willing to throw a temper tantrum and shut down the government unless he gets his way."

From the first few days of the shutdown, I'd seen the human toll it was taking. I followed Chef José Andrés on Twitter, and during the shutdown I read that he had set up a pop-up kitchen to serve hot meals to federal employees who were not being paid. I retweeted a couple of his posts, and soon Chef Andrés reached out via direct message and asked me if I'd be willing to come to the kitchen to serve food.

"Of course," I told him, and showed up the next day. In my job, it's not unusual to serve food to the masses. I do it at church events, around the holidays, and at homeless shelters. But never, ever, in my wildest dreams, could I have imagined serving hot food during a cold winter to unpaid federal workers. In the food line that day, I saw uniformed FBI police officers, federal public defenders, and National Park officials. It was hard to look them in the eye. Even though this was strictly and entirely a Donald Trump shutdown, these were hardworking folks who only expected and needed their elected leaders to budget for their work. They shouldn't have been standing in that line.

I worked the whole shift. I told Chef that more of my colleagues needed to see what I saw, and I posted about my experience on all of the socials. Soon, elected officials from both parties were showing up to serve meals. That was all Chef wanted. Sure, he had his beef with President Trump, but he never made it *about* President Trump. All Chef cared about, like any effort he'd worked on prior to this, was feeding people in need.

During the shutdown, I flew to Atlanta for the Martin Luther King Jr. Day celebration. Going back to Washington, I sat at a restaurant bar inside the Atlanta airport waiting to board a delayed flight. As I was texting back and forth with my wife, a customer stepped up to order a drink. The bartender carded him. The customer shot back a dirty look. He was clearly well over twenty-one. I looked at the customer and told him not to be offended; I wasn't asked for ID, but I wished I had been. He looked at me and said, "Well, you're not on the business end of the government shutdown." He went on to tell me that he had served in the Coast Guard, was behind in his mortgage, and had come to Atlanta for a funeral he couldn't afford to attend, and he'd had to borrow money to make it. I wanted to hear how the shutdown was affecting him without his response being colored by his knowing what my job was, but finally, I told him. "Man, it's just not right," he said. He didn't really care about the politics or who was responsible. He just needed the shutdown to end.

Leave it to Speaker Pelosi to get the shutdown ended. She'd seen right through Trump. It wasn't hard. The man was all id. If you ignored the nonsense he was spouting, it was obvious what mattered to him: whatever big, shiny thing was dancing in his eyes at any given moment. In this case, that big, shiny thing was obvious: He was fixated on the bump he thought he'd get by delivering his annual State of the Union address before both houses of Congress, a speech carried live on all the networks, a forum for him to pout and yell and insult and do all those things he so enjoyed doing.

To which Speaker Pelosi replied, in effect, no, thank you. She let him know that he was not, in fact, invited to give the State of the Union. She did it politely, citing the cost of security during the government shutdown, when security officials weren't even being paid, but she struck her mark. You could almost see the White House vibrating as, somewhere inside, our man-child President went into full tantrum mode, shouting, "She can't do that! She can't do that! She can't do that!"

Yes, she could.

Trump lost his mind. His advisors let him occupy himself with non-starter ideas, like trying to organize his own State of the Union. But even Trump must have figured he'd look like a dope trying that. He understood the power of the office and knew how unpresidential it would have looked to deliver the address from anywhere but the Capitol. So he ultimately caved and reopened the government, having gained nothing.

When Trump finally did deliver his State of the Union address, Speaker Pelosi was right there to keep an eye on him. Amazingly, unlike the three Presidents before him, who all lost the House and made gracious mentions of that fact early in their speeches, Trump made no mention of the power shift in Washington. He did not want to acknowledge the obvious new reality, that the Democratic-led House was going to be a force. Still, he knew, as everyone did, that a new day was at hand. The single most iconic image that emerged from Trump's speech that night was of Speaker Pelosi, elegantly evoking the suffragettes in her cream-colored suit, extending both arms out to applaud Trump after he said he claimed he would avoid "the politics of retribution." Thanks to social media, it was the clap heard 'round the world.

CHAPTER 22

"HE IS A RACIST. HE IS A CON MAN. HE IS A CHEAT."

Say what you want about longtime Trump fixer and attorney Michael Cohen, but he showed more courage than many in the Trump orbit. It took real courage for Cohen to testify, in late February 2019, before the House Oversight Committee and say what he said. The committee, chaired by Elijah Cummings, was tasked with investigating ties between Trump affiliates and the Russians. Cohen testified despite a threat Florida Congressman Matt Gaetz made the day before on Twitter, a tactic that would become a hallmark of the Trump brigade in their quest to intimidate witnesses at every turn.

"Hey @MichaelCohen212—Do your wife & father-in-law know about your girlfriends? Maybe tonight would be a good time for that chat. I wonder if she'll remain faithful when you're in prison. She's about to learn a lot."

Cohen knew he had his own credibility issues, and he'd brought documentation to back up what he said. His description of the shame and disappointment he felt for having helped Trump had the ring of truth. (Knowing he would be appearing before the House Intelligence Committee, I went to Oversight and sat in a section reserved for members to take in Cohen's testimony.)

He apologized to his family and to the entire nation for the wrong he had done in service of Trump. "Never in a million years did I imagine, when I accepted a job in 2007 to work for Donald Trump, that he would one day run for President, launch a campaign on a platform of hate and intolerance, and actually win," Cohen said sadly. "I regret the day I said yes to Mr. Trump. I regret all the help and support I gave him along the way. I am ashamed of my own failings, and I publicly accepted responsibility for them by pleading guilty in the Southern District of New York."

Of course, his testimony was intended to help him knock time off the three-year prison sentence he'd already been handed for lying and various financial crimes, but he was offering a compelling glimpse into a sordid world. "I am ashamed of my weakness and misplaced loyalty—of the things I did for Mr. Trump in an effort to protect and promote him," he continued. "I am ashamed that I chose to take part in concealing Mr. Trump's illicit acts rather than listening to my own conscience. I am ashamed because I know what Mr. Trump is."

Michael Cohen knew, and he was ready to tell the country all about it.

"He is a racist. He is a con man. He is a cheat."

This was the President of the United States he was talking about. Even if we all already knew those things, it was still shocking to hear them said out loud.

"He was a presidential candidate who knew that Roger Stone was talking with Julian Assange about a WikiLeaks drop of Democratic National Committee emails."

Later in his opening statement, Cohen walked the nation through Trump's approach to lying—for example, the way he had lied as a candidate when he said he had no business interests in Russia even as he was actively pursuing a massive development project in Moscow that would bear his name. The project was so important to Trump, in fact—he was obsessed with it—that it's probably on target to assume that he ran for President in part in the hope of gaining leverage to close that deal. Cohen confirmed—believably, I still say—that Trump never thought he would get the Republican nomination, let alone wind up in the White House, but that his campaign would be the greatest infomercial ever.

"The last time I appeared before Congress, I came to protect Mr. Trump," Cohen said, referring to his testimony in 2017 before the House Intelligence Committee and our Senate counterparts. "Today, I'm here to tell the truth about Mr. Trump. I lied to Congress about when Mr. Trump stopped negotiating the Moscow Tower project in Russia. I stated that we stopped negotiating in January 2016. That was false—our negotiations continued for months later during the campaign. Mr. Trump did not directly tell me to lie to Congress. That's not how he operates."

So how did Trump operate? By maintaining deniability and making sure his people knew what he wanted of them.

"In conversations we had during the campaign, at the same time I was actively negotiating in Russia for him, he would look me in the eye and tell me there's no business in Russia and then go out and lie to the American people by saying the same thing," Cohen said. "In his way, he was telling me to lie. There were at least a half-dozen times between the Iowa Caucus in January 2016 and the end of June when he would ask me 'How's it going in Russia?' referring to the Moscow Tower project."

Cohen's one day of truth-telling testimony was not going to rehabilitate his image, but he was bold enough in what he said to capture the attention of the country.

His revelations to the Intel Committee behind closed doors the next day were, if anything, even more dramatic. His tone was similar, but in that private session with us, he offered a riveting and startling explication of serial corruption on a mind-boggling scale. Most important, he offered plenty of specifics that could open up new lines of investigation.

For example, at one point, I asked about mob-connected Russian-born businessman Felix Sater, one of many whom Trump tried to pretend he didn't know. "I've seen him a couple times," Trump said in a 2013 deposition.

"Did Mr. Sater have a Trump Organization business card?" I asked Cohen.

"At one time, yes," he said.

"How would that happen if he wasn't working for the Trump Organization?"

"So, his card stated," Cohen said. "I believe it said, 'Senior Advisor.'"

"Was he actually a senior advisor?"

"His card said so," Cohen said.

I also asked a series of questions about the planned Trump Tower in Moscow that was an obsession for Donald Trump.

"Would Mr. Trump talk to you about his understanding of what Mr. Putin's role would be in any deal in Russia?" I asked Cohen.

"He knew that," Cohen said. "We have had conversations where he knew as well that everything runs through the Kremlin."

Cohen pledged to return to the committee the following week with corroborating documents. During a break in his all-day testimony to the Intel

Committee, he came over to me to make small talk. He and I had messaged each other a little before then, with Twitter DM, going over the details of some of his travel that he wanted to clear up with me. He had even reached out the previous December to wish me a Merry Christmas and a happy and healthy New Year.

This day, Cohen's mood was conciliatory. He actually had some nice things to say about me, telling me that I was performing a valuable public service. I told him in turn that I thought he was doing the right thing by telling the truth about Trump and helping the public understand just what a threat he represents to the American people and the American way of life.

"You know, this guy, he really wants to be a dictator," Cohen told me in that brief private conversation. "He admires Putin and Erdoğan because they're dictators. Part of why I'm doing this is I worry that's where we're heading."

It was chilling to hear such a blunt assessment from someone who knew Trump better than almost anyone. Cohen had been the keeper of Trump's secrets for years and years. Not anymore. He shared with me his deepest worry—it wasn't about not being able to see his family because he was doing jail time; it was about the future of the country.

"I fear he won't accept the outcome of the next elections," Cohen told me. "So do I," I said.

I found Cohen credible. To me, this was a liberated man. His whole demeanor had changed. When he testified in October 2017, he was still Trump's guy, doing everything he could to protect him. Being straight with us didn't seem like a priority then. Now that had changed. He knew what he had done wrong, he knew Trump was a bad guy whom no one could trust, and he had a clear sense of purpose. He was hoping to avoid doing time, or to do as little as possible.

Cohen couldn't avoid prison. My wife and I would talk about this: Just imagine how it must be for Cohen. He'd come forward and told the truth about Donald Trump, and what did it get him? He was behind bars, his family going on with their lives without him. Meanwhile, Trump continued to get away with it, all of it.

CHAPTER 23

RUNNING FOR PRESIDENT

My wife, Brittany, and I talked about it after Trump was elected and agreed on the urgency of thwarting the Trump agenda in the years to come. We knew that could take many forms—late nights, trips away from our young family, and risk-taking. That discussion also included the possibility of me running for President. There was a clamor for fresh voices and change agents. I felt it. I saw it. So did my Chief of Staff, Alex. I believed in running on issues, not running for specific offices. Find an issue, learn it, fight for it, and the office will find you. That was how I would run for President. I was inspired by the class of 2018, particularly their energy. Of the new members, twenty-nine were in their forties or younger. I wanted to make sure the issues that appealed to young people had a big voice on a big stage.

So, there I was in early April 2019, sitting in the Ed Sullivan Theater in New York, with Stephen Colbert staring back at me with a look of intense interest. I was tugging at my wedding band and tried to forget for a minute how nervous I was—which was hard, since I'd never been more nervous for a TV interview. I hardly even talked to Brittany in the green room beforehand, which showed her how nervous I was. This was a big deal. This was like stepping up to the first tee for the first day of the U.S. Open and just hoping you wouldn't shank the ball and send it dribbling off into the trees.

"You've been very critical of Donald Trump," Colbert said. "You've called him a wrecking ball, you've called him a Russian agent. You're a Congressman. What can you do to try to fix what you see as wrong with this country?"

What could I do? I was ready for the question.

"I've already done a lot, but I can do more," I started. "I've been in Congress for six years. I've defended our country from the Intelligence Committee while democracy has been on the ropes. I took a group of young members of Congress, started a group called Future Forum. We've gone all over the country to listen to and stand up for the next generation of Americans."

I remembered to speak slowly, not rushing anything, and raised my hand for emphasis. Colbert was staring back at me so intently, I mostly tried not to think about where I was, but at one point, I stopped and thought to myself, *Holy shit! I'm talking to Stephen Colbert!*

"I see a country in quicksand, unable to solve problems and threats from abroad, unable to make life better for people here at home," I continued. "None of that is going to change until we get a leader who's willing to go big on the issues we take on, be bold in the solutions we offer, and do good in the way that we govern. I'm ready to solve these problems. I'm running for President of the United States."

"Now it's official," Stephen said, smiling.

"Boy, did it feel good to say that!" I said, slapping my thigh for emphasis. Back to my golf comparison, it felt like I'd hit my tee shot right down the middle of the fairway and I'd live to swing for another hole.

Running for President is a test of confidence—confidence in yourself, your ideas, and your supporters. Finding that easy confidence in myself was the most challenging part. It's not a natural act, running for an office like that. Feeling like I belonged was hard.

Speaker Pelosi was supportive of my run for President. "I'm happy you're doing this," she said. "You have a case to make, a story to tell. I'm just worried about your family." Leader Pelosi was the only person I can remember, outside of family and staff, who acknowledged how a presidential run would eat into precious time with Nelson, Cricket, and my wife. That just shows you how genuine and caring she is.

Not long after Colbert's show, I qualified for the June presidential debates in Miami. It would be ten of us at a time on back-to-back nights. I would be on the second night in a debate group with Senator Bernie Sanders; Senator Kamala Harris; Vice President Joe Biden; South Bend, Indiana, Mayor Pete Buttigieg; Senator Michael Bennet; Marianne Williamson; Senator Kirsten Gillibrand; Andrew Yang; and former Colorado Governor John Hickenlooper.

Given the lineup, I figured my best gambit would be to contrast myself with Biden. He was the clear front-runner at the time, a veteran of many campaigns who had run for President more than once. I was thirty-eight, and he was seventy-six. If I wanted to make a generational case for running, a retort to Biden was my best shot. My signature issue was ending gun violence, and I was going to make sure to speak up on that.

My wife and I watched the first night of the debates together after we put our kids down to sleep at her family's home in West Palm Beach. The worst tactic at a debate, we realized, was to give an awkward wave to show the moderators you wanted to speak. All night long, candidates were waving their hands. I was reminded of being at a crowded college pub with everyone trying to get the bartender's attention. It didn't work in either place.

It was night two, and backstage the MSNBC debate team frantically tried to track the location of candidates as we approached showtime. They put us in order of our podium positions and wanted us to walk out accordingly. They reminded us a number of times of how awkward it would look if we screwed this up, as Ben Carson did in 2016. We candidates nervously greeted one another in a narrow hallway backstage. The only one I knew well was Kamala Harris, a fellow alum of the Alameda County District Attorney's Office.

Suddenly, there was a wave of panic from the debate staff. We had an AWOL candidate. "Where's Biden?" staffers kept asking. We all looked around, as if it were our collective duty to turn up the former Vice President. Right before we were to take our places, he showed up. He had been walking around greeting the production crew. No one was surprised.

"That's Biden," one of the candidates said.

I smiled. I loved the guy, one of the most genuine public servants I'd ever met. But I was prepared to make the case that it was time to turn the page toward a new generation.

As we were breaking for lunch at our prep session the day before the debate, I had an idea for how to frame my question. Biden had run before. He had to have made the generational case himself as a presidential candidate.

"Find me a quote," I told Kyle Alagood, an ace researcher on my team.

I was sure one was out there. Kyle came back after the forty-five-minute lunch break with a litany of quotes. The best was from the 1987 California Democratic Convention, where presidential candidate Joe Biden quoted President John F. Kennedy, arguing that it was time to "pass the torch" to a new generation of leadership. Jackpot!

Nothing could have prepared me for walking out for the start of a presidential debate. The hall was filled. I saw my wife in the front row with my other guest, Fred Guttenberg, whose daughter Jaime was killed in the Marjory Stoneman Douglas High School shooting in Parkland, Florida, on February 14, 2018. Spread throughout the auditorium were other supporters from California, Indiana, Alabama, but I couldn't make out any of them from where I was standing.

If you listen to pollsters and consultants, they'll tell you that for a debate, a man should wear a Navy suit, white shirt, and a red or blue tie. You don't deviate from that. I chose an orange tie as a nod to the End Gun Violence movement, which encouraged supporters to wear orange to raise awareness of the issue. I also wore an orange ribbon that Fred had given me for his charity, Orange Ribbons for Jaime. Later in the evening, I would learn that "orange ribbon" was a top Google search term during the debate.

With the debate under way, I took my first shot at weighing in, without being called upon, when the topic turned to student loan debt. This was an issue that was personal to me.

"I've got about a hundred thousand dollars in student debt," I said. "I'd like to say something about this."

The moderators did not look over. There were hands waving everywhere and others trying to speak. My staff and I had practiced this. You had to be willing to just talk, unrecognized, for an uncomfortable amount of time. I kept going.

"You can't count on the people who have been in government for the last thirty years, who were around when this problem was created, to be the ones to solve it," I said. "It's going to be the next generation, the forty million of us who can't start a family, can't take a good idea and start a business, and can't buy our first home. This is the generation that's going to be able to solve student loan debt. This generation is ready to lead."

I felt relieved. That would be my most nervous delivery of the night, but I had to get it out. As uncomfortable as it was to horn in on the conversation, I was gratified to have made the first generational point of the night.

I was also ready when moderator José Díaz-Balart turned to me, after an Andrew Yang answer about automation. "What would you do to help people get the skills they need to adapt to this new world?" he asked me.

My tactic was to get to the most important points early. I answered the question about automating, talking about the need to make sure technology creates more jobs than it displaces, and about modernizing schools and valuing teachers. Then I saw an opening to pivot to my theme of generational contrast.

"But José, I was six years old when a presidential candidate came to the California Democratic Convention and said, 'It's time to pass the torch to a new generation of Americans.'"

I looked across the stage. I saw a look of "Where is this going?" The only other person in the hall who knew where it was going was my wife, nervously watching from the front row.

"That candidate was then-Senator Joe Biden," I said, and looked at the Vice President. He smiled and even gave a good-natured nod.

"Joe Biden was right when he said it was time to pass the torch to a new generation of Americans thirty-two years ago. He is still right today. If we are going to solve the issues of automation, pass the torch. If we are going to solve the issues of climate chaos, pass the torch. If we're going to solve the issue of student loan debt, pass the torch. If we're going to end gun violence for families who are fearful of sending their kids to school, pass the torch."

Díaz-Balart, quick on his feet, turned to Biden. "Well, Mr. Vice President, are you ready to sing a torch song?"

Biden was still smiling. "I would," he said. "I'm still holding onto that torch."

Biden didn't take the line personally. In fact, during the first break, he came over and put his hand on my shoulder. I figured he was going to rib me for the torch line, but he asked about my daughter. I'd mentioned in the debate that our family knew a thing or two about health insurance bills, having recently had a daughter in the intensive care unit. Biden picked up on that and wanted to know how Cricket was doing. That was kind of him. It also showed that Biden in person is every bit as genuine as people who have never met him probably hope he will be.

The torch line would be one of the few opportunities I'd get to speak that evening. During the final break, while most of the candidates were racing to the bathroom, I stayed at my lectern and thought about how I'd broach the topic of ending gun violence. All night long, I'd been glancing to my right to where Brittany and Fred were sitting.

Suddenly, I saw Fred fly out of his seat and move toward the moderator table. I could hear him shouting, but couldn't make out what he was saying. Brittany gave me a look like *What could I do? Do you really think I could stop him?* Soon, a half-dozen security guards were swarming him, and he was ushered back to his seat. I still had a minute before the break ended, and I hurried over to him and Brittany.

"Fred, what the hell is going on?" I called out from the edge of the stage.

"Eric, they haven't asked about gun violence," he said, agitated. "They need to ask a question about gun violence."

I agreed. What would it mean for our movement if such an important issue was not even raised?

"Fred, we're going to talk about it," I told him. "If they don't ask a question and I can't work it in, I'll devote my entire forty-five-second closing statement to it."

Right out of the break, Rachel Maddow asked me about my plan to have government buy every assault weapon in the country. "How do you envision that working, especially in states where gun rights are a strong flash point?" she asked.

This was the pitch I'd been waiting for all night, and I was ready to take a swing. I wanted every family and every community affected by gun violence to know that I was there for them and that we were saying, "Enough is enough."

"Keep your pistols, keep your rifles, keep your shotguns," I said. "But we can take the most dangerous weapons from the most dangerous people."

I also wanted to give a shout-out to the advocacy groups that had gotten us to the momentous occasion when gun violence proposals were being addressed on a presidential debate stage. "We have the NRA on the ropes, because of the moms, because of the Brady Group, because of Giffords, because of March for Our Lives," I said, and the crowd applauded their work.

"I'm the only candidate on this stage calling for a ban and buyback of every single assault weapon in America," I said, and explained my ideas. Wrapping up, I added, "We don't have to live this way. We must be a country who loves our children more than we love our guns."

I said it exactly the way I felt: from the heart, from experience, but from a resolve that we could do better. I didn't know where the race would take me, but I'd raised gun violence on the highest stage in the country that night. I was coming to learn that the road to change is paved with small victories.

When I dropped out of the race two weeks later, Vice President Biden was the first candidate to call me. He asked how I was doing and told me he knew from past experience what it was like to make a decision like that. He wished me luck and talked about the campaign.

"I don't know how far I'll go in this," he said, "but I want you to know, if I become President, I fully intend on passing the torch and putting leaders like you and many others in positions where you can make the difference you've talked about."

I thanked him and told him I was sure he would. Biden spoke from his heart. I appreciated that he understood how important passing the torch to the next generation was to me. And I believed him when he said it was important to him as well, and to the country.

"I just want to make sure that my generation, too, is stepping up to lead," I said.

I had mixed feelings. I hated to give up on anything I had set out to do, but I was glad to be getting back to Washington to focus fully on Congress. I knew I was going to have a big role to play on both committees as we continued to dig for more evidence of Trump's epic wrongdoing. Now I could fully prepare. If I was going to get out of the race, I'd chosen a good time.

CHAPTER 24

BEYOND MUELLER

I was the first person to greet Robert Mueller on July 24 when he stepped out of the holding room where he'd been sitting and walked toward the dais where he'd be answering questions for most of the day.

"Director, thank you for coming," I said.

"Nice to see you," he said.

The morning session went the way we had prepared for it to go. Mueller stayed within the four corners of his report, referring back to the text rather than offering interpretations that went beyond it, and wasn't going to read aloud from it. He was going to need to be directed to different portions of the report. Jerry Nadler was quite effective in his opening statement in covering the topline issues.

Then Republicans came at Mueller with batshit crazy conspiracy theories so convoluted and unlikely, they made your brain hurt. Representative Matt Gaetz of Florida made some sort of argument suggesting the Steele dossier was actually a Russian false-flag operation, and Nunes dutifully ranted about the professor who approached a Trump campaign advisor with an offer of Russian assistance actually being an intelligence operative for an undisclosed "Western" country. I don't know that Mueller was prepared to go down all those rat holes. He knew the report. He knew the truth. But when the Republicans brought up anything not covered in the report, you could see the special counsel wasn't tracking—and they started using that against him.

I observed that Mueller did best when you spoke slowly and loudly, and when the questions were brief.

"Director Mueller, going back to the President's obstruction via Corey Lewandowski, it was referenced that a thousand former prosecutors who served under Republican and Democratic administrations with twelve thousand years of federal service wrote a letter regarding the President's conduct," I said. "Are you familiar with that letter?" I was one of the few on Judiciary who was discussing things not in the report.

"I've read about that letter, yes."

"Some of the individuals who signed that letter, the statement of former prosecutors, are people you worked with, is that right?" I continued.

"Quite probably," Mueller said. "Yes."

"People that you respect?"

"Quite probably yes," he said.

"And in that letter, they said all of this conduct, trying to control and impede the investigation against the President by leveraging his authority over others, is similar to conduct we have seen charged against other public officials and people in powerful positions." I pressed on. "Are they wrong?"

"They have a different case."

I had to go for it. "Do you want to sign that letter, Director Mueller?" I asked.

He didn't really answer, not at first. He said, "Uhhh," or something like that, then courteously dismissed my question by repeating, "They have a different case." Still, I could see that the question had reached him. It was subtle, but he cracked a faint half-smile and gave me a look.

I knew that my colleagues on the Intelligence Committee, who I'd later join to question Mueller in the afternoon session, were watching the Judiciary Committee. So during one of the Republicans' questions, I stepped out and called down to the Intel room to speak with Dan Goldman, our lead investigator.

"I don't know if it's coming across on TV or not, but he's having a hard time hearing," I told Dan. "We have to speak loud and slowly and short."

Judiciary ran longer than Mueller's team had negotiated with our staff. I think our staff wagered that it was better to beg forgiveness than ask permission, so we kept Mueller in his seat a little longer than planned. During the break between hearings, Mueller went into the holding room. Schiff spent some time in there with him, and thanked him for coming, then reemerged.

As I sat with Schiff in a conference room adjacent to Mueller's, our staff reported that Mueller's team was not happy that Judiciary went over time. They wanted to make up for Judiciary's going long by cutting some of Intel's time.

You could tell that our Intel staff was panicking. "He's saying he's not going to come out unless you agree to take twenty minutes off the time," they told the Chairman. "We don't know if we want to call his bluff!"

I've always observed Schiff to be made of steel. The guy doesn't flinch. He wasn't going to give up twenty minutes on our side for something this big. The way we figured it, we had Mueller here once. He was never coming back.

"He knows how important this is," Schiff said. "We're not cutting our time. I'm not going back in there to negotiate. I'll see him when he comes out."

Mueller came back out in the end. Credit to Schiff for sticking to his guns.

We went into Intel's questioning and again I saw the preparation pay off. During my time, I focused on something I knew well, consciousness of guilt. I set the scene, just prosecutor to prosecutor, asking Mueller if he agreed that when suspects or witnesses lied, tampered, destroyed evidence, that we inferred that they were doing it because they're guilty. Mueller agreed. My question was a risky one because it was outside the report, and if he hadn't agreed with me, it would have taken me some steps to set it up again. But I knew he'd agree—every prosecutor thinks that way.

Schiff was very effective in wrapping it all up at the end.

"From your testimony today, I'd gather that knowingly accepting assistance from a foreign government is an unethical thing to do," Schiff said.

"And a crime," Mueller replied.

"And a crime," Schiff agreed.

"Given the circumstances," Mueller added.

"And to the degree that it undermines our democracy and our institutions," Schiff continued, "we can also agree that it's unpatriotic."

"True," Mueller said.

"And wrong."

"True," Mueller said again.

"You have served this country for decades," Schiff said to Mueller a little later. "You've taken an oath to defend the Constitution. You hold yourself to a standard of doing what's right."

"I would hope," Mueller said.

"You have, I think we can all see that," Schiff said. "And befitting the times, I'm sure your reward will be unending criticism, but we are grateful."

Schiff eloquently closed the hearing.

"Whether we decide to impeach the President in the House, or we do not, we must take any action necessary to protect the country while he is in office," he said. "Protecting the sanctity of our elections begins, however, with the recognition that accepting foreign help is disloyal to our country, unethical, and wrong."

We had done our jobs. I didn't know what would happen next. I did not see it as inevitable that Speaker Pelosi would pursue impeachment. She would move when she was ready. She would move when she was certain—certain not that impeachment would lead to Trump being removed by the Senate, but certain that she had exhausted all remedies and that there were no other moves left on the board. She wanted to reserve the right not to have to make that move, and I knew she might never make it. My own thinking was: Why let the Senate off the hook? If Trump had committed impeachable crimes, and by this point, I was sure he had, then we should impeach him for those crimes. Force the Senate to make some very hard decisions, especially the electorally vulnerable Senators. Why should Susan Collins and Cory Gardner and Martha McSally get a pass?

I came out for impeachment in June 2019, soon after Trump went on national television and told George Stephanopoulos of ABC that if offered dirt on a political opponent by a foreign country, "I think I'd take it." Incredible. He was boasting that he'd do it all over again. I'd already seen evidence that Donald Trump had colluded with the Russians on rigging the 2016 elections, and I knew that the 2020 elections would be at risk unless Trump were held in check.

"Congress has no choice," I tweeted on June 13. "We must begin an impeachment inquiry against @realDonaldTrump. He has invited the Russians to again sabotage our elections. And he has obstructed (& obstructs) justice. Time to be held accountable. Our democracy is worth saving."

PART 4: UKRAINE

CHAPTER 25

WHISTLEBLOWER

It was a routine meeting of the House Intelligence Committee right until the end. This was on Monday, September 9, 2019, just after Congress returned to session following our August break. At 5:30 p.m., the committee received one of our regular "Hot Spots" briefings, a weekly report on threats across the globe. But then, following the briefing, Chairman Schiff informed us that the Inspector General of the Intelligence Community had alerted Congress that a whistleblower complaint was supposed to have been forwarded to us, but had not been. We looked around at one another, confused. "Why would they not share it?" we wondered. The situation seemed more strange than ominous.

The complaint, Schiff explained to us, was being blocked from going to Congress by the Acting Director of National Intelligence, Joseph Maguire. This was unprecedented. Schiff said he was seeking to have the inspector general come before the committee that week to tell us what he could about the complaint. He also requested that Maguire brief the committee.

Some of the Republicans on the committee had been very critical of Schiff, seeking to demonize him at every turn, but this time they listened attentively. The gravity of the situation struck them immediately. Schiff talked briefly about whistleblower protections and federal law's provisions with regard to passing along complaints to Congress. A few Republicans had procedure questions, but there was no partisan back-and-forth. It was a sign to me that the Republicans were going to tread carefully on this one.

That Friday, September 13, Schiff subpoenaed Maguire, questioning the legal basis for "improperly" withholding the complaint. "The Committee can only conclude," Schiff wrote in a letter accompanying the subpoena, "based on this remarkable confluence of factors, that the serious misconduct at issue involves the President of the United States and/or other senior White House or administration officials."

Chairman Schiff went on the CBS program *Face the Nation* that Sunday and talked about the whistleblower's report. "According to the director of national intelligence, the reason he's not acting to provide it, even though the statute mandates that he do so, is because he is being instructed not to," Schiff said. "This involved a higher authority, someone above the DNI.... So, I think it's fair to assume this involves either the President or people around him or both."

On September 19, Inspector General Michael Atkinson joined us in the committee's SCIF, three levels below ground, to brief our members. We met in the Damon Nelson Room, a conference room named for the committee's former Republican staff director, who had died suddenly the year before. The Nelson room was half the size of our formal hearing room, and rather than assigned dais seating, it featured a long wooden table that allowed members to sit wherever they wanted.

We could see right away that Atkinson was a buttoned-down man. A former partner in a law firm, he had entered public service after 9/11 and served as assistant U.S. attorney. He had been appointed by President Trump to his current post and unanimously confirmed by the Senate in May 2018 after vowing to be scrupulous and diligent in protecting whistleblowers. Atkinson seemed like a balls-and-strikes kind of guy, but he was very emotional in the sense that he was frustrated about what was happening. He took his job seriously, which was to be independent and to protect whistleblowers, ensuring that they had an open line of communication to him so he could pass their complaints on to Congress if he found them both credible and urgent.

Atkinson relayed in a thousand different ways that he could not tell us what the complaint under discussion was, but he reiterated that he found it credible and urgent. There wasn't a lot more he could tell us. Then he went over the general procedures—how a complaint is received, how it's investigated, and how, once he sends it to the director of national intelligence, it must come back to Congress within seven days. There was no wiggle room in this, no room for personal discretion, no allowance given for a second opinion. If the whistleblower complaint is evaluated by the IG to be urgent and credible, and this one had been, then it has to be sent to Congress. That did not happen here. On September 2, two and a half weeks before we met with Atkinson in the SCIF, that deadline had come and gone.

"Is the complaint *still* urgent and credible?" I asked Atkinson.

The whistleblower had filed the complaint with the IG more than five weeks earlier. A lot could have changed in that time.

"Yes," Atkinson said, "the complaint was urgent and credible when I investigated it and today as I sit here with you it's still urgent and credible."

When Atkinson left after several hours of questioning, we met to weigh the importance of what he'd told us. Many of us felt this was a seminal moment in the history of the Trump presidency. The earth beneath Trump was starting to move. Within hours of Atkinson's testimony to us, the *Washington Post* and the *New York Times*, through their sources, started to report what the whistleblower complaint was all about.

WHISTLE-BLOWER COMPLAINT IS SAID TO INVOLVE TRUMP AND UKRAINE was the dramatic headline in the *Times*. "Though it is not clear how Ukraine fits into the allegation, questions have already emerged about Mr. Trump's dealings with its government," the *Times* reported that day. "In late July, he told the country's new President, Volodymyr Zelensky, that Ukraine could improve its reputation and its 'interaction' with the United States by investigating corruption." The paper also noted that "close allies" of Trump "were also urging the Ukrainian government to investigate matters that could hurt the President's political rivals," i.e., former Vice President Joe Biden and "his family."

The President blasted the story on Twitter that day. "Another Fake News story out there—It never ends!" He went on to ask, "Is anybody dumb enough to believe that I would say something inappropriate with a foreign leader while on such a potentially 'heavily populated' call? I would only do what is right anyway, and only do good for the USA!"

This President had never been interested in going after corruption, not in the United States, nor with regard to the dictators he so closely aligned us with, from Turkey to Russia to North Korea and the Philippines. But now he wanted the country to believe that he had a unique interest in denying aid to the Ukrainians and pressing them to be free from corruption—and by the way, tying it to Joe Biden. The President had plainly asked a foreign government to investigate his opponent.

Once the news hit, it seemed that, every day, a few more members of Congress were coming on board to support impeachment. We had almost reached having a majority of Democrats. That weekend, we started hearing that even many "Frontline Members," who had flipped Republican seats to win election in 2018, were ready to support the drive to impeach.

Newspaper articles don't often hit like a thunderclap, but a *Washington Post* op-ed published on September 23 did. Written collectively by a group of key freshman Democrats, all with national security backgrounds, the article was sharp and intense. "This flagrant disregard for the law cannot stand," the seven wrote. "To uphold and defend our Constitution, Congress must determine whether the President was indeed willing to use his power and withhold security assistance funds to persuade a foreign country to assist him in an upcoming election. If these allegations are true, we believe these actions represent an impeachable offense."

My colleague Elaine Luria of Virginia, a twenty-year Navy veteran who served only on combat ships and rose to the rank of commander, was a driving force behind the article. She teamed up with Gil Cisneros of California, Jason Crow of Colorado, Chrissy Houlahan of Pennsylvania, Mikie Sherrill of New Jersey, Elissa Slotkin of Michigan, and Abigail Spanberger of Virginia.

Luria says now, "All of us independently came to the same conclusion, that we needed to speak up based on what we were learning about the circumstances of the President's interaction with Ukraine, digging up dirt on an opponent, using his office for leverage against a political opponent. It was wrong, and we needed to speak up about that. We all came to that conclusion independently, and we realized our voices would be stronger together."

That op-ed, and the shifting political dynamic it represented, was seismic. Speaker Pelosi was in New York that day and read the article on her flight back to Washington.

"I think it was a turning point," Luria says. "This was a new and different group of people who had joined the conversation to say, 'This is truly an issue of national security!' and 'This is an example of using his office for political gain.' This was very clear-cut, the President leveraging hundreds of millions of dollars in security assistance. I think those new voices elevated the level of concern for many people and gave the discussion new momentum."

For all Trump's unbalanced thinking, for all his impulsive actions and tweets, through most of his time in the White House, he had avoided letting the public focus on one clear outrage for long. Whatever the crime, whatever the heat it generated, along came something else to distract. There might be a thousand reasons to impeach Trump, not just one obvious one.

Trump had achieved brilliant success in getting even very smart people to overthink how to handle him, to tie themselves up in confusion to the point where they made choices that ultimately benefited him. Think back to the 2016 election. Trump kept insisting the election would be "rigged." He said this again and again and again, all the while knowing that the Russians were actually trying to rig the election in his favor. President Obama overthought the solution, loath to play into Trump's hand and lend indirect support to his wild claims of election issues. The end result was that the Obama administration never came down hard on the Russians or even alerted the public to what was going on. Trump benefited.

Trump aggressively attacked the Russia investigation as a witch hunt, and complained almost from the day it started about how long it was lasting. He turned his whining and bitter outrage into a kind of ongoing performance art spectacle. It was inescapable. Mueller had every right in the world to subpoena Trump. In fact, he had an *obligation* to subpoena Trump, and deep down he knew that. But Trump got in Mueller's head. Mueller knew that subpoenaing the President would take time, time Trump would whine about, and in the end, the special counsel decided against seeking a subpoena. End result: Trump defined the context of the Mueller investigation. He never had to interview with Mueller, which even Trump's supporters knew would have led to his perjuring himself.

The Ukraine shakedown scheme pierced through the fog. It focused the mind and the tongue. Finally, we'd cut the Gordian knot of endless overthinking on our side. The overthinkers, trying to jump four steps ahead in a game of chess, worried that impeaching Trump could give him fodder to enflame his base and be a net political win for him. All that worry was paralyzing. Sometimes it's enough to do the right thing, knowing it's the right thing, and sort out the politics later.

CHAPTER 26

"THE TIMES HAVE FOUND US"

Nancy Pelosi had preferred to use Congressional oversight, litigation in the courts, and the power of the purse to rein in his lawless ways, but Trump was irredeemable. The day after Special Counsel Mueller testified that the President had committed ten acts of obstruction of justice—but couldn't be prosecuted under Department of Justice interpretation of the law—the President personally asked the leader of a foreign government to help him cheat on the 2020 election. Speaker Pelosi had to act. Nothing short of acting on impeachment could stop Trump and save America. Her constituents, her conscience, and her views on the Constitution demanded it—and now she had the consensus of the majority of the House.

But even as impeachment loomed, the Speaker gave President Trump every opportunity to stop stonewalling. On Sunday, September 22, she sent all of us in the caucus a letter formally giving Trump until that Thursday to follow the law and forward the whistleblower complaint to Congress, or brace for serious consequences. "If the administration persists in blocking this whistleblower from disclosing to Congress a serious possible breach of constitutional duties by the President," the Speaker wrote, "they will be entering a grave new chapter of lawlessness which will take us into a whole new stage of investigation."

With the whistleblower's complaint still under wraps, the *Wall Street Journal* reported that Trump had pushed Zelensky "about eight times" in that July 25 phone call to work with his fixer, Rudy Giuliani, to concoct dirt on Biden and his son. Rudy himself did not deny pushing Ukraine to investigate the Bidens.

That Sunday, on his way out of the White House, Trump confirmed major pieces of the story. He was, as Pelosi would later put it, self-impeaching. He talked about his phone conversation with Zelensky in glowing terms, insisting that it was a "perfect call" and "beautiful." He "admitted he'd brought up Biden 'and his son.'"

Trump's comments were his typical word salad. This is what he actually said, verbatim: "The conversation I had was largely congratulatory. It was largely corruption—all of the corruption taking place. It was largely the fact that we don't want our people like Vice President Biden and his son, creating to the corruption already in the Ukraine."

I'd noticed that Trump's syntax, like his thought processes, tended to get even more garbled and incoherent the more under stress he felt. The specter of impeachment had deeply unnerved Trump. He would play the happy warrior, grinning his way through paper-thin lies about how it all meant nothing to him. He spoke to reporters that Sunday about how he would "love" to release a White House transcript of the call with Zelensky, but that "you have to be a little shy about doing it." Trump shy? Right.

Early on Tuesday, September 24, I received word that Speaker Pelosi had called an emergency meeting of the House leadership team for 3:30 that afternoon. As a member of leadership, I was well aware what that meant. This was going to be a big day. It wasn't often that we had unscheduled meetings. I was certain the Speaker was ready to change her posture on impeachment.

She called me that morning to ask me, as co-chair of the Steering and Policy Committee, to cancel our scheduled meeting that day so we could have a meeting of the whole caucus.

"Of course," I told her.

That was Nancy, even in a crisis, taking the formal, respected steps. One point we discussed was whether it would make sense for her to create a Select Committee on Impeachment, the way, for example, the Senate had created a Select Committee on Presidential Campaign Activities in 1973 to investigate Richard Nixon's Watergate scandal.

"If there is a select committee, I want to be a part of it," I told the Speaker. "But I'd have concerns about that taking too long to put together."

"You're right," she said. "We're going to need to move fast now in light of what has happened."

Now that Trump had been caught abusing the power of his office to try to cheat on the next election, it was clear democracy itself was in danger.

We saw twin themes: We had to protect both our national security and the integrity of the election process. Pelosi expressed confidence in the Intelligence Committee's ability to lead the investigation. She had reason to be confident, considering how long we'd worked on the Russia case, how much we'd already investigated the President, and how professional we'd shown ourselves to be as a committee dealing with sensitive, high-level investigations.

Her task in sorting out the question of which committees would take up the investigation was made easier. Since the inspector general of the intelligence community had brought the whistleblower complaint to the Intelligence Committee, Intel would lead the impeachment inquiry, joining forces with other committees of jurisdiction. However, Chairman Schiff would lead and host all depositions and public hearings. For Pelosi, this was a fortuitous development. Prior to becoming minority whip, she was the Ranking Member of the Intelligence Committee, which was her pride and joy. As Speaker, she still serves on the committee. She had shown great faith in Intel's taking on the initial phase of the investigation, and we didn't want to let her down.

Pelosi split other responsibilities among five other committees, including Ways and Means, Foreign Affairs, Government Oversight and Reform, Financial Services, and Judiciary. As one of three members on the Intelligence and Judiciary Committees, I noticed that the Speaker paid tremendous deference to the committees. Pelosi was a traditionalist in her belief that the committees should do their work and report up and out to the other members of Congress about their work and findings. This was, as more senior colleagues would explain to me, in stark contrast to the way the GOP had run the top-down Clinton impeachment.

Pelosi trusted her chairs, for they reflected the will of the caucus. In our leadership meetings, I saw that she was including them in every major decision on impeachment, sometimes calling on them in the middle of a meeting to get an update. This was hard for the press to understand. I'd often be asked if I had heard this or that from Pelosi on impeachment. And I got it—the press believed that Pelosi called all the shots. Yes, she is a powerful Speaker, but she empowered those chairs to make decisions on the course of impeachment. And she made that point to our caucus every week during our meetings.

An important moment came not long after noon on that same day, September 24, when Congressman John Lewis, a personal hero to me, came out for impeachment.

"I have been patient while we tried every other path and used every other tool," Lewis said. "We will never find the truth unless we use the power given to the House of Representatives—and the House alone—to begin an official investigation as dictated by the Constitution. The future of our democracy is at stake."

John was considered the moral center of our caucus. He was in favor of impeachment. The earth truly was moving beneath our feet.

Later that day, at our leadership meeting, the Speaker announced that President Trump had called her earlier that day. He insisted that he was not involved in withholding the whistleblower complaint from Congress, and he told her he wanted to "figure something out" to make this all go away. Couldn't they bargain? He seemed shocked that Pelosi would even consider impeachment.

"I told him this was a national security issue," Pelosi said.

Trump needed to release the whistleblower complaint, she told him, and added that one may conclude that he was withholding aid to Ukraine because of Vladimir Putin.

Next was a meeting of the Democratic caucus, held in the HC-5, in the basement of the Capitol. Almost every member was there. On the flatscreen TVs on the wall the Speaker displayed a quote from President Abraham Lincoln: "Our safety, our liberty, depends upon preserving the Constitution of the United States," he said on September 16, 1859. "The people of the United States are the rightful masters of both Congress and the courts, not to overthrow the Constitution, but to overthrow the men who pervert the Constitution."

"We've crossed the Rubicon," Adam Schiff said, speaking dispassionately about why this was so important. He made the point that we did not need to establish a quid pro quo, the straw man the Republicans were using. Ukraine depends on the United States, economically and militarily, to support it against Russian incursions, and that dependence gave Trump leverage that he unscrupulously exploited out of fear that he was vulnerable in a fair election to a challenge from Joe Biden.

I spoke up as well. "If you ask a foreign government for help, that means you owe them something," I said. "If you owe them something, then when it comes time for them to collect, you're putting their interests before U.S. national interests."

The more we learned, the more it became clear that this was worse than putting another country's interests above America's. It was entirely about Donald Trump's interests, over the national interest. We could all feel how different this was from our investigation of election interference, where sometimes it seemed that you needed a PhD in Russian studies to understand the importance of every twist and turn.

This was a shakedown, Trump was confessing, and he had priors. He'd done this before.

After the meeting, Pelosi spoke before the cameras to announce a formal impeachment inquiry of Donald Trump. As she had often said to me, her work on the Intelligence Committee added to her outrage about the White House blocking a whistleblower complaint. "The law is unequivocal," she said.

The Speaker cited Benjamin Franklin's famous quote. When asked at the end of the Constitutional Convention in 1787 if we had a republic or a monarchy, Franklin replied, "A republic, if you can keep it."

"Our responsibility is to keep it," Pelosi said. "The actions taken to date by the President have seriously violated the Constitution, especially when the President says Article Two says, 'I can do whatever I want.' For the past several months, we have been investigating in our committees and litigating in the courts, so the House can gather all the relevant facts and consider whether to exercise its full Article One powers, including a constitutional power of the utmost gravity of articles of impeachment. And this week the President has admitted to asking the President of Ukraine to take actions which would benefit him politically."

The Speaker was acting out of duty, a deep sense of purpose. She'd taken flak for months, much of it intense, for holding back from a formal impeachment inquiry—this gave her added moral authority now that she had reluctantly come to the conclusion that history had left her no choice.

It might be bad politics, it might even hurt some candidates in some races in 2020, but it was the right thing to do. It had to be done.

"The President must be held accountable," she said. "No one is above the law."

I was proud of our Speaker's resolve. We had no illusions about what was coming. Although Trump was at the United Nations in New York, he seemed to be spending most of his time on Twitter, throwing a predictable tantrum.

"PRESIDENTIAL HARASSMENT!" he tweeted out that day with his characteristic lack of dignity.

The President kept saying he was going to release a transcript of his call with the Ukrainian President and that it would show he'd done nothing wrong. I thought this was like how he'd said he'd release his tax returns when he was no longer "under audit." So it was a surprise when, on Wednesday, September 25, the White House released the call summary, a rough transcript of the Trump's conversation with Zelensky. What was even more shocking was that Trump and his cronies could ever have imagined that the transcript would exonerate him. It was, in fact, a highly damning document.

You always remember where you were for major moments. I happened to be in a Judiciary Committee hearing on the assault weapons ban. The room was filled with dozens of Americans who had lost a family member to gun violence, particularly from an assault weapon, including my friend Fred Guttenberg. Of course, on one level I was aware that the Ukraine scandal was heating up, but my focus that morning was on the issue on which I had worked so passionately.

While we knew the President was releasing the call record, we did not know it was going to be this earth-shattering. I was sitting next to Representative David Cicilline of Rhode Island when staff passed out copies of the call record. Almost every word jumped off the page. I was in shock. David was in shock. We kept looking at each other.

"This is *his* version of the events?" I said to David.

It was as bad as we had feared.

"Why would he release this?" David wondered aloud.

We couldn't believe it. But I remembered something one of my brothers, Jacob, a policeman, always tells me: "Eric, we don't catch the smart ones."

CHAPTER 27

THE LESSONS OF WATERGATE

"Um, Olivia, some guy named John Dean has a question for you," our twenty-year-old intern shouted across our office bullpen to my scheduler Olivia Elkins.

It was the last week of September 2019 and I was in my Washington Congressional office. For anyone born twenty-five years after President Richard Nixon resigned in shame on August 8, 1974, it's no real surprise not to have heard the name John Dean. But any lawyer with an interest in great examples of courage in our profession knows all about Dean, a key figure in the Watergate scandal. Dean served as White House counsel for Nixon for nearly three years, starting in July 1970, and was part of the cover-up. Dean ultimately did the right thing, pleading guilty to obstruction of justice and serving as a valuable witness to the Watergate special prosecutor.

In June 2019, Dean appeared before the House Judiciary Committee to use his expertise to put the Mueller Report in context. "In many ways the Mueller Report is to President Trump what the so-called Watergate 'Road Map' . . . was to President Richard Nixon," he said. "Stated a bit differently, Special Counsel Mueller has provided this committee a road map."

Dean was not appearing before us as a "fact witness," but he did have insider information—not on Trump's crimes, but on some of the most infamous presidential wrongdoing in our nation's history. Dean has moral authority when he talks about lessons learned and how to apply them to the present, and he understands what it takes to find the personal courage to take on power even at great cost to oneself.

"I would like to address a few of the remarkable parallels I find in the Mueller Report that echo Watergate, particularly those related to obstruction of justice," he told us that day. "And I hasten to add that I learned about obstruction of justice the hard way, by finding myself on the wrong side of the law." I'd had a good idea what ground he would cover, but it still raised the hairs on the back of my neck to hear him make the connections.

It just so happened that a student from my district was in Washington the day Dean testified, and her father texted to ask if our office could give her a tour. We could do better than that! I met the student myself and walked with her through the staff area to the hearing room. I opened the door that took you to the member dais area. I told her that was as far as I could take her, but she could stand in the doorway and have the member perspective of John Dean testifying to the committee. I wasn't sure if she knew who Dean was, but she assured me she did. "This is history," she said, and in the hustle and bustle of the moment, I came to appreciate how important Dean's testimony was.

"The underlying crimes were a Russian 'active measures' social media campaign and hacking/dumping operations, which Mueller describes as a 'sweeping and systematic' effort to influence our 2016 presidential election," Dean pointed out. "The targets of the hacking were the Democratic National Committee and the Clinton campaign, from which information was stolen and released to harm the Clinton campaign and in turn would help the Trump campaign. In 1972, the underlying crime was a bungled break-in, illicit photographing of private documents, and an attempt to bug the telephones and offices of the Chairman of the Democratic National Committee, with plans to do likewise that same night with Nixon's most likely Democratic opponent, Senator George McGovern, which because of the arrests of five men at the Watergate, did not happen."

Dean went through a detailed comparison, looking, for example, at the role of White House counsel Don McGahn, which he understood better than most as a former White House counsel himself. His were important points, but what came through most powerfully was Dean's calm and detached certainty that Trump, like Nixon, had repeatedly acted in a way that demonstrated his consciousness of guilt, notably in the firing of FBI director James Comey.

"The White House dissembled on the reason for firing Comey, but President Trump later admitted in a television interview that he made the decision because 'the thing with Trump and Russia is a made-up story,'"

Dean told us. "Mr. Trump made similar remarks to visiting Russians in the Oval Office. The Comey firing echoes Nixon's firing of Special Prosecutor Archibald Cox in the infamous 'Saturday Night Massacre' in October 1973."

There was almost a Dickensian feel to the proceedings, with Dean representing the Ghost of Cataclysmic White House Scandals Past. The ultimate audience for his remarks was listening—and immediately grasped the danger to himself of Dean's perspective. Indeed, Donald Trump was so rattled that he took to Twitter immediately to beg people not to pay too much attention to what Dean was saying.

"Can't believe they are bringing in John Dean, the disgraced Nixon White House Counsel who is a paid CNN contributor," Trump tweeted, essentially guaranteeing that many who would have missed Dean's testimony would now seek it out. "No Collusion—No Obstruction! Democrats just want a do-over which they'll never get!"

After Dean and I ran into each other in Los Angeles the day the Mueller Report dropped, we struck up a friendly acquaintance. He was my first choice as a guest to have for a town hall in my district on the impeachment inquiry. I knew he'd be perfect. I just didn't know if he'd agree to participate. I called and left a message for him, wondering if I'd hear back.

That was when the intern took the call from "some guy named John Dean." We were in luck: John leapt at the opportunity. We held the town hall on October 1, 2019, at James Logan High School in Union City, California, and had a good turnout, including national reporters like John Heilemann of Showtime's *The Circus*. For me, it was an engaging way to connect with voters who wanted answers about impeachment, and I could listen and learn from John Dean all day. Our green room before the event was the high school boys' locker room, and even in there, at age eighty, Dean looked at ease and comfortable, sitting on a low wooden bench in front of a lineup of metal lockers and talking about parallels between Nixon and Trump. He didn't seem bothered at all that we were in a stuffy locker room. All he asked for was a chair, telling me his back would start to bother him if he had to stand too long.

"As Charles Wiggins, a Republican from Southern California, one of his best and strongest defenders, said, 'Nixon has in essence confessed,'"

Dean told those assembled for the town hall. "So, there is a very interesting parallel right now between where Nixon's final point was and where Trump finds himself at this moment."

This went over well with the crowd, and so did Dean's estimation of Trump's legal peril when he left office: "I'd say it's about seventy/thirty right now, in terms of him being indicted," he told my constituents.

I talked about what a dramatic reminder 2019 was of the importance of getting out to vote. "I can't imagine where we would be if the Democrats had not won the House in 2018," I told my constituents.

One person stood up and asked about the dangers of an impeachment helping Trump, if even after the House voted to impeach, the Senate ended up leaving him in office. Trump could then run on impeachment to fire up his hard-core supporters.

I talked about how impeachment was the right thing to do, that it was about the Constitution, not about perceived political gain. It was also about national security and about trying to stop the 2020 national elections from being compromised the way the 2016 elections had been.

"Doing nothing will make his behavior worse," I said, striking a chord with the audience. "I also think about future presidencies. If we do nothing, we will lower the standard of conduct."

It was tempting, with the political ground shifting dramatically toward impeachment, to want to make a wide sweep. Yes, the glaring misdeeds of Secretary of State Mike Pompeo and Attorney General Bill Barr that were coming to light demanded action. It was tempting to pursue both. But what was the goal? To spread ourselves thin running around, pointing out every offense, or to eliminate the ultimate threat, a lawless President?

Don't get me wrong. I would have loved to make sure that Barr was held accountable for lying to Congress and impeding the Mueller investigation. I'd called for impeaching Barr months earlier, and his behavior had just kept getting worse. He'd taken to jetting across the world meeting with foreign intelligence leaders as some sort of Inspector Clouseau, apparently trying to debunk the Mueller findings. We will absolutely need to impeach Barr—but all in good time.

As for Mike Pompeo, he'd clearly shown himself to be a Trump enabler. This was someone I'd thought I knew, having traveled with him to Iraq, and I believed Mike loved our country above anything else. I was wrong about that. He was just another sycophant whom Trump had bent to his will. In fact, we were just starting to get press reports that Pompeo, despite intimating otherwise, had been on the Ukraine call.

Get rid of Trump, hold him accountable, and the rest will follow. If the principal is dirty, the deputies will do dirty deeds. We had Trump pinned down. Why distract ourselves chasing after his minions? Back in Washington, before and after the town hall, I advocated that we keep impeachment simple, telling people: If we keep it simple, we impeach a lawless President. If we overthink it, we lose. We had to resist the temptation to chase every rabbit. Or as I liked to say, with great irony, citing a Russian proverb for my colleagues: "If you chase two rabbits, you catch none."

We also had to move fast. I advocated for proceeding with hearings only with witnesses ready to cooperate. If someone was willing to come forward and help the country understand Trump's lawlessness, then we wanted to hear from them. If they were not, move on. Too often, we had let Trump benefit from tying us up in court. No more waiting. We had a confession.

I had great respect for *Washington Post* columnist Michael Gerson, a former speechwriter for George W. Bush. That week, Gerson wrote in a column, "For the first time in American history, the President has pleaded guilty to an impeachable offense." In 2016, as a candidate, Donald Trump said he could shoot someone in the middle of Fifth Avenue and get away with it. He'd all but done that, and was caught holding the murder weapon. Now we would find out if his boast would prove accurate. I was wagering he was wrong.

As a prosecutor, I put a lot of value in what evidence I could find about a suspect's conduct in the seconds, minutes, and hours after he was arrested. I'd ask the police what admissible statements the suspect had made between arrest and booking. I'd spend hours, hundreds of hours, listening to recorded jail calls. Did he confess? Did he contact other witnesses or the victim to discourage cooperation? Every day, judges instruct jurors that a defendant who seeks to intimidate a witness is likely doing so because of "consciousness of his or her own guilt." Makes sense, right? Innocent people may be scared, but they generally don't panic.

There were a lot of frantic "jail calls" from this President—except, they were tweets. Since the Ukraine story broke, the President repeatedly acted guilty. He attacked the whistleblower and the whistleblower process. He suggested the whistleblower was not patriotic. He demanded "to meet his accuser," completely missing the point of a whistleblower and the concept of an "accuser." He suggested that anyone who fed the whistleblower information should be treated like a spy or a traitor and be executed. And he said that the lead investigator, House Intelligence Committee Chairman Adam Schiff, should be arrested for treason. Generally, intimidating witnesses and threatening investigators is not the path to exoneration for any suspect.

Some of my Democratic colleagues had called on Speaker Pelosi to cancel the late September recess of the House to keep everyone in Washington working on impeachment. The Speaker resisted those calls. A big believer in doing things only if they make sense, she was not about to have 435 people hanging around Washington if only a fraction of that number would be working on impeachment. Instead, my colleagues and I on the House Intelligence Committee stayed back to do our work.

Also, Speaker Pelosi believed it was critical for as many members as possible to be home with their constituents listening to their views on impeachment. The overwhelming majority of members ended up going home for the two-week recess starting the last week of September, taking the opportunity to meet with their constituents. I was eager to hear how that had gone for them. The public polling was clearly moving. A Quinnipiac poll in mid-October found support for an impeachment inquiry at a new high of 55 percent. Most important, the number of independents and Republicans supporting impeachment was growing.

We just weren't seeing much courage from individual Republicans in Congress. How could it be that these people seemed so unable to think ahead a little and imagine the future? Michael Luo wrote a piece in *The New Yorker* in late 2019 suggesting that Republicans resorting to such twisted arguments in support of a corrupt President needed to be aware that history's judgment could be harsh. He did the research and provided a chilling warning of what

Trump apologists could expect, if the example of Nixon's key defenders is any guide.

"Decades later, and long after many of their Congressional careers had ended, their support for Nixon would continue to linger over their legacies, an inalterable epitaph," Luo wrote. He pointed out that support for Nixon was a leading item in the obituaries, if not the headline, of ex-Representative Charles Sandman; former Representative Joseph Maraziti; Charles Wiggins, who led Nixon's defense; and Wiley Mayne, a House Republican who voted not to impeach.

I believed in welcoming any signs of political courage from Trump-era Republicans on the theory that at least it was a first step. I was encouraged when Nevada Congressman Mark Amodei, a Republican, told reporters on a conference call that he supported the impeachment inquiry. "Let's put it through the process and see what happens," he said in late September. "I'm a big fan of oversight, so let's let the committees get to work and see where it goes. Using government agencies to, if it's proven, put your finger on the scale of an election—I don't think that's right. If it turns out that it's something along those lines, then there's a problem."

Poor Mark. He was immediately the target of a tidal wave of vicious attacks from Trump loyalists, who branded him a RINO (Republican in Name Only), all for supporting Congressional oversight and respecting the Constitution. Badgered by Minority Leader Kevin McCarthy and the White House, Mark was forced to release a statement proclaiming, "In no way, shape or form did I indicate support for impeachment." It won't surprise you how he ultimately voted.

Representative Adam Kinzinger of Illinois, a GOP member I've been able to work with in the past, did not come out in favor of impeachment, but he dared to take on Trump, knowing full well he had poked the hornet's nest and would get stung. Kinzinger, who had served in the Air National Guard as a lieutenant colonel, simply couldn't remain silent about a September 29 Trump tweet. That was the infamous one quoting a Dallas megachurch pastor to the effect that if Congress impeached Trump and removed him from office, "it will cause a Civil War like fracture in this Nation from which our Country will never heal."

Kinzinger took to Twitter himself, calling the quote "beyond repugnant," which resulted in his not getting the "honor" of serving as honorary Illinois co-chair of Trump's 2020 reelection campaign. Kinzinger stood by his comments, though he felt it necessary to clarify them. "My view on it is this: Some people maybe took that tweet and jumped to this idea that I support impeachment," he said. "I don't. I just didn't think the President should be tweeting about civil war." Kinzinger also defended Adam Schiff against Trump's wild and dangerous charge of "treason" for doing his job as Chairman of Intel. "It's not treason," Kinzinger said. "He's a Congressman. If he violated any kind of law, then we will go from there."

At least in private, there seemed to be recognition by the more responsible Republican members that the Ukraine scandal was different. One Republican I talked to on the eve of the inquiry made clear that he was with us at least in spirit. "Look," he said privately as we were going into the Intelligence Committee room, "my one piece of advice to you guys is 'Just don't rush this.'"

"I hear you," I told him, "but if we give this guy too much time, he's going to just torch the whole place. That's his MO. That's what he does."

I had walked to votes with another Republican, from New York, as all of this was breaking, and I asked how the scandal was playing out in his district. He told me he has a competitive district, and his constituents are upset with the President. But he also had a warning for us.

"If you're going to shoot for the king," he said, "you'd better not miss."

Every Trump opponent would get a nickname. That seemed to be the constant, whether the opponent was a Democrat standing up for the rule of law or less obvious targets, like Republicans or prior Trump sycophants like Michael Cohen, Anthony Scaramucci, and Lev Parnas, who had been threatened by Trump's corrupt ways and spoken out against him. When it came to attacking Chairman Schiff, Trump didn't exactly bring his A game. In February 2018 he mocked Schiff on Twitter as "Little Adam Schiff." (Schiff is my height, about six feet, and very fit—he has competed in triathlons—so I'm not sure what that was all about.) By November 2018, after we'd taken the House back in the midterm elections, Trump was tweeting at the Chairman as "little Adam Schitt." By September 2019, he was tweeting about "'Liddle' Adam Schiff," which we found out about during a meeting of Democrats on the Intelligence Committee. We knew Schiff would be asked about the Trump tweet when we walked out of the SCIF.

"We should hold a press conference," I joked to Schiff. "We can send you out with our shortest members and staff. You'll look like a giant."

Still, there was a danger that even the clumsiest Trump ploys would pay off for the President. It seemed that many in the media, and public, couldn't shake the habit of assuming that if Fox News or Trump Republicans were stepping up their attacks on someone, there had to be something to those attacks—even if they were completely fabricated.

Many people I talked to during the 2016 election assumed that if the *New York Times* and Fox News were talking about Hillary Clinton's emails endlessly, the emails must be a scandal. During the special counsel's investigation, the Republicans threw everything they could at Mueller, portraying an honorable man who had served Presidents of both parties (and who was a lifelong Republican) as some sort of partisan hack. And they attempted to gin up scandals about the origins of the investigation and the actions of Mueller's team. As the impeachment inquiry moved into the heavy-lifting stage, Trump and his defenders went after Schiff. This desperate ploy would get them nowhere.

The case of Schiff and his would-be critics is a classic example of a right-wing attack strategy that has picked up in recent years: Assail the positives of a rival, knowing that, for at least a significant percentage of the public, truth in the end does not matter. Adam Schiff is one of the most honest, focused, and approachable people I've ever worked alongside in Washington. Most important, for the task of leading impeachment, he's also one of the smartest, with the ability both to see all sides of a problem in real time and to plot a path forward.

Very few people could have shown the leadership Schiff did during the first two years of the Trump presidency, when we were in the minority, and he kept demonstrating to the public why the Mueller probe mattered. This was crucial for leveraging public opinion to empower Trump's own aides to stop him from firing Mueller. It took a person of the highest integrity to be our general throughout that struggle. Getting things right, and doing it fairly, was always more important to Schiff than anything else.

Schiff first started drawing national headlines as a U.S. Attorney in Los Angeles in the early 1990s. One important early case he worked on gave him invaluable background for understanding the Russian attack on our 2016 presidential election. In 1990, he handled the espionage trial of Richard Miller, an FBI agent who had worked in counterintelligence and had an affair with Soviet agent Svetlana Ogorodnikova.

"This is a betrayal tinged with hypocrisy," Schiff told the *Los Angeles Times* when Miller was sentenced in February 1991. "We have here an agent who did just exactly what he was supposed to protect against."

Adam was born in the Boston area and grew up near where I did, graduating from Monte Vista High in Danville, ten miles away from my alma mater Dublin High. A graduate of Stanford and Harvard Law, he served in the California State Senate before being elected to Congress in 2000. As a young Congressman, he voted to authorize George W. Bush's war against Iraq in 2003 and showed character by later admitting that "the intelligence was dead wrong on that."

In his time as the top Democrat on the Intel Committee, Schiff has always seen the work as carrying a higher purpose, about national security and our national interest. From early on, he wanted to show that Democrats, not just Republicans, were strong on the issue.

As Schiff's Republican attackers knew, he's the opposite of a loose cannon. He's so laser focused on the job that he might come across as methodical and boring. Actually he has a great sense of humor, and I saw how that helped him weather the unending attacks. He's quick, and funnier than I think most realize.

Schiff and I have a long-standing *Dumb and Dumber* joke going back and forth. For whatever reason, a favorite thing of the right has been to take the two of us and turn us into memes. Someone photoshopped a poster for *Dumb and Dumber*, the 1994 Farrelly brothers movie, putting Schiff's and my faces there instead of Harry's and Lloyd's. (I think I'm Lloyd and he's Harry.) Schiff and I just laughed. We still send tweets and gifs to each other as Harry and Lloyd. It is good not to take things too seriously.

I've learned a lot from Schiff about being a leader, relying on a deeper strength, and having a long game rather than just getting caught up in day-to-day survival. The man has had a target on his back for years now, but if it bothers him, he's never shown it. At the start of 2019 in a public hearing, House Republicans pulled the sophomoric stunt of calling for Schiff's resignation. They signed a letter and all read from it, just to try to embarrass him. Adam didn't blink; none of it affected him. He always kept his eye on the mission at hand: holding the President accountable.

We knew going into the closed-door depositions in our impeachment inquiry that the Republicans would try to distract and obstruct, not just by attacking Schiff, but with whatever moves they could come up with. Through that whole period, their only real defense of Trump's indefensible conduct was to attack the process. So, on October 3, when the committee got started with the depositions—interviewing former special envoy to Ukraine Kurt Volker, an experienced diplomat who had been appointed by then–Secretary of State Rex Tillerson in 2017 but who abruptly resigned on September 27—we knew what was coming.

Near the end of the deposition I sat in for Schiff while he attended another meeting. I was confronted by North Carolina Congressman Mark Meadows over whether Republicans could ask questions. I was puzzled. What the hell was he talking about? I had to repeat the words "You can ask questions" five times. That didn't stop him from claiming, as a bizarre bogus talking point, that they were denied the right to ask questions. But it was all there on the official record. Not that they used their time to any real purpose.

When their time was up, I started my questioning, keeping it simple.

"Ambassador," I began, "you said it was not inappropriate for you to work with Mr. Giuliani in the way that you did. Have you ever seen in your years of service, in the Foreign Service, any person like Mr. Giuliani hold a role like he held for Mr. Trump?"

"I can't say that I have, no," Volker replied.

I pressed Volker on whether it was okay for a U.S. President to ask the U.S. Attorney General to investigate a political rival, and after some back-and-forth, he gave this answer: "As an American citizen, I believe that no one is above the law."

He also said it was "inappropriate" for a U.S. President to ask a foreign country to investigate a rival.

Volker had brought us a trove of text messages that were helpful to the investigation. When I pressed him on why he used his personal phone, not his government phone, for texting, he explained, "I couldn't figure out how to do that. . . . The password on the government phone always seemed to drop." And why did they use WhatsApp? The answer: That's what the Ukrainians "prefer to use."

One thing my experience as a prosecutor taught me was that you always wanted to frame questions in a more personal way. Late in our time with Volker, I asked him if he was embarrassed, as a career Foreign Service professional, at the way the Giuliani-led "other track" in Ukraine had undermined his efforts.

"It's very, very unfortunate," Volker said, "because we had done such good work on policy with Ukraine, pushing back Russia, supporting them, democratic transition. Things are going great. And this separate track, as you refer to it, ends up overshadowing the work that we've done and the need to continue that work going forward."

Later, to other questioning, he clarified: "I believe that Giuliani was interested in Biden, Vice President Biden's son [Hunter] Biden, and I had pushed back on that."

I have mixed views of Volker. On the one hand, I was grateful that he came forward at all, and especially that he brought so many useful text messages. Those texts led us to Gordon Sondland and opened up lines of questioning we'd never have found on our own. On the other hand, I thought, *How can someone as experienced as Volker be so naïve as to go along with Trump's corrupt scheme?*

It was a little sad, listening to Volker. He had clearly been out of the loop, and he seemed to be in deep denial that his expertise and years of experience had played second string to Rudy Giuliani's blundering. I felt bad for him as he was confronted with the shadow shakedown track Giuliani had been running with the Ukrainians.

The Republicans on the committee were also in deep denial about how damning the text messages Volker had turned over to us were. Clearly, to anyone in the reality-based world, those texts corroborated the fact that the President had indeed been running a shakedown of the Ukrainians via Rudy Giuliani. The Republicans were no doubt placing their hopes on the idea that they could try to deny that there'd been an explicit quid pro quo in the infamous call with Ukraine, and had pushed Volker to say the Ukrainians had not communicated to him an explicit quid pro quo. The risk of that strategy, as any good prosecutor will tell you, is that in harping on that point, the Republicans were elevating its importance—and setting themselves up to have their argument collapse if someone else confirmed that there had, in fact, been an explicit quid pro quo.

Often during Volker's testimony, the Republicans would lead him to say yes to anything they could, to get him to make the President look better. And then, during the Democratic questioning, Volker would say anything that our side asked that made the President's position look untenable. That made for a confusing transcript that could later be selectively cited to make opposing points.

As we sat there in the SCIF, it had been just over three weeks since Trump belatedly released the all-important security assistance to Ukraine. I raised that issue with Volker.

"I also don't want to be naïve about the security assistance that has gone through finally and the meeting that may happen at the White House," I said. "It did take a whistleblower complaint and an impeachment inquiry. I mean, that has to be a part of the context, that only once those two happened was the security assistance released." Volker agreed.

More important than anything Volker told us was the sixty pages of documentation he provided the committee. The headline of the day came from a text Volker forwarded to us from Bill Taylor, a career Foreign Service officer who had been Acting Ambassador to Ukraine until recently: "As I said on the phone, I think it's crazy to withhold security assistance for help with a political campaign." Wow! That said it all. Taylor's September 9 text had been sent to both Volker and Ambassador Sondland, a major Trump donor whose donations had earned him an appointment as U.S. Ambassador to the European Union.

On September 1, in another exchange that had everyone talking, Taylor had asked Sondland: "Are we now saying that security assistance and WH meeting are conditioned on investigations?"

Sondland's reply: "Call me."

Okay, then.

Before we started interviewing witnesses in closed-door depositions, there had been some skepticism in the press and the public of how valuable these sessions would be. Interest quickly ratcheted up thanks to Secretary of State Pompeo's latest partisan move on Trump's behalf, sending a letter to House Democrats on October 1. In it, Pompeo stated his intention to obstruct our investigation by blocking five State Department employees from appearing before us. Sounding more like a Fox News host than a U.S. Secretary of State, he railed against our investigation as "an attempt to intimidate, bully, and treat improperly the distinguished professionals of the Department of State."

It was more and more obvious that Trump apologists were afraid of the truth. Witnesses were coming forward, and their revelations were filling in the details of a damning picture of presidential corruption. As Connecticut Congressman Jim Himes joked a few days after Volker testified, "I sort of get a kick out of the President's rage on Twitter at Adam Schiff, at Nancy Pelosi, at the Democrats. As a Democrat who is in the room, I will tell you, we're like a bunch of folks in the outfield just catching pop flies."

There's a saying in politics: If you're making a process case, you're losing. When it comes to impeachment, the Republicans were losing. No one wanted to defend the underlying act: the President extorting the Ukrainians to benefit his campaign and then subsequently covering it up. That was indefensible. Instead, there was a concerted effort to whine and complain that Democrats were not following the standard impeachment process. [Narrator's voice: There is no standard impeachment process.] This was only the fourth presidential impeachment process in our country's 244-year history and only the third to make it to a vote on the Floor of the House.

Republicans, including the President, were saying they wouldn't cooperate with the House's impeachment inquiry unless the House held a vote to start an impeachment inquiry. That was just more Lucy and the football. We could have that vote, it would have Democratic and probably some Republican votes, and then the Trump team would just pull the football away again. At the end of the day, they would always fall back on a twisted, self-serving notion of executive privilege and not turn anything over, running out the clock until the election. So, it was incumbent on us to conduct the investigation on our terms, not the President's. Besides, in the history of criminal investigations, when has an investigator ever asked a suspect how he'd like the investigation to proceed? Never. And this was no time to start. We would set the terms.

CHAPTER 29

DRIP, DRIP, DRIP

After the Volker deposition, I left town for a previously scheduled Intelligence Committee trip to Brazil and Argentina. It was a relief to get away for a few days, even if the topic of impeachment followed me across the globe. At one stop, a senior State Department official pulled me aside and asked to speak "freely and without attribution."

"Of course, what's going on?"

State Department employees at all levels, I was told, were riddled with fear. Career diplomats had lost confidence that the administration had their back. This senior official reminded me that a lot was riding on the progress Schiff and I and the rest of the Intelligence Committee were making.

"Keep doing what you're doing," the official told me. "You're our last hope. And please, thank Chairman Schiff."

I felt a lot of pressure. This individual was shaken, just trying to hold it together.

"It's going to be okay," I said. "Winning the House back was the most important thing we could have done. Ten years from now, even if we win the White House in 2020, I think people will see taking the House back as the most important thing we did for our country, righting the ship and beginning the slow journey back to normal."

"Boy, I hope you're right," the senior official told me.

That conversation was a needed reminder of what was on the line and of how many people were counting on me and my House colleagues to get this right. It felt like a "You get one shot" opportunity. Don't miss.

My flight back to Washington was delayed, so I was an hour late to the testimony of former Ukraine Ambassador Marie Yovanovitch. I raced from the airport to my Washington, DC, apartment, changed from jeans and a T-shirt into a suit, and hurried back to the Capitol. Fortunately, I hadn't missed much. Much of the first hour of Ambassador Yovanovitch's appearance before Congress consisted of more airing of complaints by Republicans. During her first hour of testimony, the Ambassador's ten-page opening statement had leaked to the media. The Ambassador was grilled by Republicans about how this had happened.

Process, process, process. Distract, distract, distract. It was all they had.

I found the Ambassador to be professional and friendly, but also firm. She was markedly different from Volker, who came off as eager to please whoever was questioning him. Yovanovitch listened carefully to every question. She would pointedly correct anyone on either side if she felt a question misrepresented what had happened. She was not going to be led by the questioners. Yet nothing she told the committee was as powerful as her opening statement, which expanded on the same sentiment Volker ultimately represented: It's impossible for career diplomats to execute their duties if private citizens are out there as a wild card, undermining their work.

"My parents fled Communist and Nazi regimes," Yovanovitch told the committee, laying out the larger stakes of what had unfolded. "Having seen, firsthand, the war, poverty and displacement common to totalitarian regimes, they valued the freedom and democracy the U.S. represents. . . . It is critical to the security of the United States that Ukraine remain free and democratic and that it continue to resist Russian expansionism. Russia's purported annexation of Crimea, its invasion of Eastern Ukraine, and its de facto control over the Sea of Azov, make clear Russia's malign intentions towards Ukraine."

The Ambassador knocked down the many conspiracy theories about Joe Biden and his son Hunter. And she offered a devastating assessment of the role of Rudy Giuliani, who was running a shakedown of the Ukrainians—and who did his best to get rid of her.

"I do not know Mr. Giuliani's motives for attacking me," she said. "But individuals who have been named in the press as contacts of Mr. Giuliani may well have believed that their personal financial ambitions were stymied by our anti-corruption policy in Ukraine."

It took stunning courage for Yovanovitch even to show up. No one could have blamed her if she got cold feet after Secretary of State Pompeo ordered her not to testify the night before. That's right, Pompeo had given a direct order for her not to cooperate with a lawful Congressional investigation. When we found out about that, we issued her a last-minute subpoena, giving her cover to say she had no choice. Despite that, we all understood that in coming forward and telling the truth, she was taking an extreme risk that she would be fired from the State Department after decades of service.

On one of the breaks from her testimony, I bumped into freshman Congressman Tom Malinowski of New Jersey, who was overqualified for his seat on the Foreign Affairs Committee. He was a former diplomat who had served as assistant Secretary of State for democracy, human rights, and labor. Although Congress was still in recess, Tom talked about how important he felt it was to be there in support of Yovanovitch. He said he hoped she would see him and be a little less nervous. He also expressed concern for everyone at the State Department and how little they were being defended by Secretary of State Pompeo.

"Today, we see the State Department attacked and hollowed out from within," Yovanovitch also said in her opening statement. "State Department leadership, with Congress, needs to take action now to defend this great institution, and its thousands of loyal and effective employees. We need to rebuild diplomacy as the first resort to advance America's interests and the front line of America's defense. I fear that not doing so will harm our nation's interest, perhaps irreparably."

Giuliani was becoming such an obvious liability that Trump watchers knew what to expect. It was time for Trump to pull out the whole "Barely met the guy" routine, as he always did sooner or later. An October 12 *Washington Post* headline read TRUMP TELLS REPORTERS HE DOESN'T KNOW IF GIULIANI IS STILL HIS ATTORNEY. Rudy who? Never heard of the man. Might have met him once at a big event. Tough guy, though. But it was just Trump considering his options. He was a long way from cutting Rudy loose.

The following Monday, October 14, we heard from Dr. Fiona Hill, who had been the top White House advisor on Russia. When Dan Goldman asked Hill if she had ever asked her then boss, National Security Advisor John Bolton, about Ambassador Yovanovitch, she replied yes and recalled that Bolton's "reaction was pained" and that he told her, "Rudy Giuliani is a hand grenade that is going to blow everybody up."

Hill also told us about Bolton directing her to talk to John Eisenberg, National Security Counsel, and to inform him that Bolton "was not part of whatever drug deal Sondland and Mulvaney are cooking up on this."

Ambassador Sondland was a late convert to the Trump cause. A business-man whose company owns and manages hotels, he'd been a major Republican donor for years, was a "bundler" for Romney in 2007, and though he dropped out of a fund-raiser for Trump over Trump's treatment of the parents of Army Captain Humayun Khan, who was killed in 2004 during the Iraq War, he fell in step behind Trump, as did so many other members of his party. Sondland went on to funnel one million dollars to the Trump inauguration through four different LLCs. He had his eyes on a post somewhere as an Ambassador, preferably a German-speaking country, as his own parents had fled Germany before World War II, and he was named Ambassador to the European Union.

I made a point of getting up early on October 17 to be sure I arrived in time to get a good seat for Sondland's deposition. I had started saving seats for fellow Intel members Mike Quigley, Jackie Speier, and Terri Sewell. Quigley and I had a pact: Whoever was there first saved a seat for the other.

At about 6 a.m., I received word that we had lost my friend and colleague Elijah Cummings, Chairman of the Oversight Committee. I started getting condolence texts from all over the country. Boy, Cummings's death shook all of us in Congress. He had been such a leader, and he always brought moral clarity and thunderous passion to the push for equality and accountability. When he called out "We are better than this!" at a February 2019 meeting of the Oversight and Reform Committee, it quickly became a rallying cry for our entire caucus. Cummings had also been a faithful partner to me on the Protecting Our Democracy Act, which I wrote to establish an independent commission to investigate Russia's attack on our 2016 election.

I thought back to the year before, when organizers of the Wing Ding dinner in Iowa wanted to honor Cummings and asked me to reach out to him. Held at the Surf Ballroom in Clear Lake, the same place where Buddy Holly had his last gig before dying in a plane crash, the Wing Ding is a party fund-raiser that hit it big when candidate Barack Obama was the keynote speaker there in 2007. By the time of the ramp-up to the 2020 Iowa caucuses, it had become an essential stop for candidates and their possible supporters.

Cummings would have loved to go, but he'd undergone a couple of medical procedures and wasn't feeling well enough to make the trip. He asked me to go in his place and accept the award. Now, the funny part was the organizers of the dinner had told Cummings all about the award they give: a really nice piece of metal, ornate and heavy. Cummings told them he would make sure that I personally carried it back myself.

"Don't let it out of your sight!" he told me a couple of times.

I brought that award from Clear Lake, Iowa, to Washington and handed it to Cummings. He broke into the biggest smile, admiring that hardware. He loved that, as far away as in Clear Lake, Iowa, they recognized his work.

I thought we might delay that day's hearing, given how important Cummings had been to everyone in the caucus, starting with Speaker Pelosi, but we decided that this was too important. We had Sondland coming in, a big witness directly connected to the President in this shakedown scheme. We agreed Cummings would have wanted us to carry on. He would have insisted on it.

After a moment of silence before the hearing, Chairman Schiff spoke for all of us: "There are few members, I think, that have ever served in this body who enjoyed wider respect and love among their colleagues as Elijah Cummings," he said. "He was a dear friend to many of us. He was an inspiration to all of us."

But before we heard from Sondland, there were the usual circus antics from Devin Nunes. At least this gave me time to study Ambassador Sondland. I got the sense that he had walked in thinking he could just charm the pants off of the committee members. That's often the mind-set of Ambassadors who are political appointees, posted in countries where they are treated like royalty.

I had the sense Sondland had no idea what he was in for that day. He was in over his head. In the days leading up to his testimony, we saw all kinds of leaks to the press. Sondland was clearly trying hard to get ahead of what others had already said, trying to put himself in the best possible light, and trying to distance himself from the President. In one leak, he said he'd only met Rudy Giuliani once, back in 2016, and would never have been a part of this shakedown scheme if he had known what it meant.

In his opening statement to the committee that day, he told us, "I did not understand until much later that Mr. Giuliani's agenda might have also included an effort to prompt the Ukrainians to investigate Vice President Biden or his son, or to involve Ukrainians directly or indirectly in the President's 2020 reelection campaign."

He also tried to sell us on a cockamamie story that it had been perfectly innocent for him to text "Call me" to Ambassador Bill Taylor in reply to Taylor's question about conditioning security assistance to "investigations." He told us he prefers to talk through issues and not text. But it just so happened that the only time you see him texting anything that reads "Call me" is with regard to Trump's extortion scheme.

During one of the breaks, I headed outside the SCIF and picked up my phone to see what I was missing. I'd left it in a cubby next to where the Capitol Police watched the door, as we all did before entering the SCIF. I noticed the officers were paying close attention to the flatscreen TV near their post. On the screen was a press conference with Mick Mulvaney, Acting White House Chief of Staff, the same Freedom Caucus stalwart who had blocked my rare earth elements bill. The White House had been denying there was any quid pro quo in Trump's shakedown phone call with Zelensky. But Mulvaney confirmed it. I guess you could say the rare dose of blunt honesty was welcome, even if the content of what he said was disturbing.

Asked if the demand for an investigation into Biden "was part of the reason" Trump had withheld the security assistance, Mulvaney didn't deny it.

"Did he also mention to me in passing the corruption related to the DNC server? Absolutely," Mulvaney said. "No question about that. But that's it, and that's why we held up the money." He went on to say that this was "absolutely appropriate."

The Capitol Police and I were looking at each other, raising our eyebrows, like "Are you kidding me? Did he just admit to that?" In a press conference on national television, Mulvaney was confirming what Trump's lawyers and his handlers had been working so hard to deny.

Jon Karl of ABC pointed out, "Let's be clear. What you just described is a quid pro quo. It is funding will not flow unless the investigation into the Democratic server happened as well."

"We do that all the time with foreign policy," Mulvaney answered. He added a little later, "I have news for everybody: Get over it. There's going to be political influence in foreign policy."

At this point, Republicans were starting to walk back into the SCIF, and one by one, they would look up at Mulvaney on the screen, pause, and then just shake their heads. I started to head back in myself and noticed Jim Jordan just ahead of me.

"All right, have fun cleaning that up," I told Jordan. He just put his head down and walked in, shaking it with dejection.

Mulvaney tried to walk back his comments later that day, but the damage had been done. That clip would be played over and over throughout our public hearings.

(In a perfect example of Trump's so-much-corruption-you-can-hardly-keep-up strategy, during that same press conference, Mulvaney announced that the White House planned to host the next G7 meeting at Trump's Doral Golf Club near Miami, a clear violation of the Constitution's Emoluments Clause. For once, Trump faced criticism from both Democrats and Republicans. Two days later, Trump tweeted that he "thought he was doing something very good for our country," but "the Hostile Media & their Democrat Partners went CRAZY!" Then Trump took a break to watch the opening of Jeanine Pirro's program on Fox News. Finally, he added, "Therefore, based on both Media & Democrat Crazed and Irrational Hostility, we will no longer consider Trump National Doral, Miami, as the Host Site for the G-7 in 2020.")

Inside the SCIF, as Chairman Schiff talked about the exchange between Mulvaney and Jon Karl during his questioning, you could see that some of the Republicans were just then hearing for the first time what Mulvaney had said. They were getting upset and trying to blame Schiff, as if he were misrepresenting what Mulvaney had said. Again, their first impulse was to deny.

I was under no such burden. "Mick Mulvaney has co-signed on the President's confession to the crime," I said.

Sondland didn't make much headway with his attempts to evade blame, and his efforts to spin the press didn't work out too well, either. "Current and former U.S. officials and foreign diplomats say Sondland seemed to believe that if he delivered for Trump in Ukraine, he could ascend in the ranks of government," the *Washington Post* reported.

"Sure, people sell their souls all the time," columnist Michelle Goldberg wrote in the *New York Times*, "but why for something as small as a chance to serve a man whose depravity Sondland himself once recognized?"

To me, Sondland was something of a riddle. Why had he come forward at all if he was going to risk perjury? He clearly believed that sheer force of personality was going to get him through the day, and he seemed to see this all as some kind of game.

Sondland and I headed out of the SCIF at the same time. I didn't really want to talk to him. I was put off by his whole style. But I'd been critical of all the potential witnesses who had, in my eyes, failed a test of courage and refused to come forward and testify before our investigation. At least Sondland had done that.

"Thank you, Ambassador," I said as a courtesy to him for making the flight from Brussels and showing up. "Have a good trip back."

I thought he might shake my hand. Instead, he slapped me on the back. He's a pretty big guy and it was a hard slap, as if he thought it would put me in my place or show me who was in charge.

"We'll see you again soon, Eric," he said.

How right he was about that.

CHAPTER 30

"WHEN A BUSINESSMAN IS ABOUT TO SIGN A CHECK"

We knew a lot about Acting Ukraine Ambassador Bill Taylor's reputation before he flew in from Kyiv on October 22 to testify to us. He had gone to West Point, served in the 101st Airborne Division in the Vietnam War, and worked at NATO and for the State Department. Ten years after he'd wrapped up a three-year posting in Kyiv as U.S. Ambassador, Taylor had been called out of retirement to replace Ambassador Yovanovitch—that is, after she was ousted for resisting the shadow campaign run by Trump's personal lawyer, Rudy Giuliani. Taylor's comment that it would be "crazy" to hold up security assistance for help in a political campaign helped restore our faith in the State Department in the time of Trump. Not everyone had been in on this scheme. We were eager to hear from Taylor.

He came across as friendly and relaxed, not at all like a rigid West Point grad. He was actually smiling when he walked in for his deposition. Once the Republicans had gotten through their usual theater, Devin Nunes and Jim Jordan literally reading from the same script they'd been flogging repeatedly by then, Schiff signaled to Dan Goldman to begin his questions.

All of a sudden, Congressman Chip Roy of Texas, a Republican, stood up in the far corner of the room and started shouting at Schiff. "You're the judge and jury sitting in here deciding who can see this clown show!"

From the inception of the Trump administration, many Americans had eagerly awaited any sign of a "proof of honor" from within the Trump administration. As we watched Muslims banned from entering our country, babies separated from their mothers at our border, and Trump's full bear hug with Putin, many hoped there were honorable people serving inside the administration whom we just hadn't heard from yet. Bill Taylor represented the first glimmer of hope.

During Roy's tirade, Schiff had been gaveling and repeating, "If the gentleman will suspend" and "The gentleman is not recognized."

Now Schiff told Roy, "Sir, this witness has come all the way from Ukraine. If you could suspend so we can get to the matter at hand."

"You really don't want to hear from this witness, do you?" Val Demings of Florida demanded of Roy.

While Roy was shouting, he grabbed on to the chair of Karen Bass, a Democratic Representative from California, and as he carried on, her whole chair shook. Karen looked back at him with a look that said, *Are you losing your mind?*

"Can you please take your hand off my chair?" she finally asked.

Finally, Roy sat down, and Taylor was able to give his opening statement. And wouldn't you know it? Roy lasted about an hour in the hearing. He had been so concerned about people seeing the hearing that he had jumped up and down, but once Ambassador Taylor started to lay out the President's culpability, Roy was out of there. At least he held on longer than Devin Nunes, who bolted five minutes into Taylor's statement. Nunes had gone after Schiff in his opening statement, but then didn't even have the nerve to stick around. He had no stomach for Bill Taylor's truth telling, either. He'd rather hide.

"In August and September of this year," Taylor said in his opening statement, "I became increasingly concerned that our relationship with Ukraine was being fundamentally undermined by an irregular, informal channel of U.S. policymaking and by the withholding of vital security assistance for domestic political reasons."

Boom!

We knew where Taylor was coming from. He was a straight shooter. And he went out of his way to confirm his quote about withholding security aid in exchange for help with a domestic political campaign being "crazy."

"I believed that then, and I still believe that," he told us.

I would say the most eye-popping part of Taylor's testimony, when the room truly was aghast, came when he described his September 7 call with Gordon Sondland. This was six days after Sondland had urged "Call me" so they could discuss the sensitive quid pro quo.

"During that phone call," Taylor related, "Ambassador Sondland told me that President Trump had told him that he wants President Zelensky to state publicly that Ukraine will investigate Burisma and alleged Ukrainian interference in the 2016 U.S. election. Ambassador Sondland also told me that he now recognized he had made a mistake by earlier telling Ukrainian officials to whom he spoke that a White House meeting with President Zelensky was dependent on a public announcement of investigations. In fact, Ambassador Sondland said everything was dependent on such an announcement, including security assistance."

Sondland told Taylor that Trump wanted to put President Zelensky "in a box" by having him make a public statement about investigations.

Taylor was incredulous. For him, a serious foreign policy expert and a veteran Foreign Service officer, it was a struggle to figure out what the hell had been going on.

Another shocking part of Taylor's testimony was when Sondland explained to him the Trump mind-set behind the shakedown. It started with remembering that Trump, even as President, thinks of himself, above all, as a businessman.

"'When a businessman is about to sign a check to someone who owes him something,' he said, 'the businessman asks that person to pay up before signing the check,'" Taylor remembered Sondland saying.

Taylor was outraged. Ukraine didn't owe the United States anything. The aid package was something Congress had voted on for an ally. These funds were urgently needed for Ukraine's conflict with Russia, and the Ukrainians had every right to expect the aid would come.

At the time, there was a lot of outrage in Washington about what the Turks were doing to the Kurds in northeast Syria, and the potential ethnic cleansing going on. I was struck by how many people in the United States really cared about the plight of people they'd never met. They recognized they're humans, too, and we can't just let them die. My argument was: if you cared about what the Turks were doing to the Kurds, then you should care about what it meant to hold security assistance back from Ukraine because their people were dying at the hands of the Russians.

Taylor was persuasive as he told us of the human cost of withholding that aid. I'll never forget how emotional he was about that. When it was my turn to question, I asked him about the Donbas region of Ukraine, where thirteen thousand Ukrainians had been killed in the war with Russia.

"Can you just talk about the human element here and what it means to Ukrainians every single day that goes by where we have authorized aid, they don't see it in their bank account, and Ukrainians continue to lose their lives?" I asked.

"Congressman, the Ukrainians are remarkably focused on the casualties in the east," he said, recalling being invited to a ceremony being held outside the Defense Ministry to honor the war dead. "Every day, they have this ceremony," he said. "It's about a half-an-hour ceremony where soldiers in formation, the Defense Minister, families of soldiers who have been killed are there. . . . If we were there today, on the 22nd of October, the families of those soldiers who were killed on any 22nd of October in the previous five years would be there."

During Bill Taylor's testimony, I saw Francis Rooney of Florida, a Republican, shaking his head and putting his head in his hands. Rooney, U.S. Ambassador to the Vatican from 2005 to 2008, had told CNN in October that he might support impeachment, telling Jake Tapper, "What I've heard so far is quite troubling." Then, when that position caused a furor, Rooney announced that he would not be seeking reelection.

I would have loved to see some concerned Republicans do more than shake their heads and actually ask some pointed questions.

I asked Bill Taylor, "Is it fair to say that the sooner they would have received the aid from the United States, the fewer the casualties would've been?"

He said he was careful not to draw too direct a link. "What we can say is that radar and weapons and sniper rifles, communication, that saves lives," he said. "It makes the Ukrainians more effective. It might even shorten the war. That's what our hope is, to show that the Ukrainians can defend themselves, and the Russians, in the end, will say, 'Okay, we're going to stop.' . . . That's how we would save lives."

During a break in Taylor's testimony, I took the opportunity to step outside. I saw a heavy podium being rolled up into the outer SCIF area by three maintenance guys. That was very unusual. Most of the press conferences took place out by the spiral stairway, outside the SCIF.

"Do you need help?" I asked the workers. "Can I help you with something?"

"Mr. Gaetz asked us to bring this podium down here."

I should have known. Matt Gaetz of Florida always had something up his sleeve.

"You have to get this podium out of here," I told the workers. "We don't allow press conferences in here."

That was a big day in Washington. We knew we'd moved the needle and put the pressure on Trump. He'd egg on Gaetz and the others, to see how far they would go. I never found out where they took the podium that night, but I would find out soon enough what Gaetz had in mind.

"Who knows?" I joked to Representative Sean Patrick Maloney when I saw him a few minutes later, "maybe one day he's going to have Mark Meadows fit him into a suitcase and sneak him into the SCIF."

CHAPTER 31

TOTAL SCIF STORM

I nodded my head with a slight smile to thank Laura Cooper for coming in to give a deposition in the SCIF on the morning of October 23. I hoped to make her feel a little bit better. Cooper, the Deputy Assistant Secretary of Defense for Russian, Ukrainian, and Eurasian affairs, looked a little nervous. She struck me as a dedicated public servant who kept her head down and never expected to have to testify to Congress about something of this magnitude.

A minute after Cooper sat down, she abruptly stood up and left the room. I figured she was going to greet Chairman Schiff, who would often welcome a witness beforehand in a ceremonial gesture, thanking them for coming. But then I saw Schiff come in without her. What was up?

That was when I started to hear the chants.

"Let us in! Let us in! Let us in!" came the loud, boisterous male voices.

Boy, were they let in. Suddenly, dozens of Republicans, almost all of them old white men, crashed through and careened into the secure conference room where we were about to conduct the interview. Seeing them gave me a sinking feeling. They were blundering their way into a place where most of them were not allowed, disrupting a solemn, sensitive inquiry in a way that would forever change the sanctity of that secure location.

Bill Taylor had given us the most damning testimony yet the day before. He'd come across as credible and honest and cogent, summing up the whole mess nicely in his opening statement as "a rancorous story about whistle-blowers, Mr. Giuliani, side channels, quid pro quos, corruption and inter-ference in elections."

As Taylor was testifying, Trump summoned some of his Congressional enablers to the White House to urge them to "Fight harder," we learned from news reports. Once again, they were ready to show that when Trump said, "Jump," their answer would be "How high?"

The SCIF had long been a place where Republicans and Democrats worked together in a bipartisan way. No matter your political party, a certain level of deference was shown to that room. We all lived in fear of ever bringing something into the SCIF, or taking something out of it, that was not allowed. We were all very aware that cell phones and cameras were never allowed inside. That SCIF guarded some of the nation's deepest secrets relating to our national security, our capabilities, and our force protection for our troops.

Earlier that day, when I came into the SCIF, there had been three Capitol Police officers standing outside the room to bar any unauthorized entry. When I heard the chanting mob outside and saw them stream into the room, my first thought was *How the hell did they get through?*

Then I saw Steve Scalise, the number two–ranking Republican in Congress, among the invading group, and I was really angered by that. Steve knew better. But there he was, cell phone in hand.

Next, I saw Steve King, which was unthinkable. The man's own Republican colleagues had found his racist statements so offensive that they'd barred him from all committee meetings. This had to have been the first committee hearing Steve King had gone to—albeit pushing his way into it—in nearly a year.

I turned to Mike Quigley: "Do these morons know they're not allowed to have electronic devices in here?"

Sure enough, either the morons had no clue or they just didn't care. I looked around and spotted cell phones, iPads, and Apple watches. The room was now compromised. Our foreign adversaries would go to great lengths to be able to get into a room like that and use their capabilities to understand what we were seeing. These brazen Republican intruders were showing no regard at all for national security. Incredibly, when the Sergeant at Arms asked them to remove the offending electronic devices, some of them refused.

One member even held a public town hall, a conference call with constituents, and bragged that he was calling from the SCIF. Others sent tweets from the secure room, flaunting their contempt for security. Matt Gaetz was one of them: "BREAKING: I led over 30 of my colleagues into the SCIF where Adam Schiff is holding secret impeachment depositions. Still inside—more details to come."

Schiff was wise enough not to make it any more of a scene. Bradley Byrne of Alabama tried to get in Schiff's face and was shouting at him. Schiff was not ruffled. Nor did he back down.

I chose to just sit there looking straight ahead, trying not to engage, whispering back and forth with Maloney and Jackie Speier about how ridiculous it all was.

The Republicans were walking around the room thumping their chests, shouting at the Democratic members, accusing us of running a Star Chamber, a bizarre accusation even by their standards. A good third of the "rebels" who stormed in were actually allowed to be there, since they were on one of the three committees conducting the interview, and this was an open hearing for anyone on those committees, as they all knew. Many had actually been seated at the table and had then gotten up to go play rebel.

I was too mad to speak out, but as the group got even more bellicose, Demings confronted them.

"You should all be ashamed of yourselves," she told them. "How can you stand by this person who lies, cheats, and steals? And how are you going to look at your children to defend what you've done?"

They showed her no respect, and continued marching around and shouting.

Schiff, realizing the room might be compromised electronically, adjourned the proceedings and got up and walked away. As he left, the Republicans shouted at him some more, demanding that he stay, asking why he'd walk away, as if he owed every courtesy to a wild mob that had invaded a secure facility. I was most disappointed to see Scalise was a part of this. It was so jarring to see how much these people could be warped by a call to action from Donald Trump.

What the President meant by "Fight harder" amounted to disrupting the proceedings and intimidating the witnesses. But we showed resolve. We were not going to be intimidated. Credit to our Chairman and members for not letting them bully us or the witness.

Amid the chaos, I stepped out of the meeting room to go into Chairman Schiff's office to see how he wanted to proceed. The first concern was the room's having been electronically compromised, so the Sergeant at Arms was on his way at least to try to get the electronic devices out. Schiff had resolved not to allow the Republicans to disrupt the proceedings and also not to give them what they really wanted: the theater of being physically removed.

"What do you want us to do?" the Sergeant at Arms asked him.

"We'll wait them out," Schiff said, "but we need the electronics out."

"What do we want to do with the witness?" a Democratic member asked the Chairman.

"We'll ask her to stay and wait them out."

I saw in Schiff a strong, determined leader who was not giving in. We did not want to give the Republicans the satisfaction of intimidating the witness not to testify, or let them win the day by having her go home. The Sergeant at Arms offered another room that was just as secure, but Schiff took pride in his determination not to allow them to bully us out of our space. We weren't moving.

One fair question was: How did so many people get past the secure area? One "grizzled cameraman" described the entryway to the SCIF in a *New Yorker* article that month as "the pit of despair." At the bottom of the pit was the first set of double doors, with a big red UNAUTHORIZED DO NOT ENTER sign in front of them. Right outside those doors is where Gaetz and company held their press conference before heading en masse into the committee room.

When you go through those doors, you enter a long hallway, and at the end of the hallway on the right is the first door into the Intelligence Committee. It's a thick, heavy door just to get into the foyer of the SCIF. Before that door is stationed a Capitol Hill police officer.

The Capitol Police take a lot of pride in standing there and preventing anyone from going inside. They know what is behind those doors: the deepest secrets our country protects. So how had the Republicans breached that door?

Easier than you'd think. A GOP member held the door open, disrupted the officer's role, and let the herd of elephants in. Some have asked: Why didn't the cops stop them? The police officers are there to protect Congress from outsiders, not to protect Congress from itself.

We knew time was on our side. A House Floor vote was coming up in about two hours, so if we could wait that long, most members would probably scurry out once the vote was called. These weren't exactly the types of people who had ever really protested anything before. As predicted, when the vote was called, they left.

In the meantime, a lot of damage was done. Specialists had to do a full electronic sweep of the SCIF before we could resume. This took hours. It was also intimidating to the witness. She had looked shaken when she heard the chants. We worried about the chilling effect the incident would have on future witnesses, knowing they might see a mob come in as they testified. Still, Laura Cooper testified, courageously, and we learned some pieces of information from her that were helpful.

At one point after coming back out from a meeting with Schiff, I returned to the smell of pizza, lots of pizza. The Republicans had brought dozens of boxes of pizza into the SCIF to feed themselves. I hadn't eaten all day because I'd been dealing with the Republicans' nonsense. I walked over to one of the boxes, reached across Jim Jordan, and grabbed a slice. I was not going to be physically confrontational. But I certainly was going to eat their pizza.

CHAPTER 32

THE FREE PRESS

On November 2, I was stuck in traffic on my way to an event in my district with Speaker Pelosi when I saw the news: BuzzFeed had scored a huge scoop, obtaining a vast trove of documents from the Mueller investigation through a Freedom of Information Act (FOIA) request. I had time to read, and I dove right in, skimming hundreds of pages.

What did it say about the state of America that news organizations were able to beat the U.S. Congress to the punch in getting the redacted Mueller Report? Ever since the report was released in April, the House Judiciary Committee had been in the courts trying to get as much information about it as possible. There was a lot more to see. Of the 448 pages in the public version of the report, fully one fifth had been redacted, and there were other materials that had not been made public: forty thousand pages of 302s, the forms FBI agents use for notes and summaries from their interviews.

Along with BuzzFeed, CNN and Just Security had also gone through the elaborate FOIA process, and had been rewarded with vast troves of documents. Astonishingly, Jason Leopold of BuzzFeed had been mailed a compact disc containing five hundred pages of 302s—and BuzzFeed was told it would receive a new CD every month for the next eight years!

A lot of the material in the BuzzFeed scoop was already familiar to me after sitting through dozens of interviews in our House Intelligence Committee investigation, but a lot of it was new. Much of what I until then only suspected was now leaping off the pages: The Trump campaign expected to benefit from Russia's hacking of Hillary's emails and designed a campaign to maximize their benefit at the ballot box.

The BuzzFeed scoop shifted the focus to Trump's former campaign manager, now serving time in federal prison, right in its lead paragraph: "Paul Manafort was pushing the unfounded conspiracy theory—now part of the impeachment inquiry into President Donald Trump—that Ukraine hacked the Democratic National Committee's emails as early as 2016." And Manafort's deputy, Rick Gates, "said the campaign was 'very happy' when a foreign government helped release the hacked DNC emails."

The 302s shed further light on Manafort's work for pro-Russian Ukrainian politicians, particularly of note for our Ukraine investigation. Manafort was pushing the Russian line on Ukraine possibly being responsible for the hack of our 2016 elections as far back as 2016. "Gates recalled Manafort saying the hack was likely carried out by the Ukrainians, not the Russians," one agent's summary reported.

It fit the Russian method to a tee and reminded me of something I'd heard back in the fall of 2015. This was during an informal conversation with an intelligence community official, a routine part of my work as Ranking Member on the House Intelligence Subcommittee on the CIA, when we were just two guys talking between ourselves.

"Congressman," he told me. "I don't involve myself in politics, that's not my job. I actually abhor politics, but I have to tell you one of the candidates running for President said something that really just raised my dander."

I could tell the official wouldn't have been saying anything unless he felt strongly about it. I waited for him to continue.

"Donald Trump was asked whether he accepted that the Russians shot down Malaysian Air Flight Seventeen," he continued.

That was the Malaysian Airlines flight that the Russians shot down over eastern Ukraine in July 2014, killing everyone on board, 283 passengers and 15 crew members.

"Trump's answer was, basically, 'Maybe it was Russia, maybe it was Ukraine, we'll never know,'" the intelligence official told me.

That, of course, was just what the Russians wanted. Within hours after shooting down that plane, the Kremlin used Russian media to push all kinds of false stories to confuse and distract, including one that the downing of the plane was all a CIA plot. It was, the intel guy emphasized, a case study in how Russian information warfare works.

"Look, the Russians are never going to try to convince you that the sky is red," he told me. "The way the Russian disinformation works is they want you to question whether the sky is blue or not. Maybe it's blue, maybe it's not."

The Russians never set out to convince anyone that Ukraine was responsible for hacking the DNC and attacking the integrity of our 2016 elections. That wasn't their goal. Their goal was to create a fog of misinformation.

It was all starting to make sense. Manafort spun a tale to exculpate Russia and pin the blame on Ukraine, and what a tale it was: Ukraine had worked to undermine Trump. It did the hack and set it up to look like Russia had done it to help Trump. Of course, that was crazy talk, but it was also very Putin, twisted and dirty and complicated.

Trump still couldn't escape the asterisk on the 2016 election and the preponderance of evidence that Russia in some way had affected its outcome. So Manafort gave Trump "the real killer," Ukraine. Multiple witnesses testified to us in our Ukraine investigation that Trump would routinely say, "Ukraine is corrupt." Or: "They tried to do a number on me last election." It was crazy, but that was Trump.

In his conniving mind, Trump saw an opportunity to take this nonsense and use it against an ally to get something for himself. Ukraine owed him one now. It was due $391 million in aid that Congress approved and he had signed, and its new President wanted a White House meeting. Trump figured he had leverage, a lot of leverage. Going back to that July 25 call, Trump used the word "reciprocity."

It had all come full circle with the news in October 2019 that Rudy Giuliani, still jetting back and forth to Ukraine to manufacture dirt he could use on the Bidens, was turning for advice to none other than Paul Manafort. Giuliani had not shown up at the federal prison in Pennsylvania where Manafort was serving his term of more than seven years to speak to him directly. He'd funneled questions through Manafort's attorney "several times," which might have helped explain why "[m]any of the accusations Giuliani has been making about Ukraine recycle those that Manafort's team first promulgated."

But just to be clear, he was not trying to help Manafort. "It was all about Trump," Giuliani said. "I don't think I could exonerate Manafort." Thank God for the free press.

CHAPTER 33

WHERE'S BOLTON?

We weren't shocked when Trump's former National Security Advisor, John Bolton, stiffed us on November 8, failing to show up for his deposition in our impeachment inquiry. Bolton was playing a complicated Washington game. He teased the public that he might do the right thing and step forward, signaling that he had bombshell revelations to share about Donald Trump's corrupt shakedown scheme, then took a step back and hid. It was classic Bolton. He ducked his responsibility as a public official to come forward, but he did send a letter through his attorney boasting that, as Trump's former National Security Advisor, he had been "personally involved in many of the events, meetings, and conversations about which you have already received testimony, as well as many relevant meetings and conversations that have not yet been discussed in the testimonies thus far." Bolton would only testify under a court order, which meant the Supreme Court, meaning: potentially a delay of years.

We debated in the caucus about whether to subpoena Bolton, and ultimately decided not to—not then, anyway. We could always do it later. Under Speaker Pelosi's leadership, we had our eyes on what would happen in the Senate if we impeached Trump in the House, knowing that it would take only four Republican Senators to join with Senate Democrats to form a 51-vote majority in favor of calling witnesses. This was Washington in the Trump era, and no one took anything for granted. Senate Majority Leader Mitch McConnell had shown an ability to keep his caucus in line, but we had our eyes on a small group of Senators, including former Republican presidential candidate Mitt Romney, Susan Collins of Maine, and Lisa Murkowski of Alaska, who all had shown some minimal independence from Trump at times. We felt it would come down to public opinion. How much political pressure would individual Senators feel to support a fair trial? How could there be a fair trial without our hearing one way or another from John Bolton and Mick Mulvaney?

Bolton was a man who craved the spotlight and wanted in on the action. He thought of himself as the smartest guy around, forever having to suffer fools who didn't see as clearly as he did, and yet now he was hiding. Still, you could see the gears furiously churning. He was considering his options, looking for a way to speak to history on what he saw as Trump's disastrous Ukraine shakedown scheme without alienating his fellow traditional conservatives.

I did have a certain grudging respect for Bolton, whose upbringing in some ways reminded me of my own. My dad was a police chief; his was a fireman. Like me, he came from a working-class area and went to college on a scholarship. We both got into politics as college students, me as "Bahama Bob," Bolton at Yale, where he interned for Spiro Agnew, who would resign in shame as Nixon's corrupt Vice President.

Bolton always had an intellectual arrogance about him, and a reputation for being abrasive and having a volatile temper. He was a hard-liner in the George W. Bush administration, an ally of Vice President Dick Cheney, forever pushing aggressive military action, including against Saddam Hussein. Even after the United States invaded Iraq and found no weapons of mass destruction, proving to the world that the war was built on a lie, Bolton still defended the invasion. Bush had to sneak Bolton's nomination as Ambassador to the United Nations past Congress, as a recess appointment, given widespread concerns about his having manipulated intelligence to support his arguments. In that post, he seemed intent on offending as many friends and allies as he could. Even Bush himself later said, "I don't consider Bolton credible."

Bolton was a regular on Fox News, growing wealthy on his running shtick about weak-willed liberal elites, but it still came as a surprise when Trump named him National Security Advisor in March 2018. Sooner or later, it was clear, Trump and Bolton were going to clash—and by September 2019, Bolton was gone, seething over much of what he saw in the Trump administration. His exit was vintage Trump era: Trump himself tweeted on September 10 that Bolton had been fired, a boast reported as fact in some news dispatches, but Bolton pushed back hard, saying he had left by choice.

One day after Bolton's exit, the hold on the security assistance to Ukraine was finally lifted.

Even as Bolton was failing to show up to testify before our committee in November 2019, news was breaking that he had landed a book deal of "roughly" two million dollars with Simon and Schuster for a tell-all about his time in the Trump administration, to be published before the 2020 elections. A source told CNN that Bolton would explain in the book how he "was the guardrail" in the administration trying to stop Giuliani and Mulvaney, who were "being disloyal to the President."

Bolton was sending signals that he wanted to testify in public, and there was no question he'd love to grab the attention of a nation talking about the Ukrainian shakedown scheme, which he'd famously called a "drug deal." What held him back? In his public stance, he kowtowed to the White House assertion of "absolute immunity" for just about anyone Trump didn't want to testify. Bolton was smart enough to know we weren't going to be drawn into that obvious delaying tactic. If the White House thought Bolton's testimony would be good for Trump, they wouldn't be blocking it. The fact that they were amounted to an admission of guilt and further obstruction of Congress.

We thought Bolton could add to our case, but we never felt we had to have him. After all, three of his deputies had testified before our investigation and been very helpful. But given Bolton's long tenure in Washington, we knew his testimony could potentially help sway any Senator who was unsure about the evidence. It would be a sad state of affairs if the book deal was part of his motivation in not coming forward.

Later in November, Bolton returned to Twitter with a splash, claiming that since he resigned as National Security Advisor, the White House had "refused to return access to my personal Twitter account. Out of fear of what I may say? To those who speculated I went into hiding, I'm sorry to disappoint!" He had the attention of the Twittersphere, which was waiting for some juicy details. Instead, Bolton did his best to cash in on the attention, posting a link to his political action committee, BoltonPAC. The day he failed to testify before us, he sent an email titled "My Opening Statement." Around the country, people hurriedly clicked through to see what revelations the statement might contain, but it turned out to be just a fund-raising pitch for his PAC.

Mulvaney was scheduled to testify before our investigation the day after Bolton didn't show. And he didn't show either. I went on Fox News the following week, a good way to speak directly to Trump from time to time. "If the President of the United States is innocent, he will send the firsthand witnesses John Bolton and Mick Mulvaney to Congress," I said to anchor Martha MacCallum. "If he's guilty, they'll stop us from hearing it, hard stop."

"What about executive privilege?" she asked me. "Those people obviously work very closely with the President."

"Executive privilege does not cover wrongdoing or crimes. It certainly does not cover people who are no longer in the White House. And we're talking to other people who were not the President. . . . [T]he interest here is not executive privilege, it's CYA."

Freeing Bolton to testify wouldn't help Trump, so he wasn't going to do it. Executive privilege had nothing to do with it.

We'd finished up our closed-door depositions at the end of October with a flurry of valuable interviews, including one with a Ukrainian-born American named Lt. Col. Alexander Vindman. He had listened in on the infamous Ukraine shakedown call in his job on the National Security Council—and had known right away what Trump was doing was wrong. We couldn't wait to have Lt. Col. Vindman speak to the American people directly, along with the other witnesses we had coming. Trump had long since confessed to his crimes, and our depositions had provided a treasure trove of added detail to tell the story of his corruption to the American people in vivid detail. Now it was time for Lt. Col. Vindman to tell the country what he heard.

CHAPTER 34

WE'RE LIVE

Throughout the impeachment drama, I could count on *Saturday Night Live* to sum up Trump's predicament and give us all a few laughs. Alec Baldwin got Trump as well as anyone. On Saturday, October 26, the *SNL* cold open featured Baldwin as Trump, leading one of his rallies and urging the crowd to chant, "No quid pro quo, no quid pro quo." Baldwin as Trump attacked "Adam 'Shifty' Schiff," and brought out a representative of "Bikers for Trump," who explained, "All this man did was shake down a foreign government to get dirt on his political enemy," and asked, "Is that wrong?" The crowd yelled, "Yes," in unison.

Our "Live from Washington" moment came on November 13. The Trump defenders had droned on about our depositions being illegitimate because they were held behind closed doors, and they kept shouting on Fox News about how we were afraid to interview people in public. So, naturally, when we announced live hearings starting with Ambassador Bill Taylor and Deputy Assistant Secretary of State George Kent, Trump defenders howled with outrage that we could turn the proceeding into a public spectacle.

Taylor was the star of the morning. It was one thing for Americans to read about his testimony to us, and another for them to hear from him directly. Taylor had a deep, resonant voice, and a rare kind of instant credibility. He wasn't there before us to serve any agenda except that of representing the truth, as best he could.

"Even as we sit here today, the Russians are attacking Ukrainian soldiers in their own country and have been for the last four years," Taylor said in his powerful opening statement. "I saw this on the front line last week; the day I was there a Ukrainian soldier was killed and four were wounded. . . . the security assistance we provide is crucial to Ukraine's defense and to the protection of the soldiers I met last week. It demonstrates to Ukrainians—and Russians—that we are Ukraine's reliable strategic partner."

This was the Bill Taylor who had made a strong impression in his closed-door deposition, talking about how Ukrainians held a solemn ceremony every day marking the deaths of their countrymen at the hands of the Russians.

Taylor also made news that day by offering a startling account of a member of his staff who was near Gordon Sondland when he spoke with Trump from a restaurant in Kyiv on July 26. Taylor himself had just been informed of the explosive information the previous Friday. On that call, Taylor told us, Trump was clearly heard to ask about "the investigations" and was told by Sondland that "the Ukrainians were ready to move forward." Sondland explained to the Taylor aide after the call that "President Trump cares more about the investigations of Biden, which Giuliani was pressing for."

That was the revelation that would lead the news cycle that day. The *New York Times* called it "startling new testimony . . . that further implicated President Trump."

This proved to us that information begets information. David Holmes, a U.S. official stationed at the embassy in Ukraine, came forward after he read Taylor's original deposition and recognized that he had new information. So, he raised his hand and said, "Call me." His courage inspired us to plod ahead, hear from as many witnesses as possible, and count on their producing more breakthroughs.

Early on in my questioning of Taylor in our public hearing on November 13, I mentioned his text that called it "crazy" to condition security assistance to Ukraine on help in digging up dirt on Trump's political opponent.

"Can we also agree that it's just wrong?" I asked Taylor.

"Yes," he said.

"Why is it wrong?"

"Our holding up of security assistance that would go to a country that is fighting aggression from Russia, for no good policy reason, no good substantive reason, no good national security reason, is wrong," Taylor said.

I brought up Mick Mulvaney's confirming the quid pro quo and saying that conditioning aid on favors happened all the time, and Mulvaney's dismissive "Get over it."

"Ambassador Taylor, should we get over it?" I asked.

"If we're talking about political influence, meaning attempts to get information that is solely useful for political campaigns," he said, "we should not get used to that."

Taylor was someone not at all vulnerable to the kind of cheap attacks Trump loyalists loved to make, and yet they persisted. Trump himself tweeted, "NEVER TRUMPERS!" that morning. Apparently, that was an attempt by the President to paint Taylor, a lifelong Republican, as someone suspect.

"Ambassador Taylor, are you a 'Never Trumper'?" I asked during my time.

"No, sir," he replied, sitting up straight in his chair.

Bill Taylor was indignant about what had happened, and he didn't mind letting it show. He was unflappable, and his testimony vividly and powerfully brought alive the story we'd been seeking to tell the American people of Trump's corruption and his erratic behavior in a way that Bob Mueller never did. That was partly because the Ukraine shakedown scheme was dramatic and easy to understand. It was also because the scandal of Russia interfering in our 2016 election—and what we had learned about it in two years of investigation—had prepared us to understand what the Ukraine scandal was about: Donald Trump seeking foreign help to cheat the American people out of a free and fair election.

It was a good night to go on with Rachel Maddow and share my sense of what was important. Maddow summoned for her viewers the image of Gordon Sondland in a restaurant in Kyiv, talking to Donald Trump on a cell phone. That was a call that could have been intercepted by just about anyone. "Ding! Ding! Ding!" Maddow said. "Like red flag sirens going off in the counterintelligence world just about that, right?"

During our interview, Maddow played the clip of me asking Taylor if what Trump did was wrong, and she asked why I framed the question that way.

"There's a lot of legal terms to describe what the President was trying to do," I said. "But I think for most of us, it was just wrong. It was wrong to try to involve a foreign government in our elections. It was wrong to use our taxpayer dollars to try and get another government to investigate a political opponent. And I thought it was important to just really bring it down to earth through Ambassador Taylor's own perspective."

It had been a good day for the investigation. We were a step closer to putting a halt to Trump's crime spree from 1600 Pennsylvania Avenue, if not through impeachment and removal, then through removal at the voting booth in November 2020. I felt good about that and about all the work the Intelligence and Judiciary Committees had done to get us that far.

Most of all, I felt a surge of hope. So many in the White House knew exactly who Trump was and what he was doing and had looked the other way. Now we were hearing from a courageous few who were willing to stand up and speak out, despite the great pressure being brought to bear against them.

"They are not out to get the President, as the President and his defenders have suggested," I told Maddow that evening. "They saw wrongdoing, as Ambassador Taylor said. . . . They honored the Constitution. They came forward, and they described what legitimate U.S. foreign policy is and what they saw as irregular, illegitimate foreign policy."

I went to bed that night thinking not about the next morning, or the next day, or where the impeachment investigation would go in the immediate future. I was thinking about the verdict of history, which I knew would be damning for Trump in the end. Trump and his Russian accomplices might be able to distract a large swath of the American public for a time, but credible, powerful voices like that of Ambassador Taylor would resonate long after the distraction campaign had ended.

CHAPTER 35

THE SMEAR AND CLEAR

We understood for months that former U.S. Ambassador to Ukraine Marie Yovanovitch was a key witness in establishing the guilt of Donald Trump as well as of Rudy Giuliani and so many others in their gang. The more we learned, the more outrageous the Ambassador's ordeal appeared. As we'd seen in her deposition, she was a woman of remarkable experience and insight, one who was fighting corruption and was not going to be stopped. Born to parents who fled the Soviet Union, she grew up speaking Russian, and after earning a degree from Princeton, she studied at the Pushkin Institute in Moscow in 1980. She had a lifetime of experience to inform her expertise on Putin's Russia and its ways. One of her first postings in the U.S. Foreign Service was in Moscow.

"In 1993, during the attempted coup in Russia, I was caught in crossfire between presidential and parliamentary forces," she told us in her opening statement before our inquiry on November 15. "It took us three tries—me without a helmet or body armor—to get into a vehicle to go to the Embassy. We went to the Embassy, because the Ambassador asked us to come. We went because it was our duty."

Yovanovitch was tough and committed. She'd served in seven countries, five of them hardship posts, and had three times served as full Ambassador, twice appointed by George W. Bush, once by Barack Obama. She had built a reputation, over her thirty-three years in the Foreign Service, as a stalwart defender of human rights and as a fighter against corruption.

The latter point was precisely why Rudy Giuliani, working his Ukrainian contacts to try to create the impression of dirt on the Bidens, soon had Yovanovitch in his sights. Giuliani put a bug in Trump's ear. If Trump wanted the Bidens investigated, if he wanted the Ukrainians to try to breathe new life into the debunked theory that the Ukrainians, not the Russians, had hacked the 2016 U.S. elections, he had to get rid of Ambassador Yovanovitch. Giuliani's corrupt contacts in Ukraine wanted nothing to do with a champion of anti-corruption like her.

So, she was sent home. It was so ironic: firing a true fighter of corruption in the name of anti-corruption when your real goal is a deeply corrupt scheme to extort a foreign ally to dig up dirt on your domestic political rival. I'd dub it "Smear and Clear." Smear her good name, then clear her off the board. Yovanovitch was understandably furious at the way she'd been treated, but more than anything, this selfless public servant lamented the backward steps we'd taken in helping our key ally Ukraine fight corruption and deal with the Russian threat.

The episode was so revealing of what motivated Donald Trump to act. Like any President, he could hire or fire anyone he wanted. Why, then, did he go to such great lengths to dirty up Yovanovitch? Because the Ambassador stood in the way of his corrupt scheming. Trump had therefore felt he needed to create a justification for firing her, when otherwise he wouldn't have. His fury demonstrated he knew he was guilty.

"Perhaps it was not surprising that when our anti-corruption efforts got in the way of a desire for profit or power, Ukrainians who preferred to play by the old, corrupt rules sought to remove me," Yovanovitch told us in her opening statement. They "were able to successfully conduct a campaign of disinformation against a sitting Ambassador, using unofficial back channels. As various witnesses have recounted, they shared baseless allegations with the President and convinced him to remove his Ambassador, despite the fact that the State Department fully understood that the allegations were false and the sources highly suspect."

Going into Ambassador Yovanovitch's public testimony, we kept hoping that the Republicans might show more restraint than they had through most of the impeachment inquiry. This was a highly respected, nonpartisan public servant who came across well to the public as a sympathetic figure. To the Republicans' credit, going easy on her did seem to be their game plan—but it hit a snag.

I saw the Donald Trump tweet pop up on my Twitter feed almost as soon as it posted. Incredibly enough, though perhaps predictably, Trump attacked

Yovanovitch in real time as she was testifying to us. Even after White House staff had talked themselves hoarse claiming that Donald Trump wouldn't be watching the hearings—oh no, it would be the last thing on his mind—Trump *did* watch, and he couldn't help himself. The man is so insecure, it freaks him out to see a strong, articulate woman whom he can't intimidate.

"Everywhere Marie Yovanovitch went turned bad," Trump tweeted about an hour into her testimony. "She started off in Somalia, how did that go? Then fast forward to Ukraine, where the new Ukrainian President spoke unfavorably about her in my second phone call with him."

It was a childish, petulant display from the President. Not only that, it was a blunt act of witness intimidation. As soon as I saw the tweet, I shared it with Patrick Boland, communications director for the Intel Committee, and Maher Bitar, our general counsel. I suggested they show the tweet to Chairman Schiff, so he could read it out loud to Yovanovitch as she testified. They agreed, and printed the tweet out for Schiff.

I felt awful for her. To consider all that she had already been through, the vicious smears, the intimidation, the death threats, the shock of hearing Trump take shots at her during his infamous July 25 call with the Ukrainian President. And now she was going to hear a new threat being made in real time by the President of the United States.

Dan Goldman asked the Ambassador that day about her reaction when a transcript of the July 25 call was released in late September and she, for the first time, learned what Trump had said about her.

"I was shocked, absolutely shocked, devastated, frankly," she told us, and the entire nation.

"What do you mean by devastated?" Dan asked, as gently as he could.

"I was shocked and devastated that I would feature in a phone call between two heads of state in such a manner, where President Trump said that I was 'bad news' to another world leader and that I would be 'going through some things.' So it was a terrible moment. A person who saw me actually reading the transcript said that the color drained from my face."

Dan followed up to ask how she interpreted Trump's comment that she would go through things.

"It sounded like a threat," she said.

"Did you feel threatened?" he asked.

"I did," she said.

Dan's questioning proceeded from there. For example, he asked her who she understood to be working with Giuliani in Ukraine. She mentioned Yuriy Lutsenko and Viktor Shokin, adding, "I believe that there were also Ukrainian Americans, Mr. Parnas and Mr. Fruman, who have recently been indicted."

The Ambassador also discussed being aware of the threats made to her on Twitter by Trump's son, Donald Trump Jr., who had called her a "joker," and of how Fox News had picked up the attacks. She established that it was a malicious lie, fabricated by the corrupt prosecutor Lutsenko, that she had ever "bad-mouthed" Trump. The campaign against her was ugly and unjust, and she had assumed the Secretary of State would back her up.

"The Undersecretary for Political Affairs called me," she recounted to us. "I said, 'You know, it's really important that the Secretary himself come out and be supportive. Because otherwise, it's hard for me to be the kind of representative you need here.' He said he would talk to the Secretary."

Yet, when that Undersecretary, David Hale, passed her request on for consideration by State Department leadership on the seventh floor of Foggy Bottom, the idea of the Secretary of State showing public support for Yovanovitch was shot down. Why? It's an incredible, stomach-turning story.

"I was told that there was a concern on the seventh floor that if a statement of support was issued, whether by the State Department or by the Secretary personally, that it could be undermined," Yovanovitch explained.

"How would it—could it be undermined?" Dan asked.

"That the President might issue a a tweet contradicting that or something to that effect," she said.

Dan was aghast. So were we all.

"So, let me see if I've got this right," Dan said. "You were one of the most senior diplomats in the State Department, you've been there for thirty-three years, you'd won numerous awards, you'd been appointed as an Ambassador three times by both Republican and Democratic Presidents, and the State Department would not issue a statement in support of you against false allegations because they were concerned about a tweet from the President of the United States?"

"That's my understanding," she said.

(During an interview with NPR's Mary Louise Kelly on January 24, Secretary of State Mike Pompeo claimed that he "defended every State Department official" and "every person on this team," but when pushed, he was either unable or unwilling to point to any statements he'd made in Yovanovitch's defense. Subsequently, Pompeo berated Kelly in a profanity-laced tirade, asking her, "Do you think Americans care about Ukraine?" and bizarrely challenging her to find Ukraine on an unmarked map. Kelly did so easily.)

With heads shaking all over the chamber on November 15, Chairman Schiff took the opportunity to read the Trump tweet I'd sent to him through staff.

"Ambassador Yovanovitch, as we sit here testifying, the President is attacking you on Twitter," Schiff said.

The Ambassador nodded, with a slight grimace, as if to say, *Of course he is! What next?*

"I'd like to give you a chance to respond," Schiff continued. "I'll read part of one of his tweets: 'Everywhere Marie Yovanovitch went turned bad. She started off in Somalia, how did that go?'"

The Ambassador's eyes briefly widened, but in a composed way. She seemed shocked, yet again, but handled the moment with dignity.

"He goes on to say," Schiff continued, "later in the tweet, 'It is a U.S. President's absolute right to appoint Ambassadors.'" He looked up from the tweet. "First of all, Ambassador Yovanovitch, the Senate has a chance to confirm or deny an Ambassador, do they not?"

"Yes, advise and consent."

"But would you like to respond to the President's attack that everywhere you went turned bad?" he asked.

"I don't think I have such powers, not in Mogadishu, Somalia, and not in other places," she said. "I actually think that where I've served over the years, I and others have demonstrably made things better, you know, for the U.S. as well as for the countries that I've served in."

"Ambassador, you've shown the courage to come forward today and testify," Schiff continued, "notwithstanding the fact you were urged by the White House or State Department not to; notwithstanding the fact that, as you testified earlier, the President implicitly threatened you in that call record. And now, the President in real time is attacking you. What effect do you think that has on other witnesses' willingness to come forward and expose wrongdoing?"

"Well, it's very intimidating," she said.

"It's designed to intimidate, is it not?" the Chairman persisted.

"I can't speak to what the President is trying to do, but I think the effect is to be intimidating," she said.

"Well, I want to let you know, Ambassador, that some of us here take witness intimidation very, very seriously," Chairman Schiff said, speaking for all of us.

The GOP would later claim, ludicrously, that the Trump tweet could not be classified as "witness intimidation" because Yovanovitch was testifying at the exact moment he sent it and wouldn't be able to read it immediately. How weak could their arguments get?

Later in the Ambassador's testimony, my colleague Mike Quigley alluded to Trump's attack in reply to some ridiculous suggestions from the Republican side that Yovanovitch was doing just fine, despite having been fired from her post, as she'd ended up with a teaching position at Georgetown.

"It's like a Hallmark movie," Mike said to the Ambassador. "You ended up at Georgetown. This is all okay. But it wasn't your preference, seven, eight months ago, correct?"

The Ambassador said, "No."

He continued: "It wasn't your preference to be the victim of a smear campaign, was it?"

"No," she said.

"Wasn't your preference to be defamed by the President of the United States, including today, was it?"

"No."

Finally, he summed up what she'd been through.

"It's not the end of a Hallmark movie," he said. "It's the end of a really bad reality TV show, brought to you by someone who knows a lot about that."

When my time came, I started by responding to some of the scurrilous attacks from the Republicans, who had been making noise suggesting it was untoward of Chairman Schiff not to have the whistleblower testify.

"Mr. Chairman, a lot has changed since the whistleblower came forward," I said. "First, most of what the whistleblower has alleged has been corroborated by the witnesses that we have heard from. Second, the President—who my colleagues so shamelessly continue to defend—continues to pressure, threaten, and intimidate the whistleblower."

I was angry, and it showed. I read some press reports into the record, including a September 26, 2019, Business Insider article, "Trump suggested the whistleblower who filed a complaint against him is guilty of treason, which is punishable by death," and a September 26, 2019, *Vanity Fair* piece titled TRUMP SUGGESTS EXECUTING THE WHISTLE-BLOWER'S SOURCES LIKE "IN THE GOOD OLD DAYS."

I talked about the whistleblower's "absolute right to anonymity" and that person's understandable fears for his or her personal safety, then moved on to questions for the Ambassador.

"When you were in Ukraine, you understood that Rudy Giuliani was Donald Trump's personal lawyer, is that right?" I asked.

"Yes, that's right," she said.

"Are you familiar with a *New York Times* story on May 9, 2019, where Rudy Giuliani says that he intends to visit Ukraine and says, 'We're not meddling in an election; we're meddling in an investigation'? Are you familiar with that quote?"

"Yes," she said.

"That's eleven days before you were removed as Ambassador, is that right?" I asked her.

"Yes," she said.

I highlighted Giuliani's word choice. He said "we're" rather than "I'm," clearly indicating that he was "speaking for himself and his client," obviously meaning Donald Trump. And I mocked my Republican colleagues for trying to pretend Trump was in any way, at any moment in his entire life, anti-corruption.

"Now, this anti-corruption crusader, President Trump, who my colleagues have touted out as having such a great interest in anti-corruption—in both the calls that have been referenced today, the August 21 call and the July 25 call, isn't it true that President Trump never mentions the word corruption?" I asked.

"Yes, that's true," she said.

I also underlined that the security assistance to Ukraine was released only after the whistleblower complaint had become public. "So you don't really get points when you get your hand caught in the cookie jar and someone says, 'Hey, he's got his hand in the cookie jar,' and then you take your hand out, which is essentially what my Republican colleagues and the President are trying to take credit for."

Then it was time to address Trump's crude attack on the Ambassador that day as we were all gathered together, a "disgusting tweet," as I said to Yovanovitch.

"But I think I know who you are, Ambassador," I said. "I think the country knows who you are. He smeared you when you were in Ukraine. He smeared you on that phone call with President Zelensky on July 25. He is smearing you right now as you are testifying."

The contrast between Yovanovitch's quiet dignity and poised self-control, on the one hand, and Trump's zero-impulse-control lashing out offered a sharp reminder of just how unhinged the President was. Even many Republicans found it unnerving. "Mr. Trump did not clear his Friday tweet with top White House aides before putting it out, leaving some of his advisors deeply dispirited," the *New York Times* reported. "Privately, they acknowledged he had done himself damage."

The importance of Trump's undermining of Ambassador Yovanovitch went well beyond the fate of one superlative public servant. It was about precedent. Our Ambassadors and diplomats are on the front lines all over the world, often in dangerous situations. Theirs is a generally thankless life, which they take on because they believe in the larger mission and believe there is a higher purpose to the work of fostering better relations with other countries—and helping other countries where we can.

Diplomats need a degree of autonomy in order to do their work, and Trump's selfish motivation for removing Yovanovitch set a dangerous precedent for future Presidents. His smearing of her amounted to witness intimidation.

"If the President can do this to her, he can do it to anyone," I said that night on *The Last Word with Lawrence O'Donnell.* "And that should be of great concern that a President would use his powers to act this way. As she acknowledged, the President has every right to remove someone from office if it's for a good reason, not if it's for a corrupt reason."

The Yovanovitch testimony was important because it proved beyond a shadow of a doubt that Trump's Ukraine scam was never about fighting corruption.

I'd had to hurry to make the show, since I was coming from another deposition that had only ended at 9:41 p.m. Right after Yovanovitch's public hearing, it was back to the SCIF to interview David Holmes, the U.S. embassy official in Ukraine who had overheard Sondland's loud public cell phone conversation with Donald Trump in Kyiv. It had already been a long day, the members were exhausted, and I picked up a late-afternoon coffee before we started around 4 p.m. I wasn't the only one. We knew we had a late Friday night of work ahead of us.

Holmes's testimony was a case of just deserts for the Republicans trying so hard to confuse and block our investigation. He had come forward only because they overplayed their hand by complaining to anyone who would listen that our case was built entirely on "hearsay evidence." Holmes saw Ambassador Taylor's testimony, and he heard the Republicans raising all these misleading concerns, and he thought, *I have direct evidence. I heard the call. I should come forward.*

Holmes had been with Sondland in a Kyiv restaurant on July 26, one day after Trump's all-important July 25 call with Zelensky. Holmes distinctly heard the President asking, "So he's going to do the investigation?" and knew that referred to the push to get the Ukrainians to investigate Burisma and the Bidens and the 2016 elections. Holmes had been hearing about "the investigations" for weeks; they were Topic A. He just hadn't heard them coming directly from President Trump himself, in that distinctive voice.

"On June 27, Ambassador Sondland told Ambassador Taylor in a phone conversation . . . that President Zelensky needed to make clear to President Trump that President Zelensky was not standing in the way of 'investigations,'" Holmes told us in his opening statement. "I understood that this was referring to the Burisma-Biden investigations that Mr. Giuliani and his associates had been speaking about in the media since March."

He said he remembered the Trump-Sondland call "vividly" because it was such an unusual occurrence, "someone calling the President from a mobile phone at a restaurant, and then having a conversation of this level of candor, colorful language."

Holmes's testimony was full of vivid detail. He recalled Ambassador Sondland telling him at lunch that he was going to call Trump on his cell phone to give him an update on his meeting with Zelensky. Holmes listened as Sondland was transferred through various layers of switchboards and assistants, repeating each time that he was holding for the President. When he was connected, Holmes noticed Sondland's "demeanor change," and he also noticed him holding the phone away from his ear because Trump was speaking so loudly.

"I heard Ambassador Sondland greet the President and explain that he was calling from Kyiv," Holmes told us. "I heard President Trump then clarify that Ambassador Sondland was in Ukraine." It's not clear if the President understood that Kyiv is in Ukraine. In fact, it's the capital.

Then Sondland told Trump that President Zelensky "loves your ass." Trump asked about the investigation, and "Sondland replied that 'he's gonna do it,' adding that President Zelensky will do 'anything you ask him to.'"

As for what was discussed just after the call, Sondland had told Holmes that Trump "doesn't give a shit about Ukraine," Holmes said.

"He only cares about the big things," Sondland told him. "Big stuff that matters to him, like this Biden investigation that Giuliani is pushing."

I scribbled out a note to Dan Goldman, our counsel: "This is amazingly helpful."

Our staff lawyers touched on other topics, including Sondland's efforts, on behalf of Trump, to help A$AP Rocky, a rapper imprisoned in Sweden. Holmes's detailed recollection of that part of the conversation only added to the ring of truth.

Chairman Schiff had a flight to California that night and left at around 8 p.m., leaving me to chair the deposition in his absence. When it was my turn to ask Holmes questions, I focused on issues of credibility, asking him if he was there talking to us "to build a case to support an impeachment inquiry."

"No, not at all," he said. "I think it's my duty to be here, based on what I know."

I asked if he'd gone to the press with what he knew.

"In my Foreign Service career, I have never gone to the press about anything," he said.

I also asked if he was a Never Trumper, and he said no. I was doing what I could to inoculate Holmes against the inevitable Republican smears. I knew they would pull all their usual tricks in trying to undermine him, given that his testimony was so damaging to the President—and also to Gordon Sondland's credibility.

As I said that night on MSNBC, when Lawrence O'Donnell asked about Holmes's deposition and what it meant for Sondland, "Gordon Sondland has the opportunity to come forward and do the right thing on Wednesday, Lawrence."

We had one more deposition scheduled for the following morning, with Mark Sandy, deputy associate director for national security programs at the Office of Management and Budget, and with Schiff out of town, I was asked to chair that one as well. The Dans (our Dan Goldman and Dan Noble, both counsel for the Intel Committee) told me if it was a problem, they could lead the deposition.

"I'd better be here," I joked, "lest we spend the whole morning talking to Mr. Sandy about rap music."

CHAPTER 36

"DAD, DO NOT WORRY"

Maybe it has to do with my early memories of having a dad who was a police officer, but I've always had the highest regard for those who wear a uniform. We expected Trump loyalists would go after Lt. Col. Alexander Vindman, the National Security Council official who had been alarmed by the July 25 shakedown call with Ukraine. That's what they did.

Senator Ron Johnson sent a letter to our committee suggesting that Vindman "fits the profile" of those in government who had "never accepted President Trump as legitimate," raising without a shred of evidence the charge that Vindman might be guilty of leaking to the media or trying to "sabotage" Trump's policies. Doug Collins, Ranking Member on the Judiciary Committee, disgraced himself with a letter questioning Vindman's "credibility and judgment." Once again it was shocking to behold the lengths to which Trump apologists would go to debase themselves and do Trump's bidding.

Some Washington Republicans, including one member of the Intel Committee, even questioned whether it was appropriate for Lt. Col. Vindman to wear his uniform to appear before us. Vindman, who was born in Kyiv but left with his family for Brooklyn at age three, becoming a naturalized American, had earned a Purple Heart for his service in the Iraq War, where he was wounded by a roadside bomb outside Fallujah in 2004.

On July 10, 2019, disturbed by Ambassador Sondland's handling of a Ukrainian visit to the White House, where Sondland openly pressed the Ukrainians to investigate the Bidens, Vindman had reported his concerns. On July 25, when he heard the President shake down the President of Ukraine on that infamous call, he also reported it.

Now Lt. Col. Vindman, in full uniform, as is customary for officers when testifying in Congress, spoke in his opening statement about the courage of anyone who had dared come forward and testify to our impeachment inquiry, despite the many "character attacks." At the end of his statement, he talked about his family, and I was one of many who got emotional listening to him.

"When my father was forty-seven years old, he left behind his entire life and the only home he had ever known to start over in the United States so his three sons could have better and safer lives," he said, going on to talk about the gratitude he and his brothers felt toward their father. Then Vindman said he understood that what he was doing that day, standing up to speak truth to power, "would not be tolerated" in many countries of the world.

"In Russia, my act of expressing concern to the chain of command in an official and private channel would have severe personal and professional repercussions," he said. "And offering public testimony involving the President would surely cost me my life." This was no exaggeration.

Finally, he finished up by directing his comments to his father.

"Dad, I'm sitting here today in the U.S. Capitol talking to our elected professionals," he said. "Talking to our elected professionals is proof that you made the right decision forty years ago to leave the Soviet Union and come here to the United States of America in search of a better life for our family. Do not worry. I will be fine for telling the truth."

It was an inspiring display of moral courage. Vindman was betting on the truth, betting on the goodness of America, and putting everything on the line. That was what he had done again and again in his career.

Under questioning from Mike Quigley, Vindman said he knew of no one who worked in national security in the administration who supported the hold on security assistance.

"No one from the national security?" Quigley asked.

"None," Vindman said.

"No one from the State Department?"

"Correct."

"No one from the Department of Defense?"

"Correct."

When it was my turn to ask a question, I started with a reminder of how fraudulent it had been to claim that Trump made it a priority to crack down on corruption in Ukraine.

"Isn't it true that the Department of Defense had certified that the anti-corruption requirements of Ukraine had been met when the hold was put on by the President?" I asked Vindman.

"That is correct," he said.

Also testifying that morning, at the same time as Vindman, was Jennifer Williams, a State Department employee detailed to Vice President Pence's office to advise him on Europe and Russia. Like Vindman, she had also monitored the July 25 call. Williams was a respected career Foreign Service officer. Originally hired to work in the Department of Homeland Security in the George W. Bush administration, she moved to the Foreign Service and had postings in both the Bush and Obama administrations.

In her deposition to us, Williams had said she found references in the July 25 call to be "unusual and inappropriate" in that they were "specific to the President in nature, to his personal political agenda, as opposed to a . . . broader foreign policy objective of the United States."

Shortly before Williams came in to testify, Trump took to Twitter for yet another of his cheap attempts at impugning the credibility of someone with far more credibility than he's ever had. Maybe not understanding that Williams had heard the July 25 call live, Trump tweeted, "Tell Jennifer Williams, whoever that is, to read BOTH transcripts of the presidential calls, & see the just released statement from Ukraine. Then she should meet with the other Never Trumpers."

This was of course another clumsy smear. Williams did not consider herself a Never Trumper; she was a national security professional. Like Vindman, she took careful notes on the July 25 call, and as with Vindman's, those notes indicated President Zelensky making a specific reference to "Burisma," despite the fact that the rough transcript the Trump administration had released of the call curiously did not mention Burisma.

In my questioning of Williams, I established that we'd been told the Vice President was a "voracious reader" of his intelligence briefing book.

"And you told us that after the July 25 call between President Trump and President Zelensky that you put the call transcript in Vice President Pence's intelligence briefing book, is that right?" I asked Williams.

"I ensured it was there," she said. "My colleagues prepare the book, but yes."

"So, let's flash forward to September 1," I continued. "Vice President Pence meets with President Zelensky, is that right?"

"That's correct," she said, and confirmed that she was present for that meeting.

"President Zelensky, with Vice President Pence, they talk about a lot of things, but you will agree that Vice President Pence did not bring up the Bidens, is that correct?" I asked.

"That's correct," she said. "He did not."

"He did not bring up investigations."

"No."

I'd laid it all out. Now it was time to pull the strands together.

"Is one reasonable explanation that although Vice President Pence will do a lot of things for President Trump, that he was not willing to bring up investigations and Bidens because he thought it was wrong?" I asked.

"I'm not in a position to speculate," she said.

My friend Sean Patrick Maloney of New York took Vindman through a careful recollection of the July 25 call.

"You heard the President's voice on the call?" Maloney asked him.

"I did," he said.

"And you heard him raise that subject again, that Ambassador Sondland had raised before, about investigating the Bidens, right?" Maloney pressed.

"I did," Vindman said.

"And I want to ask you, when you heard him say that, what was the first thought that went through your mind?"

"Frankly, I couldn't believe what I was hearing," Vindman said. "There was probably an element of shock that maybe in certain regards my worst fear of how our Ukraine policy could play out was playing out. And how this was likely to have significant implications for U.S. national security."

"And you went immediately and you reported it, didn't you?" Maloney asked.

"I did," Vindman said.

Another memorable moment came when Devin Nunes addressed the witness as "Mr. Vindman."

"Ranking Member, it's Lt. Col. Vindman, please," Vindman corrected him.

Schiff seemed to build from day to day, his closing arguments gaining in force and purpose. He had an unerring feel for cutting to the heart of the matter, and ended the morning session with a step back to look at why the shakedown scheme was wrong and what it meant.

"Ukraine is fighting our fight against the Russians, against their expansionism," Schiff said in closing. "That's our fight, too—at least we thought so on a bipartisan basis. . . . That's why we support Ukraine with the military aid that we have. Well, the President may not care about it, but we do. We care about our defense, we care about the defense of our allies, and we darn well care about our Constitution. We are adjourned."

We had two more witnesses coming later, U.S. Special Representative for Ukraine Kurt Volker and Tim Morrison of the National Security Council, making for an eleven-hour day of public testimony. Volker and Morrison would add more detail to a story we'd had nailed down for us long since, but Vindman's emotional testimony and startling revelations had the most impact that day.

Watching Vindman, from his strong opening statement to his determined sparring with some of the Republicans on the committee, I kept thinking about the courage he was showing just by being there. He had so much to lose and so much to fear, but duty and love of country gave him no choice. This was who he was, a man of conviction. I thought of the courage that Vindman and Yovanovitch and the others had shown in coming forward, and I wondered why their example couldn't be more widely emulated. If they were able to find it in themselves to do the right thing, to risk their reputations and career, then couldn't my Republican colleagues somehow locate enough courage to do their damn jobs and hold this President accountable?

CHAPTER 37

SONDLAND

The Gordon Sondland who testified on November 20, 2019, was not the same cocky, grinning man who had ended his deposition with us three weeks earlier by giving my back a slap hard enough to leave a handprint. Sondland had been humbled, at least a little, by the humiliating adjustments to his testimony he had been forced to send us in the interim. As word leaked out of what Ambassador Bill Taylor and others had told us in very credible fashion, Sondland had to confront the fact that glaring gaps were opening up between their versions of events and his. Speculation in Washington was that Sondland could face perjury charges.

During our preparations for his testimony, we made a collective decision not to beat him up about this. Schiff and I, as former prosecutors, made the point to our colleagues that it was not uncommon at all for witnesses not to give the full version of events at first, for a variety of reasons. Witnesses often hold key details close to the vest, and then later start to tell the truth. No question, the testimony of others had motivated Sondland to get in gear. Just how fearful he was of a possible perjury conviction, we didn't know, but the timing of his appearance turned out to be propitious for us.

Five days before Sondland was set to testify in public, a guilty verdict was handed down in the Roger Stone trial. Stone was convicted specifically of lying to the Intelligence Committee (and other counts involving obstruction of justice), so if there had been any question in Sondland's mind about whether the public cared about witnesses lying to Congress, a jury of Roger Stone's peers had laid that to rest.

Sondland clearly did not want to end up sharing Stone's fate, but even after he updated his testimony, it was clear he was still leaving details out. The testimony of David Holmes, describing the July 26 phone call he overheard between Sondland and Trump, made that clear. Sondland's testimony to us would represent his third crack at the truth. He was stepping back up to the plate 0 for 2.

We were sure Republicans would attack Sondland's credibility. How convenient: If someone lies to protect Trump, as Michael Cohen so often had, when that person finally tells the truth, you impugn his testimony by calling him a liar. So, if we joined in those attacks on Sondland, we would only be helping Republicans. Our objective was clear: We needed Sondland to be truthful, candid, and open, and making him feel under attack and on the defensive wouldn't help. In television interviews I encouraged Sondland to come forward, and told him that when he did, the environment would be accommodating.

Reviewing Sondland's opening statement beforehand, I had the sense he was going all the way down to the one-yard line as far as telling the truth. He was still holding key details that we believed he possessed, but he made clear that there were two quid pro quos he knew about for sure.

"Mr. Giuliani's requests were a quid pro quo for arranging a White House visit for President Zelensky," Sondland's statement read. "Mr. Giuliani demanded that Ukraine make a public statement announcing investigations of the 2016 election/DNC server and Burisma. Mr. Giuliani was expressing the desires of the President of the United States, and we knew that these investigations were important to the President."

One thing that was absolutely maddening, and frustrating, was that Sondland was still insisting that Trump wanted Burisma investigated, but that Sondland himself never understood that Burisma meant Biden. That of course was absolutely absurd, and no one bought it. Still, overall, Sondland was delivering the goods. We figured: *He's rolling on the President, let's not get in his way.*

Sondland once again had a half-smile in place, and occasionally smirked, as he came out for his testimony. He sat still as the cameras all recorded the moment, no doubt trying to look solemn, but at one point he did lean over and make a joke to his attorney, seated next to him. Yet by the time Chairman Schiff was about to begin, Sondland flashed a look of anxiety. He had to have been wondering how he'd gotten himself into this fix. He hadn't even been a Trump guy, not until after he'd been elected, and yet here he was. The thought might have crossed his mind: *Can I get that million dollars back?*

Even though the opening statement had been released to the media, and we'd all seen it, there was still a jolt of electricity in hearing Sondland say, "Was there a quid pro quo? . . . The answer is yes."

The Trump defense strategy had been built on layer upon layer of denial, so much effort put into denying that there had been a quid pro quo—and that just blew away with Sondland's testimony. His words struck many as "bombshell testimony," a widely repeated phrase that day.

André Carson of Indiana, who was sitting a couple of seats to my left, told me that he noticed Sondland slouching in his seat just before I started questioning him. Then, Carson said, Sondland looked up at me and sat up straight, as if getting ready for an intense exchange. I did not plan for that. I wanted him to be comfortable, but I also wanted to see what I could do to shake out a little bit of the truth.

"Ambassador Sondland, you were told by the President and others to not show up," I said. "You showed up. I think that says a lot about you and I think history will look kindly on you doing that."

I said the words with conviction, looking Sondland in the eye, but I didn't slow down long enough to encourage him to reply.

"But there are consequences to that," I continued.

Speaking to reporters on the White House lawn that morning, Trump had done his usual distancing move when asked about Sondland, saying, "I don't know him well. I have not spoken to him much. This is not a man I know well."

That was a crock, obviously, so I read the quote aloud to Sondland and asked if it was true that the President did not know him well.

"It really depends on what you mean by 'know well,'" he said. "We are not close friends, no. We have a professional, cordial working relationship."

Sondland did admit that they spoke at least twenty times. The point was, everyone knew Sondland was following Trump's orders on this. The idea that a guy like Gordon Sondland would make any major decisions without the President's authority was laughable. That was easy enough to establish.

"Were you ever hauled into the leadership of the State Department for any actions you had taken around your work on Ukraine?" I asked him.

"No," he said.

If Sondland's demands for investigations into corruption in Ukraine were counter to what the President wanted, the Secretary of State would certainly have seen Sondland punished. He was not. The investigations in Ukraine were exactly what Trump wanted.

I needed to tie Giuliani more closely with Trump, because Sondland said some of his information came from Giuliani. So I used basic deductive logic.

"As to Rudy Giuliani," I asked, "on May 23 the President told you, 'Talk to Rudy.' . . . Did the President ever say to you, 'Stop talking to Rudy'?"

"No," Sondland said.

"Did he ever say, 'Don't any longer talk to Rudy'?"

"No."

Something Sondland had said in his opening statement had jumped out at me and a lot of other people. "We did not want to work with Mr. Giuliani," he'd said. "Simply put, we played the hand we were dealt."

I now referenced that metaphor: "On Ukraine you said that you were playing the hand you were dealt," I asked, adding, "President Trump was the dealer, wasn't he?"

Sondland looked taken back. "President Trump was what?" he asked in a confused voice.

"The dealer," I said. "In your metaphor you were playing the hand you were dealt. The dealer is President Trump, is that right?"

Sondland laughed, as if to say: You're not going to get me to call Trump a "dealer" and have that quote all over social media. But that wasn't my goal at all.

"I'll recharacterize your question by saying we followed the direction of the President because that was the only pathway to working with Ukraine," he said. Bingo!

Over the course of the questioning, I watched as Sondland's demeanor shifted drastically. As we were heading into a break, Schiff announced we would take thirty minutes for lunch. Republican counsel mentioned that Sondland had a flight back to Brussels to catch, and he would appreciate it if we could make the break shorter. Schiff said we would do our best.

I fly a lot, usually three hundred thousand or so miles per year, and I'm a flying geek. I know just about every flight that goes out of Washington, to anywhere, because I've taken most of them. During the break, just out of curiosity, I looked up flights to Brussels, to see what time frame Sondland was up against. I could see why he wanted us to rush the break. The only direct option to Brussels that day left Dulles at 5:50 p.m. He didn't have much wiggle room.

Sondland's body language completely changed as he started to sweat missing his flight. The confidence was fading by the minute. The swagger was gone. As somebody who constantly lives with the anxiety of missing a flight, I knew how he felt. I kept my eye on Sondland, and the later it got, the more he shifted in his seat, sneaking looks at the clock.

Chairman Schiff started his closing argument at about 3:45.

"It's been a long hearing and I know Americans watching throughout the country may not have had the opportunity to watch all of it," Schiff said early in his statement, then he added: "So I'm going to go through a few of the highlights." Sondland closed his eyes and shook his head slightly, as if to say, *I'm never going to make it.*

"Ambassador Sondland, I appreciate the fact that you have not opined on whether the President should be impeached or not be impeached, or whether the crime of bribery or the impeachable offense of bribery, or other high-end crimes and misdemeanors has been committed. That is for us to decide in consultation with our constituents and our conscience, that is for us to decide," Schiff said near his conclusion, and Sondland nodded his assent.

"I'm continually struck how my colleagues would suggest that because the President got caught, we should ignore the fact that he was conditioning official acts in order to get political favors in order to get an investigation against his rival," Schiff said in closing. "Getting caught is no defense, not to a violation of the Constitution or to a violation of his oath of office, and it certainly doesn't give us reason to ignore our own oath of office. We are adjourned."

With that Sondland placed both hands on the tabletop and did a brisk push-up to stand as quickly as he could, then headed for the door at top speed.

I wasn't the only one who noticed his hurried exit, and in our anteroom, I joked about it with a couple of colleagues.

"How adorable. He thinks he's going back to Brussels," I said.

Sondland had just given information damaging to Donald Trump. I couldn't see how this guy could possibly still have a job.

A reporter texted me that day, noting that Sondland was the most Trumpian of our witnesses and asking how I would compare him with Trump. It was a good question. Sondland was much smarter than Trump. He could put sentences together. Unlike Trump, I think he actually was a successful businessman. I didn't like Sondland's attitude, but at least he could laugh at himself, something Trump is incapable of. Finally, Sondland had shown up. He had held himself accountable. That was something Donald Trump would never do.

Maybe we'll never know why Gordon Sondland decided to come in and testify when so many others did not. Maybe at some point he'll write a book, and we'll get the full account, or some version of it. Who knows? I think the Sondland case shows that for some people, reputation still really does matter. Sondland still had a job when he flew back to Brussels after testifying, but it turned out I was right. Trump made an example of Sondland. He fired him as Ambassador on February 7, along with Lt. Col. Alexander Vindman and his twin brother, Lt. Col. Yevgeny Vindman.

CHAPTER 38

THE LAST WORD

My sleep was fitful the night before the last day of the impeachment inquiry. I was full of anticipation and kept thinking about what questions I would ask of our final two witnesses, Dr. Fiona Hill and David Holmes. I cleared my head by hitting the gym. For me, that's the House of Representatives gym.

"How you doing?" I said to the guy working out one spot over on the elliptical machine.

"Hi, Eric," Jim Jordan said back.

That was all we had to say to each other. It was so strange. Where else do two adversaries who will be clashing that day share space beforehand? Imagine an NFL game where the teams have the same locker rooms and suit up side by side beforehand.

The House gym has a history of providing a rare safe space in Congress. Republicans and Democrats can both go and not have to worry about cameras or being judged. As a piece in Slate put it, "What happens in the gym stays in the gym."

I made the same mistake I always make. I try to work out as hard as I can, for as long as I can, and I get all hot and sweaty, and then I have to hurry to take a shower to try to cool off, hurry to towel off and get dressed, and hurry to get wherever I'm going. That morning, I had to run over to Statuary Hall, where I had an 8 a.m. remote interview with CNN. I don't know why I do this to myself. I got there maybe forty-five seconds before the hour, out of breath and dripping with sweat—and realized I had totally forgotten that *San Francisco Chronicle* reporter Tal Kopan would be following me around for the day. I showed up with a towel I'd borrowed from the gym, and there Tal was at the CNN camera, waiting for me with my press secretary, Natalie Edelstein. Probably not a great impression for this *Chronicle* profile piece. I looked like I had just robbed a bank!

A few minutes later, I was on live TV for what I figured would be a typical prehearing, set-the-table type of interview. I was ready to focus on that day's testimony and how damning it would be (again) for Trump, but Chris Cuomo had a little bit of a curve ball for me. Unbeknownst to me, as I was finishing up on the treadmill and heading to the showers, Donald Trump had included me in his morning stream of angry, incoherent tweets.

"Why do @ShannonBream & @FoxNews waste airtime on Democrat Rep. Eric Swalwell, who recently left the Presidential Primaries," the President of the United States tweeted. "Fox should stay with the people that got them there, not losers!"

"You got to the President this morning," Chris Cuomo said to start our interview. "He's talking about you."

"It's news to me," I said.

Cuomo read Trump's Fox News–obsessed tweet out loud and CNN flashed it on the screen.

"I don't care to talk about you and your politics and running for President, good for you for making a go at it, but what does that tell you about how the President sees that outlet and sees the dialogue that you're all engaged in?" he asked.

"First off, Chris, I have to go on that other network, it's the only way my parents will see me on TV."

Cuomo was not expecting that. He laughed loud enough that I actually had to pause for a beat before continuing.

"He's clearly not working," I continued, and pointed out that besides following the impeachment, Trump could also be doing his job, focusing on critical national priorities like gun violence. I tried as often as I could to remind people that like Speaker Pelosi and the entire Democratic caucus, we were working on a range of our constituents' concerns, not only impeachment.

Next up was a huddle with my Intel Committee colleagues, to put our heads together on our strategy for the day. These meetings quickly started to feel like a tradition. We had worked so closely together under so much pressure and time constraints that we had truly bonded.

On my way into the room where we met, I stopped by a wooden table to pick up a copy of the opening statements for Dr. Hill and Holmes, each a thick sheaf of papers, and also to look at the clippings of news that had recently broken. Most interesting was a printout of a Daily Beast report that had posted overnight revealing that Devin Nunes, Ranking Member on the House Intelligence Committee, a leader of the desperate attempt to keep the truth from coming out, had himself been working with Lev Parnas, a Ukrainian American who had turned up at the heart of our investigation.

Parnas was clearly a dodgy character, but he'd been working for the President of the United States. In fact, our requests for Parnas to testify in our impeachment investigation and provide documents were at first blocked by none other than John Dowd, Trump's lawyer at the time. Dowd, acting on Trump's behalf, wrote to Congress arguing that Parnas and his associate Igor Fruman were protected by executive privilege. "Be advised that Messrs. Parnas and Fruman assisted Mr. Giuliani in connection with his representation of President Trump," Dowd's letter asserted. Not only was Dowd operating on Trump's behalf, but other documentation we obtained confirmed specifically that Trump had approved Dowd's representing Parnas and Fruman.

"Lev Parnas, an indicted associate of Rudy Giuliani, helped arrange meetings and calls in Europe for Rep. Devin Nunes in 2018, Parnas' lawyer Ed MacMahon told The Daily Beast," the article began. "Nunes aide Derek Harvey participated in the meetings, the lawyer said, which were arranged to help Nunes' investigative work. MacMahon didn't specify what those investigations entailed."

Nunes was hooked deeper into Trump's corrupt scheme. Parnas had been indicted for routing foreign contributions to Republicans in a U.S. election, and our investigation had established that he had been giving smear information on Marie Yovanovitch and the Ukrainians to Rudy Giuliani and Donald Trump. A link between Parnas and Nunes reinforced the Gordon Sondland line "They were all in the loop."

"Throughout every #ImpeachmentHearing, @DevinNunes falsely accuses @RepAdamSchiff of being a 'fact witness,'" I'd tweeted out the night before, when the Lev Parnas–Devin Nunes story broke. "Turns out, Nunes was projecting all along: a Ukrainian who was indicted around facts in our inquiry helped Nunes travel overseas for 'investigations.'"

I talked with my Intel Committee colleagues about the Daily Beast story as we each went over our planned questioning for the day, and I emphasized how potentially important I saw the Nunes-Parnas link.

"You'll be sure to make that clear in your questioning," a committee staffer suggested.

The feeling I experienced as we walked from the SCIF to the committee room reminded me of that pregame feeling I had as an athlete, going from the locker room out onto the field for a high school football or college soccer game. We walked together as a team, with Chairman Schiff usually out front, and came through the Cannon Tunnel, which connects the Cannon House Office Building to the Capitol, and out into the hearing room, where a swarm of reporters and cameras waited for us. As we walked, I happened to be talking to Schiff about football and the Oakland Raiders, his team.

"I've been trying to find a time where we can go catch a game together, but with impeachment, I don't see any dates that work before the end of the season," I mentioned. "Hopefully, they make the playoffs, and this investigation is over, and we can go see a Raiders playoff game before they move to Vegas."

After we'd taken our seats and the chair gaveled in at 9:05 a.m., the hearing got started with the ritual of dozens of reporters and photographers huddled around the witness table, waiting for the witnesses. As Dr. Hill and David Holmes entered, you could hear this rattling of *click-click-click-click-click,* all the cameras going at once.

During Holmes's opening statement, I was thinking about the Republican efforts during his deposition to try to undermine his credibility. I remembered that he had received some kind of award during the Obama administration for raising tough questions.

"Some of you on this committee appear to believe that Russia and its security services did not conduct a campaign against our country and that perhaps, somehow, for some reason, Ukraine did," Dr. Hill said in her opening statement. "This is a fictional narrative that is being perpetrated and propagated by the Russian security services themselves. The unfortunate truth is that Russia was the foreign power that systematically attacked our democratic institutions in 2016. This is the public conclusion of our intelligence agencies confirmed in bipartisan and Congressional reports. It is beyond dispute, even if some of the underlying details must remain classified."

Dr. Hill had firsthand experience of some of what happened in the shakedown scheme, but given her expertise, she also had an unmatched thirty-thousand-foot perspective to share. She beautifully articulated in her opening statement why this aid to Ukraine was so important and why we must stand against Russian aggression. She also gave the House GOP, who had spent weeks spinning Russian propaganda, a well-deserved dressing down.

I used my time questioning Dr. Hill to put into layman's terms some of the basic points about talk of a "quid pro quo."

"Dr. Hill, yesterday I think a lot of Americans were scratching their heads as Ambassador Sondland testified that on September 9 he calls the President of the United States and just says broadly, 'What do you want from Ukraine?'" I began.

"And," I continued, "the President says, 'There's no quid pro quo, there's no quid pro quo.' Like being pulled over for speeding and being asked, 'Do you know how fast you're going?' And saying, 'I didn't rob the bank, I didn't rob the bank.'"

Dr. Hill, clearly nervous, nodded slightly, but mostly had a look of fierce focus, no doubt waiting to see where I was going with this.

"But your testimony today is that on July 10 of this year, you told one of the President's lawyers that you had concerns that a White House meeting was linked to investigations, is that right?" I continued.

"That's correct," she said, "based on what Ambassador Sondland said in the wardroom."

"And so, as early as July 10, the President's lawyers had knowledge that there was at least concern by a presidential employee about a linkage, is that right?"

"That's correct," she said.

No wonder the President had a guilty reflex of saying, "There was no quid pro quo."

I also wanted to make the connection between Devin Nunes and Lev Parnas. I used some of my time to read into the record the first sentences of the Daily Beast article linking Nunes and Parnas and asked for unanimous consent to record the article.

"Mr. Chairman, you have been falsely accused throughout these proceedings by the Ranking Member as being a quote-unquote 'fact witness,'" I said. "Now if this story is correct, the Ranking Member may have actually been projecting and, in fact, he may be the fact witness if he is working with indicted individuals around our investigation."

Devin Nunes didn't have much of a reaction. He just kept his head down, trying to ignore the stares he was drawing from all over the room.

Then I turned to David Holmes, an honorable public servant with a proven track record of independence of mind and bipartisan service. "I want to go to what this is really all about," I said to him. "First, it's your credibility, Mr. Holmes, and can you tell us and confirm that in 2014, you received the William Rivkin Constructive Dissent Award from the Obama administration State Department?"

"Yes, sir," he said.

"And that was for dissent that you brought up against an administration policy, is that right?" I continued.

"That's right," he said.

It was important to show that Holmes, just like all the other witnesses, was no "Never Trumper." He was the type who spoke truth to power, no matter who was President, and had no dog in this fight.

Finally, since our investigation had so far not included any pictures of Ukrainians on the battlefield, I wanted to put one in the record. I couldn't find a better image than President Zelensky visiting Eastern Ukraine on May 29, 2019, wearing body armor and standing with Ukrainian troops.

"It was his first visit to the front lines of Donbas as President," I said to Holmes. "Can you just tell taxpaying Americans why it's so important that our hard-earned taxpaying dollars help President Zelensky and the men standing beside him fight against Russia in this hot war?"

"Absolutely, sir. President Zelensky was elected on overwhelming majority to defend Ukraine interests," Holmes said. "This is at a time when Ukrainians are defending their sovereignty, their territorial integrity on Ukrainian soil from Russian-backed soldiers who are attacking them. And they said fourteen thousand Ukrainian lives lost in this war so far, as I mentioned, a few this week already. . . . This is a hot war. This is not a frozen conflict. People are shooting at each other and dying, being injured every single week and despite the ongoing war, they're still trying to pursue peace."

That was my last question in the inquiry, and a good place for me to end. I had been concerned all along in our inquiry about what the withheld assistance at the heart of the scandal meant to Ukrainians on the ground. This wasn't just money we had voted to send to Ukraine. The assistance was a matter of life and death.

A highlight of each day of hearings had been Chairman Schiff's sizzling closing statements, all without notes, all unscripted. Committee members and staff were waiting to hear what he'd come up with on this, the final day, and his words made me proud to stand with him. He was speaking not just to the Republicans, not just to Americans watching at home in every corner of the country, but to history.

"We all remember that debacle in Helsinki, when the President stood next to Vladimir Putin and questioned his own intelligence agencies," Schiff said in his closing statement. "I wish I had heard just some of the righteous indignation we heard in the committee today when the President questioned that fundamental conclusion of our intelligence agencies, but of course they were silent when the President said that. They'll show indignation today, but they will cower when they hear the President questioning the very conclusions that our intelligence community has reached."

I wish I could reproduce the whole statement for you here in this book—to me, it was that important—but I'll focus on what Schiff said after he pointed out the Republican smears against Dr. Hill, against David Holmes, against Lt. Col. Vindman.

"One question posed by your testimony, Mr. Holmes, is what do we care about?" Schiff continued. "Do we care about the big stuff like the Constitution, like an oath of office, or do we only care now about the party? What do we care about? . . . We learned that a dedicated public servant, Marie Yovanovitch, known for fighting corruption, widely respected throughout the diplomatic corps, was ruthlessly smeared by Rudy Giuliani, by the President's own son, by their friends on Fox News, and a whole host of other characters.

Her reputation was sullied, so they could get her out of the way, which they did. And you're right, it was gratuitous; the President could have gotten rid of her anytime he wanted—but that's not enough for this President. No, he has to smear and destroy those that get in his way, and someone fighting corruption in Ukraine was getting in his way, so she's gone."

He moved on to compare our impeachment inquiry against Trump with the impeachment inquiry against Richard Nixon when Howard Baker, ranking minority member of the Senate Watergate Committee, famously turned against the President.

"The difference between then and now is not the difference between Nixon and Trump, it's the difference between that Congress and this one," he said. "And so, we are asking, where is Howard Baker? Where are the people who are willing to go beyond their party, to look to their duty?"

And here is how he closed, finishing with an homage to Elijah Cummings: "This President believes he is above the law, beyond accountability, and in my view, there is nothing more dangerous than an unethical President who believes they are above the law. And I would just say to people watching here at home and around the world, in the words of my great colleague, 'We are better than that.'"

With that, Chairman Schiff's powerful, impassioned closing argument, we closed the hearing. Just afterward, we went into the anteroom, and Chairman Schiff thanked the members and staff for months of hard work. We'd all come a long way together.

PART 5: IMPEACHING THE PRESIDENT

CHAPTER 39

COUNTDOWN TO IMPEACHMENT

When I first walked into the hearing room the morning of Saturday, December 7, I immediately spotted Professor Laurence Tribe of Harvard Law School standing behind the witness table. My Judiciary Committee Democratic colleagues, tasked by Speaker Pelosi with drawing up the articles of impeachment, were in for a long weekend of prep work for the coming week's impeachment hearing, and Tribe was there to help. I went right over to say hello. I've admired Professor Tribe's work since I was a law student at the University of Maryland. Professor Tribe and I had appeared a number of times together on television news programs, but had never actually met, even though it felt that way, given the various friendly messages we'd exchanged. Often during the Russia and Ukraine investigations, he had reached out via Twitter DM to share ideas with me.

"I've spent my entire life defending the Constitution," Professor Tribe told my Judiciary Committee colleagues and me that morning, "and I've never seen a time where there is such a need to do so."

He walked us through the various articles of impeachment the President could be on the hook for, which ranged from abuse of power, bribery, obstruction of Congress, and obstruction of justice. Tribe emphasized that with this President, we had to focus on pattern evidence. Pattern evidence on soliciting foreign assistance and pattern evidence on obstruction. I followed up on a few points, including whether a President's failing to comply with a judicial order could in and of itself be part of an article of impeachment. Tribe said no, not effectively. Better to work such instances into a larger story of abuse of power.

On the obstruction charges, Tribe was careful to note that a President's merely going to court was not impeachable; that was his right. What made

Trump different was that his statements about impeachment cooperation had been "categorical assertions that he won't cooperate."

Talking later for this book, Professor Tribe made the point that for all the insistence from Republicans and some in the media that the impeachment effort was all about partisanship, for him, it was anything but. Trump's abuse of power was so widespread and so beyond the pale, Tribe believed—as I do—that it would demand dramatic action whether a Democrat or a Republican was in the White House.

"I try to be nonpartisan about this in my role as a constitutional lawyer, but I have no doubt that I would be publicly urging for the impeachment of Hillary Clinton if she behaved like this," Professor Tribe told me. "I also think it's important to remember that the reason this is so partisan is essentially that the Republicans have lined up like lemmings, right down to the last man and woman, behind Donald Trump."

Tribe had recently coauthored a book on impeachment with Joshua Matz, counsel to the Judiciary Committee, who was also helping draft the articles of impeachment. *To End a Presidency: The Power of Impeachment* was one of many volumes I had pored over in preparation for the impeachment inquiry. Published in May 2018, the book warned against using impeachment as a tool without sufficient cause. "The impeachment power is not a tool for Congress to eject a President solely because of disagreement with his policies," they wrote. "It's easy to envision how a successful partisan removal could unleash a cycle of bitter, destructive recrimination."

Throughout this impeachment process, under the leadership of Speaker Pelosi, we reminded ourselves at every turn of the solemn constitutional responsibility driving us to impeach a President. That was no mask we wore for public consumption; it was how we talked among ourselves in private and what we discussed with families or old friends who knew us best.

"Even though impeachment is unfortunate and dangerous," Professor Tribe told me, "and something we should try to avoid, that everybody in favor of impeaching is in the opposite party of the President, it's even more dangerous to have a partisan lineup behind a President who has clearly abused his power. The coin has two sides. You can't blame the Democrats for the fact that there are no Republicans who are going along, especially since, privately, a number of Republicans say that the right thing to do is remove the guy, but politically, they're constrained from doing that."

We'd started the long weekend of preparation on Saturday morning at 11 a.m. Word was to dress casual, and I did: jeans, sneakers, a sweatshirt, and a blue puff coat. Lots of layers. I took some ribbing, but hey, I was fighting a cold. Debbie Mucarsel-Powell, a freshman representing Miami, Florida, asked me if I was hitting the slopes after the prep. It turned out the joke was on her. The room was freezing. Members were scrambling to find the heating ducts or sending staffers to collect scarves and blankets.

Right before lunch that Saturday, a committee staffer came over to me. "I'm sorry we let you down for lunch, sir," he said.

I stared back quizzically. I had no idea what he was talking about. "Sorry?"

"I just read in the *New York Times* that you were hoping for something other than pizza. Sorry, today's lunch is pizza."

A few days before, I had given a "What is it like in there?" interview to Mark Leibovich of the *New York Times*. There wasn't much I could offer Leibo without telegraphing our approach to the Republicans, so we talked about what we ate, which had been mostly pizza.

"I'm just looking for a break from pizza," I was quoted in the article.

Suddenly I was pizza's Public Enemy No. 1. How dare I attack pizza! Texts came in from all over the country in defense of pizza. I even got a Twitter notification that &pizza, a popular DC pizza parlor, had begun following me on Twitter. Minutes after that, the &pizza account was tweeting at me, "@RepSwalwell say the words + we'll send you some warm 🍕 for those late nights." Then I saw that my press secretary, Natalie, had responded to their tweet: "Staff here: we'll take it" and my Chief of Staff, Michael Reed, wrote, "Please Help," with a gif. I texted Leibovich about the fuss my answer had caused and about the &pizza tweet. He replied, "impact journalism."

Saturday afternoon's prep session was a wild one. Phil Schiliro, a veteran former House Oversight Committee staffer assisting the Judiciary Committee with the investigation, played the role of a disruptive Republican member, interrupting the Chairman and the members along the way, pulling out all the stops to throw us off our game. The proper response was *always* to ignore the GOP stunts and stay focused. I didn't have much of a voice, given my cold, and it was probably the quietest I'd ever been at a committee meeting.

The next day, our discussion of articles of impeachment ran long, and we had to rush to our lunch.

"I'm sorry, but you guys only have fifteen minutes to eat," Amy Rutkin, Judiciary Committee Chairman Jerry Nadler's Chief of Staff, announced.

This time lunch was falafel, kebab, and salad from Roti Modern Mediterranean.

"Who says you can't fight city hall and win?" I joked.

We turned it into a working lunch, going over the schedule for the upcoming week, but even then, we had to rush.

"We have to keep moving," Rutkin told us ominously. "Let's go back to the hearing room. The Phils have some trouble planned."

Phil Barnett, another staffer assisting the committee, also played Republican members. The two Phils would object, interrupt, and make endless points of order, causing as much disruption as they could to see how we would react. They also were very good at preparing the Chairman for their disruptive acts, so Nadler was ready to gavel them down when they crossed the line. We wanted to show order in contrast to their circus.

"Our strength is what the President did, his acts," Phil S. told us. "Let's focus on the acts that are not in dispute." He then listed about a dozen acts that Trump took that were not in dispute, from calling from the White House lawn for China to investigate the Bidens to Mulvaney's damning press conference. The President's strength, Phil S. continued, is "the absence of his words"—meaning, while there was strong evidence of what Trump had actually done, there was little evidence of what he'd actually said. As I had in my questioning of Dr. Hill, Phil S. used a bank robbery example. If you have the crime on videotape, showing the robber waving a gun and taking the money, you don't need the robber saying, "I'm robbing the bank," but the President and his defenders will argue that you don't have Trump actually saying, "I'm abusing my power to force you to help me cheat."

Then Phil S. slipped into character for the mock hearing and set about portraying a very disruptive Ranking Member Collins making accusations at Nadler and the two Intelligence Committee members, Val Demings and me. The two Phils hammered away at Nadler. Motions to adjourn. Points of order about process. They even asked to go into a closed session to get the name of the whistleblower. Still role-playing, Phil S. warned, "If you don't vote for this motion—to hear the name in private session—you are voting to out the whistleblower."

Phil S. played a better Doug Collins than Doug Collins would ever play. First, we could understand everything he was saying. Collins has a tendency to scream and speak fast, which makes it incredibly hard to track his words. He also has a habit of making up or merging words. "Irregardless" was one of his favorites.

Phil pressed on, at one point asking Nadler if he could ask each Democratic member if he or she knew the name of the whistleblower. Nadler, a tough New Yorker who represents parts of Manhattan and Brooklyn, jumped all over him.

"I am not going to allow you to cross-examine your colleagues," Nadler said.

The Phils looked at each other. Our Chairman was ready.

Midway through our mock session, Representative David Cicilline from Rhode Island nudged me with his elbow and pointed to his iPad screen. A friend had sent him President Trump's latest tweet, which I read on his screen: "Don't get why @FoxNews puts losers on like @RepSwalwell (who got ZERO as presidential candidate before quitting), Pramila Jayapal, David Cicilline and others who are Radical Left Haters? The Dems wouldn't let @FoxNews get near their bad ratings debates, yet Fox panders. Pathetic!"

I couldn't believe it. As I was sitting with those very two members, preparing to impeach the President, he had volleyed a tweet our way. We leaned back in our chairs to devise a response. I suggested that we take a selfie, with Pramila, and tweet it back at Trump. It would be part "We see you" and part "We are working; what are you doing?" Joe Neguse from Colorado told us that the Trump campaign had tweeted at him, too, earlier in the day. "Come on in," we told him. Now we had a foursome picture to send back.

We tweeted, "While you're tweeting at us, Mr. President, we are working to uphold our Constitution and keep you accountable." We shook our heads, had a laugh, and continued on late into the night.

CHAPTER 40

WE PRESENT THE EVIDENCE

It was time for the Judiciary Committee to receive the Intel Committee's evidence. I'd thought all weekend about how best to use my five minutes of questioning time during the presentation of evidence that Monday, and was leaning toward a focus on explaining how Trump's acts had hurt our national security. I wanted to show everyday folks why this mattered so much. Even if you didn't necessarily care about Ukraine not getting the $391 million in aid it was counting on, you needed to know that Trump's actions had flat-out made us less safe at home. Staff urged me to stay flexible during Intel Committee investigator Dan Goldman's presentation of the case against Trump.

A potential line of questioning had been kicking around in my mind since our Saturday prep session. All weekend, I kept thinking back to how Phil Schiliro had listed acts Trump had committed that were not even in question. I went to Phil on Monday morning, before the hearing, to let him know I was keeping my options open. I told him I might focus on the facts no one could dispute. Just the facts—or "Just the (f)acts," as I wrote it out.

"I thought you might say that," Phil told me.

He reached into his coat pocket and pulled out a piece of paper. He'd written out all the acts.

"I wrote these down," he said. "For no one in particular, but I was hoping you'd want to use them if it was appropriate."

The slip of paper listed eleven acts Trump had taken that no one could dispute, many of them on video or in the call record the White House had released. Phil also pointed out to me that Ranking Member Collins had noted in his opening statement that there were no Howard Baker moments here, as in "What did the President know and when did he know it?"

"The reason that's the case is because the President knew everything," Phil said.

I wasn't even born when Richard Nixon resigned as President in August 1974 rather than suffer the humiliation of being impeached in the House of Representatives and convicted in the Senate. Even for people my age, it was still chilling to hear Howard Baker's words from that time repeated. Baker, from Tennessee, was the senior Republican on the Senate Watergate Committee and at first was skeptical of the effort to impeach his fellow Republican. "It's not going to amount to much," Baker thought at the time, "it's just a Democratic effort to embarrass him." But then, after he talked to Nixon and realized the gravity of the situation, Baker told himself that "You better just put your head down and charge into this thing and let the facts fall where they will." He served as an honest broker, and the facts led to Nixon's downfall.

In his questioning of former White House counsel John Dean, Baker posed the question "My primary thesis is still, what did the President know, and when did he know it?" and Dean's response was the beginning of the end for Nixon.

I thought I could walk Goldman through each of the different acts with a series of straightforward questions that would cut through the White House's misdirection and obfuscation and denials. "Who was the person that . . ." I'd begin, with the answer always being "President Trump." The line of questioning would depend on Goldman giving crisp replies. If he stuck to "President Trump" for each answer, we could lay out each undisputed fact, and use the power of repetition to hammer home the truth.

We gathered Democratic members of the Judiciary Committee for an 8:30 a.m. huddle with Chairman Nadler.

"I've never given a pep talk before," he told us, starting a pep talk. "We will all be acquitted by history for the work we are doing here to defend our Constitution. Now, let's go defend it."

That was Nadler: No words wasted. Straight to the point. His opening statement in the hearing was equally strong and clear.

"As we heard in our last hearing, the Framers of the Constitution were careful students of history and clear in their vision for the new nation," he said. "They knew that threats to democracy can take many forms, that we must protect against them. The debates around the framing make clear that the most serious such offenses include abuse of power, betrayal of the nation through foreign entanglements, and corruption of public office. Any one of these violations of the public trust would compel the members of this committee to take action. When combined, in a single course of action, they state the strongest possible case for impeachment and removal from office."

Collins had his turn, and was more emphatic than he was clear or convincing. It was hard to understand half of what he said.

"For anyone to think that this was not a baked deal is not being honest with themselves," he said. Huh? At one point, probably revealing more than he intended, he added, "And as we have talked about before, this is a show."

At 10:47 a.m., Goldman's turn came to give his opening statement, and it was crisp and powerful.

"We are here today because Donald J. Trump, the forty-fifth President of the United States, abused the power of his office—the American presidency—for his personal political benefit," Goldman said. "President Trump directed a months-long scheme to solicit foreign help in his 2020 reelection campaign, withholding official acts from the government of Ukraine in order to coerce and secure political interference in our domestic affairs."

After the first break of the day, just after 11:30 a.m., Republicans on the committee doubled down on their various antics. Goldman bore the brunt of the Republican diversionary attacks, with Collins repeatedly cutting him off and barking, "You're done! You're done!" We couldn't say we were shocked, but it was insulting and craven of Collins and so many others to demean the staff presenters.

(Greg Steube of Florida, the final Republican asking questions, would refer to House majority counsel Barry Berke as a "New York lawyer," a clear anti-Semitic trope. We were horrified. After the hearing, Berke commented, "I am an Irish New York lawyer! Get your insults straight!" Steube's comment would also inspire me to write an op-ed in the Jewish American digital publication *The Forward* about the rise of anti-Semitism.)

For Goldman, who like all of us had prepped to avoid sinking to the level of the Republicans, it wasn't always easy to hold his fire, but he never let the predictable stunts get to him.

Still, when it came my time to question him, I knew I wanted to give him an opportunity to make a plain case to the American people. It didn't take me long after Chairman Nadler gaveled the hearing into session to decide I'd go with my list of questions. I started by swatting down an idea the Republicans had tried to plant. Shortly before it was my turn, Republican Guy Reschenthaler of Pittsburgh complained about the timing of the impeachment report, saying, "We received less than forty-eight hours ago over eight thousand pages of documentation."

"Mr. Goldman," I began, leaning into the question, "would you welcome the problem of having eight thousand documents given to you from the White House?"

"It would be a wonderful problem to have," he said.

"How many have they given you?"

"Zero."

I turned to minority counsel Steve Castor.

"Mr. Castor, you said earlier that 'They got the aid, they got the aid,'" I began, lifting both hands in the air and sitting up higher in my chair as I emphasized the words. "No harm, no foul, they got the aid," I continued. "But you would agree that, although Mr. Sandy said that the presidential concern was European contributions, nothing changed from when that concern was expressed to when they actually got the aid, right? You agree on that? Europe didn't kick in a bunch of new money."

"No, but they did a study," he said in a pleading tone. "I mean, they—"

"Oh, a study," I said, my sarcasm light. "Okay. But they didn't kick in new money. Do you agree on that?"

"Ambassador Taylor discussed that they—" He was eager to filibuster.

"Okay," I cut in. "You talked a lot about the anti-corruption President that we have in Donald Trump, the person who had a fraud settlement relating to Trump University, the person who just recently with his own charity had a settlement related to fraud. Let's talk about that anti-corruption President of ours."

My tone was even, almost gentle. I was walking a fine line in how aggressive to be with Castor. Like so many of the visible defenders of Trump on impeachment, Castor came into these hearings looking like a man intent on showing how over-the-top angry and petulant he could come across. It was weird. When I was growing up, men like my father and relatives who were Republicans believed in projecting quiet strength. Ronald Reagan might flash anger in a public setting—"I'm paying for this microphone!" he famously said at a presidential debate—but he preferred to project a genial, easygoing persona. That was out the window in the Trump era. Republican men now seemed to be in a contest to see who could sound the surliest and most emotional. I was going to stay cool and firm and professional, just as I would in court, even when I was pressing a point.

"Take a wild guess, Mr. Castor," I continued. "How many times has President Trump met with Vladimir Putin or talked to him?"

"I don't know the number," Castor said, sounding like a distracted high school student given a pop quiz.

"It's sixteen," I said.

"Okay," he said, nodding slightly, as if he were worried I was trying to trick him.

"How many times has President Trump met at the White House with President Zelensky?"

"Um . . ." Castor said, though the distracted high school student routine was obviously an act. He was well aware of the answer.

"It's zero," I said. "And who is President Trump meeting with at the White House tomorrow? Do you know?"

"Um, I'm not, I'm not—" he started, cocking his head sideways with an odd grin.

"It's Russian Foreign Minister Lavrov," I finished for him. That was all I had for Castor.

Next, I needed to torpedo the "Trump is an anti-corruption crusader" nonsense and show that Trump's would-be defenders, when pressed, were helpless to defend him. I turned to Goldman.

"Now, Mr. Goldman, withholding aid from Ukraine obviously hurts Ukraine," I said. "It hurts the United States. Does it help any country?"

"The witnesses said that that would help Russia," Goldman said calmly, folding his hands in front of him.

"Did you also hear testimony that these acts by the President, while being wrong and an abuse of power, also harmed U.S. national security?"

"Yes," Goldman said firmly.

"Did you hear anything about how it would harm our credibility?" I continued. "And I would turn you to a conversation Ambassador Volker had on September 14 of this year with a senior Ukrainian official where Ambassador Volker is impressing upon that official that President Zelensky should not investigate his own political opponents. What was thrown back in the face of Ambassador Volker?"

Goldman replied in a calm but forceful voice, "After Ambassador Volker suggested to Mr. Yermak—again, who is here—that they should not investigate the prior President of Ukraine, Mr. Yermak sent back: Oh—said back to him: Oh, like you're encouraging us to investigate Bidens and Clintons," he said.

It was going well. Goldman and I were on the same page. It was time to go for it with the line of questioning Phil Schiliro had helped me put together.

"During Watergate," I began, "the famous phrase from Senator Howard Baker was asked, 'What did the President know, and when did he know it?' There's a reason that no one here has repeated those questions during these hearings. We know what the President did, and we know when he knew it."

The room was quiet. I could feel my words resonating with people and knew I had a rapt audience.

"Mr. Goldman," I continued, "who sent Rudy Giuliani to Ukraine to smear Joe Biden?"

"President Trump," he said, maybe not quite as crisply as I was hoping, but close.

"Who fired the anti-corruption Ambassador in Ukraine, Marie Yovanovitch?"

"President Trump."

"Who told Ambassador Sondland and Ambassador Volker to work with Rudy Giuliani on Ukraine?"

"President Trump," he said again, and even gave it a slight nod for emphasis.

"Who told Vice President Pence to not go to President Zelensky's inauguration?"

"President Trump."

"Who ordered his own Chief of Staff, Mick Mulvaney, to withhold critical military assistance for Ukraine?

"President Trump."

"Who refused to meet with President Zelensky in the Oval Office?"

"President Trump."

"Who ignored on July 25 his own National Security Council's anti-corruption talking points?"

"President Trump."

"Who asked President Zelensky for a favor?"

"President Trump."

"Who personally asked President Zelensky to investigate his political rival, Joe Biden?"

"President Trump."

"Who stood on the White House lawn and confirmed that he wanted Ukraine to investigate Vice President Biden?"

"President Trump."

"Who stood on that same lawn and said that China should also investigate Vice President Biden?"

"President Trump."

"As to anything that we do not know in this investigation, who has blocked us from knowing it?"

"President Trump in the White House."

I'd half-expected the Republicans in the room to knock over a chair in the background or otherwise do something to prevent me from having all the questions in a row in a clean sequence for history to record, and for people watching at home to track clearly, but they were quiet as I wrapped up with one final question.

"So, as it relates to President Trump, is he an incidental player or a central player in this scheme?" I asked Goldman.

"President Trump is *the* central player in this scheme," Goldman said.

"There is a reason that no one has said, 'What did the President know, and when did he know it?'" I concluded. "From the evidence that you have presented, Mr. Goldman, and the Intelligence Committee's findings, we know one thing, and one thing is clear: As it related to this scheme, the President of the United States, Donald J. Trump, knew everything."

It had gone perfectly. I'd achieved my goal of resetting the hearing and bringing us back to what the President had done. For one of the few times in my Congressional career, I had left about thirty seconds of time on the clock. There was no need to vamp. Like a quarterback taking a knee when his team is up at the end of a game, I felt no need to run another play.

"I yield back," I said.

My exchange with Goldman was soon being cited as an important sequence, one that framed the case against Trump in a crisp, concise way that people found immediate and understandable. It also helped take the heat off Goldman—and short-circuited the Republican strategy of staging various distractions and turning a solemn hearing into a sideshow.

That night after the hearing, I ran into Jeffrey Toobin, the former Justice Department lawyer who had long worked as a legal analyst for CNN and *The New Yorker*. He told me the series of questions with Goldman had come across well.

"Dan did a good job of selling it, too," he remarked.

I smiled. "Dan didn't know what I was going to ask," I told Jeff.

He didn't believe me.

"No way," he said, "you guys scripted that."

We really hadn't.

"Why not?" he asked. "You're allowed to talk to him."

True. I certainly could have planned it with Goldman, but as I told Toobin, I wanted the exchange to be natural, not forced or scripted. I had confidence in two things: that Goldman knew the case, and that at his core he was a prosecutor. He would see quickly where I was going and stick to the cadence. That was just how it played out, too.

The House leadership held a meeting at 5:30 p.m. Even though I was part of the leadership, normally I would have skipped the meeting to stay in the hearing. This time, though, Amy Rutkin, Nadler's Chief of Staff, pulled Representative Ted Lieu, Representative Hakeem Jeffries, and me aside.

"I know there are a few members on our committee who have to get to the leadership meeting," she said. "Typically, I'd say I need you to stay at our hearing in case there are more procedural stunts by the Republicans. But I'd like the three of you to go to the leadership meeting to make the case to Speaker Pelosi that the Chairman would like us to have the articles markup on Thursday at the earliest," she said, referring to the process of amending the forthcoming articles of impeachment in preparation for their presentation to the Senate.

We hurried off to the leadership meeting. Our message was that we'd had a good hearing but were hoping to hold off on starting the markup of the forthcoming articles of impeachment until Thursday, December 12. Any sooner, we feared, would not give us or the American people time to consider the weight of the articles. There were also issues with Judiciary Committee bills due to get a Floor vote, which posed obstacles for us holding a simultaneous impeachment markup, and oddly enough, at that time we didn't have a room to use! Ways and Means had its own work and needed its room back, and we had outgrown the Judiciary Committee room, considering the intense public and press interest in our hearings.

When I had a chance to present the case later, I told the Speaker the preference was to go on Thursday at the earliest, and why. The Speaker was intent on doing everything she could to keep the process moving along. The longer we waited to start the markup, the more risk of our spilling over into Friday. Congress wasn't set to be in session, and she was hesitant to have only the Judiciary Committee in Washington on something so consequential. She said she could move the other votes, and the room issue could easily be solved. She would keep us in the historic Ways and Means Committee room.

After the hearing, and the 6:30 p.m. votes session, we reconvened for a Judiciary Committee huddle. The evidence from Intel was now received formally by our committee. Until then, any discussion of possible articles of impeachment had been theoretical. After all, it would have been irresponsible to draft the articles of impeachment before all the evidence was before the committee.

As we walked into the Judiciary Committee conference room, I saw that my pizza protest was continuing to pay off. Tonight, the food was Chinese. We ate as we waited for Nadler to finish his meeting with Speaker Pelosi. It had been a long three days. We sat around the tight conference room table, taken up mostly by the Chinese food, exasperated. *What was next?* we wondered. But we knew. Now we had to put pen to paper and impeach the President.

The Chairman arrived and told us that in the morning, he and the other five chairpersons with jurisdiction (Schiff of Intelligence, Maxine Waters of Financial Services, Richard Neal of Ways and Means, Carolyn Maloney of Oversight, and Eliot Engel of Foreign Affairs) would join Speaker Pelosi at 9 a.m. to announce that we were moving forward on two articles of impeachment. One on abuse of power and one on obstruction of Congress. We would see the text of the articles in the morning, Nadler promised. He and our lawyers would work through the night to write and produce them to be introduced in the morning. He also thanked us for our guidance throughout the weekend, and said our suggestions had been relayed to the Speaker's team drafting the articles. Finally, he encouraged the members to get some rest and be ready to reconvene at eight o'clock the next morning.

No rest for me yet. That was the night we'd planned for my annual dinner with my DC staff to thank them for the incredible work they do all year long, and I didn't want to reschedule. We went to my favorite restaurant in DC, St. Anselm, a steakhouse with great food and service. My staff had been through a lot in 2019, and I wanted to show them as much gratitude as they deserved for all their hard work on everything—we took the majority, I ran for President, the Mueller investigation happened, and then came July 25, which changed everything. All my staff and their significant others joined us. I raised a toast to their commitment not just to me, not just to our office, but to the country—at a time when we needed people of courage and moral clarity.

CHAPTER 41

THE ARTICLES

The impeachment committees focused on the big picture, which was how the impeachment would be processed over time by the public and how its impact would be remembered, not the daily up and down of news media and social media swings. History's verdict would be the ultimate test. If we had not defied the many skeptics and demanded accountability of Donald Trump through the impeachment process, we were all very aware we would have left Trump unchecked. We would in effect have been encouraging him to cheat in another national election and offering him countless more chances along the way to put his personal interests before those of the country. The painful truth lurking in the background at every turn was that if Trump was able to prevail in another election, corrupt as he was, we as Americans had truly crossed the Rubicon. As reliant as Trump was on lies, misinformation, and the help of sworn enemies of the United States, the U.S. experiment in democracy would never be the same if he were given a pass. From Speaker Pelosi to Chairman Schiff to every member of the investigating committees—we all knew that history would judge us for how we handled this challenge.

That was why the idea of pushing to censure Donald Trump, rather than impeaching him, was a nonstarter. Some moderates had floated the idea, but our investigation wasn't about slapping Trump on the wrist and hoping he'd feel bad. After all, Trump had demonstrated time and again that he was incapable of remorse or empathy or, apparently, shame. This was about the viability of our system of government. If ever there was a test case of whether a power-mad would-be monarch running amok as U.S. President could be stopped through the constitutionally mandated provision of impeachment, this was it. Our very real and justifiable concern was that if we didn't impeach Trump for this conduct, then, really, what was the point of having impeachment available at all?

I'd talked privately with many members in tough, vulnerable districts. I'd helped many of these members by visiting their districts and supporting their campaigns, so I knew what they were up against. I'd also learned a lot about the country while on the road as a presidential candidate. The concern expressed to me most by vulnerable House members was this: "We know we have to hold the President accountable. Doing nothing is not an option. But we have to show our constituents that we are not *only* focusing on impeachment."

It was a valid concern, one constantly emphasized by Speaker Pelosi, and we had done all we could to demonstrate our commitment to working on behalf of voters to get things done. We had been holding up our end in the House and more. It was the Senate that was blocking action. While the President was undergoing impeachment proceedings, the House had passed and sent to the Senate more than *400 bills,* 275 of which were bipartisan. The subject of the bills ranged from equal pay for equal work, to ending LGBTQ discrimination in the workplace, to requiring background checks on all firearm purchases.

The night before we announced the articles of impeachment, Speaker Pelosi held a meeting of the Democratic leadership. We'd been making major progress on a trade deal with labor leaders on the pending United States–Mexico–Canada trade agreement, and Pelosi said that an announcement was imminent. This was an essential part of honoring our commitment to keep working for voters, not just holding Donald Trump accountable. As the Speaker put it during that meeting, "How could we walk away from a win for our workers?"

Our lawyers worked hard through the night on the articles of impeachment. We had decisions to make. Should we go with a broader abuse of power charge, contemplating all the crimes the President had committed with one charge? Or should we enumerate all the crimes? Bribery? Extortion? Obstruction of justice? I advocated that we keep the articles focused, to reflect the urgency of what the country faced. This was a crime spree in progress. The President had committed a lot of other crimes, from the Mueller obstruction to violating the Constitution's Emoluments Clause to soliciting foreign contributions to his campaign. But most of those crimes had occurred in the past. The abuse of power represented by inviting a foreign government to help him cheat represented a clear and present danger. Time was ticking by. The election was fast approaching. We couldn't wait for court cases to protect an election he was trying to rig. We were at risk of losing everything.

I believed we could write articles of impeachment that referenced the President's prior conduct, particularly asking for Russia's help in 2016 and obstructing the investigation that followed. "A leopard doesn't change its spots," I argued. When I was a prosecutor and was assigned a case, the first thing I'd do was look at a defendant's rap sheet. "What are the priors?" I'd ask. Priors always had a story to tell. They showed the jurors patterns. They demonstrated, "This is what the defendant does." This was particularly effective with domestic violence cases, where the average victim is abused seven times before calling police. (Indeed, I was a little startled at how often the arguments I heard from Republicans in the impeachment investigation echoed what I used to hear in domestic violence cases. Over and over, they would harp on the fact that President Zelensky said he felt "no pressure." I thought they had to be kidding with that argument. To me, it was obvious that Zelensky would say he'd felt no pressure from Trump. He desperately needed our $391 million in aid to defend his country from Russian aggression. What else was he going to say?) President Trump had priors, and whether he was charged with them or they explained his current conduct, we were going to make sure they were part of the public record we were laying down.

Remarkably, every member was on time for the Judiciary Committee's 8 a.m. meeting to finalize the articles of impeachment. Tired we were, but we were also eager to see where the Speaker and constitutional lawyers had landed, based on the guidance we had provided. Each of us was given a copy of the final draft, but told we had to leave it in the room. To my right was Representative Hank Johnson of Georgia, and to my left, Representative Karen Bass of California. For ten minutes we all read in silence, the only sounds the slow turning of pages, or pens quickly scribbling notes.

The articles argued that Donald Trump had abused his power by asking a foreign government to help him cheat in an election. And by doing so, he had jeopardized our national security and the integrity of our elections. It also alleged that once he was caught, and we launched our investigation, President

Trump had gone to great lengths to obstruct Congress. And, thankfully, it included the Mueller pattern evidence. After the weight of the articles set in, we looked up at our army of staffers. The articles were crisp and they were potent, but we still had questions. We needed to make sure we could defend them to our constituents.

First up was the question: Why not charge the President for his obstructive acts in the Mueller investigation? We were told by Joshua Matz, our in-house constitutional scholar, that we would continue to pursue the obstruction of justice investigation on the Mueller matter in the courts. He also said that if we were successful in the courts before the President's trial in the Senate, we would seek to introduce the pattern evidence via witnesses like former White House counsel Don McGahn. We anticipated that the press, naturally, would obsessively ask why the obstruction of justice article was not included? Were Democrats in retreat? Was this to appeal to moderates? I cautioned against taking that bait or accepting the premise of that question. We had two serious articles, and that should be the focus.

"Let's not get caught up in the ticktock process story of how we got here," I said. "We are here. And that's what's most important."

We had to avoid process traps. Next, we anticipated that Republicans would try to run with the spurious argument that there were "no federal crimes charged here." I'd heard it repeatedly over the past few weeks. "You can't impeach a President who didn't commit a crime!" my GOP colleagues claimed. It was a trap of an argument. First, the President's own Department of Justice policy made it clear that the President couldn't be charged with a crime. We'd learned our lesson on that from Mueller. Most prosecutors believed that once President Trump left office, he would indeed be charged for many crimes. Finally, and most important, the President had committed the highest of crimes, crimes against the Constitution. And in America, the Constitution is the supreme law of the land. Oversight consultant Norm Eisen insisted we focus on that argument if pressed about the President's crimes. He reminded us: All laws are derived from the Constitution, not the other way around.

Before we left the committee room, Amy Rutkin reminded us we still had to sort out when we would formally debate the articles of impeachment in our committee. Would it be Wednesday or Thursday? We wanted to allow at least twenty-four hours between presenting the articles of impeachment and starting the first hearing. That was for everyone's benefit: ours, so we could let the articles sink in, process them, and defend them; for the public; and out of fairness to our colleagues.

Cedric Richmond, my colleague from Louisiana, offered a compromise: Let's start Wednesday night, in prime time, so the American people, especially working people, could hear our opening statements. That, Cedric said, was what had occurred with Watergate. It was a brilliant idea, but would it be well received by Speaker Pelosi? Within fifteen minutes word came that Cedric's idea was a go.

"Be real with me, you just wanted to play a night game," I later kidded Cedric, a former college star pitcher who is also our best player in the annual Congressional Baseball Game for Charity.

"Yeah, who doesn't love a night game?" he joked.

Chairman Nadler headed to the Sam Rayburn Room, a large space just off the Floor of the House, "to join Chairmen Schiff, Neal, and Engle, Chairwoman Waters and Maloney, and Speaker Pelosi for a press conference announcing the articles of impeachment. In the caucus rooms where we were meeting, the televisions were turned on with the volume up, as we waited for the press conference.

After the Speaker made her announcement, she joined us at the caucus meeting. But she didn't come to talk about impeachment. She told the caucus that she had just struck a deal with labor and Mexico that would give us the United States–Mexico–Canada trade deal that would help American workers. She also said we would be voting this week on a bipartisan, bicameral agreement on the defense spending bill. Then she told us to get ready for the prescription drug reform bill, which we would debate and vote on either this week or next. Oh yeah, she mentioned, we were also passing a farmworkers bill, to allow more rights for those who toiled away to put food on our tables. To Pelosi, sure, we were working on impeachment, and that was important. But she was hell-bent on showing that impeachment wasn't going to define her or our caucus. She wanted us all to go back to our districts before Christmas ready to show our constituents that we were hard at work for them.

A confused reporter asked me as I left the caucus meeting about the USMCA deal: "How can you work with the President when you're impeaching him?"

I had expected as much, but the question made no sense; it was a product of reporters buying into story lines pushed by defenders of the President. No, impeachment was not driven primarily by partisanship. That was a false narrative, one history would have little trouble dispensing with. But if the media took the easy way out again and again, and flogged the story line that everything was Democrats versus Republicans, Pelosi versus Trump, feuding politicians, then it followed that substantive, important developments like the trade bill would be treated as secondary. If you're only looking for drama, you're going to miss a lot. I get that a certain amount of cynicism, assuming the worst, is always going to be endemic to the Washington press corps, but the reality is that most members of Congress came to Washington to try to get something done. And most of us understood that this meant taking wins where we could get them, even if political foes won, too. That's okay, so long as the American people win.

Speaking of taking wins and not just staying focused on impeachment, also that morning, I attended a Science, Space, and Technology Committee hearing. I was allowed to sit in as a guest member for the hearing on the rare earth elements bill I'd authored in 2014. With the majority, we were finally in the position to pass it and move toward leveling the playing field against China. I walked into the committee room, noticing that it was much smaller than the Ways and Means room where I had spent most of the last month. It was also much quieter. Other than the members and witnesses, there were only a handful of people in the audience. Just an hour before, I had been reading yet-to-be-introduced articles of impeachment against the President of the United States. Now I was asking questions of four scientists about the seventeen rare earth elements. I'd seethed over Mick Mulvaney's intervention to kill the bill years earlier, a painful lesson for me in how little Washington creatures like Mulvaney, ever in thrall to right-wing interest groups, cared about their responsibility to the public, but now the bill was finally moving forward.

That afternoon, once the articles of impeachment were actually introduced, and my copy delivered to my office by Judiciary Committee staff, we convened again to prep for Wednesday's opening statements. This time, we were back in the Judiciary Committee hearing room. Rutkin asked me to explain my idea of forming a "strike team" to respond to baseless GOP attacks on process or in defense of what the President had done. I had recommended that we not take the bait for every crazy defense the GOP made or every attack they lodged. I urged that, instead, we plan on having a few members ready to respond on particular issues. Let the Republicans be crazy and all over the place. We'd be surgical and purposeful. After all, it was the discipline we showed that had gotten us here, I argued. Let's keep it going. Hakeem Jeffries and I had talked about this the day before. He was a big supporter of the idea and backed me up. The next day, Rutkin would assign four of us to the strike team. Me, Hakeem, David Cicilline, and Val Demings. We were each given subject matter areas, and each would be responsible for responding if the Republicans "went there." I was to respond to any "How can you impeach someone who hasn't committed a crime?" argument. It was the perfect task for me to take on. I couldn't wait.

That night, I was back on *Hardball with Chris Matthews*. He'd read the articles of impeachment and found them tightly argued and powerful. Thinking like a former Hill Chief of Staff, he was having a hard time understanding what defense the Republicans were going to use.

"How does a Republican colleague of yours . . . how does somebody defend the charge that Trump has obstructed, when he hasn't turned over a single piece of paper or a single live witness?" Chris asked. "How do you deny that's defiance and obstruction of the Congress?"

Not a tough question for me. "They have actually never defended that, Chris," I said. "Actually, in all of the hearings you have seen, it's just attacks on us, as members. It's attacks on the process. No one has defended the President's cheating scheme with Ukraine. No one has defended him refusing to give us documents."

I made the added point that the upshot was how to think about what the President had done. "We know what he did," I said. "It's about what *we* should do. Should we do *nothing*? Should we allow this to continue? Should we allow future Presidents to do this? Or should we say we have a duty under the Constitution to act, and now is the time to act?"

The next evening, when we started the televised debate on the articles of impeachment, I decided to make my argument as relatable as possible and talk about my Iowa childhood, once I'd called my father to clear the idea with him first.

"When I was five, my dad was the police chief of Algona, Iowa," I said. "He was and still is a law-and-order guy, everything by the book. So, that year, when the county fair was going on and the fire chief called him and told him that cars were parked illegally in the fire lane, it wasn't a close call for my dad. He knew what to do." And right there, during the debate on the articles of impeachment, I told the story of how my dad was told to fix the tickets and refused. No one was above the law, not even the mayor, my dad's boss.

"We packed up our little family and moved west," I continued. "It was my first lesson in politics, abuse of power, and executive arrogance. And watching these proceedings, and watching my colleagues across the aisle ignore and deny facts in blind defense of the President of the United States, I'm certain that had they been in Algona, they, too, would have supported that local mayor."

I talked about the courage of Ambassador Yovanovitch and Lt. Col. Vindman and Dr. Hill in standing up for the principle that no one is above the law, and closed by talking about knowing right from wrong. "Imagine you're a kid with a paper route, it's the first job that so many Americans have held, and the owner of the local paper tells you, you're due for a raise, and I'm going to give you that raise, but first, I need you to remove our competitors' paper from every house on your route," I said. "A ten-year-old should know right from wrong, but our children will only know right from wrong if we lead by example. Wrong is wrong, from your workplace to the White House. There's no time to spare here. No time to waste. This is a constitutional crime spree."

CHAPTER 42

DEBATE NIGHT

The morning of our epic fourteen-hour debate on the articles of impeachment, I was up early. Nelson started crying at 5:30 a.m. and wanted to watch Blippi, a children's YouTube personality. It was way too early for Blippi. I could barely stand watching Blippi during daylight. This was going to be a long day, I knew, even if we did have one ray of hope. There was no time limit for the end of debate, and we were ready to go as long as we needed, but we'd found out the Republicans were all hoping to be out of there between 5 and 7 p.m., to attend the White House Christmas party. We weren't going to let them know we knew.

That morning at the House gym, I ended up one treadmill over from Doug Collins. On another day, we might have said hello and exchanged "I can't wait to get home for the weekend" small talk. Not that morning. Collins didn't even acknowledge me, nor I him. We'd both seen more than enough of each other during the impeachment investigation.

Collins carried on with a surly, put-upon attitude that made clear he liked to think of himself as some kind of victim. He took things personally when that made no sense at all. In our first few years in Congress, our offices were near one another in Cannon and we'd talked fairly often. We had a rapport based on mutual respect for one another's legal experience and perspective. That changed during the Trump administration. Collins went out of his way to be nasty, and even tried to mock me whenever he could.

From the gym, I hustled to a CNN camera for an 8:15 a.m. Wolf Blitzer interview, and then down to the Intel Committee space. The night before, we were notified that Chairman Schiff had obtained new, classified information regarding Pence advisor Jennifer Williams's testimony to Intelligence Committee members. During Williams's deposition, we had asked her about a September 17 call between Vice President Pence and President Zelensky.

Williams had said she couldn't talk about the call because it was classified. This had struck us as fishy. We pressed and pressed, but she would not tell us more.

We finally devised a work-around. The Vice President had refused to declassify the call, so the Intel Committee made an arrangement with Williams to come into the SCIF with her lawyer and write out a detailed description of it. Even though the Vice President was blocking her from declassifying what she'd heard, she could transmit the information to us through classified channels like the SCIF. Schiff then sent a letter to Vice President Pence, arguing that a review of the information Williams had shared showed that the call was not in fact classified, and again requesting that Pence declassify the information. Again, he refused.

This felt familiar. Pence's refusal to declassify the call record was consistent with the National Security Council's unusual decision to move Trump's July 25 call with President Zelensky into a top-secret classified server. The law forbids the government from using classified servers, or the classification process generally, to shield a President and his administration from embarrassing information.

Judiciary Committee members would have to come in and view the materials "in camera," meaning read-only, at the Intel spaces. We couldn't take any notes outside the room or discuss the contents of what Williams had shared. It wasn't as if we didn't already have enough to do. I knew this was important, but I was weighing whether I should make time in a crazy schedule that day to review the materials right away, or wait until after the committee voted to impeach.

"Mr. Schiff believes every Judiciary Committee member should see this before they vote," an Intel staffer told me.

I can't reveal any details, but what I saw when I went to the Intel space at around 8:20 that morning only reinforced for me the real-time need to protect our country from the President's effort to work with a foreign government to cheat our election. Because I was on both committees, I was bombarded with texts from Judiciary Committee members, asking, "Should we go see it?" I texted them all back to say, "Yes, it's relevant."

When the committee huddled in the anteroom of the Ways and Means Committee room before taking our seats, I had one last chat with Barry Berke.

My assignment on the strike team was to emphasize that the President had committed not only crimes against the Constitution but also, if he were to have an honest Department of Justice investigating him, statutory crimes.

"These crimes have been vetted by the Speaker's lawyer?" I asked Berke, not for the first time.

"Yes," he assured me, "I just checked again."

I was committed to being a team player, and that meant not getting ahead of others on the team, particularly the Speaker. Barry's words were my green light. It was 8:55 a.m. Amy Rutkin started circling the members.

"I need everyone to go out to their seats so the Chairman can come out," she told us.

"Places, people!" I yelled, joking that it felt like we were back in high school theater. I'd been saying the same thing at the start of every hearing, but it still brought quizzical looks.

"I should have known you were the high school drama type," Rutkin said with a smile.

I smiled back. "It didn't last long."

I took my seat, armed with the first Starbucks Grande Mocha of three I'd drink that day. We had prepared for weeks to make our case. Now we had to rise to the occasion—and not take the Republicans' bait.

"There are no crimes here?" I started, my voice rising. "That is the defense my colleagues across the aisle are putting forward?"

I paused as if waiting for an actual answer.

"How about the highest crime that one who holds public office could commit, a crime against our Constitution?" I continued, listing his offenses as "abusing his office, cheating in an election, inviting foreign interference for a purely personal gain while jeopardizing our national security and the integrity of our elections." I summed up: "After all, we in Congress are not criminal prosecutors, we do not prosecute crimes. We protect the Constitution."

From there, it was my chance to go back to the place I have always felt most comfortable, the courtroom. I enjoyed it. For a prosecutor, it's a satisfying feeling to have the facts and the law on your side. You can make your case with confidence and conviction. I started with bribery of public officials, and explained that it occurs when a public official "demands or seeks anything of value personally in return for being influenced in the performance of an official act." I continued: "President Trump demanded and sought the announcement and conduct of politically motivated investigations by President Zelensky," I said, and then went through the various specific requirements of the law and how they matched up with Trump's behavior. As I summed it up, "President Trump behaved corruptly throughout this course of conduct because he used his official office in exchange to seek a private benefit."

Then I described a second crime Trump had committed, honest services fraud, as defined in 18 U.S. Code §1346. "President Trump knowingly and willfully orchestrated a scheme to defraud the American people of his honest services as President of the United States," I said.

Before I could say much more, I was interrupted by a Republican member, asking if I would yield for a question. Why would I do that? Process, process, process, obstruction, obstruction, obstruction.

"I will not yield," I said. "Clearly the July 25 phone call constitutes a wire communication," I added, a necessary component to establish honest services fraud. "There you have it," I said. "At least two criminal statutory crimes. However, all of these conversations about statutory crimes are moot because the President of the United States refuses to allow his own Department of Justice to indict him. So the President may be charged with crimes one day, but that's not what we're doing here on this day."

I closed, talking about Trump "jeopardizing the integrity of your vote for a purely political purpose and a purely personal gain," and my time was up.

Our debate lasted all day and into the night, so commentators had plenty of time to pore over our words. On CNN, Jake Tapper called it an "interesting moment" when, as a former prosecutor, I laid out Trump's actual statutory crimes. He asked his guest, CNN legal analyst Laura Coates, what she thought of the case I'd articulated. She called it "a good one and very persuasive," but pointed out that we had more work to do to "show the American people . . . what constitutes an abuse of power" and needed to hammer home what was at stake.

Watching news coverage and checking social media, I kept seeing this basic struggle over constitutional authority reduced to a "clash" of "partisans." Sometimes I'd almost think they had it right. I'd challenge myself: *Could I really be so sure that I wasn't just enflamed by passion, riled up and blinded by the heat of the moment? My side against their side?* Actually, I could.

There were a lot of tells. Which side was running scared, worried more about a sharply worded tweet than about what voters back home thought? Which side tended to yell most of the time and made a point of ignoring most of anything anyone else said? To me, if you're calm and reasonable and solemn about doing your job, you're probably on firmer footing than the loudmouths trying to intimidate and bully.

Two hours before we convened that day, the President of the United States had taken to Twitter to attack a sixteen-year-old girl with Asperger's syndrome. Yes, it was a new low for a man committed to forever plumbing the depths of bad taste, all to get a reaction. *Time* magazine had named Swedish teenage climate activist Greta Thunberg "Person of the Year." Trump was, as we knew, obsessed with the cover of *Time,* and it was clear he was going to throw a temper tantrum over this.

"So ridiculous," Trump tweeted that morning. "Greta must work on her Anger Management problem, then go to a good old fashioned movie with a friend! Chill Greta, Chill!"

I wasn't worried about Thunberg—she would be just fine, and knew how to laugh off the demented attacks of bitter old men clueless about climate change—but it was embarrassing to have a President who was so self-obsessed and vain.

"In my colleagues' efforts to defend this President, you want him to be someone he's not," I told the Judiciary Committee that night just before 8:30 p.m. "You want him to be someone he is telling you he is not. You're trying to defend the call in so many different ways, and he's saying, 'Guys, it was a perfect call.' He is not who you want him to be."

Every time I entered a courtroom as a prosecutor, I always did my best to take a step back and make sure that I showed a healthy respect for human dignity and human life. There are things you just don't do, like talk loudly and disrespectfully at a funeral, or smirk and joke when someone is talking seriously about people dying. Yet that is exactly what Collins did when I spoke about the ultimate consequences of Trump's denying military aid to Ukraine.

"And let me tell you how selfish his acts were," I continued. "Ranking Member Collins, you can deny this as much as you want. People died in Ukraine at the hands of Russia. And Ukraine, since September 2018, when it was voted on by Congress, was counting on our support. One year passed, and people died. You may not want to think about that. It may be hard for you to think about that, but they died when this selfish, selfish person withheld the aid for his own personal gain."

I wasn't mincing words. Collins had been horsing around all day, mumbling in that meandering auctioneer voice of his, carrying on like he was a rowdy schoolboy, not a U.S. Congressman. He even had the temerity to claim it was the Democrats who lacked solemnity. (Though he didn't put it quite that way. As the *New York Times* noted, "Collins, on three occasions questioned what he called the 'solemn-enity' that Democrats kept claiming they were bringing to these proceedings.")

Collins was stung by my comments, as I expected him to be, but I didn't think he'd ramble on quite so incoherently, bouncing from a lame charge that I was speaking "untruths" to the random notion that I had only said what I did because I wanted to be an impeachment manager. True, like many of my colleagues, I'd let the Speaker know I would love to be an impeachment manager and felt that as a member of both the Judiciary and Intelligence Committees, as well as a former prosecutor, I'd be a strong asset to the team, but I knew Pelosi would weigh many factors in her choice and make a great decision. This was vintage Collins, making accusations of ambition. *He's projecting again,* I thought. But none of it showed that he cared about the real-world consequences of the corrupt actions of a President he had protected at every turn.

It was a grueling day. We headed to the Floor for votes at one point, taking a short break, and then came back to continue the debate. Riding in a crowded elevator, I heard Republican Congressman Mike Johnson of Louisiana comment offhandedly to another member, "The White House wants us to wrap this up, so I don't know how much longer our hearing will last."

I didn't know what to make of his comment. Was that really the view of the White House? After all, we were kicking their asses in the debate. The Republicans were complaining over and over about process. We were hammering home point after point about what the President had done and why people should care.

The later it got that evening, the more we wondered if the Republicans were really going to wave the white flag so they could get to their White House Christmas party. In the days leading up to the debate, a few reporters had gently probed for information on how long it would last, asking questions like "How long do I have to stay?" or "When do you think you'll be done on Thursday?" or even "Won't the Republicans want to make it to the White House?"

I played dumb and shrugged. I'd been to plenty of White House Christmas parties. Men wore tuxedos. Women wore gowns. A day or so after, you were emailed your high-resolution picture with the President. Post it to social media. It's a big deal. We needed no further proof than Mrs. Doug Collins, sitting in the hearing room dressed to the nines in a gown and ready for a ball. *So why were they continuing on and on, making the same points?* we wondered. We soon got our answer.

"We are ready to go all night," Collins said during the debate. "We have plenty of balls we all can be invited to."

I went to the back anteroom, where the staff had assembled. Rutkin told me she had learned that the press had figured out the Republicans intended on ending before the White House party. They were caught. To show that this was wrong—they weren't going to flee such an important debate for a party—they had to do the opposite and engage like mad. It was like we were caught in a loop: "Biden. Burisma. Schiff. Whistleblower. No harm, no foul. They got the aid. No quid pro quo." Over and over they went.

We'd all agreed we would not vote in the dead of night on impeachment, but our team was under instructions from the Speaker's office to avoid, if we could, dragging the debate into Friday. Back in the anteroom, I told Rutkin that I thought we had to move to end the debate as the only alternative to a dead-of-the-night vote. Ending the debate had its risks. It could appear that we were railroading the President. I argued, however, that as we neared

9 p.m., we'd been debating almost twelve hours. The same points were being repeated over and over. Most Americans would agree that that was long enough. A few of my colleagues who had served much longer than I argued that we had to debate as long as the Republicans insisted. It would set a bad precedent, they argued, to cut off the debate.

My impatience was showing. "They're not saying anything new," I said. "They got caught trying to end early for the White House ball and now they want to make us take this to the dead of night for a vote."

I suggested we reach out and put the updated situation to the Speaker, to see if she would sign off on having the impeachment vote on Friday. I called her. No answer. I texted. No response. It turned out Pelosi was in New York that night being honored—along with *Harry Potter* creator J. K. Rowling—as one of the recipients of the Robert F. Kennedy Ripple of Hope Award. Barack Obama was part of the ceremony, via a video clip he'd put together to honor Pelosi. "She is tough, she knows her stuff, listens and understands," the former President said. "She has a moral compass and knows what's important."

No wonder she wasn't picking up. We were reaching a panic. Rutkin, Jeffries, and I huddled and agreed to take a thirty-minute break, the first in twelve hours (besides that brief break to vote). We'd have dinner and then regroup.

"She's okay with a morning vote," Rutkin told us during the break. Fortunately, our staff had reached the Speaker's staff, and the Speaker had given us the green light.

For the past few hours we had been keeping our powder dry, hopeful the GOP was ready to vote on the articles of impeachment and make their party. We resisted the temptation to respond to their myriad insane arguments. But we also knew—and were lamenting on our group text—that our not responding had allowed the GOP to own the airwaves. They were going five-minute block to five-minute block without any Democrat responding to torpedo their wild conspiracy theories. Now that we had permission to vote in the morning, we were not on any time limit and could start fighting back again. We felt liberated. We agreed that we would not tell the Republicans that we were voting in the morning. We figured if we got all the amendments out of the way, they'd lose steam, and we could recess at a late hour to a morning vote. Sure enough, as 11 p.m. approached, it was clear the Republicans were throwing in the towel.

We had made our points—and worn down the Republicans. After Collins made his close, Val Demings made ours. She made thunderous points about right and wrong and law and order. Then it went back to Nadler. He was brief. He noted that it'd been a long day and we'd been debating for more than fourteen hours. He recommended we get some sleep, consult our consciences, and vote in the morning. Then he loudly pounded the gavel.

"We stand in recess," he proclaimed.

The Republicans were stunned. I never saw so many shocked looks. They had wanted a late-night vote so they could cry foul. Nadler got up, and we all walked back to the anteroom. Collins was shouting; Louie Gohmert joined in. They'd be raked over the coals on Twitter and the press. They were essentially complaining they'd have to work on a Friday, a complaint almost no American could identify with. They were caught, doubly caught. Caught trying to end the evening early for a White House party and caught trying to have a late-night vote.

CHAPTER 43

"IF WE CAN JUST GET THROUGH TOMORROW"

One day in the midst of the impeachment process, my phone started lighting up with texts from colleagues, friends, and reporters, all asking me variations on "Is it true?" and "Would he really leave??" and "WTF." I had no idea what they were talking about.

Then I went on Twitter. A freshman Congressman from New Jersey, Jeff Van Drew, had decided to ditch the Democratic Party and cast his lot with the Republicans. This wasn't entirely out of the blue (so to speak). Van Drew had been one of two Democrats to vote against opening the impeachment inquiry. Every story that mentioned Van Drew always referenced how "vulnerable" he was—that is, terrified of being tweeted at by the President. Trump had carried his district 50.6 percent to Hillary's 46 percent.

His vote on the inquiry had disappointed me. It didn't take much courage to stand for accountability, as no one thought a vote in favor of holding an inquiry in any way amounted to a commitment to vote for impeachment. How in the world could your reaction to the epic, unending corruption of the Trump years be "Nothing to see here!"

I'd never talked in detail with Van Drew about his political thinking. I knew he had worked for years as a dentist and came from South Jersey. I knew he liked to wear shiny suits with pocket squares. I also knew he wasn't at all shy about hitting me up for money every chance he could. He didn't even bother to make a pitch, just handed me a three-by-five card he expected me to read. I am not making this up. Since Van Drew was so "vulnerable," and I as a good Democrat did not want us to lose his House seat to a Republican, the card directed me to please donate $1,000 or $2,000 to his reelection fund before the end of every fund-raising quarter.

"Hey, Eric, I hope you can help," he'd say after thrusting another of those cards in my hand. Then he'd work the caucus and hand out dozens more.

We had a lot of "Frontline" Democrats in vulnerable districts deserving of special help. In the 2018 midterm elections, we'd picked up an amazing forty-one seats, our biggest net pickup in the House since the 1974 elections. Thirty incumbent House Republicans lost their seats to Democratic challengers. Thirty-six Republicans chose not to seek reelection, including Frank LoBiondo of South Jersey, compared to just eighteen Democrats, leading to thirteen Democratic pickups in formerly Republican districts, including Jeff Van Drew, who won LoBiondo's district. In 2016, the district had gone for Trump, but in four out of five previous presidential elections, it had been solidly Democratic, twice giving Obama an eight-percentage-point margin.

I didn't understand what Van Drew was seeing that I wasn't. What was he seeing differently from countless other Democrats in vulnerable districts who had gotten behind impeachment because it was the right thing to do? After all, we had launched our impeachment inquiry on the steam of the "National Security Dems," the seven freshmen who wrote that op-ed in the *Washington Post*. They were supporting an impeachment inquiry. If they could do it, why not Van Drew?

During the investigation, we'd often checked in with the National Security Dems, or they checked in with us, telling us how our inquiry was being viewed in their conservative districts. They impressed upon us the need to be careful with our language when describing the President, to resist partisanship, and always, when on television, to talk about other non-impeachment issues we were working on in Congress. I kept these concerns in mind anytime I did an interview. I had no idea what it was like to be a Frontline Member. My situation was the opposite: If I was ever going to face a primary challenge, it would come from my left, and if I lost, the party would not lose a seat, and the balance of power in Congress would not shift. We needed these Frontline Members. Without their winning in 2018, we wouldn't have been in the position to hold the President accountable. Without their winning, we would never have known about the July 25 phone call.

New Jersey Governor Phil Murphy and other state Democrats were outraged that Van Drew was opposing the impeachment inquiry, and they made clear he was unlikely to have their support. Fewer than 30 percent of Democratic voters believed Van Drew deserved reelection and over 60 percent said they'd vote for someone else. Van Drew wasn't leaving the party out of some principled concern. He was leaving because he just wanted to keep his job. He didn't see a path to keeping it as a Democrat. So, he would seek to do so as a Republican.

"Jeff stabbed us in the back, certainly," Atlantic County Democratic Chairman Michael Suleiman told the *Philadelphia Inquirer*. "It's disgusting. It's a disgrace. Good riddance."

Van Drew's move was exactly what bothered me about Washington: No one was willing to lose their job for doing what they believed was right. If he truly believed we shouldn't impeach, he should have stuck to his guns and then paid the price, whatever it was. But to switch parties because he couldn't stomach losing as a Democrat—that was cowardice. Van Drew had voted with President Trump only 7 percent of the time, and now he was running to Trump for political cover. I viewed this play as no different from that made by Republicans unwilling to speak up and risk losing their jobs by being challenged in a primary. It was a blatant lack of courage.

I'd been reading up on one of the great formative displays of courage in our nation's history. It's not a well-known chapter, but still an important one. In 1797, John Adams was in his first year as U.S. President, only the second President in the young country's history after George Washington. France had been a crucial ally in the War for Independence, but tensions had built up, and we were about to enter into an undeclared war with the French called the Quasi-War, mostly featuring attacks at sea. Adams sent three emissaries to France, the far larger and more powerful country, to try to negotiate peace, only to find that the French foreign minister, Talleyrand, was demanding a "favor"—sound familiar?—in the form of a sizable bribe, before he would even begin negotiations.

"Faced with this shakedown, Adams didn't shrug and pay the bribe," I wrote in an op-ed for NBC News. "Instead, he asked Congress to arm American vessels, shore up our coastal defenses, and manufacture more arms, all as prelude to potentially waging war against France. . . . Adams publicly released the letters he'd received from his envoys laying bare Talleyrand's extortion, bribery, and abuse of power. The only redaction he made was to change the French agents' names to 'X, Y and Z,' respectively." I found Adams's courage inspiring. Studying the XYZ Affair, as it came to be known, offered me a sense of what it's like to be the smaller, weaker country and have something like that done to you.

The night before the House vote on whether to impeach Donald Trump, we had a meeting of the Democratic leadership. Speaker Pelosi had always encouraged me to speak up if I had something to bring to her, so I did.

"Speaker, you don't need any homework from me, you're busy enough," I told her that night. "But I was reading about John Adams and I came across the XYZ Affair."

She knew immediately what I was talking about.

"It was the 1797 version of 'I would like you to do us a favor, though,'" I said.

"That's right," she said quickly, smiling.

As she was wrapping up the meeting, looking at how far we'd come since she'd made the decision to support an official impeachment inquiry, she said something that surprised me. "If we can just get through tomorrow, I think we'll come out in okay shape," she said.

I didn't hesitate to push back.

"Speaker, come on," I said. "'Okay shape'? You're downplaying how you've handled this. I think history will judge us well for how we've done this, start to finish. Speaker, we're going to come out more than okay."

She did not respond to that.

Nancy Pelosi has never done an end zone dance. No one has ever seen that. I understood her mind-set. She meant that we had done our jobs and borne a historic burden. In a process fraught with so many pitfalls and land mines, and so much incoming from the other side, we will have come through this without having made errors or let anything throw us off. It would be up to history to judge our ultimate effectiveness.

CHAPTER 44

FOREVER IMPEACHED

Donald Trump, whatever you might have heard, absolutely hated the idea of being impeached. I never for a second bought into the notion that he didn't care or actually wanted to be impeached. No way. Trump was offended deep down at the idea of being branded in history as a loser. He hated the word *impeachment*. He called it dirty and ugly. If Trump understood anything, it was branding. For all his work to create a public image for himself, he knew that if the House voted to impeach him, and he became one of only three Presidents ever to carry that badge of infamy, his obituaries would all mention this permanent stain on his record in their lead paragraphs.

If anyone needed to be reminded of his true feelings, Trump himself helpfully unleashed a tirade just before his impeachment that demonstrated how desperately he hated what was about to happen to him. For some odd reason—and you know there's a colorful backstory on this one—Trump decided it was a good idea to send a six-page screed to Speaker Pelosi complaining about—well, just about everything. It read like a compilation of tweets, a Christmas letter compendium of some of Trump's more unhinged social media verbiage from the previous year, all marinated in his distinctive style of outraged self-pity.

"You have cheapened the importance of the very ugly word, impeachment!" Trump declared high up in the letter.

What did that even mean? It hurt the brain to try to figure out what he thought he was conveying.

Stephen Colbert read that line out loud on CBS, in his Trump voice, then switched to his own voice to say, "Happy now, Nancy? You've cheapened something very ugly. That goes against everything Trump stands for, making very ugly things extremely expensive."

But it wasn't at all funny; it was scary—or, as Speaker Pelosi put it, "really sick."

In his letter, Trump touched on some flimsy, not-even-close-to-persuasive lines of defense, bemoaned the "great damage and hurt" Pelosi had supposedly inflicted on him, and rolled into a public display of denial so transparent that it almost seemed like a cry for help. This was a fanboy President who idolized the authoritarian style of Russian President Putin and had helped him at every turn, including by denying Ukraine the nearly $400 million in security assistance to fend off Russian expansionism. It was a little rich to read Trump's refrain in the letter: "I have been far tougher on Russia than President Obama ever even thought to be."

The impeachment process wasn't about hurting anyone. It wasn't about inflicting damage on Trump or his family members. It was about respecting the democratic traditions of this great country, and insisting on holding a rogue President accountable. Trump had confessed to the crime, and the only issue was whether he was above the law.

Elsewhere in the letter, Trump claimed that he was writing it for history, "to put my thoughts on a permanent and indelible record." I'm writing this book for history, for the history my son, Nelson, and daughter, Cricket, will live, and for the history their children and grandchildren will study.

I woke up on the morning of December 18, 2019, Impeachment Day, feeling the weight of history. I had two minutes to speak that day for the debate on the House Floor, and I knew I'd be speaking to history. How did I want to use the time? I went back and forth on that.

I always thought back to what worked for me as a prosecutor, and sometimes that helped give me ideas. I knew just what I would have done that day if I'd have been arguing the case against Trump in a courtroom: I'd have taken the ten questions I'd asked Dan Goldman, each with the answer "President Trump," and put them on poster board puzzle pieces. One by one, I'd have read the questions and pulled off a puzzle piece Velcroed to a picture underneath—and at the end, when all ten pieces had been removed, nothing would be left but a picture of Trump. I loved the idea, but it just wouldn't. have worked on the House Floor.

Finally, I decided it was time to stop kicking ideas around and put pen to paper. Without staff or anyone else, I sat at my desk and wrote in longhand on a yellow legal pad, as I always do. Sometimes the temptation is to put extra pressure on yourself, thinking you have to come up with something new every time, something original and surprising, but the truth is that, for a prosecutor, repetition is one of your greatest weapons. My ten questions to Goldman had resonated and been widely cited. I knew I wanted to bring them back in a new way.

This was about the Constitution and about the vision of the Founding Fathers. That's what we went back to in shaping the articles of impeachment. We wanted to hold the President to account on what we thought was the highest of high crimes, abuse of power. The worst thing someone in power can do is abuse their power and betray the public trust. I used the second half of my two minutes to put Trump's crimes into a deeper context, with a call to stand up for the Constitution.

Just in the last couple of days, as we neared the culmination of all our work, I'd been thinking about how best to convey why impeachment was absolutely necessary. The argument we had kept hearing was: *Why do this if the outcome in the Senate is a foregone conclusion? Why not wait for the election and vote Trump out?* Putting aside the urgency to act and stop Trump from trying to rig the 2020 election, as he was actively seeking to do—a code red urgency on its own—an even better point was: Donald Trump is a bully, and like most bullies, he is also a coward. When people pushed back, Trump backed down. We'd seen it time and again.

I remembered what my father had taught me when I was a kid: "If someone bullies you around, you stand up to them." My dad was right when I was in middle school, and his words were still true today.

Trump was challenged on illegally withholding much-needed security assistance to Ukraine, and he backed down. The Republicans kept saying, "No harm, no foul, they got the aid." Nice try. The only reason the Ukrainians got the aid was that Trump had gotten caught. The lesson was: Keep catching him. Hold him accountable, and he just might do the right thing. We all have to stay on him, and that goes for Congress, it goes for the women and men of the media, and it goes for every American at home. We may not stop everything, we may not catch everything, but standing up to him works.

I finished the text I was going to read that day and sent it to three people for feedback: Dan Goldman, whom I'd worked together with so closely on the Intel Committee, and Judiciary staffers Barry Berke and Sarah Istel. All three had a good sense of where I was and what we wanted to communicate to the public. Over the course of the day, they helped me tighten up the text.

A couple of moments from that day stand out. One was when I had a chance to get in a quick workout. I got down to the gym to find that it had been decorated for Christmas—there were snowflakes and garlands all over the place and the songs "White Christmas" and "Jingle Bells" and "Let It Snow!" were playing on the sound system. It was jarring to say the least. It took me thirty seconds before it really sunk in how bizarre this was: Upstairs, where a historic impeachment vote was about to happen, Democrats and Republicans were anything but merry, but down here, in the House gym it was like Rockefeller Center over the holidays.

I also told my staff I was going to leave to go see Nelson at his preschool, and the idea did not go over well. I knew I'd get home late and not be able to put him to bed that night, so I really wanted to see him. But this was maybe forty-five minutes before I was scheduled to speak on the Floor. "Do not leave!" my staff implored me. "Please, just wake him up when you get home. If you get called on and you're not there, it's going to be really bad." The school was only five minutes away. I raced over there.

It was funny, I had the impeachment debate going on and I arrived at the preschool in my suit. Everyone else was picking up their kids in sweats or whatever else they'd had on. It was cool to see Nelson. He had no idea what was going on. Why would he? He was just happy to see me.

"Daddy!" he called out and came running to me.

I asked his preschool teacher if he'd taken his nap, because that's always the first question you have as a parent. No, he hadn't. I gave him a kiss and helped my wife put him into the car seat. He'd be cranky, and I felt extra bad for Brittany. She had to go home with a toddler who hadn't had a nap. I was about to go back and listen to a lot of Republicans who sounded like they hadn't taken one, either. I wasn't sure who had it worse.

It had been agreed that I would follow Chairman Schiff and have my two minutes during the afternoon Intelligence Committee time, following the Judiciary Committee earlier. Back from Nelson's preschool, I went to the Floor and sat in the front row while Schiff spoke, partly because I was next, but also because I wanted to be right there, as close as I could. Anytime Schiff speaks, you listen. His arguments have the quality of being almost poetic, in the sense that every word is so well chosen, so purposeful, and there is always a deeper meaning behind his words and a structure to his arguments that put him in a league of his own. My Republican colleagues were so outmatched that they would bristle when he spoke. You would hear them making outbursts, against all protocol, which they don't do for many others, but it just showed how effective Schiff was.

But that day, as Schiff solemnly stepped up to the lectern, saying he was rising to support the impeachment of President Donald J. Trump, the chamber was silent and still. He opened his argument that day with a quotation from the 18th century.

"'When a man unprincipled in private life, desperate in his fortune, bold in his temper, possessed of considerable talents, having the advantage of military habits, despotic in his ordinary demeanor, known to have scoffed in private at the principles of liberty, when such a man is seen to mount the hobby horse of popularity, to join in the cry of danger to liberty, to take every opportunity of embarrassing the general government and bringing it under suspicion, to flatter and fall in with all the nonsense of the zealots of the day, it may justly be suspected that his object is to throw things into confusion that he may ride the storm and direct the whirlwind.'

"Those are the words of Alexander Hamilton written in 1792," Schiff continued. "Could we find a more perfect description of the present danger emanating from 1600 Pennsylvania Avenue? The Framers crafted a Constitution that contemplated free and fair elections for the highest office in the land, but also afforded the Congress with the power to remove a President who abused the powers of his office for personal gain, who compromised the public trust by betraying our nation's security, or who sought to undermine our democratic system by seeking foreign intervention in the conduct of our elections. I would say that the Founders could have little imagined that a single President might have done all of these things except that the evidence has sadly proved this is exactly what this President has done. Hamilton, among others, seems to have predicted the rise of Donald Trump with a staggering prescience. Having won freedom from a king, the drafters of our Constitution designed a government in which ambition was made to check ambition, in which no branch of government would predominate over another, and no man would be allowed to be above the law, including the President, especially the President, since with whom would the danger be greater than with the officer charged with being our commander in chief."

I was asked by Goldman to stay near the Intel table after Schiff finished his commanding and magisterial argument, just in case Republicans started making personal attacks against the Chairman, as we expected they would. In that case, we could have stood and objected to the out-of-order comments, but ultimately, we decided that it was better to just let them go, even though they were violating the rules of the House.

Jason Smith of Missouri sarcastically complimented Schiff for his "frothy eloquence" and then, like so many Republicans, skipped out on any real defense of Trump's wrongdoing and, instead, started talking about unemployment and trade agreements. At least he didn't start reading from a phone book, an old filibuster trick.

Then my moment arrived. "Donald Trump is using the presidency to put his own personal gain above our national interests," I began. "He is using our taxpayer dollars and foreign interference to cheat the next election, and it jeopardizes our national security and integrity at the ballot box. And not a single fact in this case is seriously in dispute."

I paused, and looked around briefly.

"I ask my colleagues 'Who sent his personal lawyer to Ukraine to investigate his political rival? Who fired an Ambassador, who stood in his way? Who conditioned a White House meeting on investigations that only personally benefited him and not the national interest? Who cut off military aid to an ally that desperately needed it? Who pressured President Zelensky to conduct those investigations? Who stood on the White House lawn and asked not only Ukraine to investigate his rival, but also China? Who has buried evidence and blocked witnesses from testifying? And who is still today sending his personal lawyer to Ukraine to dig up dirt and rig an election?' The answer to all of these questions is President Donald Trump."

Now it was time to take a step back and put Trump's actions in a larger context.

"This is a crime spree in progress, but we know how to stop it," I continued. "Courage. Yes, this investigation has shown us how corrupt President Trump is, but it's also shown us the courage of some of our fellow patriotic civil servants who have used their courage to not only stand up around the world to extinguish corruption, but also to extinguish it at the White House. How? Well, my colleagues argue, 'No harm, no foul. Ukraine got the aid.' Wrong. Trump cheated. Patriots caught him. *Then* Ukraine got the aid. Standing up, turns out, works."

I was almost there. I'd always seen this as a story of courage, of finding the best within us, and this was my chance to have that point resonate.

"Now is the time to summon the courage of those patriots and to summon the courage that they showed against Donald Trump," I said. "If they can risk their careers, even their lives, to do the right thing, can my colleagues also do the same? After all, more is on the line than just military aid to an ally. Our national security is at stake. Stand up for that. Our election integrity is at stake. Stand up for that. And our Constitution's at stake. Stand up for that."

I tried to be there that day for as many of the arguments as I could. I remember sitting for a while next to David Cicilline. We don't take ourselves too seriously, and he was showing me some funny tweets and the texts his constituents were sending him.

The challenge of the day was not to get riled up when Republican speakers were up there trying so hard to rile us. We kept telling each other: *Don't have it out. Don't react. You really want to.* Anytime Cicilline and I were together, we checked each other to make sure that didn't happen. Don't get riled, but sometimes get even.

As Kevin McCarthy was speaking, and really going after Schiff, I just shook my head, like, *You've got to be kidding.* I wrote out a note on a yellow legal pad: "It was McCarthy who said Putin pays Trump." I gave that note to Nadler to show to Schiff. McCarthy had not just been quoted saying he thought Putin paid Trump, the quote was captured on tape. McCarthy had even added, "Swear to God." To reach a wider audience than the two chairmen, I also tweeted out the hypocrisy: "Just a reminder it was in 2016 that @GOPLeader McCarthy said Putin pays Trump."

I took a bathroom break and, on my way out, ran into Doug Collins. He seemed to want to joke around with me.

"You know, every time I step off the Floor, I don't see Schiff ever responding in his comments to what our side is saying," he told me. "He only does it when I'm on the Floor."

I was thrown. What was he trying to say? Did he think Schiff was making it personal? That would have been ridiculous.

Then, as soon as Collins got back on the Floor and spoke, I thought: *Is there something to what Collins is saying?* Schiff just then started responding to their side's argument. I was thinking, *Oh man, Schiff doesn't even know how much he's getting under Collins's skin.*

"Impeachment is a form of deterrence," my California colleague Ted Lieu said that day. "Our children are watching. No President wants to be impeached. Whether Donald Trump leaves in one month, one year, or five years, this impeachment is permanent. It will follow him for the rest of his life, and it will be included in all future history books. And the people will know why we impeached. It's very simple: No one is above the law. Not our commander in chief. Not our President."

For the actual vote to impeach, I could have just voted electronically for the impeachment of Donald J. Trump, but I wanted to fill out a card; I wanted to physically sign my name to impeachment. I delivered my card to the clerk for the first article of impeachment and then, like other members standing around me, watched the board to see how people were voting. The system was slow. A card vote wasn't verified immediately. We knew the number of votes we needed to impeach was 213. I waited a good ten minutes to see my name turn green up on the screen, indicating my vote had been tallied. Now, as I watched, the count stood at 212. Then, at the exact moment my name flashed green, the number turned to 213. It was nothing I'd planned or thought about, but it just might have been my vote that first put us over the top on impeaching Donald Trump.

CHAPTER 45

WHAT DO WE DO NOW?

I felt a little like I was reliving that scene from the movie *The Candidate*, just after Robert Redford's character wins his election. He put so much into running, he'd looked ahead to Election Day with total focus, and now it had come and gone, and he'd won. He looks at his campaign manager and asks, "What do we do now?" That was a little how it seemed now that we had voted, on December 18, to impeach Donald Trump.

We did not even know at that point when impeachment managers would formally march the articles over to the Senate in preparation for a trial. The assumption had always been that it would be automatic, more or less, but now that we had voted, the situation had changed. Senate Majority Leader Mitch McConnell, a shrewd reader of the political terrain, understood all too well the potential for Republicans to pay a price with voters for protecting and defending a deeply corrupt President. McConnell could smell danger—to himself and his position, though apparently not to the presidency or to fair elections—and he had concluded that it was best to get this over with as soon as possible, push through as short a trial as possible, and acquit the President by the time of the State of the Union address in early February.

McConnell took to Fox News on December 12 and told Sean Hannity, "Everything I do during this, I'm coordinating with White House counsel." He added, "The case is so darn weak coming over from the House. We all know how it's going to end. There is no chance the President is going to be removed from office."

No way? Not one chance in a million? McConnell knew better. He knew that the only way that would be true was if he was rigging the trial in the Senate. He knew just how crooked and corrupt Trump was. He was fully aware that if a Democratic President had coerced a foreign ally into digging up dirt on a domestic political rival, the way Trump had, McConnell and

Fox News would have attacked like rabid dogs, with impeachment the least of their demands.

Then McConnell went even further. Talking to reporters on December 17, he, incredibly, uttered these words: "I'm not an impartial juror."

McConnell made this statement knowing full well that he would soon be swearing an oath, administered by Supreme Court Chief Justice John Roberts, who would ask him, "Do you solemnly swear that in all things appertaining to the trial of the impeachment of Donald John Trump, President of the United States, now pending, you will do impartial justice according to the Constitution and laws, so help you God?"

Now, as an attorney, every time I went into a courtroom and heard someone sworn in, the oath ending with "so help you God," I always saw that as an almost sacred ceremony. But McConnell was now admitting that he would take that oath and mean not a word of it.

The rules of the Washington game had changed in the Trump years, and McConnell had changed along with them. During the Obama presidency, McConnell was devious and made an effort to disguise his intentions. In steadfastly refusing to give a hearing to Obama Supreme Court nominee Merrick Garland, a naked power grab that was met with predictable outrage, McConnell tried to say it would be improper during a presidential election year. This was "about a principle, not a person," he insisted at the time. Now McConnell felt emboldened to say the quiet parts out loud. He didn't have to pretend he cared about principle. He could admit that he was coordinating with Trump's attorneys. He didn't have to be an impartial juror. Trump had created an environment where McConnell could just blurt out the ugly reality of what he was doing.

McConnell's insistence on pushing to have a sham trial gave Speaker Pelosi little recourse once the articles were passed in the House. She'd handled herself with dignity throughout the process. This was something we as the Democratic Party had pursued because we had to, or Trump would have kept on cheating. We could not wait, as Republicans kept insisting, for the next election, if Trump was already trying hard to rig that election. There was no glee in impeachment, no joy. Pelosi struck a perfect tone, presiding over the vote to impeach in a black suit adorned with a symbol of the House of Representatives, a gold Mace of the Republic brooch.

As she announced, "Article One is adopted," and firmly gaveled, the Speaker heard some cheering from the upstairs gallery. Pelosi, wanting to be sure no Democratic members were making the noise, memorably glared and waved the vote tally card in her hand to make clear she wanted decorum and respect for the weight of the occasion.

Back in my office soon after the vote, watching a replay with staff, I said, "Oh my gosh, that look from the Speaker!"

This was one more unforgettable Speaker Pelosi moment in her ongoing confrontation with Trump, one right up there with her clapping motion at his 2019 State of the Union, which was in no way disrespectful and yet somehow made Trump look the lesser figure.

"We were hoping for a clap, but that look from her was even better," Natalie Edelstein of my staff said.

Between the first and second impeachment votes, I asked colleagues about the cheering, worried it was from one of our members. "It was from the gallery," my pal Ruben Gallego, a three-term Congressman from Arizona, assured me. "Not a single member clapped."

During the press conference after the vote, the Speaker evoked Elijah Cummings, as I and many others had hoped she would. "He said, 'When the history books are written about this tumultuous era, I want it to show I was among those in the House of Representatives who stood up to lawlessness and tyranny,'" Pelosi said, and I nodded along with her. "He also said, somewhat presciently, 'When we are dancing with the angels, the question will be, what did you do to make sure we kept our democracy intact?' We did all we could, Elijah. We passed two articles of impeachment. The President is impeached."

Answering a question about sending the articles over to the Senate, Pelosi referenced the obvious credibility problem Majority Leader McConnell had created in not announcing the rules for the Senate trial and in signaling that it would be a sham trial coordinated with Trump.

"So far," she said, "we have not seen anything that looks fair to us, so hopefully it will be fair, and when we see what that is, we'll send our managers."

We had one more day in session, and then it would be home for the holidays, so in actuality, "holding the articles" was at that point largely symbolic.

But the symbolism was potent, and it focused attention on the crooked "trial" McConnell was planning for the Senate.

Holding back the articles was an idea I had first heard from John Dean and Professor Tribe, expressed both privately to me and to some Judiciary and Intelligence Committee colleagues. The two had also made a public case on Twitter and in television news appearances. To be honest, I wasn't sold on the idea at first. I thought it might seem like a gimmick, something we wanted to avoid, and I thought the public would be strongly behind sending the articles over immediately. The public also—by an overwhelming majority, it turned out—wanted to hear from witnesses in the Senate trial. The last thing the public wanted was a rigged trial. If it took holding up the articles to try to push for a fair trial, that was in line with what the public wanted.

This wasn't about bucking tradition. This was only the third time a U.S. President had been impeached, so it was not as if there was some natural order to how these things went. But if the Speaker was thinking about precedent, maybe she wanted to ensure that if a President was ever impeached again, the Senate outcome would not be rigged ahead of time. And by holding the articles back, she did just that.

Professor Tribe had been in touch with the Speaker and published a December 16 op-ed in the *Washington Post* arguing against letting McConnell "conduct a Potemkin impeachment trial," pointing out that McConnell was signaling that he planned to hold "not a real trial but a whitewash, letting the President and his legal team call the shots." And Pelosi later mentioned John Dean raising the idea on CNN.

Credit to Tribe and Dean for getting the idea out there in the national conversation. I received dozens of text messages and direct messages on Twitter and Instagram saying, "Do this!" It showed the weight of their words. I had not heard holding the articles discussed internally among the House leadership. That's not to say the Speaker wasn't thinking about it, but if she was, she wasn't sharing it with us. Then, at our last leadership meeting before the vote, she told us that she was considering not sending the articles until she had assurances that there would be a fair trial in the Senate.

Once again, Nancy Pelosi was showing boldness and foresight. The entire reason we had elected her as Speaker was revealing itself now. As I often tell people, "My default is 'Don't doubt Pelosi.'" The Speaker operates on a plane few will ever understand. She sees everything—not just the urgent and important, but also the future. And she's patient, and will rarely bend to public pressure. She hears the questions from reporters, sees the tweets, watches the evening news and cable shows. It's not unusual for her to text or call me or another member after we've done an interview. Sometimes I wonder if she sleeps at all, as one time she referenced an interview I had done on *The 11th Hour with Brian Williams*. Even I was barely awake for it!

Pelosi argued that she could not make informed decisions about how to constitute her team of impeachment managers without knowing what the rules of engagement in the trial would be. It was a strong point. But it meant more time for speculation.

"Are you a manager?" I'd been asked for weeks by every journalist. Enterprising reporters looked for the slightest clues. They stood outside Pelosi's office to see whom she was meeting with and watched conversations on the House Floor to see whom she was talking to. "I don't know" was all I could say. And I didn't know. No one knew. I had made my personal appeal to the Speaker and left it at that.

Sending the articles over and naming managers was really of concern, especially over the winter holidays, only to Washington insiders. To Speaker Pelosi, why not try to get some assurances from Senator McConnell, stoke public demand for a fair trial, and allow more time for documents and witnesses to come forward? We'd been investigating Trump long enough to know from experience that, with this man, the more you looked, the more shocking, depraved revelations you would find.

Day after day, the strategy bore more fruit. McConnell moved off his initial position of considering an outright dismissal of the impeachment articles. He was now talking about the "Clinton rules." Those rules, at least in the perverse and highly idiosyncratic way McConnell interpreted them, were still not helpful to our case. But they were a hell of a lot better than an outright dismissal.

Public sentiment for a fair trial continued to increase and represented a clear repudiation of McConnell's statement that he would not be impartial. A FiveThirtyEight/Ipsos poll in early January found that 86 percent of respondents said that Senators should seek to be "impartial jurors" and examine the evidence.

John Bolton could read a poll as well as the rest of us, and he must not have wanted to come off as a guy who cared only about selling books. All of a sudden, he came out of nowhere to declare that he was ready to testify. On Monday, January 6, he caused a political earthquake in Washington by saying that if subpoenaed by the Senate, he would come forward. "Mr. Bolton's surprise declaration," the *New York Times* reported, "was a dramatic turn that could alter the political dynamic of the impeachment process in the Senate and raise the risks for Mr. Trump of Republican defections."

Most Democrats disagreed with almost every one of Bolton's foreign policy views, but we were savvy enough to know he was appalled by the amateur hour, Giuliani-led Ukraine shakedown scheme. There were continuing doubts about how much he would actually choose to say in an impeachment trial, but I thought Bolton could be a devastating witness against Trump, given what he knew, given his credibility in conservative circles—Fox News loved the guy, or used to—and given his colorful and vivid way of making a point.

As to managers, Speaker Pelosi would tell our leadership team she did not want to name them until she "knew the arena they were going into." She would say this often. She'd go on to explain that without McConnell telling her if there would be witnesses, she didn't know what types of members to send over. She even mentioned that she didn't know if she could send non-members, alluding to staff members Barry Berke and Dan Goldman, who had so skillfully questioned witnesses during the impeachment inquiry. Some saw the delay as clashing with the urgency case so many of us had made as to why we had to impeach, but that missed the point.

National security and election integrity were on the line, we argued. We couldn't wait for years and years of court cases to compel witnesses Donald Trump was blocking to come forward. But Pelosi wasn't worried about a single argument. She wanted to use the leverage she had to get the fairest trial possible. She also believed it would be irresponsible to send articles over for a rigged outcome. If she could give the managers even the slimmest shot to make their case and earn a conviction, she was going to seek that. History was her judge.

CHAPTER 46

TRUMPED-UP WAR

I was on a much-needed, four-day family vacation over the New Year's holiday when I checked my Twitter feed to find images of our Baghdad embassy being stormed by protesters, some chanting, "Death to America." I immediately thought back to visiting that embassy in April 2015 with Mike Pompeo, then a House Intelligence Committee colleague, and waking for the sunrise Easter service on an outdoor patio of the embassy. I couldn't believe what I was seeing. I'd toured that well-guarded fortress, the most expensive embassy in the world. How the hell had this happened? How did the protesters have their run of the outer areas?

The flare-up in tension started on December 27, when U.S. contractor Nawres Waleed Hamid of Sacramento, California, lost his life in a missile strike on an Iraqi military base near Kirkuk. The Trump administration blamed an Iranian-backed militia for the attack, and on December 29 retaliated with airstrikes that killed at least twenty-five members of the Iranian-backed Kataeb Hezbollah militia, as the Associated Press reported. Then, on December 31, after a funeral for the militia members, a group of protesters broke through the main door of the U.S. embassy compound in Baghdad, started a fire in the reception area, and spray-painted anti-America graffiti.

I was relieved to see that the protesters had left by that Wednesday. I assumed the steam had been let out of the pot on the Iraqi side. I should have known it was still boiling in Trump's. Later that week, news reports made it clear that the United States had killed Iranian major general Qasem Soleimani, a man some considered next in line to be the country's President.

Not once during those first hours did it ever cross my mind that the strike on Soleimani had any connection to Trump's impeachment. My first thought was always national security considerations. I separated the two completely, even though Trump had lied to Americans so often that he didn't deserve the benefit of the doubt.

I questioned the judgment behind the decision to kill Soleimani, but I viewed it above all as the act of a reckless, childish President with no understanding of how the world works. It worried me because I knew how little consideration Trump was able to give to strings of consequence. He just didn't have the attention span. My first reaction was to see the attack as impulsive and dangerous, but not corrupt.

I should have known better. Soon, the *Wall Street Journal* would report that in the days leading up to the strike, Trump had told many of his guests at Mar-a-Lago in Florida that killing Soleimani would help him with the Senate in his impeachment trial. Of course, that's why he'd done it! For Trump, everything was always about him.

Now he was in a mess of his own making, and he would lie and lie to try to dig himself out. First was the lie that Iran was planning an "imminent" attack. That defense lasted about a week, before it collapsed when Secretary Pompeo admitted about the alleged planned attacks by Iran, "We didn't know when, and we didn't know where."

"It's coming," Pompeo told CNN's Kaitlan Collins when asked what exactly "imminent" meant.

"So is New Year's Eve 2020," I told Wolf Blitzer on CNN. "In three hundred and sixty days. That doesn't mean it's imminent."

Then Trump shifted the defense by claiming the Iranians were going to attack four of our embassies. It was soon revealed that only the Baghdad embassy was on any sort of high alert, as it had recently been stormed by protesters. No other embassy was on heightened alert. So, either that was also a lie, or Trump was being dangerously negligent.

It didn't take long for the "four embassies" defense to collapse, as we knew it would. On January 12, Secretary of Defense Mark Esper went on *Face the Nation* and told host Margaret Brennan that he had seen no specific evidence of four embassies being threatened. The best he could come up with was "probably" and "my expectation." On the CNN program *State of the Union* that same day, Esper told Jake Tapper that the President "said he believed that they probably, that they could have been targeting the embassies in the region."

Of course, Trump said that's what he believed. He'll say anything to save himself. He's done it time and again, backed up lies and misrepresentations by saying he "believed" something was true. Reality is his to mold like clay.

It was clear, to me and everyone, that the Iranians were not going to take the Soleimani strike on the chin. The question was not *if* Iran would hit back, but *when*. Imminent attack was at the top of my mind on Sunday, January 5, when I joined the congregants of Eden United Church of Christ in Hayward, California, for a Tres Reyes celebration. When asked to speak, I offered a prayer for peace and for every parishioner to keep our service members abroad and their families at home in their hearts and prayers.

The best part of the day was seeing a Nicaraguan immigrant family that had been recently reunited. Under Trump's family separation policy, the father of the family had been in a detention center, awaiting resolution of his asylum claim, for over a year. I'd come to know the family and had had my staff and our lawyers advocating on their behalf. The family's little boy, Wilmer (nicknamed "Yo-Yo"), was the same age as Nelson. I couldn't imagine Nelson not having me in his life. It angered me. I'd often tear up when I saw Yo-Yo. But there were thousands more families just like theirs in the same position. This motivated me every day as I took on the Trump administration, and throughout the midterms as I fought for candidates to deliver the majority. I knew, up close and personal, what was on the line.

I learned of Iran's retaliatory attack in Iraq when we were all back in Washington on January 7 for our first day in session. I was sitting next to Speaker Pelosi, co-chairing the Steering and Policy Committee hearing. Top of mind in our caucus was the future of the impeachment articles and the case Speaker Pelosi was making for the value of continuing to hold the articles to get the fairest Senate trial possible. She had the full support of our caucus.

As she was talking about the benefits of having held the articles, her phone kept ringing, but she did not sit down or look at her phone, and continued to address the caucus. Her phone would stop ringing, and then start to ring again right away. After a few minutes of this, an aide handed her a note saying the Vice President was calling.

She knew it must be important if an aide was interrupting her, but she continued standing. It was something to see: Speaking to about fifty of our colleagues, articulate and forceful, the Speaker continued with her remarks even as she looked down and read the note, all without missing a beat. She hammered home her point about impeachment, obviously having given great thought to exactly what she wanted to say to that room on this crucial first day back, and then added, "The Vice President is on the phone."

She sat back down and told her aide, "Tell him I'll call him back."

My phone was blowing up, too, with Twitter alerts that U.S. troops at Al Asad Airbase, in Iraq, were under attack from Iranian missiles. I scribbled the news quickly onto a white "House of Representatives" notepad in front of me and slid it as discreetly as possible to the Speaker. She glanced at it and turned her microphone back on.

"Your Chairman has informed me that the news is reporting U.S. troops are under attack in Iraq from Iranian missiles," she announced. "Pray." She then walked out of the room and was briefed by Pence.

I felt sick. Our troops, thousands of miles away from home, were running for their lives as Iranian missiles rained down on them. I prayed silently for their safety and thought of their family members here in the United States and the anxiety they must have been feeling. By the grace of God, our forces were able to scramble into bunkers, and none died. I feared Trump took the wrong lesson, though: We killed the Iranians' general; Iran responded and missed us. To him that was "We win."

No Americans were killed in the attack on Al Asad Airbase, but many were wounded. And predictably, Trump lied about that, too, claiming that no Americans were harmed by the Iranians. That was the first story we heard. By January 17, it was being reported that, although the U.S. military had reported no injuries, eleven troops were being treated for concussions. Five days later, in Davos, Trump would minimize their suffering, saying, "I heard they had headaches . . . and I can report it is not very serious." By

January 24, the Pentagon was announcing that *thirty-four* service members had been treated for traumatic brain injury following the missile strikes on Al Asad. On February 10, the Pentagon released a statement saying that 109 had been diagnosed, and 30 percent had not yet returned to duty. Not very serious. Whatever.

Our first week back in Congress in 2020 ended as chaotically as the year before, and I knew this foreshadowed a long year ahead. On the impeachment front, Speaker Pelosi and Leader McConnell were in a public back-and-forth about what a Senate trial would look like. Speaker Pelosi had the support of her caucus to hold back on the articles, but the same wasn't true of all Senate Democrats. Throughout that first week back, Senators started to ask for the Speaker to send over the articles. They were eager to begin the trial. Senator Richard Blumenthal of Connecticut and Senator Dianne Feinstein of California called on the Speaker to send over the articles that Wednesday, though one day later, Feinstein told the *San Francisco Chronicle* she was walking back that comment, saying she did not see any downside to holding back on the articles, and adding, "I don't know what happened there. . . . I did not mean to say that."

At a birthday party that Wednesday evening, I ran into a friend in the Senate who holds a "vulnerable" seat. "Tell your Speaker to send those articles over," he said in a friendly, polite way.

"But look what we've already gotten," I said, smiling.

I understood the pressure was building.

At her Friday press conference, Speaker Pelosi announced that we would be voting on naming the managers and transmitting the articles the following week. There you had it. Certainty. Of course, for the Washington press, this meant endless questions of "What day next week?" and especially nonstop speculation over the managers—how many there would be, who they would be, and when their names would be announced.

Speaker Pelosi had kept that one close to the vest. Washington is known for leaking, but the names of the managers never leaked. That makes me conclude that the managers themselves never knew until right before they were named. They didn't need to know. Speaker Pelosi assured her leadership team at every meeting that her lawyers and Schiff and Nadler and their staff had worked throughout the winter recess on impeachment. Her message was: Don't worry, we are going to be ready.

That Friday afternoon, the Speaker sent out a "Dear Colleague," a caucus-wide communication announcing that managers would be named the following week and a vote would take place to send the articles to the Senate. But first, the Speaker wanted to discuss what was next with the caucus at our regularly scheduled Tuesday morning meeting. All 232 of us would meet in our Caucus Room, at HC-5 in the Capitol basement.

Many of us thought Pelosi would use our leadership meeting on Monday, January 13, to announce the names of the managers. She didn't. And in classic Pelosi fashion, she moved on to other business we had, possibly passing an infrastructure bill as well as one to protect drinking water from chemicals used in firefighting foam and some houseware products. I knew the naming of the managers would be one of the hardest decisions she'd have to make as Speaker. There was no shortage of people who wanted the job, and no shortage of talent. The Clinton trial had thirteen managers from the Republican side. That was too many for Speaker Pelosi. And that was all I knew as far as how Pelosi viewed who the managers would be: They would be fewer than thirteen.

Our caucus meeting the next morning had a turnout I hadn't seen since the day the Speaker called a special caucus session to announce the impeachment inquiry. Our members wanted to know what was next and to offer their feedback. The Speaker went through what we had achieved since voting on the articles and then holding them back. Public sentiment for a fair trial: up. Bolton's hand: now up. Hidden documents: released to Just Security. We had achieved a lot, she said, by holding back the articles. But she believed it was time to send them over.

And the managers? All in good time.

She turned the microphone over to Chairman Schiff, who laid out how the case had factually developed since our recess, including the new information we had obtained from Lev Parnas. That afternoon, at 3 p.m., the Judiciary Committee met in our conference room. I joked that it was nice to see the band back together. Believe it or not, I had missed spending so much time with the committee. Chairman Nadler told us he had no information on the impeachment managers, but that he would be leading the debate the next day on the House Floor to send the articles over.

Finally, the next morning, we found out who the managers would be—first on Twitter, of course. Manu Raju, one of the hardest-working reporters on the Hill, staked out Pelosi's office that morning and tweeted out the names of the members going in. Pelosi would hold a press conference at 10 a.m., with the managers at her side. Manu had it right: out walked Schiff, Nadler, Zoe Lofgren, Hakeem Jeffries, Val Demings, Jason Crow, and Sylvia Garcia.

I watched the press conference only later, on replay. At 10 a.m., when it took place, I was walking into the SCIF for an Intelligence Committee briefing. With no access to my phone or a television, I was able to deduce, based on who was missing from the briefing that morning, who was and was not on the team.

I was disappointed I hadn't been chosen, but this wasn't about me. I wanted to help the team convict a corrupt President who had put his personal interests above our national security and election integrity. But I also would miss not being on the investigation team, working with other members, with the staffers I'd go to when I wanted to talk through a new thread to the case. I'd miss the late-night phone calls and text messages when I had an idea I wanted to share, or when someone wanted to bounce one off me. We all had become very close. We had a country to save and had bonded trying to save it.

To me, the impeachment wasn't a months-long investigation. It had really started with the Russia investigation. So much of what had happened with Ukraine was previewed by what we learned in our years-long Russia investigation. That's why we referenced the President's Russian conduct in the articles of impeachment we voted on.

Besides, more and more information was coming in from the Parnas evidence trove. Ten hours after the managers were named, I was on *All In with Chris Hayes,* making the case for the Senate to give our managers a fair trial. Before I came on, Chris used his opening to preview an interview that would air an hour later, of Rachel Maddow talking with Parnas, an interview that would end up snagging the biggest audience ever for a Maddow program.

This was the clip that aired shortly before I came on:

MADDOW: What do you think is the main inaccuracy or the main lie that's being told that you feel like you can correct?

PARNAS: That the President didn't know what was going on. President Trump knew exactly what was going on. He was aware of all my movements. . . . I wouldn't do anything without the consent of Rudy Giuliani or the President.

It was the ultimate proof of the wisdom of Speaker Pelosi's decision to hold on to the articles of impeachment—more information kept coming out all the time, and still more would come out. That information sharpened the case the managers would present to the Senate, but just as important, it would make it more and more untenable for Senators to claim that there wasn't enough evidence to prove Trump's wrongdoing.

"Documents beget documents, and witnesses beget witnesses," I told Hayes. "And Mitch McConnell should understand that—that if you allow documents in this case from the President, if you ask for witnesses like John Bolton, and other relevant witnesses, like Mick Mulvaney, to come forward, you're going to learn more and more about the President's corrupt scheme. So, hopefully, it inspires at least four Senators on the Republican side to say that."

It was safe to assume that Trump and his circle were purposeful in knowing what to block. The gaps in our knowledge no doubt represented information that would be still more damning to Trump. So, the more we learned, the more gaps we filled, and the more guilty it would make Trump look.

CHAPTER 47

SCHIFF SHINES

Every good prosecutor is a good storyteller. Facts are useful, facts are essential, but a fact on its own can be disputed, twisted, undermined. A fact that's a part of a story becomes a larger narrative that can't be touched. I knew that when it came time to argue the impeachment case against Donald J. Trump before the United States Senate, my friend and colleague Adam Schiff would use his eloquence to tell a larger story. I was excited, the way you are when some incredibly talented musician you've been into for years is going to finally get the attention of the whole country.

The day the impeachment managers were picked, Schiff went out of his way to find me on the Floor, and asked, "Eric, can we chat for a second." The Floor is a chaotic place, members and staff hurriedly moving in all directions. I asked if we could go somewhere that was a little more private. We went to the bench that sits along the back wall of the Floor. On the other side of the wall is the Democratic cloak room.

"I want to thank you for everything you've put into the investigations," Schiff said. "I've enjoyed working with you and hope you'll help us in the public messaging that we'll need as the managers and our case come under attack."

I told Schiff I would do anything to continue helping the team. I also told him I felt like this wasn't a four-month investigation we had been a part of—referencing the Ukraine inquiry that started in September 2019—but rather a three-year investigation that started with Russia. I told Schiff that there was no better person in America to make the case than him and wished him well. While my expectations for how he would present the evidence were stratospheric, he somehow cleared them.

Schiff's electrifying series of speeches in the impeachment trial of Donald Trump will go down in the books as some of the most important oratory in the history of this country because he reclaimed the long view. He was not looking for headlines, and he was not looking to force the Republicans doing crossword puzzles during the trial to open their minds. He was telling a story of the country to the country and for the country. He was taking all that we on the committee had gathered in our investigation, pulling it together to achieve a critical mass of insight and outrage and moral authority to declare, unforgettably: This was wrong. We are better than this.

"Colonel Vindman said, 'Here, right matters. Here, right matters,'" Schiff said in his emotional summation at 10 p.m. on Thursday, January 23, during opening arguments. "Well, let me tell you something, if right doesn't matter, . . . it doesn't matter how good the Constitution is. It doesn't matter how brilliant the Framers were. Doesn't matter how good or bad our advocacy in this trial is. Doesn't matter how well written the Oath of Impartiality is."

Schiff's words had an emotional power that was riveting. There was a fury to his words that was painful and beautiful and true, all at once.

"If right doesn't matter, we are lost," Schiff told the nation. "If the truth doesn't matter, we're lost. [The] Framers couldn't protect us from ourselves, if right and truth don't matter. . . . No constitution can protect us, right doesn't matter any more. And you know you can't trust this President to do what's right for this country. You can trust he will do what's right for Donald Trump. He'll do it now. He's done it before. He'll do it for the next several months. He'll do it in the election if he's allowed to. This is why if you find him guilty, you must find that he should be removed. Because right matters. Because right matters and the truth matters. Otherwise, we are lost."

Schiff had spent most of that day—as he would spend most of the trial—arguing fact by fact why Trump was guilty, but at key moments he brought the discussion back to what really matters, raising the important deeper questions, like *Is this who we are?* He spoke the words "otherwise we're lost" with such emotion, they instantly struck a chord all over the country. No one wants to be lost. That is a terrifying feeling. And no one wants their country to be lost. America should be the shining city on the hill, a lighthouse, a beacon to help others find freedom, opportunity, and integrity.

It made me think of what that intelligence official had told me about the Russian style of disinformation and the canny understanding of human nature on which it was built: Don't try to convince anyone that blue is red, just mix in a little doubt about whether they can even know if red is red, blue is blue. I would literally hear that official's voice in my head, "They want you to question," echoing over and over. To be honest, it got pretty annoying. The Russian disinformation strategy against the U.S. has paid off spectacularly because it found a way to give Americans a sense of being lost, unable to rely on the fixed points of previous generations. Up until that day, we didn't have an answer to that attack. Chairman Schiff gave us that answer.

"Certainly, the most permanent moment of the entire impeachment lay in Schiff's performance before the Senate as the lead House manager," author Adam Gopnik wrote in *The New Yorker*. Gopnik extolled Schiff's "carefully paced intelligence that one might have thought had vanished entirely from the American lectern," and concluded he was "without exaggeration, Lincoln-like. . . . He turned legal argument into moral practice."

For many Americans, they were just starting to get to know Schiff as he thundered home point after point to the Senators. For those watching him for the first time, they were treated to an honorable public servant, prepared with the facts, passionately making his case, and doing it with integrity. I was happy to see so many of our fellow citizens getting to know the leader I had been able to serve with since joining the Intelligence Committee.

Soon #rightmatters and #adamschiffhasmyrespect were trending on Twitter and the video of his speech was on fire. I heard from many people who all expressed a variation on what actress and activist Debra Messing said via Twitter: "I am in tears. Thank you Chairman Schiff for fighting for our country." People kept asking me if we could have Schiff run for President against Trump.

A lot had changed for Schiff since Russia attacked our democracy in 2016. I think he'd agree that at the time most Americans didn't know his name. He held an important role in Congress. But outside of Washington and his own district, he was largely unknown. And, typically, that was on purpose. All of that changed after Russia attacked our democracy. Americans started to realize Schiff was effective at making the case as to what Russia did, who they worked with on the Trump team, and why it matters for democracy.

Even as his profile grew, and he became a household name, to us he was always the same Adam: serious, prepared, and ethically centered, but never taking himself too seriously. Mike Quigley and I often tried to egg him on during meetings to get a few good jokes out of him. Throughout the Russia investigation and through Ukraine, he never changed. Schiff was always accessible, always laughing at himself and the lighter moments the investigations turned up. And that's what got us through it, and kept us behind him all the way.

Schiff's plea to remember our better natures as a country was not about Democrat versus Republican. It had nothing to do with how anyone felt about Donald Trump. This was bigger than that, much bigger, and honest analysts—including Republicans—acknowledged that.

"I have to say, Schiff is very, very effective," Republican Senator James Inhofe told reporters.

Another Republican Senator, John Kennedy of Louisiana, offered a particularly bizarre and damning admission, saying that he and other Senators had "learned a lot" listening to Schiff and other impeachment managers. "Everybody has. Senators didn't know the case. They really didn't. We didn't stay glued to the television. We haven't read the transcripts."

Among those praising Schiff was Senator Lindsey Graham, the man who had famously called Trump a "kook" and "crazy" and "unfit for office," then groveled before him at every turn. Graham made a point of shaking Schiff's hand after one of his ringing arguments to congratulate him. "Good job, you're very well spoken," Graham said.

Trump and Fox News went after Schiff for one reason: He was effective. He was everything they feared, because he was made up of everything they weren't: courage, integrity, patriotism, and independence. Oh, and he was just smarter than all of them. It was like watching the Harlem Globetrotters play the Washington Generals. Schiff kicking their asses every single day.

"I can't watch Schiff battle these guys anymore," Brittany told me. "I'm starting to feel sorry for them. It's not even fair."

Trump prized loyalty over competence and for his defense went with his private attorney, Jay Sekulow, known more for hosting a talk radio show than for any legal excellence he'd ever demonstrated; White House counsel

Pat Cipollone, who should have recused himself given his own role in White House obstruction of our investigation, and his two deputies, Mike Purpura and Pat Philbin; and, finally, celebrity lawyer Alan Dershowitz, forever linked to pedophile Jeffrey Epstein, and Ken Starr and Robert Ray, both independent counsels during the Clinton administration.

It was Trump's idea of a joke, but his allies were horrified at the incompetence of the team, in stark contrast to the professionalism of Schiff and his colleagues. Matt Gaetz offered an honest assessment, grousing that the Trump defense was so shoddy, it looked like "an eighth grade book report."

At that stage we were still hoping that four Senators would listen to the American people and vote to have John Bolton and Mick Mulvaney and other essential witnesses testify before the Senate. We understood Mitch McConnell's objective was to rig the outcome, but we thought the combination of public pressure and basic honor might open the way for at least that basic nod to a fair trial. Otherwise, the Republicans opened themselves up to devastating charges of being part of the Trump cover-up, which they knew could cost them more Senate seats in the November 2020 elections.

I went on Fox News with Martha MacCallum on January 23 to make the case. "If the Senators truly want to give the American people a fair trial and show that this President did not jeopardize national security, then what is the harm in allowing these witnesses to come forward?" I said. "It's not like Mr. Schiff's not asking for those witnesses to come forward. He's putting motions forward to ask them to come forward. And I just think that trials have witnesses and that if this trial does not have witnesses, it's a cover-up for the President. . . . This should not be up to Donald Trump. Mitch McConnell should say, 'John Bolton, if you want to come in, here's your subpoena, come in and then let them decide whether this President put his own interests above the country's.'"

CHAPTER 48

"YOUR HEAD WILL BE ON A PIKE"

One of my favorite Schiff presentations was when he pleaded with the Senators not to be afraid to stand up to President Trump. "CBS News reported last night that a Trump confidant said that key Senators were warned, 'Vote against the President and your head will be on a pike,'" Schiff said on Friday, January 24, adding that he hoped the report was not true and if it was, those were the words of a king. Immediately, the mood in the chamber shifted. Some Republican Senators snickered. Some groaned. Senator Susan Collins of Maine shook her head at Schiff and said, "Not true."

I'm not sure I've ever seen a more comical display of fake outrage in my whole life. First off, how could any of them know what had been said privately to every single one of their Senate colleagues? Their "shocked" routine reminded me of that scene from the movie *Casablanca*, when Captain Renault says, with a glint in his eye, "I'm shocked—shocked—to find that gambling is going on in here." The entire Ukraine saga was filled with examples of Trump threatening people. Why would the Senators be spared from Trump's intimidating tactics?

"I thought he was doing fine with moral courage until he got to the head on a pike," Alaska Senator Lisa Murkowski said. "That's where he lost me."

Uh-huh, right. It was bad political theater, put forth in bad faith. Of course these Senators neck deep in the Trump cover-up would pretend to take the wrong lesson away from Schiff's warning to not be intimidated. And, boy, way to show you're not scared of the defendant, by doing exactly what he wants you to do.

That weekend came a bombshell in the *New York Times* that shook up the impeachment trial. According to the *Times*, John Bolton would throw Trump under the bus in his book, due for publication on March 17, 2020. Trump, the book would reveal, "told his National Security Advisor in August that he wanted to continue freezing $391 million in security assistance to Ukraine until officials there helped with investigations into Democrats including the Bidens," the *Times* reported in a story that had everyone talking.

The details of the story increased the pressure on the Senate to do the right thing and subpoena Bolton and other witnesses. Bolton's book would reportedly also offer damning testimony against Mulvaney, Bill Barr, and Mike Pompeo, among others. Trump had claimed he'd fired Bolton, when Bolton insisted he'd resigned, and it was clear Bolton was serious about making Trump pay for having crossed him.

The problem was gravity. No matter how bad the Republicans looked in denying witnesses, no matter how many problems they created for themselves in the upcoming elections, they knew they simply could not afford to start letting the truth about Trump's monstrous corruption be revealed to the public. As we'd been saying on the Intel Committee for months, evidence begets evidence. If Bolton appeared and told even half of what he knew, it would not only be explosive and damaging to Trump, it would also open up new lines of questioning. Despite the unending talk of how "everyone" knew the result of the Senate trial in advance, Mitch McConnell was afraid that if Bolton testified, they all might be exposed, the whole gang of them. Trump might go down, and so might all of them. So their only option was to keep mouthing the same lame talking points, in the same droning, pompous tones, and deal with whatever damage they were inflicting on themselves.

It didn't take long for a head to end up on a pike. Within minutes of the vote on witnesses, the Conservative Political Action Committee (CPAC) tweeted a picture of Mitt Romney—who had just voted as one of two Republicans for witnesses—with the words "NOT INVITED" above his head. Too often throughout impeachment, Schiff's warnings would come true. This was one I'm sure he didn't want to be right about. The GOP Senators would show almost no courage, and the one Senator who did would be immediately publicly disowned by his own party.

Senator Lamar Alexander of Tennessee went on *Meet the Press* that Sunday to justify his vote. It didn't go well. "If you have eight witnesses who say someone left the scene of an accident, why do you need nine?" he told Chuck Todd. "I mean, the question for me was 'Do I need more evidence to conclude that the President did what he did?' And I concluded, 'No.'"

This was his argument against witnesses. Alexander then talked to Todd about how guilty the President obviously was. "He called the President of Ukraine and asked him to become involved in investigating Joe Biden," he said. "But he admitted that. The President admitted that. He released a transcript, he said on television. The second thing was, at least in part, he delayed the military and other assistance to Ukraine in order to encourage that investigation."

Apparently Alexander was ready to be the first Senator to announce Trump had committed both offenses as charged. But—and it was a big but— Alexander did not believe they warranted removal from office. It was "wrong" what Trump did, and "inappropriate," but somehow not enough to remove him from office—and not enough to have a real trial, instead of a sham.

Back to the "Head on a Pike" line, Alexander even toed the party line and pretended that Trump, if acquitted in his impeachment trial, wouldn't feel emboldened to do whatever he wanted, including retribution.

I will give Alexander this. He was one of the few Republican Senators brave enough to actually justify their vote on witnesses and acquittal. Most of them cowardly tried to echo Trump's "hoax" complaints, but couldn't attack the evidence. It was just too overwhelming. So Trump's defenders focused on process, personal attacks against Schiff, and spinning Russian conspiracy theories. The problem with Alexander's logic was it only worked if Alexander was the sole juror in the case. If he was the only juror, and believed he had heard enough to show Trump was guilty, but it didn't warrant removal, that was one thing. But he was projecting how he saw the case onto fifty-two other GOP Senators, most of whom had endlessly protested there wasn't enough evidence.

CHAPTER 49

COURAGE

No matter how frustrating the outcome of the impeachment trial, this is a story about courage. As the Trump administration came to power, and moved quickly to ban Muslims, cage children, and demolish the rule of law, many Americans recoiled in horror. They hoped that inside every government building there were men and women of honor who would have the courage to stop Trump's wrecking ball.

This is the story of the courageous voices that did just that: Lt. Col. Vindman and the others didn't write books. They didn't leak to the press. They trusted that institutional channels would work, even as the institutions we've trusted for so long were crumbling. I was looking for signs of courage when Congress started investigating Donald Trump's corrupt ways, knowing that courage is the only answer to the contagious spread of craven, self-serving opportunism, and I've found it. Again and again, I've been inspired by the courage of a few brave souls. The courage of an Ambassador to fight against corruption abroad. The courage of a few public servants who came forward to stop a crooked scheme. And the courage of leaders in Congress—empowered by vulnerable freshman members who would risk paying a political price at home—that led to the impeachment of Donald Trump. And in the end, I was so happy, and honestly, relieved, to see Mitt Romney turn impeachment into a story of the difference one courageous man could make.

The night before the acquittal vote, Donald Trump addressed Congress for the State of the Union. It was the last place in the universe I wanted to be. It felt much like Inauguration Day three long years earlier. Thank heavens there was no dinner with Kellyanne Conway and Sheldon Adelson! But it was as awful as I or anyone else could have imagined. Trump disgraced the House Chamber with his usual mix of lies and empty boasts.

The White House billed it as a "unity" speech, but all I heard was the same old politics of division he rode to power in the first place. In a line we will use in many campaign ads against him, Trump flat out lied and said, "We will always protect your Medicare, and we will always protect your Social Security." And also said, in another whopper: "We will always protect patients with preexisting conditions."

I could have boycotted. I considered it. And I respected those who did, as I supported those who walked out in protest, including Tim Ryan of Ohio. "I've had enough," Ryan tweeted. "It's like watching professional wrestling. It's all fake."

Representative Alexandria Ocasio-Cortez of New York also took a principled stand in boycotting: "After much deliberation, I have decided that I will not use my presence at a state ceremony to normalize Trump's lawless conduct & subversion of the Constitution," she explained via Twitter.

I went to that State of the Union for the same reason I went to Trump's inauguration: I wanted to stand and be counted. I wanted him to see me, know I was in the room, and know I stood against him. He could be certain I was going to do all in my power to check and stop his corrupt presidency, whether it was through impeaching him if he broke the law, or working to remove him from office at the ballot box, as I had worked so hard to elect a majority during the midterm elections. I was there in Washington working for my constituents before he arrived on the scene. I was going to be there once he was soon gone. That was my resolve. That's why I showed up. And I had to remind myself of that every word he spoke. It was like trying to get through a root canal.

During the speech, I sat next to my pal David Cicilline, who was on the aisle, three rows back. We were too close to the parade of corruption that would walk right past us: the Senators, led by Mitch McConnell; the cabinet of crooks, including the President's lawyer—not America's—Bill Barr; and then, last, and certainly least honorable, the President of the United States. *What hell has this man brought to our great country*, I thought.

I did not fan-boy as the various notables marched down the center aisle of the House Chamber to the front of the room—except for one person, Senator Mitt Romney of Utah. He walked slowly down the aisle, wearing a blue suit, white shirt, and blue patterned tie. Cicilline was talking to other members, so I had a clear path to lean into the aisle.

"Senator," I said.

Romney looked over. I extended my hand, and he grabbed it.

"Thank you for your courage," I said, and he smiled before moving ahead.

I said those words to Romney not knowing what he would decide to do the next day. Romney had already done the hardest part, bucking the pressure of Trump and the Republican power structure in voting for the trial to have witnesses. He had basically gotten himself there, as far as I was concerned. *Team Trump was always going to consider him a traitor*, I thought to myself as I watched Romney walk up the aisle, *so he might as well do what he thinks is right.*

The last day of the impeachment saga did not turn out as expected. Sure, Donald Trump was acquitted. That was not a surprise. The trial was rigged, with the jury foreperson, Mitch McConnell, openly colluding with the defendant, Donald Trump. When it looked like enough Senators might show enough courage to say yes to witnesses, and no to a sham trial, McConnell whipped them into line by urging dirty self-interest over principle: "We can be smart or we can be stupid," he told wavering Senators, doing his best to sound like the tough-talking mob boss in an old movie, according to the *New York Times.* But he couldn't control the narrative.

Romney turned the story of that day into a story of courage. He was brave enough to break ranks with his fellow Republicans and vote that Donald Trump was guilty of Article One.

Romney's speech that day on the Senate Floor was a bright light on a rocky, dangerous coast. As I watched Romney speak, and heard him choke up early on, declaring, "As, a Senator-juror, I swore an oath, before God, to exercise 'impartial justice'," adding, "I am a profoundly religious person," the words hit me with the force of honest conviction and true bravery.

"This verdict is ours to render; the people will judge us for how well and faithfully we fulfilled our duty," he said.

"The grave question the Constitution tasks Senators to answer is whether the President committed an act so extreme and egregious that it rises to the level of a 'high crime and misdemeanor'," Romney said, and for many listening, there was still an element of doubt.

"Yes, he did," Romney continued. "The President asked a foreign government to investigate his political rival. The President withheld vital military
funds from that government to press it to do so. The President delayed funds
for an American ally at war with Russian invaders. The President's purpose
was personal and political. Accordingly, the President is guilty of an appalling
abuse of the public trust."

Every other Republican may have voted to acquit Trump, but one man
stood up to him, making it a bipartisan vote to impeach this President. Within
seconds Donald Trump Jr. was tweeting that Romney should be expelled
from the party. He wanted his head on a pike! I texted a dear Republican
friend the point about the last two nominees casting two of the biggest votes
against Trump. And I told him, pointing to the Don Jr. tweet, "This is the new
Republican Party." My parents and so many Republicans I grew up around
were of the McCain-Romney brand of Republicans. This new iteration was
completely unrecognizable to so many of them.

The evening of Donald Trump's rigged acquittal we had late votes on
the House Floor. I was fortunate to find both Chairmen Nadler and Schiff. I
thanked them both for all they had done, and congratulated them on being
able to reach Romney. I told Nadler that while his 1999 words were used
against him throughout this process—he said impeachments should be
bipartisan—he was acquitted with Romney's vote. Just as Nadler had told us,
huddled in the Ways and Means anteroom before we voted to send articles
to the full House, that we, as a committee would be acquitted by history for
our work. While we didn't get the outcome we had hoped for, impeaching
Donald Trump revealed not only how corrupt he was, but also how courageous some of us could be.

PART 6: A SECOND IMPEACHMENT

CHAPTER 50

THE 2020 ELECTION

"You going to watch Biden's speech tonight?" I asked a conservative family member the day Biden was to accept the Democratic nomination for President of the United States.

"I cannot wait," he said. "Dementia Joe is going to forget where he is five minutes into the speech. I bet he won't even be able to find his way to the podium. What do you want to bet me?"

"Dementia Joe," "Sleepy Joe"—I had heard it all from my conservative family members as it became clearer earlier in the year that Biden was going to be the Democratic nominee. I had basically given up on pushing back. I knew the then Vice President. I had worked with him when he was Vice President and, of course, encountered him on the trail when I ran for president. Biden was anything but sleepy; he had boundless energy. But it was a waste of time explaining this. I was overmatched by President Trump, who endlessly claimed that Biden had dementia. Trump's false claims were amplified by Fox News and then retweeted on Twitter and shared on Facebook. Over and over. Day after day. It felt like truth no longer mattered.

After Biden's home run acceptance speech in Delaware, I called my conservative family member to see what he thought. His wife answered. I asked her what her husband thought. "He walked out a few minutes into the speech," she said.

Biden was nothing like what my relative had been promised by Fox News. It occurred to me that that speech was probably the first time this family member had ever seen an unedited version of Biden. Everything prior had been packaged for him and other conservatives by Fox News, his preferred news choice. There were about two months to go in the campaign. Biden promised to unite the country if he won, but talking to this family member, I worried that the country had become too divided.

Even in a pandemic, I was doing all I could to get across the country safely to help the Democrats sweep the election. I launched an effort called "Remedy" to help candidates in key Senate and House races. I was all in, and so were my volunteers. We had enlisted thousands of Americans to help us make phone calls, send text messages, and make small contributions to help us save the country. The name "Remedy" was the brainchild of Anthony Shore, who had helped me name Future Forum. The idea was that if we won the White House, Senate, and House, it would be the remedy to the hell Trump had brought upon the country. Incidentally, we came up with the name before the pandemic, but as we lurched into that crisis under Trump's inept leadership, "Remedy" took on even more significance.

I asked the Biden campaign how I could best help. "Philly is the firewall," I was told by a Biden confidant. "If we win Philly, we win Pennsylvania. If we win Pennsylvania, we win the election." He was right. Hillary Clinton underperformed Barack Obama in Philadelphia in 2016. Donald Trump overperformed Mitt Romney in the suburbs and rural areas. And we lost a pivotal Democratic state. I was directing all our volunteers to the Philadelphia Democratic Party. My team dubbed our efforts "the Philly Project."

With the support of volunteers and donors from across the country, Remedy had the resources to help Biden and about a half-dozen Senate and House candidates. We were busy. With resources pouring in, we expanded our voter outreach beyond Zoom calls and phone banks. With the help of a talented producer and the editing team from Eleven Films, we invested in digital persuasion ads to be played across social media feeds.

Early in the pandemic, I was fortunate to connect with Hollywood producer Tracy Falco. Falco had made the feature films *Blow* and *Rounders*, but she had never produced a campaign ad. Our first project was in May 2020. Our goal was to highlight Trump's failure to contain the novel coronavirus COVID-19. At that point, the virus was spiraling out of control. Trump was in way over his head. And like any bullshit artist, he was doing anything he could to try to escape responsibility.

We had seen other digital ads hitting Trump on this, but we wanted to be purposeful. Even then, it was apparent that the dynamic of the 2020 election had dramatically been altered. The entire race would be a referendum on how Trump handled COVID-19. The first impeachment trial was only a few months old when the pandemic hit, and it would not be mentioned once during the remainder of the campaign by Biden or his team. The election was entirely about who could lead the country in a crisis.

For this first spot, we had a targeted audience in mind: Republican women. Poll results and anecdotes indicated that Republican women were fleeing Trump. "He has a suburban woman problem," I told Tracy. I saw it in my own family. Women who had held their noses and voted for Trump in 2016—because he "wasn't Hillary"—were having deep regrets. Trump tried very hard to paint Biden as corrupt, but Americans, who saw from the first impeachment the lengths to which Trump would go to gin up evidence of that supposed corruption, weren't buying it. Trump may not have been removed from office in the Senate trial, but his playbook had been exposed.

Republican women were now fearful for their lives and the lives of their family members as Trump bungled the COVID-19 response. On our early planning calls, we talked about doing something no spot had yet done: feature a COVID-19 victim's family. Put a face to the struggle. My Twitter and Facebook feeds and direct messages were full of heartbreaking COVID stories. I remember having messaged with a Denise Jorgenson of New Jersey, who lost her father. He had been rehabbing from a broken hip at a nursing home where there was an outbreak; according to a report on CNN, twenty-one residents there died of COVID-19. I called Denise and asked if she would share her story on camera as we conveyed her loss and connected it to Trump's failure to defend the country against the virus. She wanted to do all she could to help: "I don't want to see anyone else go through what we went through."

To help with production, Tracy brought in cinematographer Wally Pfister, who had won an Oscar for the film *Inception*. Tracy and Wally interviewed Denise and produced a gut-wrenching ad. It was a side-by-side of Trump golfing, going to a NASCAR race, and giving Rush Limbaugh the Medal of Freedom as the COVID-19 case and death rates rose. The viewer was then introduced to Denise, who shared her father's story. It was hard to watch. It still is, five hundred thousand COVID-19 deaths later. Denise closed the piece by saying, "In November, we are literally voting for our lives." The screen showed faces of deceased COVID-19 victims and faded out with text stating, "They Can't Vote. Will You?"

I felt it was the first COVID-19 ad that told the viewer what exactly was at stake: Life. Loss. I was so proud of the work and believed so much in the cause that we ran the ad on Fox News to really target the Republican woman voter, who, we hoped, would identify with Denise and her loss.

In the fall, with just weeks until the election, Tracy reached out to me and pitched me on a "closing argument" piece. "What if we got Taylor Swift on board?" I laughed. Anyone who knew me knew my favorite artist was Taylor Swift—and that was before I had a daughter. I was, in fact, unapologetic about it. I'd been to concerts, knew every song, had followed Swift's evolution from country to pop. Not to mention that, every night, after we bathe Nelson and Cricket, we hold Taylor Swift dance parties to get their energy out. (And it's probably not lost on anyone that the title of this book is also . . . a Taylor Swift song!)

"Sure, knock yourself out. Maybe she could do a duet with John Legend," I joked—as in, *That's never happening.*

A week later, Tracy messaged me. "Taylor is on board."

I was blown away. "Taylor Swift? *The* Taylor Swift?"

Taylor had never previously allowed her music to be used in political ads, but her team agreed that they would review any ad Tracy made and consider licensing the Taylor Swift song that would serve as the musical piece. We chose the song "Only the Young," which was a tribute to the next generation, positing that if we wanted true change, only the young could deliver it. I loved the song. It spoke to me and everyone who believed that the next generation was our best hope for change.

The Eleven Films team went to work. The piece started with a voice-over of Kamala Harris asking, "Why are so many powerful people trying to make it so difficult for us to vote?" The goal was to uplift people and move them to the polls. The ad showed everything we had suffered through since Trump was elected, but it also showed how we had persevered: the marching, the change at the ballot box, the leaders who'd inspired us, like Ruth Bader Ginsburg and John Lewis. And, of course, it showed Biden as a healer at a time when we needed to heal. I cried every time I watched it. What a four years we had experienced! And we had this final shot to make it all right. Only the young could help us do that.

The video would be seen by more than ten million people on Twitter and millions more on other platforms. It was retweeted by Biden, Harris, Michelle Obama, and a who's who of celebrity and athlete influencers. We released the ad about one hundred hours out from Election Day, but nowhere close to closure.

I spent Election Night in Pleasanton, California, with a few friends, aides, and campaign supporters. We were masked and distanced, but bonded together in our hope that the country would climb out of the four-year hole we'd found ourselves in. The early numbers did not look good for Biden. He was behind in every key state: Wisconsin, Michigan, Pennsylvania, Georgia, and Arizona. It felt like 2016 all over again. Even Florida felt that way, starting the return of results with Biden ahead. But then the western part of the state came in with numbers that quickly put Biden behind. Could our country weather four more years of Trump? I was nervous.

Alex Evans, my former Chief of Staff, presidential campaign advisor, and national pollster, saved everyone from losing their minds on Election Night. "Nothing to worry about," he said. "Biden's got this."

We were sitting spread out in an empty banquet room, nervously eating and watching the returns. Every five minutes, someone would call out, "Alex!" as the latest unfriendly numbers came in.

Alex, picking at his food, with his reading glasses at the tip of his nose, had his head in his laptop. "We're fine," he said.

No one believed him.

At some point he became a party trick. Friends were convinced I had brought him in to keep the room calm. That was true, but it wasn't blind faith. No one knew numbers better than Alex. And he knew every precinct that mattered in America.

"Detroit isn't even in yet," he said. "Just wait."

We went to bed at 2 a.m. Brittany and I had an early flight with the kids the next morning. I didn't really sleep, but I woke up to see that the numbers had moved favorably—as Alex had predicted—in Biden's direction. The early Trump-leaning returns were turning out to have been a "red mirage."

Months before the election, political pundits had predicted that Trump would be ahead on Election Night, but that as absentee ballots were counted, Biden would surge and win. How could that happen? Well, it was a crisis of Trump's own doing.

As COVID-19 made in-person congregating dangerous, states had scrambled to make it easier for people to vote without going to the polls. Nearly every state had allowed no-questions-asked absentee voting. (Prior to 2020, a majority of states allowed mail-in voting, but many had limitations. You had to show medical necessity or some other reason you couldn't go to the polls.) Trump had railed at the concept of no-questions-asked absentee voting. He knew his biggest existential threat was voter turnout. If people voted, he was toast. His job was to suppress the vote. When that became impossible, he shifted to seeding the idea that the only way he could lose was if the election were rigged.

On Election Night, when Trump's team must have seen what Alex saw, Trump made an absurd speech in which he claimed victory and declared, "This is a major fraud" and "We'll be going to the Supreme Court."

Thus, the "Big Lie" was born.

We were in the endgame. On November 7, after nearly every vote from across America had been counted, every major network declared Joe Biden the winner of the presidential election. Soon, CEOs and foreign leaders would call and congratulate Biden. In a poll, 80 percent of Americans would acknowledge Biden as the rightful winner. The election was over—to everyone except Donald Trump and those who wanted or needed to enable him, that is.

For two months, Trump would pour kerosene on the "Big Lie," telling more and more outrageous tales of his victory having been stolen. He claimed that dead people had voted, that cities had had more votes than people. He even claimed that votes were being sent up to the sky. Trump would go on the biggest losing streak of any incumbent president in U.S. history. He lost every substantive case in court—more than *sixty times*. The Supreme Court— which he had stacked with three justices whom he believed were there to be loyal to him—had consistently ruled against him. Trump-appointed judges in lower courts had thrown out his suits. The Department of Justice had issued a statement that there had been no fraud that would have changed the outcome of the election. (Naturally, Attorney General Bill Barr would soon be out of a job.)

Despite all this, most Republicans in Congress stuck with Trump, afraid to buck him and call Biden the victor. So did many Republicans who had voted for Trump. The brainwashing I had seen in friends and family members was a harbinger of what lay ahead. The Republican Party was no longer a party. It had become a cult. And it no longer had policies or principles. It was fueled only by grievances. The latest grievance was that their victory had been stolen. It didn't matter that Chris Krebs, who ran election security for the Department of Homeland Security, called November 3, 2020, "the most secure election ever." Trump fired him via Twitter.

The truth wasn't piercing the veneer of Trump's lies. Indeed, the intransigent Republican support only emboldened him. He'd retweet his adoring supporters in Congress, adding to doubts about a peaceful transition of power. Thankfully, Joe Biden had done the hard part and won the election. And while we lost seats in the House, Democrats would keep the majority and be in a position to stop any efforts by Trump to go around the Electoral College and have Congress declare him president.

Nancy Pelosi was as smart as Trump was corrupt. Even before the election, seeing a Biden win as likely, she had prepared her leadership team for the various plays Trump could make to overturn the election. "Are you ready to play hardball?" she asked her leadership team.

After the Electoral College votes were certified by every state on December 14, Trump's final play was the January 6 joint session of Congress. Vice President Pence would preside over the session in the House Chamber. Pelosi would be seated next to him. Pelosi told the leadership team that she would remain at the Rostrum the whole time: no funny business was going to happen on her watch.

Trump had other plans. On December 18, he had an hours-long meeting at the White House with his lawyers Sidney Powell and Rudy Giuliani, along with Michael Flynn and, for some reason, former Overstock.com CEO Patrick Byrne. Powell made ludicrous claims about Dominion Voting Systems machines, arguing that the Trump campaign hadn't actually *lost* those

sixty-plus cases—many of them had been thrown out for lack of standing—
and proposed that Trump declare a national emergency.

Later that night, at 1:42 a.m., Trump sent out a tweet saying it was
"statistically impossible" that he had lost the election and calling on his
supporters to come to Washington for a rally before the joint session. "Be
there," he wrote, "will be wild."

"There is no path for Donald Trump to the presidency through the
House of Representatives" Pelosi told us after Biden was declared the victor.

In chess, the endgame is the final stage of a match. With the election
called by the media and certified by every state legislature, Trump had been
checkmated. He would spend the next eighteen days pressuring Vice President Pence not to certify the election, but he was boxed in. He had no moves
left. Yet, sore loser that he is, he wasn't going to stop trying. He was going to
try to flip over the board.

CHAPTER 51

THE ATTACK

On the morning of Wednesday, January 6, 2021, with just under fifteen days left in office, Donald Trump was facing a likely censure vote in the House of Representatives. Well over one hundred members of Congress were in support of Representative Hank Johnson's censure resolution against Trump for his shakedown phone call of January 4 with Georgia's Secretary of State. In that call, Trump had made a series of outrageous and nonsensical claims, issued vague threats, and said, "I just want to find 11,780 votes."

"So, what are we going to do here, folks?" he had asked on the call. "I only need 11,000 votes. Fellas, I need 11,000 votes."

Most of us on the Judiciary Committee believed the call was probably an impeachable offense, but we recognized that there was probably not an appetite among all our colleagues to go through another impeachment so close to Trump's departure, especially with a Senate that would almost certainly acquit (again). But we wanted to be on record condemning Trump's unlawful act.

I was helping Hank Johnson get cosigners to his resolution, hoping the bill would be brought up in a swift manner for a vote. That week, I was on Mehdi Hasan's show on MSNBC, and Mehdi rightfully pushed me as to why I wouldn't support impeachment. I told him, "We should impeach him every day of the week and twice on Sunday. But it won't happen, which is why I'm supporting a House censure resolution." I also recommended a presidential crimes commission to look at all of Trump's actions and at those people who had enabled any that were illegal. On January 5, Hank Johnson kindly sent a clip of my interview to our House Judiciary Committee colleagues, hoping we could get more support for his resolution. Little did we know that in just over twenty-four hours, our committee would be working on its second impeachment resolution.

While Hank's censure push was seeing momentum, Donald Trump was on a losing streak. He had lost the election. He had lost dozens of times in the courts. He had failed to disrupt the December 14 Electoral College certification votes among all fifty states. And on December 15, he even lost Senate Majority Leader Mitch McConnell, who finally acknowledged that Joseph R. Biden was going to be the next president of the United States. It was all over except for the ceremony—first, the January 6 joint session of Congress to certify the states' Electoral College count, and then, the inauguration two weeks later.

Under normal circumstances, and among normal candidates, no one would have viewed the certification of the Electoral College count on the sixth as anything like a last shot. It's Congress counting the state's ballots. We literally count and say, "Yes, that adds up." It's not a forum of last resort—unless you're a legal terrorist like Donald Trump.

Somehow, Trump became convinced that if he could persuade Vice President Pence, who would sit as President of the Senate and preside over the joint session's count, to decertify the Electoral College count, he could remain President. Of course, the Vice President had no authority to do this, just as the Secretary of State of Georgia had had no authority to "find" 11,780 votes. But these facts didn't stop Donald Trump from putting in motion a pressure campaign, including on Twitter, starting with that 1:42 a.m. statement, "Be there, will be wild!"

The sixth wasn't any old day. And Trump wasn't assembling any old protest. He knew that January 6 was the joint session, and he believed (wrongly) that it was his last chance. For eighteen days leading up to the sixth, Trump sent a flurry of tweets regarding the date. His campaign spent over fifty million dollars in online advertising around the theme "Stop the Steal." The ads were set to run all the way up to January 5. Trump knew what he was doing. This was a premeditated assembling, inflaming, and inciting of supporters.

And Trump wasn't just working his followers into a fury. He was publicly calling for the Vice President to decertify the election results. "They're not taking this White House. We're going to fight like hell," Trump said at a rally in Georgia on Monday, January 4, for the Senate runoff elections the following day. "I hope Mike Pence comes through for us, I have to tell you . . . Of course, if he doesn't come through, I won't like him quite as much."

In our weekly House leadership meetings, we were prepared for any effort by House or Senate Republicans to try to decertify the election. Our team was led by Representatives Schiff, Lofgren, Raskin, and Neguse. They had worked for weeks to master the procedural maneuvering necessary to thwart any Republican trick to overturn the will of the American people. They had also worked with the state delegations whose votes were likely to be challenged: Arizona, Georgia, Michigan, Nevada, Pennsylvania, and Wisconsin.

The Democratic Caucus's approach, led by Speaker Pelosi, was not to use the forum to attack Donald Trump. In our collective mind, he was a loser. Why make him more significant than necessary? Rather, we would hold up the integrity of each state's elections. Week by week, the January 6 team of Schiff, Lofgren, Raskin, and Neguse would update members on how the Floor debate would play out. They also emphasized how important it was that each of us attend the joint session and be ready to vote down Republican efforts to overturn the certification. While we were allowed to vote by proxy for most of 2020 (in light of COVID-19), the rules for the joint session required in-person voting. This meant that no one could get sick, as our margins in the House and Senate were very close.

Of particular irony during our January 6 planning meetings, in leadership and among the Democratic Caucus, was that Republican members were going to object to their state's certification, but not to their *own* election. Here's what I mean. Mike Kelly of Pennsylvania had filed a lawsuit in Pennsylvania challenging Biden's victory. However, Kelly had been elected on the very same ballot and through the very same process as President-elect Biden. He was essentially in the position of arguing that the result at the top of the ballot should be thrown out, while the result down ballot, the election for House of Representatives, should be honored. I had suggested that we not seat any member who was challenging their own state's outcome, as they were essentially saying that their own election or reelection was fraudulent. Why should they be there? Other members expressed the same sentiment. Had there been more of a likelihood that Republicans could have prevailed in decertifying the Electoral College results, there would have been more pressure not to seat Republicans from the six states being challenged. We were ready to play hardball if necessary.

I started January 6, 2020, at the Rayburn House Office Building; I was in the health unit to receive my second COVID-19 vaccine. I ran into Senator Brian Schatz of Hawaii and congratulated him on the double Georgia win from the runoff of the night before. With the twin wins for Raphael Warnock and Jon Ossoff, Democrats had taken control of the Senate. I was still bleary-eyed from watching the returns. When my wife went to bed at midnight, the race had still been too close to call. I stayed up and ultimately passed out on the couch, waking up at around 5 a.m. to see that the race had been called for Warnock and that Ossoff had taken a commanding lead. Schatz was thrilled and told me we had lots to catch up on.

I've always seen Senator Schatz as a generational peer, fighting in the Senate for many of the same issues I cared about (climate change, student debt, gun violence). After my COVID vaccine, I had to be under observation for fifteen minutes. I sat next to a member of the Sergeant at Arms staff whom I see often in the House Chamber. You can't miss the guy. He's about six foot four, slender, and has a long beard. He'd later play a big role in keeping the House Floor secure during the attack, was present when one of the attackers was shot, and was the first to attend to her and give aid. Hours later, we'd find ourselves together again in the tight isolation room where we were held with hundreds of members of Congress until the Capitol was secured.

Just before noon, I entered the House Chamber. Speaker Pelosi asked me to open the session as Speaker-designate. I would be gaveling in the start of the session. I was honored to be asked, recognizing how historic a day was ahead of us. At 12:01, I gaveled in the session. The Chaplain, retired Rear Admiral Margaret Grun Kibben, offered a prayer, recognizing the gravity of the moment. Kibben was the first woman to hold the position and had been sworn in only the previous weekend. Then, I appointed the "tellers" for the Electoral College count that would soon occur.

Shortly after I had gaveled in the session, Speaker Pelosi presided over the House Floor to welcome the Vice President, who would preside over the joint session. Hours before presiding, Pence had issued a statement, a "Dear

Colleague" to members of Congress, that he would not decertify the Electoral College votes. It was a blow to the outgoing President. Trump would go on to tweet at Pence and call him out at the rally just a mile down the road, outside the White House.

Because of COVID-19 restrictions, the House Floor was not as crowded as for a typical joint session. Speaker Pelosi had asked members of her leadership team to be on the Floor. That team consisted of Speaker Pelosi, Majority Leader Steny Hoyer, Majority Whip Jim Clyburn, and others, ranging from Caucus Chair Hakeem Jeffries to me, as co-Chair of the Steering and Policy Committee. In addition to leadership, members from the states being challenged were to be on the floor at the time the challenge was raised. The states are counted alphabetically, so the Arizona delegation was on the floor and ready to go. Any member who was not part of leadership or the challenged delegations was allowed to watch from the Gallery, one floor above the House Chamber. I noticed the that Gallery was pretty packed. Democrats were determined to see Joe Biden's victory over the finish line.

Little has been more maddening post–January 6 than to hear police leadership declare that they didn't have intelligence justifying a tighter security posture. In the week leading up to the certification of the Electoral College results, a number of family and friends reached out to me, expressing concern for my safety. To be clear, these are people who did not have security clearances or access to intelligence briefings. They were using their common sense and were reading with their own eyes that Donald Trump was assembling, inflaming, and inciting a mob to come to Washington and "Stop the Steal." Social media posts by members of the Proud Boys, Oath Keepers, and other white nationalist groups had made it plainly clear that they intended violence on the sixth.

I, too, was aware of the threats and of the President's rhetoric, but I naïvely assumed that the Capitol and those inside it would be protected— protected by Capitol Police leadership, protected by the National Guard. Never in a million years did I imagine that my personal safety or the safety of others would be threatened.

On the sixth, once the Arizona vote was challenged by Representative Paul Gosar (who was himself reelected on the very ballot whose validity he was disputing) and Senator Ted Cruz, the joint session was suspended to allow debate in both the House and Senate Chambers over the validity of Arizona's count. Speaker Pelosi returned to preside over the House. Many of us on the floor were focused partly on the debate over Arizona's votes and partly on our smartphone screens. I was sitting with my Steering and Policy co-Chairs, Cheri Bustos and Barbara Lee, sharing with Cheri images of what was happening outside the Capitol.

The mob had moved from Trump's rally at the Ellipse, up Pennsylvania Avenue, to the Capitol. Trump had told the rallygoers that he was accompanying them to the Capitol. We would later find in our investigation for the Senate impeachment trial that this gave the mob a false sense of permission. In their poisoned minds, if the President of the United States said he was going, then they had permission to storm the Capitol. Yet, as was clear later, Trump was only feigning solidarity.

On the Floor, we scrolled through Twitter to see the Capitol perimeter from different vantage points. Nothing of what we were seeing was encouraging. The mob was breaching the perimeter, with some scaling walls to enter the complex. Indeed, many had come with climbing gear. And they appeared ready for combat: We saw rioters carrying pepper spray, stun guns, and long poles. Many were wearing body armor and helmets, and some looked like they were in color-coordinated uniforms. And why not? Only minutes before they arrived, the President's lawyer, Rudy Giuliani, had said to them, "Let's have trial by combat."

As the debate continued, our phones were also blowing up with alerts from Capitol Police. My House office building, Cannon, was the first to be evacuated. Pipe bombs had been found just outside it, at the offices of the Republican National Committee. They'd also be found outside offices of the Democratic National Committee.

I still felt safe. After all, I was sitting inside the Chamber of the House of Representatives, at the United States Capitol, the seat of government for the most powerful country in the world. Why wouldn't I be safe? I expected that there was a phalanx of officers arrayed around the Capitol to meet the threat.

We would soon learn that there was not. Not even close.

Earlier in the debate, Congressman Ruben Gallego's wife, Sydney, had reached out to me to see if Ruben was okay. Ruben is my best pal in Congress; I told her I was with him. I knew she was also worried that Ruben, having served in Iraq, would run *toward* the mob rather than away from it. After texting with her, I moved over to Ruben, to stay with him. I told him I had talked to Sydney and that he and I would be leaving together.

As I watched what was unfolding outside on my phone, plainclothes Capitol Police officers rushed toward the House Rostrum, the elevated area on the Chamber Floor where the Speaker presides. It was 2:14 p.m. I saw Keith Stern, the Speaker's Floor Director, tell the Speaker, "Ma'am, we've got to go." And just like that, she was off the Rostrum. (Pelosi would later recall that she was moved off so fast that she left her cell phone behind.) I assumed this was a precautionary measure. Speaker Pelosi is second in line to the presidency, behind Vice President Pence.

Chairman Adam Schiff was nearby when Pelosi was taken out. I joked to him, "Well, that was humbling. I guess the rest of us know where we stand in the pecking order." Gallows humor would get many of us through that day.

Rules Committee Chairman Jim McGovern stepped up to take Speaker Pelosi's place. Next, I noticed Leader Hoyer and Whip Clyburn being ushered out of the Chamber by their security detail. Other members started to get anxious. We were uncertain of what was going on, and the images on our phones showed that things beyond the Chamber door were growing more and more violent. McGovern was interrupted by a Floor security officer wishing to make an announcement. We were told that the mob had breached the perimeter and was now inside the building. We were also told that tear gas had been disbursed in the Rotunda, just a few hundred feet from the Chamber, and that we should take out the gas masks kept beneath our chairs.

Gas masks? I was stunned. I had no idea we even had gas masks.

I asked Ruben, a former marine, "What the hell do I do with this?" He ripped open the outer packaging, took out the mask, and showed me how to open it. I noticed that others were watching. I helped Debbie Dingell of Michigan open hers, and Ruben started to help other members.

In the midst of all this, McGovern gaveled the session back in. I respected his style. *Let's not panic, let's keep going.*

A few minutes later, the security officers returned to the lower lectern at the Rostrum. We were advised that we should be prepared to duck under our desks if protestors came in, in case there was gunfire.

"What?" I said incredulously to Ruben. How would they get inside? Why weren't they being stopped?

At this point, you could hear the mob. They were screaming, chanting, pounding. They were banging on the center door that leads into the Chamber—the same door the President walks through for the State of the Union address, after the Sergeant of Arms yells out, "Madam Speaker, the President of the United States." That same door was now shut, locked, and being barricaded with furniture from the House Floor.

At the other end of the Chamber, just behind the Rostrum, is the Speaker's Lobby. On each side behind the Rostrum is a set of doors to enter the lobby. In normal, pre-COVID-19 times, the lobby is filled with journalists seeking to get an interview with a member. On this day, Capitol Police and Sergeant at Arms staff were stacking chairs against the outside doors leading into the lobby. Those doors were made of wood and glass. The glass was tall and wide enough to allow anyone to enter if they smashed their way through.

My sense of security was in a free fall. I looked at Ruben and said, "Time to lose our coats." I figured if we were going to fight or run, we couldn't be in stuffy suit jackets. I took off my coat, lost my tie, and loosened my collar.

"Look for a pen," Ruben said. "In case we have to stab someone in the neck to protect ourselves."

I have to say, as intense as these moments were, Congress members were remarkably poised and did not panic. We listened to the security officers and awaited orders. There was no stampede off the floor. It seemed as if there were widespread recognition of the gravity and fragility of the situation—with one exception.

During one of the security announcements, a Democrat sitting in the Gallery screamed toward the Republicans one floor below, "This is all your fault! Tell Trump to stop this! Tell him to call it off!" That really shook the place. Members from both sides seated on the floor stood up, faced the Gallery, and told those shouting, almost in sync, "STOP. STOP. STOP."

I knew it was Trump's fault. I knew many Republicans had contributed to inflaming the mob. But I also knew that this was not the moment to litigate that point. Whether I wanted to be in that Chamber with Republicans or not—especially if these were my last seconds on earth—we were stuck there together. And we would need to get out safely together.

At this point, I could hear rioters screaming, pounding on the front and back doors leading into the Chamber, and glass being smashed. Up in the Gallery, members panicked. They were trapped. The mob had made its way up to the third floor and were just outside their doors. Yet, the members had been locked in, ostensibly for their safety, by Capitol Police.

I had been in touch with Brittany throughout the day. It was actually me, at first, asking *her* what was happening. Across town, she was glued to news coverage and relayed to me what she was hearing, and I was relaying back to her by text message what I was hearing from Capitol Police. But it was jarring when she asked me if I was still on the Floor.

Unannounced, the Chaplain approached the lower lectern at the Rostrum. She offered a prayer for peace. That's what got me: Not the images on my phone—because I falsely believed the building was secured. Not Speaker Pelosi's being ushered out—because I assumed that such a move was just precautionary. Not even the gas masks, unprepared as I was for them—I figured it was a break-glass-in-case-of-emergency measure. But when Chaplain Kibben offered her unsolicited prayer, I was shaken. I knew she had served in Afghanistan and had a decorated career spanning more than three decades. I figured she had seen a lot. That *she* was praying, from a lectern that only a select few people are permitted to use, hit me. It felt like last rites.

As I was listening to the Chaplain's prayer, over the banging and other noise, I remembered that I hadn't answered Brittany's question, "Are you on the floor?" I didn't want to worry her, but what might happen next was uncertain. I had a gas mask in my hand. My coat was off. A Capitol Police officer had advised that tear gas had been disbursed, pipe bombs had been found, and that we needed to be prepared to duck in case of gunfire. And the House Chaplain was praying. At that moment, there were an awful lot of warning signs and flashing lights.

I texted back to Brittany that I was still on the Floor. "They apparently have bombs. I love you very much. And our babies." I didn't know what else to say. I wish I had called her. But that, I feared would have been worse. She would have heard the chaos, the pounding, the praying, the humming of a hundred gas masks. I didn't want that to be the last thing she heard from me.

"Babe, what?" she responded. "Don't say that. Are you okay?"

I couldn't text her back for about a half hour. It was agonizing. Things had intensified, and I had to put my phone down to follow directions.

After the Chaplain's prayer, a security officer told us police had secured an evacuation route out of the Chamber. We would leave from the end opposite the Speaker's Lobby, where the mob was smashing windows and trying to push their way past the locked, barricaded doors. Being a rule follower, I was ready to go. I was on the opposite end of the exit path, standing with Ruben. I started to take my place in the long line out. I could hear Ruben shouting to members in the Gallery, helping them find a door that wasn't locked.

"Ruben! Ruben! RUBEN!" I yelled. "Time to go! We have to get out of here." But he wasn't leaving, and I wasn't going to convince him. "How can I help?" I cried out to him.

"Help the Gallery," he said. He was standing on one of the leather House chairs, pointing and shouting. I yelled with him, trying to assure the members in the Gallery that it was going to be okay.

With most members off the Floor, Ruben stepped off the chair, and we both headed toward the exit. As I was leaving, I witnessed a few scenes I'll never forget.

At the center doors entering the Chamber, Capitol Police were standing guard as the mob tried to push their way in. A few Republican members, also with their coats off, stood with the police. I also noticed that the door to the Speaker's Lobby was being crushed by the mob. It was a chaotic scene. The rioters were loud, angry, forceful. They wanted in. Most notably, I observed the professional Floor staff packing up and collecting relics of the House including the bill hopper and carrying them out via the evacuation route. One Sergeant at Arms staffer picked up and packed away the Mace of the Republic, a symbol of the legislative authority of the House, and of order, which had been used for more than 150 years. Fittingly, the current Mace was created to replace one that was destroyed when British forces burned the Capitol Building in 1814.

As we were fleeing the Chamber, I let the Chaplain go out in front of me and asked if she was okay. Kibben, who is just a little taller than five feet, looked at me, smiled, and said, "This is not my first rodeo in a riot."

Ruben and I stepped into the Speaker's Lobby, which was being protected by just a few Capitol Police officers; they were standing guard and ushering members through the evacuation route. "Let's go! Let's go! Let's go!" the officers yelled.

As I was exiting at the opposite end of the Speaker's Lobby from the mob, I heard a gunshot. I moved faster . . . but into a logjam of members. Our path out was a narrow one: down staircases, through narrow hallways and tunnels. I saw members carrying various pieces of House property they had clearly collected along their path, perhaps hoping to have something they could use for protection. One member was carrying a hand-sanitizing station. On the route, the line could move only as fast as the slowest member. I tried to move as fast as I could, to make way for anyone behind me, but not too fast that I'd contribute to any crush.

At various times, I found myself next to Republicans who had been at Trump's "Stop the Steal" rally or who had actively stoked the "Big Lie." I was so angry with them. But here we were, all of us running for our lives. One Republican member noticed me in the crowd and joked, "Stay away from Swalwell. They'll kill him first."

At one point, I was next to Liz Cheney; she was walking fast and on the phone. I heard her say "Dad" a number of times, and I thought of her father, Vice President Dick Cheney, and his famous route out of the White House on September 11, 2001, grabbed by his belt by Secret Service agents.

As I entered the secure room that was our destination, the noise of the humming gas masks became louder. The room was smaller than the House Floor, and we were packed more closely together, hundreds of us in a space the size of an auditorium. The constant din was disorienting. One of the first members I talked to once we were safe was Adam Schiff. He was calm—though, I was not surprised. Over the last few years, I'd been in a few foxholes with Adam. Nothing shakes him, not even an insurrection. He's also got a pretty good sense of humor—exactly what you need when you've survived a coup and want to reclaim your seat of government.

Adam and I agreed that we had to get back to the Floor as soon as it was safe. A fear among many Democratic members was that Trump would use the evacuation of the Capitol as an excuse to declare martial law, and then God only knew what would come next. More and more people started to come into the room—not just members who had been on the Floor, but also some who had been watching the proceedings from their offices, waiting for a vote. There were even members of the press who had been in the third-floor Press Gallery.

While we waited in the secure room, we received intermittent updates from the Sergeant at Arms. It started to feel like we were stuck in an airplane waiting on the tarmac. With each announcement, we hoped we'd be going back. Instead, it was hours of "Police are working to clear out and secure the Capitol. It will take a couple hours."

During our exit, Ruben and I had gotten separated. I reconnected with him in the safe room and was happy as hell to see him. Ruben was still working. He saw a microphone, walked over to it, and made the first announcement in the room.

"Colleagues, colleagues. I want to talk about how to use your gas mask." He then gave a three-minute demonstration and asked anyone among the members who had served in the military to raise their hands and offer themselves up as resources.

Pretty soon, there were announcements every few minutes from the microphone. Liz Cheney, Chair of the House Republican Conference, was the most senior member on their side in the room. Hakeem Jeffries was the most senior on our side. Both gave updates, working together. Other members walked up to the mic and offered prayers. Some members wanted to talk about what had just happened. The speeches varied, but they were all collegial.

I joked to Schiff, "It's become Open Mic Night."

At around 5 p.m., I got an alert from NBC News that the outstanding Georgia Senate race had been called. I showed my phone screen to Schiff and Joe Neguse and jokingly asked, "What would happen to this room if I walked up to the open mic and announced that the Ossoff race has just been called and Dems control the Senate?"

The attack had brought us together, at least temporarily—and with one exception. We were still in the midst of a pandemic. And even those of us who had received vaccine shots had only just gotten them. We were nowhere near immunity. Yet that wasn't enough, apparently, to persuade dozens of Republican members and their staff to wear masks. At first I thought, *Well, we've just gone through this harrowing attack. Give them a few minutes to collect themselves. Maybe they just need a breath.* But then minutes turned into hours. Members were becoming anxious.

A senior member of the California delegation came over to me visibly troubled. "Eric, they're not wearing masks." She was pointing to a herd of maskless Republicans. "Can you make an announcement?"

I knew that probably wouldn't work, so I went over to the Sergeant at Arms, Paul Irving, and passed along the members' concerns, thinking perhaps the Republicans would listen to him. Irving made an announcement, asking everyone to wear their masks. The Republicans eye-rolled him. Not a single one obeyed. My colleague Lisa Blunt Rochester, of Delaware, picked up a stack of new masks and tried passing them out to the maskless. She had a little bit more success than Irving, as some grabbed them and put them on. Others, like Marjorie Taylor Greene, refused.

I couldn't believe it. We had just run for our lives. People had just died in the Capitol, and hundreds of thousands of Americans had already died from the pandemic, and some of my colleagues were acting in a way that could kill the most vulnerable in the room. I was disgusted. (And in the following two weeks, at least eight members of Congress would test positive for COVID-19.)

As the hours dragged on, members grew tired, hungry, and anxious about our safety. Were we safe? Would we be back on the Floor that day? Cell phones were dying. There was a single bathroom for hundreds of people. Thankfully, because of hardworking custodial and food service staff at the Capitol, bottles of water and snacks were brought into the room.

During the wait, I went and checked on Speaker Pelosi's staff. I wanted to know how the Speaker was doing. I asked about her personal effects. Many photographs of her as a girl, with her father, a former Congressman, were displayed on the walls of her office. One of them depicted a young Nancy Pelosi meeting President Kennedy. The Speaker treasured that picture.

The Speaker's staff told me they had seen smashed glass and knew the Speaker's Office had been vandalized and some items stolen. At this point, I became much more concerned about the staff. I could tell they were badly shaken. As the world would see at Trump's second impeachment trial, many of Pelosi's staff had locked and barricaded themselves inside a small conference room that was part of the Speaker's Office. Rioters kicked down a door to try to get in. Staffers pleaded with Capitol Police to come help and were stuck there for hours.

I couldn't believe it. I wish I had known. One of the Speaker's staffers who helps me with the Steering and Policy Committee told me, "Don't worry sir, I saved and took with me the Steering and Policy binder." I started to tear up. Even under attack, this loyal staffer had had the presence of mind to grab a binder containing decades of knowledge that had helped the Speaker advise the Steering and Policy Committee on committee assignments. We had always joked that it was "the magic binder," a physical representation of the Speaker's institutional knowledge of every member's committee aspirations. And these staffers had saved it from the mob.

Early in the evening, Speaker Pelosi and Steny Hoyer entered the secure room and the room erupted in applause. Just like Schiff, the Speaker didn't look shaken one bit. She launched right into a "We are getting back to work" speech. She condemned the mob, declared that they had failed, and told us we were finishing the count. Again, the room applauded. The Speaker was happy to hear from Hakeem Jeffries that he and Liz Cheney had worked together inside the secure room while we waited for the Speaker to come back.

Just after 8 p.m., I headed back toward the Floor. I took the Cannon Tunnel, which connects the Cannon House Office Building to the Capitol. It goes right under Independence Avenue. Going through the tunnel, I was stopped by Madison Cawthorn, a freshman member from North Carolina.

"What was it like running for president?" he asked.

I was a little confused by the question. We had just survived a coup, and he wanted to know about that? "Brief" I quipped.

As he was talking to me, I remembered seeing on my Twitter feed that Cawthorn had been at the Trump "Stop the Steal" rally. My blood started to boil again. He kept droning on and on about my having run for president, concluding, "I think you did a great job."

Cawthorn, paralyzed from a car accident, was in a wheelchair, and as we approached a ramp, he looked up at me: "Do you mind pushing me up?" As angry as I was at him and so many others who had incited the attack, of course I was going to push him up the ramp. This was another reminder of how odd a day it was. I was among not only the victims, but also the inciters.

It was an eerie scene, walking into the Capitol. National Guardsmen were everywhere. The lighting was probably the same as on any night there, but it felt much darker. I thanked every Guardsman and officer I saw. Everyone looked bewildered. There was only one way onto the House Floor, through the center door that the mob had tried to knock down hours before. There was still glass on the floor.

"Be careful," a Floor staffer advised me, pointing to the damage to the door.

On the Floor, I noticed an FBI forensics team taking measurements and photos. Trump's mob had turned this sacred space of democracy into a crime scene.

Just after 9 p.m., the Arizona debate resumed. I sat with Ruben Gallego, who was up soon to speak to defend Arizona's count. I had gone back to sitting exactly where I'd been when the mob reached the Chamber. Somehow, a brown accordion file I'd forgotten was still in the seat where I'd left it.

Because of where I was sitting, directly behind the Floor speakers, I'd end up being in the TV shot for much of the evening. I was there until about 4 a.m. At the time, I had no idea that many people would stay up late into the night to watch the proceedings. It was heartening that so many networks carried the debate live and that so many fellow citizens watched and even messaged me. They cared very much to see their government still functioning.

Late into the morning, Pennsylvania's vote was challenged, with the objection raised by that state's Representative Scott Perry and Missouri Senator Josh Hawley. Members were tired; and understandably, many had left for the night, as it was all but settled that the votes would be certified. But I figured I had made it that far; I might as well stay and see it through to the end.

As I and others were about to nod off, Conor Lamb stepped up to the lectern. In defense of Pennsylvania's vote, he gave the best speech of the night. Conor is a marine and a former federal prosecutor. He's relatively soft-spoken, but his speech indicted the Republicans for their irresponsible challenging of the Electoral College vote. He said the objections didn't "deserve an ounce of respect, not an ounce," and he pointed out that it had been a *Republican-controlled* legislature in Pennsylvania that had "passed a Republican bill" setting the state's voting rules for the election.

Lamb's strong remarks woke up the Republican members; they wanted his "words taken down." This is a rarely used Floor request in which a member's speech is stricken from the record, erased essentially, and the member is forbidden from speaking for the rest of the day. Speaker Pelosi ruled that the request had come too late—it has to be made at the time the remark deemed offensive is uttered. Republican Representative Andy Harris of Maryland tried shouting down Conor's words from the back of the Chamber. Members on our side told Andy to let Conor speak. Representative Al Lawson, from Florida, seconded this, and Andy started challenging Al.

Big Al, who is six foot seven and a former professional basketball player, got up and walked over toward Andy, as did Colin Allred, Democrat from Texas, who played linebacker for the Tennessee Titans. Allred told Andy to be respectful, but Andy wasn't hearing it. That's when I got out of my seat to make sure there wasn't an incident.

"Andy," I cautioned. "Colin tackles people for a living. You don't want to do this."

We ultimately had two votes that night: one to block the objection to Arizona and the other to block the objection to Pennsylvania. Thankfully, the vote was overwhelmingly to accept the counts from Arizona and Pennsylvania. But it was disturbing that a majority of the GOP Caucus voted to overturn the outcome of the election in both states.

After the final vote for Pennsylvania, the rest of the states still had to be certified. I stayed to watch until the bitter end. I encouraged my colleagues to stay, too—even though there would not be another vote—so we could all watch Pence declare Biden and Harris the winners. My neighbor to the North, Barbara Lee of Oakland, was ready to go after the Pennsylvania vote. She had told me earlier in the day that she'd worn sneakers to the joint session, having a bad feeling that we were going to be under attack and that she was going to have to run. I encouraged her to stay for the remainder of the count. We were both tired. She agreed that it was too important to miss. I was glad she stayed. We both wanted to show ourselves, the terrorists, and the world that we would not bend and that a peaceful transition of power would, ultimately, occur.

It wasn't until 4:30 a.m. that I walked through the door of my DC residence. Brittany was waiting for me. She was emotionally shaken. We hugged for some time. Our babies were upstairs sleeping, and thankfully, at three and two years old, they were none the wiser about what had just occurred.

CHAPTER 52

IMPEACHMENT II

By late afternoon on January 6, 2020, Donald Trump would have been lucky if all he faced was a Congressional censure. But Judiciary Committee members were already working—from a secure, undisclosed location—to impeach Trump for inciting the attack that had suspended the count. The effort was being led by David Cicilline and Ted Lieu. The duo had the unanimous support of every Judiciary Committee member, with whom they were in touch throughout the afternoon via group messages.

From our perspective, the Capitol attack had been completely foreseeable. For weeks, Donald Trump had promised that January 6 would be "wild." He'd retweeted supporters who promised "The Calvary [*sic*] is coming." We had seen footage of Trump at the rally that morning declaring, "If you don't fight like hell, you're not going to have a country anymore." As we huddled in that secure room, we knew who was responsible: Donald Trump, inciter in chief.

In the days following the attack, we had a number of leadership meetings to sort out what to do next. Speaker Pelosi was firm in her resolve that Donald Trump could no longer be president. And although he had only about two weeks left in office, Congress was being briefed on new threats to the coming inauguration. Simply put, every second that Donald Trump remained in office was a risk to life and our democracy. He had to go.

Speaker Pelosi saw three options: First, Trump could resign. She argued that it was the quickest way to get rid of him, but she acknowledged it as the unlikeliest of scenarios. Second, Vice President Pence could invoke the Twenty-Fifth Amendment and have Trump removed. While this was also unlikely, it made sense. After all, Pence was nearly killed during the attack. Members of the mob had repeatedly chanted, "Hang Mike Pence," and had erected an actual gallows outside the Capitol. We figured that if Pence had any dignity (or even self-preservation), he would want to see Trump gone.

Pence never did this. Perhaps, in time, we will learn that he tried to rally the Cabinet to remove Trump. Or, maybe, like so many others around Trump, Pence was just afraid to cross him, fearing the political consequences. In Trump's mind, once the election was called for Joe Biden, Pence had one job: to reverse the outcome. He hadn't done that. He couldn't have even if he had wanted to.

On Sunday, January 10, Pelosi wrote to say we would be bringing a resolution to the Floor that would call on the Vice President "to convene and mobilize the Cabinet to activate the 25th Amendment to declare the President incapable of executing the duties of his office." She asked Pence to respond within twenty-four hours, or she would act on the third option: impeachment. On Tuesday, January 12, Pence responded in a letter to Pelosi, writing, "I do not believe that such a course of action is in the best interest of our nation . . ."

So, for the second time (and a first for any U.S. President), we sought to impeach the President. The charge would be a simple one: incitement of insurrection, one simple charge that also happened to be the single-greatest offense ever committed by a President against our Constitution.

The Republicans would accuse us of bringing a "snap" impeachment, one that was too rushed. We should conduct more investigations, they argued, call witnesses in the House. Except that, as House Democrats would argue, when members of the House are all witnesses and victims to the President's act, you don't have to conduct a months-long investigation. Also, we were in a race against time. The inauguration was approaching. We felt strongly that we had to (again) check Trump. It was our best chance to prevent another violent attack on the Capitol, the site for the upcoming inauguration. Also, we had learned that Republicans would criticize our approach no matter what we did. In the first impeachment, we were "obsessed with impeachment," they claimed, and they accused Chairman Schiff of running a "Star Chamber," or secret trial. The essence of their argument was that it was taking too long. We were dragging it out to embarrass the President. And now, with what we would all call "Impeachment II" we were accused of rushing it.

With hindsight, we know that there was no additional violence at the Capitol between January 6 and Inauguration Day, January 20. So, did we overreact in believing we had to impeach Donald Trump, in part, to prevent another attack? Or did our impeaching him, and the threat of removal, temper him? Certainly, as a parent to five kids, Speaker Pelosi knows that children behave best during the "sentencing phase." You know, that period between when you get caught and when your punishment is meted out. You're always on your best behavior then. Impeaching Trump could ensure, in part, that he wouldn't wreak more havoc, specifically at the upcoming inauguration.

After all, he was soon kicked off Twitter. (The company would reaffirm this decision, banning him for life after the Senate impeachment trial showed how blatantly and flagrantly Trump had violated its terms of service to propagate the Big Lie and incite violence.) And only once Trump was impeached did he really go into a hole. It also was not lost on us that before January 6, Trump had flirted with pardoning himself and his family members. After January 6, that was off the table—not because he'd suddenly found a conscience, but because, as the media were reporting, he was being advised by his lawyers that a self-pardon could expose him to legal liability for his role in the January 6 attack. Essentially, a pardon could be viewed as consciousness of guilt.

Speaker Pelosi scheduled two votes, one on the resolution calling for Pence to activate the Twenty-Fifth Amendment and then, ultimately, one on impeachment. I spoke on both. For the Twenty-Fifth Amendment vote, I argued, "The most essential function of the President is to protect life and uphold liberty. Donald Trump has failed to do that, and is *failing* to do that, so Vice President Pence must invoke the Twenty-Fifth Amendment."

With impeachment unfolding so fast, I didn't give much thought to what role, if any, I'd play in a potential trial. During the first impeachment, I had a lot of time to think about it. After all, I was on both committees with jurisdiction, and I was in the thick of the investigation. I wanted to be a part of the trial. I regarded it as my seeing the task all the way through. In Impeachment II, I really didn't give it much thought beyond remembering Adam Schiff's quip, "Maybe he'll be impeached again." Perhaps I was still coping with what had happened on January 6.

On the afternoon of January 12—the day before we would vote on impeachment—I spoke with my friend Barry Berke. Barry had been lead counsel for the first impeachment trial, and he thought my experience with law enforcement, and as a prosecutor, could help the team. After we hung up, I sent a message to Speaker Pelosi and told her I'd be honored to help the team and that I would bring to it my experience as a prosecutor, as a son and brother to police officers, and as someone who had worked with hate crimes. I thought the hate crimes experience was important, as one potential defense for Trump would be that his words couldn't be considered a crime. For years, I had worked to prove that, in some cases, it's just the opposite. It's the old law school lesson: Free speech has limits. You cannot, in fact, yell "Fire!" in a crowded theater.

Before the evening Twenty-Fifth Amendment vote, I took Brittany to dinner. We went to our favorite sushi restaurant in DC. I was coming from the Hill, so I got there first. Brittany was still working, so she told me to get us a table outside and she'd meet me. While I was waiting for my wife, Speaker Pelosi called. I was instantly filled with anxiety. Was she calling to make me an impeachment manager? Was she going to reject me?

"Hi, Speaker" I nervously answered.

"Hi, Eric. Of course, I want you to be an impeachment manager. We will announce it tonight before the vote. Thank you, dear."

And that was that. The call lasted less than two minutes. I was stunned. I had the same feeling I'd had at twenty-four, when my dad called to tell me I had been hired as a clerk in the Alameda County District Attorney's Office.

Within a few hours, I was back at the Capitol for the vote. As I was walking onto the Floor, the Speaker sent out a press advisory announcing the impeachment managers. She had picked nine of us to prosecute the case. Leading the team was Jamie Raskin of Maryland, a fellow Judiciary Committee member. Jamie had been through a lot. Just two weeks before, on New Year's Eve, he had lost his son, Tommy, to death by suicide. Brittany and I were with my in-laws at their home in South Florida when we heard the news about Jamie's loss. We were absolutely crushed for him. I messaged Jamie to express our condolences. I didn't expect him to respond. He immediately wrote back, thanking me for reaching out and telling me to "hug Nelson and Cricket tonight for me."

Jamie's loss was unimaginable. Tommy had still been in law school at the time of his death—Harvard Law School, Jamie's alma mater. Jamie had been so proud of Tommy and spoke of his son's influence on his own speeches and writings. Just a few days later, Jamie's daughter and son-in-law came to watch him lead our Floor effort to make sure the electoral votes were certified. They were worried about whether it would be safe, given Trump's calls to his supporters, but they wanted to witness the historic event. It had been "a devastating week for our family," Jamie later said, and they "wanted to be together."

The impeachment team was rounded out by Diana DeGette, David Cicilline, Joaquin Castro, Stacey Plaskett, Ted Lieu, Joe Neguse, and Madeleine Dean. Some of us had worked on the first impeachment, while others had hoped to be picked for that team. Now we all had a second shot to hold Donald Trump accountable.

The next day, the House would impeach Donald Trump. As the vote was taking place, Speaker Pelosi called the maiden meeting of the impeachment managers. We met in her conference room. The attack had been exactly a week before. As I sat at the end of the long conference room table, with Pelosi at the opposite end, I looked around the room. A week earlier, the whole world was introduced to that room through social media, and the world had watched in horror as the mob ransacked the Speaker's Office and terrorized her staff. Now we were in the same room, laying out a plan to try the president for his role in bringing the rioters to the Capitol and her office.

The biggest question on all our minds was when we would send the articles of impeachment over to the Senate. How soon we could remove Trump was our priority. The Speaker wanted to send them as soon as possible. Our team was fired up and ready to try the case. Hell, we were confident we could have tried it the next morning if we had to. The problem? The Senate would not be in session again until January 19, 2021, the day before the inauguration. And although the Democrats had won the Senate in the Georgia runoffs, Jon Ossoff and Raphael Warnock had not been sworn in yet. Technically, it was still Mitch McConnell's Senate. Also, it had been made clear to us that if we sent the articles over on January 14, the Senate would not receive them. When Minority Leader Chuck Schumer proposed to McConnell that the Senate reconvene immediately to receive the articles, McConnell refused. We faced the prospect that we would be impeaching Trump while he was president but trying him as an ex-president. We all knew that this would invite constitutional challenges from the Republicans.

During the manager meeting, the Speaker asked each manager to offer their thoughts on the case. We were all so honored and humbled to be in that room, and we were all still shaken by what had happened a week earlier. When I spoke, I said this would be unlike any trial that had ever been tried in the history of the world: the jurors were also the victims, and the courtroom was also the crime scene. I noted that this vote would essentially be a chance for a deathbed conversion for Republicans. For four years, they had enabled Trump, and when they weren't enabling him, they had looked the other way. And many of them were partially responsible for the attack on the Capitol. This trial was their last off-ramp, their last chance to cure themselves of their Trump delirium. Our job was to make them confess, vote "guilty," and convict the inciter in chief.

Throughout the meeting, Speaker Pelosi kept turning around to watch the C-SPAN feed on the small television behind her. The vote on impeachment was under way. I knew what she was watching for. It wasn't Democratic votes; we were unified. She wanted to see how many Republicans would come along.

As the Republican "aye" votes came in, Pelosi counted them off.

"That's five . . ."

"That's six . . ."

She already had a sense of who was going to vote yes.

"We expected her to do that."

She told us she hoped that at least ten Republicans would vote yes.

"That's double digits."

As the meeting wrapped, we had eight Republican "ayes."

I walked back to the Floor to make sure I voted. It occurred to me that it would be a bad look if I were named impeachment manager, met with the team, and forgot to vote. I'm capable of doing that.

Just as I had one year earlier, I stood in the well to watch Speaker Pelosi retake the Rostrum to gavel in the final vote. By a vote of 232 to 197, the House stood up again to Trump, making him the first president in U.S. history to be impeached twice.

As the Speaker stepped off the Rostrum, I thanked her again for naming me as a manager. She was looking at the electronic vote board. We both did the math.

"We got ten of them" she said.

In the end, ten Republican Representatives had voted to impeach. The Speaker, as she usually does, had correctly called the count.

I knew the Senate would be much more challenging. It was just a matter of how soon we could take our best shot.

CHAPTER 53

THE TRIAL

"I hope this is the last time anyone walks this path" I told David Cicilline. It was January 25, 2021, and David and I were lined up with the seven other managers just outside the House Chamber to take an all-too-familiar walk over to the Senate. We were delivering the articles of impeachment for Donald Trump. Again. Much of what was ahead for us was uncertain. But as we planned out the processional, our fearless leader, Jamie Raskin, told us, "We will walk en masse, we will stand en masse. We will stand shoulder to shoulder. Sister and brother."

This processional would look a little different from the one that took place almost a year earlier. For one, for this walk, we'd be masked and socially distant. We were headed into the second year of the COVID-19 pandemic.

"Two-minute warning everyone," Drew Hammill, Speaker Pelosi's Deputy Chief of Staff, told the team.

It was a solemn moment. The chatter among the managers halted. With just under a minute until we were live and marching, Jamie turned around and recited a few words by Thomas Pain. "These are the times that try men and women's souls. The summer soldier and the sunshine patriot will shrink at this moment from the service of their cause and their country but everyone who stands with us now will win the love and favor and affection of every man and every woman for all time. Tyranny, like hell, is not easily conquered but we have this saving consolation: the more difficult the odds, the more glorious our victory."

We were ready.

Although I had watched the processional from the first impeachment, there's no way to prepare for the two-hundred-or-so-yard walk from the House Chamber to the Senate Chamber. The walk takes you through Statuary Hall (the second House Chamber, from 1801 to 1859), where the location of

Lincoln's desk is marked; into the Rotunda, where statues of Presidents keep watch; past the Old Senate Chamber, used in the middle of the nineteenth century; and finally, to the Senate Chamber. I knew each of the waypoints well, having given hundreds of tours of the Capitol as a summer intern., but this walk was different. There were dozens of reporters and cameras, bulbs flashing and lenses panning. Each manager looked straight ahead, laser-focused on getting to the Senate without tripping. This was something I'd found harder to do in the time of COVID-19; the building was erected in 1801, so there are not many smooth floors, and masks can be disorienting, limiting one's field of vision. I had already tripped on stairs and over bumps in the floor. So, while I was determined to try the President for insurrection, I was also personally determined to prove to the world that I knew how to walk straight.

We had a lot of difficult decisions to make with regard to the trial. I didn't expect that one of them would be what masks we wore. The topic came up during a manager Zoom meeting the weekend before the processional. Julie Tagen, Raskin's Chief of Staff, suggested we all wear the same type of mask. We agreed. That was easy. But what would it be? We went back and forth. Should we find and buy the same pattern?

One of the managers noted that she wanted to make sure her mask matched her attire, joking, "I guess that's just a concern for us women."

I jumped in to note that my wife didn't let me leave the house if my mask didn't match my suit and tie.

We were at loggerheads. Julie suggested we wear House of Representatives logo masks. This sparked a debate about whether the Senate would find this disrespectful—that is, our coming onto their turf essentially wearing our jerseys. Jamie made a smart executive decision: we would all wear black masks.

When we arrived at the doorstep of the Senate Chamber, the Senate Clerk greeted us and announced us to the Senators. We walked in. The Chamber Floor is slightly elevated. The center pathway is essentially a ramp you walk down to get into the well. The Clerk pointed each of us to a designated spot to the left of the Chamber, in front of the Democratic members. Patrick Leahy was presiding as President of the Senate.

A U.S. president's trial commands the Chief Justice of the Supreme Court to preside. Our preference was to try the case before Chief Justice Roberts. The managers worried that anyone else presiding would create the appearance that the trial was not legitimate. But Roberts wanted nothing to do with the trial. With Trump as a former president, Roberts had a convenient escape hatch not to appear. The duty fell to the most senior member of the Senate, Patrick Leahy.

Leahy read some ground rules for the trial and then asked Raskin to present the articles. For about ten minutes, Jamie read the articles and our justification for appearing before the Senate. The room was much smaller than I'd imagined. As an intern, I was allowed to give tours only from the Senate Gallery. The Chamber had looked palatial from that vantage point.

I looked around at the Senators. Per the custom of impeachment trials, they were all in their seats. Attendance was mandatory. An absent Senator risked losing their vote. It was a little surreal to look across the Chamber and see so many familiar faces. Many in the room had run for president against Donald Trump, either in the 2016 Republican primary or the 2020 Democratic primary. There were Ted Cruz, Rand Paul, Marco Rubio, and Lindsey Graham. On the Democratic side, Bernie Sanders, Elizabeth Warren, Michael Bennet, Amy Klobuchar, Kirsten Gillibrand, and Cory Booker. And of course, there was Mitt Romney, the 2012 nominee so often panned by Trump, and Tim Kaine, Hillary Clinton's vice-presidential candidate. That's over 10 percent of the body connected electorally to the man being tried for impeachment.

"They don't want you there, and they don't want to be there" had been the constant refrain from our lead counsel, Barry Berke. He had said this to remind us that we couldn't waste a word or a second with the "jurors." Everything we did had to be purposeful. And boy, was Barry right. The second we walked in, we could feel the impatient looks. As soon as Jamie was finished speaking, we were promptly escorted out.

We didn't have much time to prepare for the trial against Donald Trump, but we made the most of the twenty-five days we had in between impeaching him in the House and trying the case in the Senate. As one of the youngest members of the team, I was first tasked with creating a group text for the members and staff, an effort that reminded me of my early days in Congress, when I felt like the IT Help Desk. I resisted welcoming everyone with a GIF.

For weeks, we met every day on Zoom to plan the trial. Each meeting started with an update from Jamie, then from Barry as lead counsel, and then from relevant staff on the various issues we faced. The best part of each meeting was the last half, when Jamie would go around the room, always in a different order, to get member input. He was the leader of the team, but he made sure to lead with a first-among-equals approach. He valued our input. And time and time again, I saw member feedback, including my own, make its way into the overall trial strategy.

Jamie had a unique, pre-Congress connection to a few of the managers. In 2002, I interned for a nonprofit on whose board he sat, the Center for Voting and Democracy (now called FairVote). Stacey Plaskett had been his law student at American University. After a few Zoom meetings, she told me, "These meetings feel just like Jamie's law school classes." It wasn't exactly the Socratic method, but Jamie could call on you at any time to ask you what you thought of a particular trial tactic. Because of this, I was always on my toes, ready to help the team.

"Here's our pathway to victory, but we can't call it 'the pathway to victory,'" Barry Berke told the group on January 19, during one of our first trial strategy sessions. Barry, having survived the first impeachment, had become a careful student of impeachment managers, impeachment jurors, and impeachment optics. We were in good hands. He made the case that we should break up our presentation into three acts:

Act 1: The Provocation;

Act 2: The Attack on the Capitol; and

Act 3: The Harm.

As we were preparing for the case, it soon became clear who was not preparing for the case: the defendant. At our January 20 meeting—only hours after Joe Biden had been sworn in as the forty-sixth president—we learned from House Counsel Doug Letter that Trump had not yet chosen his own counsel. This led to a conversation about who would represent Trump and what we would do if Trump chose not to participate. I asked our constitutional law expert Joshua Matz if there'd ever been a Senate impeachment trial in absentia—that is, without the defendant participating. Without missing a beat, Josh shared with us such an example, from the Civil War, involving a federal judge who defected to the Confederacy. I also asked, "What if he goes pro per?" That is, what if he represented himself? I wanted us to be prepared for the worst. That's how you always had to prepare for Trump.

The first legal hurdle for us to clear was the constitutional question of whether you could even try a former President. Essentially, if he is already out of office, why bother? We believed that the Founders intended to hold a president accountable all the way up to his or her last day in office. Otherwise, we feared, it would create a "January exception," in which a president could commit crimes in the final weeks of their presidency and not be held accountable because a Senate trial might not commence while they were still in office. Fortunately, in addition to the Founders' intent, we also had some precedent on our side. Because of the learned Joshua Matz, we all received a crash course in the 1876 impeachment trial of Secretary of War William Belknap. Belknap, accused of selling government appointments, had resigned, but he still stood trial in the Senate (where a majority, but not the required two thirds, voted to convict). Our concern was that Senators who knew that Trump was guilty on the merits of the case would twist themselves into pretzels to give him a legal loophole to avoid conviction. Indeed, before the trial even started, Senator Rand Paul had moved to dismiss the case on these grounds. Only four GOP senators voted to allow the case to move forward.

We knew we had a mountain to climb. But as Barry Berke would remind us over and over in our Zoom sessions, "We have the goods"—overwhelming evidence that should move most reasonable jurors to convict.

Once we hammered out our three-act presentation, we had to break each act down into chapters to tell the story effectively. For example, with "The Provocation," we wanted not only to show Trump's inciting words at the January 6 speech, but also the months leading up to the speech, during which he had said that if he lost the election, it would be only because the election was rigged.

Each chapter had a manager assigned to it. We wanted our case to be seamless, ever mindful of Barry's "They don't want to be here" guidance. Impeachment 1 managers had been given twenty-four hours for opening statements. The Senate rules for Impeachment II provided sixteen hours. Both sound like a lot of time for an opening statement. But "opening statement" is a misleading title for what we were doing. In a typical trial, an opening statement is followed by witnesses and a closing argument. Here, we weren't guaranteed witnesses. The vote on that would come after the opening statement.

So, the goal was to be so persuasive in our opening statement that, if we had witnesses, the Senators would vote to hear from them. And while we were given eight fewer hours for our opening statement than the Impeachment 1 managers had, we still wanted to come in way under that.

As I looked at the three acts and the underlying chapters, one in particular leapt off the page: "The Attack on the Capitol," which included the threat to Congress and violence against police. As I thought through what this chapter would encompass, I remembered my criminal prosecution days in a courtroom. This was exactly what I would do with a complicated homicide case: piece all the evidence together and connect with the jurors in such a way that they understood the crime scene. This was a little bit easier, as every juror for this case was sitting in the crime scene, but it was also challenging in that the Capitol Complex is massive. Thousands had attacked it. There were hundreds of victims of the attack. We would have to collect all the evidence and present to the jurors, in an easy-to-digest way, who had done what when and where.

As the son of a police officer and brother to two police officers, I felt a special connection to law enforcement. The crimes against the cops made on January 6 were personal to me. I know what it's like to worry about a family member's safety. I wanted to present the chapter in such a way that the jurors and the world would know exactly what Donald Trump's actions had led to.

As the jurors and Americans would later see, Jamie's assignment of the chapters perfectly fit each member's experience and skills. I was assigned two chapters, chapter 3, the post-election statements by Trump leading up to January 6; and chapter 7, the threat to Congress and violence against law enforcement. Chapter 7 was itself broken up into two parts: the threat to the joint session (Pence/Pelosi) and the threat to Congress and violence against law enforcement. I'd split the chapter with Stacey Plaskett, also a former Deputy District Attorney.

The challenge of presenting the attack was in the overwhelming amount of evidence that needed to be condensed to, essentially, a ninety-minute presentation, split between Stacey and me. To say that a lot of powerful evidence was left on the editing room floor would be an understatement. Culling from publicly available footage—much of it captured by the rioters and some by members—our hardworking Judiciary Committee and Oversight Committee staff were able to obtain never-before-seen Capitol security footage that helped us better understand, and therefore better communicate, the nature of the attempt. They also were able to obtain new footage of the House Floor. Although C-SPAN must go black once Congress recesses, quick-thinking House Video Gallery staff had thought to turn the cameras back on once it was obvious an attack was under way. Their judgment provided valuable images that helped us depict the terror of that day. Barry, a seasoned trial lawyer, recommended creating a digital model of the Capitol that could help Stacey and me move our presentations along.

In the midst of trial prep, a former Alameda County District Attorney's Office colleague, Casey Bates, reached out to me. "I assume you thought of this, but the radio traffic of the police would be compelling evidence at trial." He was absolutely right. The police had been completely overrun on the day of the riot. From my experience as a prosecutor, I knew that radio traffic from dramatic events could put jurors in the crime scene and help them track what was going on. I asked one of our most dogged Judiciary Committee staffers, Arya Hariharan, to help me track down this audio. During our years of oversight of the Trump administration, the Judiciary Committee had benefited from Arya's "never take no for an answer" mindset, and she didn't let me down now. Arya unearthed hours of haunting radio traffic. She and her team listened to hours of officers in distress, being overpowered by the mob. They pulled out the calls that best told our story of how the mob had moved from the Ellipse to the Capitol and then inside its halls.

We were working eighteen-hour days to pull together evidence on tight deadlines, as we planned to have a few dry runs in the coming days. I was really starting to feel like I was back in an Alameda County jury trial.

"Why are there zip ties on my dining room table?" my wife asked late one night when I returned home from impeachment prep.

"Oh yes, the zip ties."

Rioters with zip ties in the Senate Chamber was one image I could not get out of my head. *Who were the zip ties for?* I wondered. *And what would the mob have done with anyone they restrained?* To get a better sense of how they could have been used, I had my staff go out and buy zip ties that were identical to those that at least two different rioters were seen carrying inside the Senate Chamber. What I learned was that calling them "zip ties" minimized their ability to detain someone. "Zip ties" are what parents use to seal the liquor cabinet when they leave the kids home alone. What those rioters were carrying were actually "flex cuffs," the type of restraints police use to make mass arrests.

"Get those out of our house," my wife said.

Their presence was quite jolting. I was considering using the flex cuffs in my "Attack on the Capitol" presentation. I wanted to hold them up for the senators. I wanted them to experience the same discomfort my wife felt. That's what I would have done in a jury trial. If you have the murder weapon, you show it to the jury.

I had two concerns, though. First, I was mindful of not gilding the lily. We had the goods. The "Attack on Congress" chapter was going to challenge the emotions of everyone in the room, including the guy presenting it. Second, some of the rioters had claimed that they did not bring the flex cuffs to the Capitol that day, but had found them. This was not completely implausible, as the police may have had flex cuffs, and the police were overrun. It's not outside the realm of possibility that, in the chaos and confusion of that day, they would have dropped some. But when staff made this argument to me, I pushed back: "The rioters weren't picking them up to throw them away. We should assume they intended to use them."

I called one of my trial mentors from the Alameda County District Attorney's Office, Paul Hora, and laid it all out for him. "Would you use them?"

"Absolutely" he urged.

I liked Paul's trial style. It was like my own. Now I was really torn. I called Phil Schiliro, a Judiciary Committee advisor from Impeachment 1 who was also helping us for Impeachment II. Phil said there are very few demonstratives you could use on the Senate Floor, and this was one that you could. He gave me the best advice:

"It's a game-time decision. Read the room. Then decide."

He was right. My first read of the Senators was my presentation of chapter 3: "The Provocation." A minute into my presentation, I observed that almost every Senator was paying attention. They were following our presentation—probably because it involved them. I wasn't going to need to show them the flex cuffs to get their attention.

Indeed, for the whole trial, we would have their near-undivided attention. We wondered, though, if we would have their vote.

"You're going to be asked a lot about witnesses in this impeachment trial. You were one of the loudest voices for witnesses in the last impeachment trial," my communications director Josh Richman ominously cautioned.

No two trials are alike, but Josh was right. The press doesn't care about such hair splitting. And they loved to catch any elected official in an inconsistent statement. I wanted Impeachment II to include witnesses. After all, it would be incredibly helpful to know what Donald Trump was doing while the insurrection was taking place. What was his state of mind? The decision was not entirely in our hands, though. We could request witnesses, but the Senate had to vote to allow them. Of course, we now had a Democratic Senate (barely), and we had a few conviction-curious Republicans. If we had the right witnesses, we believed we could get a vote to allow them.

The team believed, first and foremost, that the best, most relevant witness would be the inciter himself, Donald Trump. For days, we went back and forth on our Zoom sessions about the pros and cons of asking Trump to testify. I liked the move. It was an aggressive, outside-the-box strategy. Force Trump into the spotlight, his favorite place. I cautioned that we had better be ready if he said yes. Trump is a showman, and if he saw an opportunity to hijack the proceedings, he would take it. Ultimately, we decided to put the ball in his court. If he refused to testify, it would only make him look guilty.

On February 4, we sent a letter to Trump's counsel inviting the President to testify. We chose to invite him rather than subpoena him, because we knew he would tie us up in court to fight a subpoena. If he had an innocent explanation for his conduct on the sixth, he'd come tell us. Within hours, he rejected our offer. We were ready to hammer him, in the court of the Senate and of public opinion, with the inference of guilt.

"I just talked to Officer Fanone. Not one Member of Congress has talked to him. That's messed up." The major network news anchor who was advising us to make the courtesy call had gotten to know Officer Michael Fanone of the Metropolitan Police Department. Fanone, a twenty-year plainclothes narcotics officer, had responded to the Capitol attack after hearing multiple distress calls. He hadn't worn a uniform in over a decade. Fanone had given multiple television interviews about his experience. He shared a stirring recollection of being dragged by the mob, pummeled and beaten, and then tased with a cattle prod, an assault that led to a mild heart attack. The news anchor asked if I wanted Fanone's contact information.

"Absolutely," I said, and called Fanone immediately to thank him for what he'd done on the day of the attack. For someone who had gone through what he had, he sounded in good spirits. But he wanted to make sure his fellow officers were thanked. I promised him they would be.

For the next few weeks, Fanone would also assist me in analyzing and understanding the radio traffic we had pulled. During the trial, I would feature his experience and play some of the interviews he'd given to reporters. After a long criminal trial, I used to treat the officers who assisted me in prosecuting the case to dinner, to thank them for helping me prepare for trial. In this instance, Fanone called me and asked if he could buy me a beer.

"Not in a million years," I told him. "But I'll buy you one."

We met up and, for a few hours, talked about what he had experienced. We shared our different vantage points inside the Capitol. I learned that Officer Fanone had four daughters. I couldn't imagine how they'd felt that day, as their father ran into the mob to save others. As I was sharing my experience, describing how close the mob had come to me and my colleagues in the Speaker's Lobby, I asked Fanone, "What would these guys have done if they had been able to break through that door?"

"They would have hanged every one of you."

The Super Bowl happened to land the weekend before the trial was to commence. But there was no bean dip and beers for us. We started our day at 9 a.m. in the House Judiciary Committee Hearing Room. With nearly twenty chapters of presentation on the Provocation, the Attack, and the Harm, we had a long day ahead. It was our first full rehearsal from start to close.

After each manager's chapter, he or she would take feedback from Barry, the other managers, and the rest of the staff. Sometimes this felt a little bit like standing before the judges of *American Idol*. Because of security concerns, we had Capitol Police officers with us for our transportation to and from the Capitol. While waiting for us to finish, they'd assemble in the committee staff space behind the dais. At one point, while on a break, I ran into a bunch of them, and it occurred to me that these poor guys were stuck protecting us on Super Bowl Sunday. So, I turned the big-screen television in our conference room to the pre-game coverage. I also wanted to watch, so I'd sneak back there as often as I could.

We wrapped up just before 8 p.m. We were ready to make our case.

The next day, we did a walk-through of the Senate Chamber. We thought it was important to get a sense of the "courtroom." It felt so strange to be standing on the Senate Floor and practicing my presentation from a Senate lectern. We each stepped up to the lectern to make sure we knew how to adjust it to our height. We also ran through our visual slide presentations to get comfortable with the setup, which was a little awkward with the screens the Senators would be watching located behind us.

Then there were more practical problems. "Where do we put our masks" many asked, not wanting to keep them in their hands when they took them off to speak on the Floor. I suggested putting them in the plastic sheet inside the binders we would use at the lectern. Problem solved.

After the Floor walk-through, Senate staff showed us the room we would work out of: S-219. It was the Senate Committee on Rules and Administration Room. It was about fifty feet away from the Senate Chamber. Because of

COVID-19 restrictions, only two managers would be allowed on the Floor at a time. The rest of us would work out of S-219. It was a comfortable room with a couch, refrigerator, conference table, and two large televisions. An IT team showed us how to use the printer and photocopy machine they had brought into the room. I asked one of the IT aides for help.

"Is there a Wi-Fi network we can use?"

"Yes sir. It's your own network. It's called 'Managers'"

I thanked the young aide. "It's impressive how quickly you stood up this workspace for us," I conveyed.

"Sir, we were the same team that helped with last year's impeachment. We left the tech infrastructure in place because we figured you guys would be back."

He wasn't joking, but I couldn't stop laughing. This team was not made up of partisans. They were professional, nonpartisan staffers who just happened to work at the center of national politics. And even they knew who Donald Trump was: a serial constitutional offender.

At noon on February 9, the second impeachment trial of Donald J. Trump was under way. Up first was a motion to dismiss on constitutional grounds. It was similar to the motion Senator Paul had made before the trial started. This motion was brought by the President's lawyers. Managers Raskin, Cicilline, and Neguse handled the pre-trial motions for our team. The rest of the managers watched from the ceremonial Senate workroom. After four hours of argument on the motion, the Senators would vote whether to dismiss.

We didn't expect to lose, and we fully expected to keep the five Republicans who had voted against Senator Paul's earlier motion. The managers huddled around the television to listen to the vote. Each Senator's name was called. Aaron Hiller, Senior Counsel for the House Judiciary Committee, told the managers that a "grand slam" would be if we added any Republican senators. We were all skeptical. What had changed constitutionally from Paul's motion of a few weeks ago?

To our surprise, Senator Bill Cassidy of Louisiana voted against dismissing. In our book, that put us one Senator closer to the seventeen we would need on the GOP side to vote to convict. Cassidy was at least showing a willingness to hear our case. He went into the hearing with an open mind, listened to both sides, and voted with the side that made the best case. What a concept! But could we pull eleven more along?

Having survived the motion to dismiss, we were ready to deliver the goods. We kicked off again at noon. The managers arrived in the holding room at 11:00 a.m. Before Lead Manager Raskin went to the Senate Chamber to give his opening statement, Manager Dean offered to lead us in a prayer. We huddled in a circle and bowed our heads. Then we were ready to go. Raskin left us for the Senate Chamber.

Even at full volume, the flat-screen television in the managers' room was hard to hear with the managers and staff around it. You had to be absolutely quiet. We watched in silence as Raskin masterfully launched our case. Trump was "singularly responsible for inciting the attack." He had "praised, encouraged, and cultivated violence." "And when his mob overran and occupied the Senate and attacked the House and assaulted law enforcement, he watched it on TV like a reality show. He reveled in it, and he did nothing to help us as commander in chief. Instead, he served as the inciter in chief, sending tweets that only further incited the rampaging mob."

Raskin had chapter 1, the opening statement. He would be followed, by Neguse, who would lay out the road map for what the evidence would show. Chapter 3, split between me and Castro, would lay out "The Provocation." Our chapter would be the first pieces of actual evidence the jurors would review.

"What you just heard from my colleague, Manager Castro, about President Trump's lies and actions *before* the election, to paraphrase Winston Churchill, was not the end of his efforts, it was not even the beginning of the end, but it was perhaps the end of the beginning." I had made sure to get the quote right, with about a hundred rehearsals, to be sure not to flub it in front of the Senate. And I didn't glance down at my notes while delivering it. I wanted to look the Senators in the eye.

The Senator whom I first noticed was Minority Leader Mitch McConnell. He was seated closest to me and was looking right at me as I spoke. I wanted to convey that Donald Trump was so unreasonable that his complaints about the election did not end when the election was over. Instead of conceding, he had done the opposite: He had ratcheted things up.

For weeks, the manager team had been trying to land on the right metaphor to use to describe the provocation. Raskin and I both liked the fire analogy, but we didn't want it to be too cheesy. Raskin argued, building on Liz Cheney's description of Trump's actions, that once Trump had assembled the mob, his speech at the Ellipse was the dropping of the lit match. Jamie and I were determined to find the right words, and we went back and forth in phone calls and texts. We finally found them:

Trump was assembling a fire, which would ultimately be the January 6 attack. But fires don't just come out of nowhere. First, you have to gather the tinder and kindling: Those were the pre-election lies. Then you must place logs on the kindling for greater fuel: After it was clear that Trump had lost the election, the lies became bigger. And once the elements of the fire are assembled, you apply the lit match: That was when Trump called his supporters to his rally and delivered his inciting speech.

I used my presentation to lay out this case. For evidence, I showed tweet after tweet, video after video, of Trump telling more and more outrageous lies to inflame his supporters. Although I'd practiced this presentation dozens of times, it was still unbelievable to me how much time and effort Trump had spent trying to overturn the election. I feared that we had all become numb to what he was doing.

In preparation for this chapter, we kept paring down the material, worried it would be too much. I'd never before had a case for which I had *too much* evidence. This was a first.

Barry told us that during Impeachment 1, rarely did the Republican Senators pay attention. They doodled, they stepped into the cloak room, they showed no interest. That was hardly what I observed this time. And I was no favorite of many of the Republican Senators in the room. Cruz, Graham, Hawley, Rubio, and Paul all routinely Twitter-trolled me. But I had to put that aside. And because all the Senators were themselves victims, it appeared they had put that aside, too. Regardless of how they would ultimately vote, they were interested in the trial because . . . well, it was about them. We saw that as an opportunity.

"We have to be careful of guilt creep" was a constant refrain among the lawyers advising our team. They argued that if we connected the Senators who had also perpetuated the "Big Lie" to Trump, we would put them in the position of voting to convict not only Trump, but also themselves. The whole team felt very strongly that Senators like Cruz and Hawley bore some responsibility for what had happened on January 6. Even Senator McConnell had refused to acknowledge that Joe Biden won the election until after the December 14 Electoral College certification by all fifty states. But these Senators weren't on trial; Trump was.

During the Provocation chapter, I was tasked with making a distinction between what the Senators had done the day of the riot and what Trump had done. I hated that I had to say it: "What Trump did was different than what each of you did here on January 6: peacefully debate the integrity of election." I meant it when I said it, but I didn't want anyone to believe that those Senators shouldn't be held responsible in a different forum. And I believe the best forum is the court of public opinion: they should be judged by being voted out of office. And in my mind, I vowed to work to see them out as soon as the trial was concluded.

Of course, Senator Hawley took the wrong lesson from my presentation. On an afternoon break, he told a reporter that I had made the best presentation and that I was the only manager he agreed with because I had acknowledged that he had not done anything wrong. Hawley, after all, had already spent about a month in the barrel for his fist-pumping encouragement of the mob on January 6. He lost a book deal. Hotels were canceling fund-raising events he had booked. His mentor, former Senator John Danforth, had said that supporting Hawley was the "greatest mistake of his life."

Hawley thought I was throwing him a life raft. I wasn't. Just because I wasn't accusing him of being the inciter in chief, it did not mean I was nominating him for the Nobel Peace Prize. Quite the opposite: I look forward to getting to know Missouri quite well as I campaign across the state to help usher him out of office in 2024.

I knew that Castro and I had delivered the goods when it was announced after our presentation that Twitter was permanently suspending Trump's account. Our presentation of Trump's inciting tweets made it clear that he should never be allowed on the platform again. More people would die.

I had a few hours after my Provocation presentation to get ready for the Attack chapter. Judiciary staffer Sarah Istel was tasked with syncing the slide presentation with our remarks. It was a stressful job, and it wasn't her only one. She had organized and helped write most of the remarks the managers were delivering. And chapter 7 was going to be the hardest presentation to sync up. It had the most forms of media: video, audio of radio calls, photos, and a 3-D model of the Capitol. Because Sarah had been so busy with each chapter, we didn't get to do a run-through of my chapter, but I had confidence in her.

Right before Stacey was to begin chapter 7, I found Sarah and said, "All you need to know is that the cops start and end my chapter. If we get that right on the syncing, we'll pull this off." I was referring to my chapter starting not with me speaking, but with the audio of a radio call from an officer in distress. I thought that would grab the attention of the jurors as I moved into what would be an emotional roller coaster of slides. It's also how I used to begin most felony trials. If I had a 911 call of an officer in distress, I would start a trial, in the opening statement, with the victim's words rather than my own—making sure the purpose of the trial was never lost on the jury. It wasn't about me or the other managers. This case was about the victims who had suffered because of Donald Trump.

I walked up to the lectern as Stacey concluded. She had just shown never-before-seen footage of Vice President Pence being escorted out of the Senate Chamber. The jurors also saw Speaker Pelosi's staff running into the conference room where they would turn out the lights and barricade the door. Later footage showed the mob pour into Pelosi's office and bang on that door. Layered over that was a voice mail left by Pelosi's staff pleading for Capitol Police to assist them. It was chilling. Plaskett had set the bar high for me to close out the Attack chapter. I didn't want to do anything to undermine her impactful presentation.

I looked at Sarah and gave her a slight nod.

Cruiser Fifty: they've breached the scaffolds. Let Capitol know they have breached the scaffolds. They are behind our lines.

The room was still. The Senate television screens showed the text of the officer screaming in distress as his call was blared throughout the Senate Chamber. I let the harrowing words sink in and took a beat.

"Shortly after two p.m.," I said, "the Capitol Police and Metropolitan Police were overwhelmed by President Trump's mob. The perimeter was broken. The Capitol had been breached."

I also wanted to make sure the jurors and Americans understood why this attack was so offensive. It wasn't only an attack that threatened members of Congress. It wasn't only an attack that killed police officers. It was an attack that threatened every American's vote. The officers who were killed or injured that day were protecting the election that was being certified. I didn't want anyone to lose sight of this.

Using a digital model of the Capitol, I walked the Senators through the attack on the complex. It was not easy for me to do so. The videos depicting the threat to the House side were the most difficult to get through. They reminded me of how I'd felt inside the Chamber as the mob approached: the fear, the uncertainty, the texts to my wife.

During the rehearsal, I had teared up before the House. I knew I had to pull it together to present this case on the Senate Floor. It was still difficult.

I told the Senators about the House Chaplain's prayer for peace and the text message to my wife. And I started to tear up. Then I went off script. To control my own emotions, I projected my feelings onto the Senators, suggesting, "I imagine many of you sent a similar message to your loved ones." I know they did. We all did.

I then showed the Senators unseen footage of a hallway on the first floor of the Senate, depicting Senators running away from the mob. The silent video lasted about a minute. The first group of Senators walk hurriedly; the middle and final waves sprint. I could tell from the looks on the jurors' faces that they were shocked by this new footage. I asked Sarah to play the video again. I figured that the second time, the Senators would try to see where they were in the footage.

In the video, you can see each Senator looking to their right as they run. Two days earlier, when the managers did our Senate walk-through, I went to the location of this scene. In the footage, you can see the police at the top of the screen holding off the mob. I paced off the distance between where the Senators were exiting to where the officers were attempting to fend off the mob.

"Fifty-eight paces," I told the Senators. "I know because I counted them."

I also showed never-seen footage of Senator Schumer, with his security detail, leaving the Capitol. In it, he walks up a ramp, goes off camera, and then, a second later, runs with his detail back down the ramp. The security detail shuts the glass door, and then two officers put their bodies against the door to protect the Majority Leader. It was terrifying.

The Attack chapter ended with the attack on law enforcement. I told the Senators about my dad and his law enforcement service, and about my brothers, who still serve today. I shared that in most law enforcement families, when we hang up the phone with our police family member, we don't say only "I love you." We also say "Be safe." I wanted them to know that this attack was personal to me. I knew what it was like to worry about a family member's safety as they walked the beat. There were thousands of family members who worried about their loved one's safety on January 6. And we must never forget that.

I concluded my presentation by introducing the jurors to Officer Daniel Hodges. Officer Hodges was a Metropolitan Police Officer who, on January 6, was helping protect an entrance to the Capitol. I showed a video of Officer Hodges being interviewed, describing what he had experienced. Before I closed with the footage of Hodge's experience, I read a prayer known to every law enforcement family. Matthew 5:9 says, "Blessed are the peacemakers, for they shall be called the Children of God." I told the jurors that we were blessed to have a peacemaker like Daniel Hodges protecting us that day. And I implored them, "This must never happen again." Then I closed my binder as the video screen displayed footage of Officer Hodges being crushed by the mob: His head is stuck between two closing doors. Rioters pulled at his helmet. He screams for his life.

It was haunting. I wanted that image to be the last thing the Senators saw with regard to the attack. The video faded to black.

I looked at them, taking another beat. Then I took my seat.

The room stirred with emotion. Leader Schumer asked the President of the Senate to adjourn for an hour. We all needed a break.

I walked into the managers' room feeling like I had finally processed what had happened on the sixth of January. I had never really had the chance to. After the attack, we impeached Trump. After the impeachment, I was tasked with being a manager. After that tasking, we swore in President Biden. After the inauguration, we prepared for trial. I had merely moved from one waypoint to another, without fully thinking about what we had all experienced. It was as if my therapist's couch was the Floor of the Senate and the jurors my therapist. I wasn't only telling them what we had experienced; I was processing it myself.

The next day, we moved from the Provocation and the Attack to the Harm. Managers described the harm Trump had caused to life and limb, recounting the stories of those who were lost or injured. They described the harm to our democracy. And they described the harm Trump's incitement and attack had caused to America's standing in the world. We thought it important that we impart upon the jurors that we had a special responsibility not only to ourselves but also to the world, which looks to America as a leader in democracy. Trump failed America that day. And it was on all of us to hold him accountable for that.

At the end of our summation of the evidence on Thursday, the managers met in the Senate workroom. We were relieved. We had seamlessly presented a blistering case against Trump. We had kept the evidence moving. There'd been no preaching or speechifying. Everyone had known their act and scene. It was a team effort.

We were in the managers' room when I heard Wolf Blitzer's voice from the television: "We have breaking news as it relates to Donald Trump and the attack on the Capitol." I pointed to the TV. Raskin, who was talking about what was ahead, paused. We watched the screen.

Our House colleague, Jaime Herrera Beutler, a Republican from the State of Washington, had issued a statement about Trump's knowledge of the mob's attack. Herrera Beutler had been told by Minority Leader Kevin McCarthy that McCarthy had called Trump while the attack was happening and told him to call off the mob. And Trump had mocked McCarthy, telling him that maybe the mob cared more about the election being stolen than McCarthy did. This was shocking new evidence about

Trump's state of mind at the time of the attack, the type of evidence we did not have.

For the next twelve hours, the managers would discuss whether we should seek to call in Herrera Beutler as a witness. In light of this new evidence, we felt we had to.

I was also given a lead that night: that we should reach out to Vice President Pence's aide, Marc Short. Short was with Pence at the Capitol on January 6, my tipster told me, and could shed light on what Trump knew vis-à-vis communications with Pence. I scrambled to get a cell phone number for Short. I found it and called him. He didn't answer. I left a message. He called back.

I was jolted. Was he going to help us? I asked.

Nothing.

"Hello? Marc? Hello?" He didn't say anything. The other end of the line had gone dead.

I texted him, telling him that we were seeking his testimony and now had an opportunity to seek witnesses. Other lawyers on our team had been in touch with lawyers connected to Short. They had been trying to connect with him for weeks. We pressed late into Thursday evening. Short never got back to us.

On Friday morning, Raskin went to the Senate Floor and asked the Senate to vote to allow the testimony of Herrera Beutler. The defense counsel Michael van der Veen lost his mind—on the Senate Floor. It was embarrassing. He threw a temper tantrum and threatened to call one hundred witnesses, including Speaker Pelosi. He even threatened to depose them all in his office in "Philly-delphia." The entire Senate burst into laughter—on both sides of the aisle. Van der Veen looked puzzled. Then he doubled down, adding, "I don't know why you're laughing." It was an epic meltdown. A bipartisan vote allowed us to move ahead.

The next question was how long it would take for us to get Herrera Beutler in. Back in the managers' room, Barry Berke bee-lined over to me and Stacey Plaskett. "Get ready to do this deposition," he told us. This was, after all, why I had asked to be on the team: to use my prosecutorial experience to interview witnesses. I pulled out a yellow legal pad and jotted down lines of questioning I'd want to pursue. I saw Herrera Beutler as a cooperative witness, so we would not have to put the screws to her. Still, it would be awkward to interview a colleague.

As we were preparing for the interview, we were also trying to get a hold of Herrera Beutler. It was just before 9 a.m. on the West Coast. We figured we should give her some time to get back to us. Meanwhile, defense counsel came to their senses and agreed to stipulate to Herrera Beutler's testimony, meaning they would allow her statement to be entered into the trial record.

At about the same time, Barry was told by a contact he had that under no circumstances would Marc Short be a cooperative witness. We would have to subpoena him. Other managers asked Barry, "What about other Trump aides, or Secret Service around Trump or Pence?" Barry and the legal team conveyed that we had reached out to all of them and were blocked at every approach. If we wanted any of them, we would have to subpoena them and then fight it out in the courts.

The name "Don McGahn" kept coming up. The managers from the Judiciary Committee were familiar with the former White House counsel. Since the summer of 2019, we had sought his testimony in the Mueller investigation. We hadn't even made it to the Supreme Court; we were still waiting for lower courts to rule. Our thinking was that if we subpoenaed Short and others, we would have to wait at least eighteen months to get a ruling. We didn't have that kind of time. Most important, we had made a powerful, uncontradicted case to the jurors.

At the same time that we were learning about Short and waiting on Herrera Beutler, McConnell sent an email to GOP senators informing them that he would be voting to acquit Trump. He said he believed that the whole trial was unconstitutional, as Trump was no longer in office. It was a maddening loophole McConnell had found for himself. The Senate had already voted that the trial was constitutional. For McConnell, or any other Senator, to do this was the equivalent of jury nullification—as when a juror in a criminal trial refuses to follow the law to put their own personal beliefs ahead of the instructions for deliberation. In an ordinary trial, such a juror would be excused. This was anything but an ordinary trial, though. Still, this helped us reach a decision on pursuing witnesses. If McConnell was telegraphing that he believed the whole exercise unconstitutional, then he and others like him didn't need more witnesses; they needed more spines.

We agreed to the stipulation and were prepared to rest our case. We finished our presentation with a closing argument. I sat on the Floor next to Barry to watch Jamie close the case. It was powerful. He compared Trump to an arsonist who had not only lit a fire but had also poured more fuel on it and watched it "gleefully." He said that Trump "must be convicted for the safety and security of our democracy and our people."

Immediately following the closing arguments, the Senators were asked to vote. I remained on the Floor, next to Barry and Jamie. The Senators were seated at their desks. The clerk read out each name. Each Senator stood as the Senator before them was called, stated their vote, and then sat back down. It was like watching a bunch of jack-in-the-boxes pop up.

"Senator Burr" the clerk said.

"Guilty." We were not expecting that. Burr had voted twice that the trial was unconstitutional.

Cassidy would also vote guilty, showing that he had evolved from the original Paul motion.

Toomey also voted guilty.

In the end, seven Republican Senators would vote guilty. Three would change their votes from the original Paul motion to side with the prosecution. But we were ten short for a conviction.

President Leahy read the vote total. Trump was "acquitted." The managers were then promptly excused.

It was like closing time at a bar, when the lights come on and the music stops. The Senate staff ushered us out the same doors we had marched the articles through a few weeks earlier and we were catapulted back to the House side. Later, we returned to the managers' room to collect our belongings. We were all stunned. It was over.

We were also exhausted. Jamie sat down in the same chair, in the center of the room, that he had sat in for each day of the trial. I typically sat in the chair just to his left. He wore a look of disbelief, a look of "How could this happen?" He started to tear up. Managers took seats in a circle with him.

Tears in his eyes, Jamie apologized to us, "I'm sorry we couldn't get it done." I felt awful. What a good and decent person we had in our Lead Manager.

But at first, I was confused. Did Jamie think, after the McConnell statement before the vote, that we were actually going to get a conviction? Once McConnell put that statement out, I had come to terms with the fact that we were going to lose. As we each told Jamie he had nothing to apologize for, it struck me: he had believed, even up to the vote on Trump's guilt, that the jurors would be honest about the evidence he'd presented. It wasn't naïveté. It wasn't Jamie being a Pollyanna. He believed in our case. And despite how awful things had been on him and his family over the past forty-five days, he still saw the best in all of us. He believed that we had proved, beyond all doubt, that Donald Trump had incited the attack on the U.S. Capitol. He was right. And I was sadder than hell that not all the jurors had deliberated in good faith.

We hung around the managers' room for another hour. We thanked the staff and the IT team for their commitment to our cause. But our work was not done. Speaker Pelosi's team had asked us to appear at a post-trial press conference. There, we would make our final closing argument—this time, in the court of public opinion.

At the press conference, we were bombarded with questions about witnesses. To the public, seeking witnesses was an opportunity to get Trump and his gang under oath. To us, it was something to do only if necessary. We had delivered the goods. If we could find a cooperative witness, we were down for that, but there were none. So, I understand the gap between how we were proceeding and what people expected. But we didn't want the public's focus to shift from the thundering case we had brought. Fortunately, the stories about trying to obtain witnesses were overshadowed while we were holding the press conference.

Minority Leader McConnell was on the Senate Floor laying into Trump. In an admonishing address, he laid the blame for the attack at Trump's door. "There's no question, none, that President Trump is practically and morally responsible for provoking the events of the day."

While it was vindicating for us to hear McConnell essentially say we had proven our case, we didn't need his compliments; we needed his vote.

Trump later lit into McConnell, and when asked, McConnell said that he would "absolutely" support Trump if he were the GOP nominee in 2024.

In the end, we won the trial. Fifty-seven Senators voted to convict Donald Trump. It was the largest bipartisan vote for conviction ever at a presidential impeachment trial. Sure, we did not reach the 67-vote threshold to disqualify Trump from holding office again. But 57 out of 100 for guilt feels a hell of a lot more like a conviction than an acquittal. Day after day, we had shown the American people how Donald Trump assembled, inflamed, and incited the mob that attacked the Capitol. Even when Trump was acquitted, I was convinced he could never win another election. In a PBS *NewsHour*/NPR/Marist poll of registered voters, 57 percent said they would vote against Trump.

We had won. And I thought it was important that we carried ourselves that way. We had nothing to apologize for. As we were leaving the press conference, I told Jamie, "We will be vindicated for this trial. Over time, our case will age like wine, and Donald Trump will age like milk."

With the impeachment trial over, so was our four-year quest in Congress to hold Donald Trump accountable. He was no longer president. But to paraphrase Churchill again, this was not the end of holding Donald Trump accountable. It was not even the beginning of the end. Perhaps it was the end of the beginning.

About a month after we walked the articles of impeachment over to the Senate, I filed a civil suit in DC federal court against Donald J. Trump, Donald Trump Jr., Rudy Giuliani, and Representative Mo Brooks for their role in inciting the January 6 attack.

On January 20, 2017, I had sat on the inaugural platform to watch Donald Trump take the oath of office. Four years later, I would prosecute him before the Senate for violating that oath. In between those two events, I spent more time than I wanted in Congress holding him accountable for his corrupt acts.

Trump was a bully who tested America and her principles every single day he was in office. Unfortunately for him, I was raised by Eric Nelson

Swalwell, who taught me, from my earliest memory, the importance of standing up to bullies.

Standing up to Trump was the least I could do for our country. After all, I wasn't being asked to throw my body in front of the Capitol, like Officer Fanone, to defend it and the people inside. I merely had to follow the oath I'd taken to defend the country against all enemies, foreign and domestic.

On the day of the verdict, I texted Fanone to tell him the witnesses we had hoped to call didn't want to come in. He quickly wrote back, "Tell them I said grow a pair and do what's right. If I can endure the ass kicking of a lifetime, then they can deal with a little political fallout. Tell them it's their penance."

That could have been my father texting me back in 1986, when he stood up to that corrupt small-town mayor. "Do what's right." That's what I signed up to do. That's why Officer Fanone raced to the Capitol. And that's why I'm going to hold Donald Trump accountable for all his crimes.

ACKNOWLEDGMENTS

I'm most grateful to my wife, Brittany, a loving partner whose support makes me a better Representative. Professionally, Brittany is on a meteoric rise in hospitality sales and still manages to be the best mom Nelson and Cricket could ever have.

I'm grateful to my constituents, the hardworking and big-hearted people of California's East Bay. You remind me every day that freedom is on the line.

Thank you to my colleagues in Congress who proved there are still patriots in public service who put country over self. Our caucus was fortunate to have been led by the fearless, indomitable Speaker Pelosi. It was an honor to serve with Chairman Schiff, a friend and mentor to me these past trying years. To my colleagues and staff on the Intelligence Committee, who have toiled away to keep our democracy standing. Especially grateful to staff director Tim Bergreen, lead investigator Dan Goldman, chief counsel Maher Bitar, and Kathy Suber. Same for the Judiciary Committee, led by our Chairman Jerry Nadler and a top-notch staff, including Chief of Staff Amy Rutkin, Aaron Hiller, Arya Hariharan, and former counsel Barry Berke, Norm Eisen, and Sarah Istel. And thank you to my own staff, led by chiefs Ricky Le, Alex Evans, and Michael Reed, and District Director Mallory De Lauro, for their faithful service to our constituents. I've had a great communications team throughout the investigation, including Josh Richman, Cait McNamee, Natalie Edelstein, and Celia Olivas. Andrew Ginsburg has been our office's chief lawyer, assisted by Kyle Alagood.

I was able to help prosecute the case against a corrupt President because of the training and principles I learned at the Alameda County District Attorney's Office. Thank you, District Attorney Nancy O'Malley, and all of my friends in the office.

I learned about the rule of law from my dad—saw it enforced at home growing up by my multitasking mom—and see it carried out today by two brothers who wear the badge, Jacob and Chase. Thank you for your service.

My in-laws, Drs. Will and Kathy Watts, are lifelong Republicans in Southern Indiana. They couldn't be more welcoming when I visit and our spirited, but respectful conversations help me stay open-minded to other perspectives. I think I can get at least one of them to vote Democratic this fall!

And thank you to some of my closest friends who always keep me centered, Chris Michel, Jeff Crawford, Ruben Gallego, Tim Sbranti, Bryan Vann, Eric Olson, Anna and Adam Connolly, Chris Doyle, Lisa Tucker, Shannon and Glen Fuller, Paul Mandell, and my brother, Josh.

David Larabell of CAA is the kind of agent who jumps at a problem any hour of the day, and tackles it head on and with his sense of humor intact.

I had a great editorial team at Abrams led by Jamison Stoltz, who has shown himself to be a smart, resourceful publisher with vision. The whole team at Abrams did amazing work to make this book happen: Michael Sand, Peggy Garry, Sarah Robbins, Mary O'Mara, Anet Sirna-Bruder, Sarah Masterson Hally, Jennifer Brunn, Jessica Wiener, Deb Wood, and Devin Grosz. Thanks to Steve Kettmann, who first started talking to me for a *New York Times* article he was writing in 2018 and then agreed to offer some advice and guidance. He and his wife Sarah run a small writers retreat center in Northern California, the Wellstone Center in the Redwoods, and he works with writers there, and has helped out on six *New York Times* bestsellers and counting.

Finally, thanks to all of you for reading this book and for standing up for truth and accountability. Our country is what we make of it.